GOVERNMENT MARKETING

General Editor
Steven E. Permut
Yale University

Praeger Series in Public and
Nonprofit Sector Marketing

GOVERNMENT MARKETING
Theory and Practice

Edited by
Michael P. Mokwa
Steven E. Permut

PRAEGER

PRAEGER SPECIAL STUDIES • PRAEGER SCIENTIFIC

Library of Congress Cataloging in Publication Data

Main entry under title:

Government marketing.

Collection of papers from the the May 1979 workshop held
at Yale University, co-sponsored by the American
Marketing Association.
Includes bibliographical references.
1. Government publicity—Addresses, essays, lectures.
2. Public goods—Addresses, essays, lectures.
3. Marketing—Addresses, essays, lectures.   I. Mokwa,
Michael P.   II. Permut, Steven E.   III. Yale University.
IV. American Marketing Association.
JF1525.P8G64   351.81′9   81-308
ISBN 0-03-058316-0   AACR1

Published in 1981 by Praeger Publishers
CBS Educational and Professional Publishing
A Division of CBS, Inc.
521 Fifth Avenue, New York, New York 10175 U.S.A.

© 1981 by Praeger Publishers

123456789   145   98765432

Printed in the United States of America

For Susan, Matthew and Andrew
—M. P. M.

For Joanna and Lisa
—S. E. P.

CONTENTS

SERIES EDITOR'S FOREWORD

Government Marketing is the second volume in the Praeger Series in Public and Nonprofit Sector Marketing. It marks a time of considerable interest in the application of marketing theory and practice to nonbusiness situations. This volume, along with the series itself, reflects a strong scholarly commitment to explore the limits of marketing thinking far beyond its traditional boundaries within the private, for-profit world.

The Praeger series was created to foster in-depth scholarly research and pragmatism in a wide variety of areas of pressing contemporary concern. Volumes currently in progress focus, for example, on marketing of government programs and services, urban transportation, higher education, and ideas and social issues. In each volume, the authors have attempted to expand marketing thinking and, at the same time, "map" the rather extensive unexplored domain that has just begun to engage the imaginations of marketing professionals.

Although marketing has well served the for-profit sector for many years, there are those who feel that its greatest and most meaningful contributions are likely to be found in the public and nonprofit arenas. This is not to suggest that concepts, theories, and marketing practice can simply be transferred wholesale to these other sectors. Rather, it is to recognize explicitly that we are only beginning to sense the benefits of applying marketing in new and unusual ways to the problems and challenges that affect our public institutions, social systems, and very way of living in the modern world.

The series will publish scholarly work that contributes in a meaningful way to either the theory or practice of marketing in nonbusiness sectors. It will not offer textbooks, case books, or books of readings, although we hope that volumes in the series will find their way into the classroom and onto the desks of practicing managers.

PREFACE

Government, at all levels and across all policy areas, faces challenging pressures to think more responsively and to operate more effectively. Marketing issues are an inherent dimension of most public policies and of all public programs in which citizens interact with their government; however, most public sector marketing decisions are formulated implicitly. There is little regard for strategic or technical precision. The power, problems, and potential of an explicit marketing perspective in government have largely been ignored, possibly evaded.

Marketing as a field of study and practice focuses on the development of exchange relationships through purposeful benefit configuration, communication, facilitation, and evaluation processes. As such, marketing can contribute to government policy development, but the complex nature and scope of its role require thoughtful articulation and elaboration.

Most advocates of a public sector marketing orientation have not been trained in political science or public administration. They have not been elected to office, appointed to a public position, or managed a public agency. They need to learn much more about the ideologies and problems of our hybrid federal-democratic government. Few public policy makers or administrators have exposure to formal marketing thought. They must have the diligence to change naive, often negative, perceptions about marketing and to investigate it enthusiastically and openly. Together, marketing advocates and public decision makers must have the foresight and courage to learn cooperatively through communication, experimentation, and formative evaluation.

This volume initiates a necessary dialogue. The intricate problems and complex context of public sector marketing are explored constructively. The tone is firmly but cautiously optimistic. Marketing is not presented as a panacea, nor as a set of commercial principles and recipes for their use in government. Rather, it is presented as an applied social science and strategic art. It is treated as a field of knowledge possessing its own ideological, technical, and empirical foundations. Consequently, the basic concern of this volume is the development, transfer, use, and evaluation of marketing knowledge in an underdeveloped and poorly explored marketing frontier— the public sector.

A pervasive theme throughout the volume is a pragmatic and scholarly *struggle* to identify and understand the dimensions and dynamics that distinguish government marketing from conventional contexts, processes, and perspectives. Another important theme is *demonstration*. A diverse range of public policies and programs applying marketing methods are described and intensively analyzed. Federal, state, and municipal-level programs are presented, as are comparative international analyses featuring British and Canadian programs. Policy areas include military recruitment, welfare, postal services, rail transit, social services, energy policies, and currency introduction. Yet another noteworthy theme is *challenge*. Many novel ideas, provocative research questions, and interesting policy frameworks are outlined. Clearly, the challenges are implementation and continued scholarship. Both indicate the need to sustain the momentum that produced this volume.

Government Marketing incorporates the collaborative efforts of nearly 50 scholars and practitioners representing both marketing and public sector interests and backgrounds. In May 1979, these specialists were invited to participate in a national workshop and conference held at Yale University and sponsored by the American Marketing Association and the Yale School of Organization and Management. Invitations were based upon both commitment to and expertise in the field. A list of conference participants is presented in the Appendix. Each participant contributed significantly.

The purpose of the conference was expressed in its title; "Exploring and Developing Government Marketing." The conference objectives were basic but ambitious: (1) to establish a "state of the art" through dynamic analysis rather than traditional static description and reviews; and (2) to shape the path for future development and research through a formulative blend of theory and practical analytical frameworks. The chapters of this volume attempt to accomplish these objectives by communicating the spirit and substance of the Yale conference. Each contribution was prepared specifically for the conference with this volume in mind. Each was presented and then enriched through constructive discussions and reviews.

The volume has been divided into four major parts. Each part begins with a short introductory commentary and brief overviews of the chapters. Part I, "Developing Perspective and Marketing Practice," establishes the tone for the other sections of this text and for future efforts. Here, marketing and government are described as institutions confronting challenges to their social legitimacy. Is a more conscious marketing perspective truly appropriate for government? Next, the generic nature and scope of marketing are discussed and the characteristics of government goods and services are outlined. But are public policy makers really serious about marketing? Marketing methods are conceptualized as a policy innovation within government, and the adoption behavior of public administrators is analyzed. Then, what are the basic problems in applying conventional marketing wisdom to public programs? These are described and carefully illustrated.

In Part II, "Exploring Government Programs," the chapters focus on detailed descriptions and constructive analyses of government marketing programs. The effort to generate an all-volunteer military force, the operation of the national food stamp program, and government's disjointed attack on energy problems are among the topics. Two very interesting comparative analyses are presented in this section. Both add an international dimension.

"Using Marketing Research" is the topic of Part III. The use of citizen survey techniques as a source of information for guiding public planning and evaluative decisions is demonstrated and debated. Federal consumer research programs are outlined, and the impact of increased government use of marketing studies on their quality and relevance for managerial decisions is examined. This section concludes with a discussion of the characteristics of knowledge, specifically focusing on insights related to the transfer and use of marketing knowledge.

Part IV, "Extending Marketing Practice and Investigating the Consequences," emphasizes novel issues, important linkages among concepts, and evaluative concerns. For example, the novel concept of marketing laws as an alternative to coercive enforcement is presented. The relationships between theory and strategy formulation and between program implementation and evaluative field research are demonstrated in a social program context. A marketing audit is used to evaluate a state development program, and a strategic program is formulated. Public service advertising is reviewed critically as an important dimension of many public sector marketing efforts. In conclusion, controversial issues in public management competence, the appropriate scope of government market involvement, the potential need for regulation of government marketing, and ethics are all thoughtfully investigated.

Many individuals have supported and contributed to this project. Above all we acknowledge with great thanks the enthusiastic and competent work of the contributing authors. Next, we recognize the commitment and special involvement of all participants at the Yale conference. Their comments and encouragement sharpened our thoughts and influenced the final form of many chapters.

Professors Ben Enis of the University of Missouri and Len Berry of the University of Virginia were particularly helpful channeling the support of the American Marketing Association for the conference. Dean William H. Donaldson of the Yale School of Organization and Management provided support staff and facilities for the conference, along with his personal enthusiasm for this project. Professor Clayton P. Alderfer, then Director of Professional Studies at Yale, provided welcoming remarks as well as expert consultation in the creation of a workable program format.

Michael Mokwa would like to express personal appreciation to the Graduate School of the University of Wisconsin—Madison for supporting his early efforts in this project and to his colleagues at Arizona State University for their genuine interest and encouragement as the project was concluded. A very special thanks to teachers, colleagues, and friends in the field of government: while idealism remains entrenched, it is within the swamps of reality!

Steven Permut would like to express personal appreciation to Professor Larry Isaacson of Yale for untold hours of discussion on the merits and problems of public sector marketing and to Professors Jagdish N. Sheth of the University of Illinois and Christopher H. Lovelock and Stephen A. Greyser of Harvard for scholarly insights and observations that continue to have a major impact on his own thinking in this emerging field.

M. P. M.
S. E. P.

I

DEVELOPING PERSPECTIVE AND MARKETING PRACTICE

INTRODUCTION TO PART I

All organizations, both public and private, engage in marketing. Simply expressed, marketing is an exchange of values. Marketing policies are concerned with developing, facilitating, executing, and evaluating exchange relationships that are mutually accommodating and potentially satisfying. As such, marketing decisions are a fundamental dimension of organizational policy. However, organizations practice marketing with distinctive styles and strategies, with different degrees of precision, and with varied levels of consciousness. It is a relatively recent development to consider and study explicitly the marketing behavior and practices of noncommercial organizations, particularly government organizations.

Marketing methods are being selectively applied by a growing number of public sector organizations to a diverse range of issues and problems. Successful applications toward the resolution of public problems such as mass transit, higher education, health services, social action, and postal services have been documented. Currently, some public policy makers and administrators are eager, at times even overanxious, to employ marketing techniques; most are not. Few public policy makers and administrators truly understand the scope, demands, or impact of a marketing orientation. Even fewer have specific training in marketing, and most approach the topic with apprehension or, at the least, strong reservation. Furthermore, many marketing scholars and practitioners may be guilty of selling marketing without a clear comprehension of their product or market—the realities of public issues, political processes, and bureaucratic norms of administration. Change is necessary but it will be difficult.

Philip Kotler, the noted marketing management scholar, states, "Marketing thinking is not easy to introduce into an organization. It tends to be misunderstood, easily forgotten. . . . Marketing is characterized by a law of slow learning and rapid forgetting" (1977). If the task of introduction and adoption is difficult and often frustrating in an organization, then introduction, adoption, and diffusion throughout a sector—"government"—will be more difficult and often more frustrating. Nonetheless, the time has come to generate a learning curve for public sector marketing.

In Part I, the most basic issues for developing government marketing are discussed. These include the importance of formulating a scholarly and pragmatic perspective; comprehending and enriching marketing theory; understanding the scope and nature of government products and services; perceiving and managing marketing as innovative policy technology; and challenging conventional marketing concepts in public sector contexts.

The sudden expansion of interest in public sector marketing has been marked by a regrettable void of any sense of the role of government as an institution. Research, theory formulation, and practice throughout this field are likely to be myopic, sterile, or naive when "perspective" is absent. Chapter 1, "Marketing, the State, and Legitimacy," by Frederick Sturdivant, is a diligent exploration of the social challenges confronting the traditional commercial character of marketing, the state as a broker of power and allegiance, and the precarious marriage of marketing practice and the state. The concept of institutional legitimacy is proposed as a premise to encourage and structure perspective. A set of propositions outline differing perceptions regarding the nature of government. Libertarian, elitist, pluralist, welfare, and bureaucratic value orientations are presented. In a spirit of commencement rather than conclusion, vital questions are advanced regarding the evolving character of marketing as a major social and political institution.

Building on the challenge of these questions, Michael Mokwa presents "Government Marketing: An Inquiry into Theory, Process, and Perspective," Chapter 2. Providing a strong admonition for more public sector marketing scholarship, conscious practice, and education, the author attempts to structure a foundation for encouraging dialogue and elaboration. A selective review of the state of practice and literature leads into a critical discussion of the adequacy and accuracy of current theory. A generic concept of marketing is described and policy implications are provided. The author warns that government is not a homogeneous sector and approaching it as such produces naive prescriptions ignored by policy makers. The distinctive contexts and dynamics of government are probed with the aim of delineating interdisciplinary directions for further development.

The production and consumption characteristics of public goods are generally recognized in economics and political economy, particularly in discussions of welfare or public choice. In Chapter 3, Thaddeus Spratlen discusses "Government Goods and Services: Characteristics and Concepts for Marketing Analysis." Selectively, the author outlines basic classification frameworks using industrial, functional, and product attribute/marketability criteria. Careful note is made of the frequently confused difference between marketing *to* government, wherein government is the "buyer," and marketing *by* government, wherein it is the "seller." The chapter produces a sense of the pervasive and differentiated scope of government product and market domains and the complexity of product and market attributes. The adequacy of market characterizations based upon simple industrial typology or classic enonomic logic is an underlying issue. Can an exchange framework of marketing be used to generate innovative and valid taxonomies? Would these be adopted by public sector policy makers and scholars?

"An Innovation Adoption Perspective for Marketing in the Government" is set forth by Dale Achabal and Robert Backoff in Chapter 4. Given the growing advocation of marketing's public sector potential, a fundamental concern is the minimal response by government policy makers and educators. An innovation-diffusion definition of the dilemma produces rich insights into the problem and a framework for a responsive solution. The authors see an environment that creates a climate conducive to policy innovation in public organizations. The context and innovation attributes of marketing are identified. Marketing advocates are encouraged to assume a change-agent role. Appropriate agencies must be selected as target markets. Agencies' perceived needs, values, and entrenched policy dynamics must be the frame of reference when initiating change. The relative advantage and compatability of marketing approaches must be clearly communicated and demonstrated. One basic barrier is semantic confusion, and a simple list of "equivalent" policy terminology is constructed demonstrating the compatibility of basic marketing management concepts with those from public administration.

Although marketing methods can provide relative benefits in public sector policy processes, Paul Bloom and William Novelli constructively outline the "Problems Applying Conventional Wisdom to Social Marketing Programs." The marketing decision process is employed as a frame of reference to delineate the features of social marketing problems and management practices. Many examples document the difficult tasks faced by social marketers. The authors suggest that social marketing is a continuous struggle requiring hard work, perserverance, and considerable skill—a struggle possibly more difficult than commercial marketing.

REFERENCES

Kotler, Philip (1977), "From Sales Obsession to Marketing Effectiveness," *Harvard Business Review* (November–December): 67–75.

1

MARKETING, THE STATE, AND LEGITIMACY

Frederick D. Sturdivant

Charles E. Lindblom concluded in *Politics and Markets*, "It has been a curious feature of democratic thought that it has not faced up to the private corporation as a peculiar organization in an ostensible democracy. . . . The large private corporation fits oddly into democratic theory and vision. Indeed, it does not fit" (1977, p. 356) If marketing scholarship is viewed as either charged with the study of certain institutions or with serving those institutions, then *legitimacy* deserves careful consideration. Although this concept will be developed more fully, it should be noted that marketing's traditional institutional subject/client—business—has not been well served in this regard. While marketing has been enormously successful in the cultivation and delivery of materialism and its progeny, what has it done for corporate legitimacy? As the Lindblom quote suggests, in the eyes of many students of American society, the answer is "Not much." Assuming that legitimacy is somehow related to an institution's compatability with the basic tenets of a society, the corporation, as the most powerful manifestation of American business, faces serious problems in this regard.

Thus, in spite of the substantial attention given in recent years to consumer attitudes, consumer satisfaction, the marketing concept, and so forth, marketing seems not to have convinced many observers of the corporation's compatibility with America's sense of purpose. Given the apparent enthusiasm for applying marketing concepts and tools to government, one might appropriately ask about the broader implications of such efforts. To assess these implications, it will be necessary to consider the notion of institutional legitimacy.

THE LEGITIMACY CHALLENGE

"From the perspective of history," according to Willis Harman, "the mightiest force for social change is the unproclaimed power of society's citizens to challenge and withdraw legitimacy from any or all of society's institutions" (1976, pp. 115–16). If one keeps in mind that institutions are the creation of mankind, then the critical relationship between institutions and societal values should be clear. Institutions exist because they provide people with something, be it security, structure, hope, a sense of integrity, identification, guidance, or other benefits. In many respects, institutions are the depositories of a society's values. As long as they offer a good return to their "investors," those value banks will enjoy support. Should they get seriously out of phase with society, there can be the equivalent of a run on the bank as citizens withdraw their support. Whether it be the corrupt Roman Catholic Church of the Middle Ages, slavery, colonialism in the post-World War II era, Jim Crow legislation and traditions in the South, or the monarchy in Iran, no institution can survive in the long run if it lacks legitimacy.

Robert Dahl (1963, p. 19) and Edwin Epstein (1969, p. 254), among others, suggest that legitimacy may be defined as a belief in and acceptance of the rightness, propriety, moral goodness, or appropriateness of an institution. Such evaluations are made, of course, within the context of a given society's value system. As Harman notes, "Major historical transformations often seem to stem from values and beliefs changing at a different pace from, and getting out of step with, changes in the sociopolitical structure" (1976, p. 117). He goes on to say, "Legitimacy of a social system and its power concentrations is fundamentally based on its (1) being duly constituted, (2) adherence to adequate guiding moral principles, and (3) effectiveness in achieving agreed-upon goals" (p. 117).

MARKETING AND LEGITIMACY

With these dimensions of institutional legitimacy in mind, it may be of some value to consider the influence of marketing on society and business. Notwithstanding a strange reluctance on the part of marketing scholars to address issues such as those raised by David Potter a quarter of a century ago in *People of Plenty*, it is clear that societal values in the United States have changed and that these changes have been influenced in part by marketing activities. The late historian argued, "Advertising now compares with such longstanding institutions as the school and the church in the magnitude of its social influence" (1954, p. 167).

The shaping of the American character and our society's political and economic structure have been of interest to observers at least since Alexis de Tocqueville wrote *Democracy in America* in 1835. Whether it be another

Frenchman over one hundred years later—Jean-François Revel (1971)—or the English writer D. W. Brogan (1944) near the end of World War II, the treatment of the American character by foreigners has tended to be both favorable and optimistic. Revel, who visited the United States in the late 1960s with the intention of writing an account of a corrupt and decaying society, returned to France and wrote:

> The United States is the country most eligible for the role of prototype-nation for the following reasons: it enjoys continuing economic prosperity and rate of growth, without which no revolutionary project can succeed; it has technological competence and a high level of basic research; culturally it is oriented toward the future rather than toward the past, and it is undergoing a revolution in behavioral standards, and in the affirmation of individual freedom and equality; it rejects authoritarian control, and multiplies creative initiative in all domains—and allows the coexistence of a diversity of mutually complementary alternative subcultures. (1971, p. 183)

American writers have often been less positive. For example, in 1970 Andrew Hacker wrote that the United States had entered a period of decline at the end of World War II. Hacker pointed to accelerating technology, higher incomes, expanded self-respect, and rising expectations as the bases of the decline. He pointed to serious, unanticipated consequences for American society growing out of these seeming strengths. Material prosperity freed Americans from traditional controls and personal limitation, and, in turn, human character was transformed. According to Hacker:

> Tensions and frustrations are bound to arise when 200 million human beings demand rights and privileges never intended for popular distribution. It is too late in our history to restore order or re-establish authority: the American temperament has passed the point when self-interest can subordinate itself to citizenship. Calls for enlightened attitudes and concerted action will continue, but with little ultimate effect. Our history shaped our character, and that history will now run its course. (1970, p. 8)

In view of the less than successful efforts of a series of presidents to engage citizens in the voluntary battle against inflation and given the lack of enthusiasm for waging the so-called moral equivalent of war in the continuing energy crisis, it might well appear that self-interest has prevailed over citizenship. Hacker would point to these problems, among others, as substantial evidence that the American people are now incapable of making the personal sacrifices required to sustain domestic order or international authority. Americans no longer display that spirit which transforms a people into a citizenry and turns territory into a nation. We have become a loose aggregation of private persons who give higher priority to personal pleasure than to community endeavors.

One might appropriately ask, therefore, if the fundamental rationale of marketing—consumer sovereignty—and its commitment to satisfy virtually every need, want, and whim has served us well. Perhaps this notion coupled with the traditional emphasis on shareholder primacy has caused us to view the role of the corporation too narrowly. Such a restrictive force may well have delayed serious consideration of the issue of corporate governance. For example, the link between this broader view and corporate legitimacy is suggested by the following quotation from Neil Chamberlain's, *The Limits of Corporate Responsibility:*

> The corporation has become, by virtue of its size and scope, more of a public institution than a private one. Its management . . . exercises a political function no less than an economic one, responding to and coordinating contentious public-interest and special-interest groups. Even if its discretion is limited, even if it is constrained by the system of which it is a part, it now operates within a social context in which increasingly it can legitimate its authority only by assuring its numerous and often conflicting publics that it is doing its best to act responsively. (1973, p. 204)

Chamberlain articulates the reality of an institution whose constituency is by no means limited to the customers who purchase its products and services or to the shareholders of the corporation. The social and political consequences of corporate policies and practices are simply too diverse and profound for other groups to be classified as irrelevant in shaping corporate plans. In this respect, the large private corporation has come increasingly to resemble a public agency.

As the adaptive/responsive mechanism of the corporation, marketing would appear to bear a particular burden in this regard. Chamberlain, Hacker, Potter, and a host of other social commentators have noted the pervasive influence of marketing. For example, Chamberlain contends, "Television, more than any other medium, has dramatized and glamorized the gospel of consumption" (1973, p. 29). He goes on to say, "To sustain a consumer-oriented, egalitarian society requires cutting the disadvantaged in on televised goodies for the masses" (p. 29). Chamberlain hypothesizes that the resultant social pressures led to the rapid expansion of the welfare system in the 1960s.

In a more familiar vein, Hacker asserts, "Materialism is not uniquely American, nor is the high valuation placed on material possessions entirely the result of management decisions. However, the perpetuation of this system of values . . . is due to corporate judgment about what sales are needed" (1970, p. 46). While Hacker's words on corporate power may suffer from Galbraithian overstatement, his and other social critics' views of business are firmly supported by the sharp drop in public confidence in the institution since the late 1960s. In 1966, 55 percent of the American public expressed "a great deal of confidence" in major companies. In 1979 that figure was 18 percent (Harris 1979). Since a number of marketing scholars proclaimed in the late 1960s that "this is the era of the dominance of marketing in the management of business enterprises in the United States" (Sturdivant et al. 1970, p. 1), one should wonder about the rush to bring the glories of marketing to the central state. This question is not based on the assumption that marketing is an overwhelming force that could alter the nature and course of the state. Rather it is intended to suggest that the state as an institution may be facing an even greater test of legitimacy. Marketing may help or may compound the problem. Regardless of one's assumptions about the potency of marketing, researchers should enter the arena with a realistic view of the state as an institution.

THE STATE AND LEGITIMACY

Social philosopher Robert Nisbet has observed, "In most ages of history some one institution—kinship, religion, economy, state—is ascendant in human loyalties. Other institutions, without being necessarily obliterated, retreat to the background in terms of function and authority" (1975, p. 13). Nisbet suggests that "when major institutions die or become weak, it is ultimately by virtue of their loss of power to command respect and allegiance. That loss of power is manifest today in the state" (p. 14).

The state's loss of legitimacy might seem far more improbable to a late twentieth-century American than it would have to his counterpart at the time the Republic was founded. The Federal Convention held in Philadelphia during the summer of 1787 drafted the Constitution in such a way as to emphasize liberty and severely limit the powers of the central state. Quite simply, the state traditionally had been something to fear. As R. M. MacIver notes in his classic study, *The Modern State:*

> The state has always been peculiarly associated with force. In its origins, in its growth, in its present control over its members and in its relation to other states, force is proclaimed to be not only its last resort, but its first principle, not only its special weapon, but its very being. . . . The state, conceived in violence, was born to power. (1929, p. 221)

The issue to be addressed is one of perspective. The literature that has grown out of marketing scholars' research and consulting ventures with the state could be characterized as myopic, sterile, or at least naive in its failure to acknowledge differing views of the character of the state and the relationship between the government and the governed. It might be constructive if marketing scholars who are working these fields or plan to do so were to develop such a perspective. An abbreviated framework for sorting through alternative perspectives might be based on the following propositions.

First Proposition: The state is inherently inclined to collect power and control unto itself. It stresses social order rather than freedom. The year following the Federal Convention, Thomas Jefferson wrote to a friend, "The natural progress of things is for liberty to yield and government to gain ground." In a very thoughtful book on Constitutional freedoms, Richard Harris comments on Jefferson's observation by suggesting, "That progress has been inexorable in America, and of all the tyrannical threats to the individual today none is more powerful or menacing than the threat posed by its oldest enemy: government" (1976, p. 4).

Proponents of this *libertarian* view would point to the fact that in spite of the spirit and protective qualities of the Constitution and the Bill of Rights, this government engaged in genocide against native Americans, endorsed first slavery and then segregation, illegally deported U.S. citizens (most dramatically during Attorney General A. Mitchell Palmer's raids in 1919), engaged in extensive illegal surveillance, conducted syphilis, hallucinogenic drug, and other experiments on unsuspecting people, unleashed a number of secret and undeclared wars, and on and on. The modern welfare state represents an effort to extend control and reduce personal freedom in the eyes of libertarians.

Second Proposition: The state is merely the instrument of the rich and powerful, who use it to dominate society. From this perspective, the state is seen as a tool of those who are in positions of economic power. Their objective is to continue their dominance. As political scientist Edward Greenberg explains:

> Through its control of the media and educational institutions, but most important, through its control of the forms by which people labor and earn their living, the dominant class finds its ideas permeating the social order. In feudal society, for example, ideas conducive to the stability of the feudal order, such as the sanctity of land, of the serf-landlord relationship, and of mutual loyalties, dominated social thought. In capitalist societies, ideas requisite to the maintenance of capitalist economic arrangements dominate social thought: the rights of private property, competition, free enterprise, consumption, and individualism. (1974, p. 24)

Those who subscribe to this *Marxist* view of the state would point to the preferential treatment white collar criminals receive in the courts as well as to tax laws and loopholes. Indeed, even "progressive" legislation is often cited as an example of business manipulation of the state. A number of writers have argued that periods of social reform, such as the Progressive Era and the New Deal, leading to the passage of the Food and Drug

Administration Act, the Federal Reserve Act, the Wagner Act, and so forth, were manipulated by business leaders to stabilize markets, reduce uncertainty, and combat mounting radicalism.

Third Proposition: The power of the state is limited by the power of organized public opinion and large special-interest groups; the influence exercised by any one group is counterbalanced by others. One of the most prominent exponents of this view is political scientist Robert A. Dahl. Instead of seeing the United States as a society controlled by an elite, he sees widespread participation in decision making. He does not argue that a pluralistic society is one that assures perfection; rather its imperfections are a reflection of its people, not a handful of power brokers and manipulators. He argues:

> The greatest obstacle to democratization and reducing inequalities in the United States is not that bugbear with which the Left, old and new, is invariably so obsessed, an elite of wealthy men, or even that military-industrial complex so much referred to these days, but rather the military-industrial-financial-labor-farming-educational-professional-consumer-over and under 30-lower/middle/upper class complex that, for want of a more appropriate name, might be called the American people. (1970, p. 110)

According to Greenberg, a central feature of *pluralistic* thinking is the emergence of a "picture of the state as a fragmented, internally competitive institution (or more correctly a set of institutions)" (1974, p. 19). Thus, instead of one federal government, in a sense there are several federal governments. The comptroller of the currency may testify in opposition to a bill requiring fuller disclosure by banks while a representative of the Securities and Exchange Commission may argue forcefully in favor of the same bill. More dramatically, a government employee called the special prosecutor may sue the president to gain access to tapes and documents, with both parties turning to some other federal employees (the Supreme Court justices) to resolve the conflict. The end result, in the eyes of pluralists, is a remarkably dynamic and healthy society.

Fourth Proposition: The state is an unselfish instrument of the common welfare; it is designed to alleviate potential hardship caused by economic displacements, technological change, and the like. From this vantage point, the state is seen as a positive entity. As Sidney Fine explains in the preface to his *Laissez Faire and the General Welfare State*, "The theorists of the general welfare state . . . believed that the state could benefit society by a positive exertion of its powers and that it should therefore act whenever its interposition seemed likely to promote the common well-being" (1956, p. vii).

This *welfare state* perspective is especially common in Western Europe. Writers on this side of the Atlantic tend to treat the welfare state in pejorative terms and have frequently forecast doom and gloom for such states. For example, in *The Culture of Narcissism*, historian Christopher Lasch points to the rise of the political ideology of welfare liberalism as a threat to national survival. By no means a pamphlet from the National Association of Manufacturers, this thoughtful book argues that an ever-expanding bureaucratic state, steeped in paternalism, robs a society of confidence, dignity, and initiative. His thesis represents a sobering link between the malaise of corporate America and the state: "Having over-thrown feudalism and slavery and then outgrown its own personal and familial form, capitalism has evolved a new political ideology, welfare liberalism, which absolves individuals of moral responsibility and treats them as victims of social circumstances" (1979, p. 281). Britain has been an especially popular target for pessimistic prognoses. *Britian—A Future That Works*, by Bernard D. Nossiter (1978), a writer for the *Washington Post* who lives in London, offers, however, a much more optimistic view of the British welfare state. Nossiter cites numerous statistics to counter common assumptions about the plight of British society. For example:

> When the Queen celebrated her Silver Jubilee in 1977, twenty-five years on the throne, each of her subjects on average enjoyed an income commanding four-fifths more in goods and services than his parents. Even allowing for the great rise in prices, "real" and not inflated incomes after taxes had grown 88 percent from 1952 through 1976. (p. 75)

> A wealthier Britian could afford to, and did, spend more on the arts and take longer holidays. When the reign began, subsidies for opera, theater, concerts and other forms of expression and creation were £887,213; by 1977 this figure had jumped to £41.7 million, or about $80 million. Only 3 in 100 Britons took more than two weeks' holiday in 1952. By 1977, two in three were enjoying holidays of three weeks or more each year. (p. 77)

In sum, Nossiter's book provides a testimonial to a positivistic state which he argues might serve as a model of economic and social progress to the rest of the world.

Fifth Proposition: The state is controlled by professional bureaucrats and politicians and is self-serving, exploitive, and often incompetent. Of the five propositions, this one is the least formal in the sense of analysis and professional appraisal. However, it is a view of the state often expressed by those frustrated with red tape, rising taxes, interference, and waste. It is a frustration born of impatience with greed, stupidity, meddling—not conspiracy. This *cynical* view does not assume that the state is purposely out to steal freedom from the people. It does assume, though, that politicians are generally crooked and deceitful, that public officials are lazy, and that the public is generally being taken for a ride. Indeed, the public seems even to be weary of almost daily warnings that yet another cancer-causing agent has been found. In short, the size and scope of government are expanding at such a rate that no one can stop or even control it.

The cynical view may lead to the conclusion that, if you cannot alter or control it, you can get on board and participate in the largess. Or you can cheat it. Perhaps the best evidence of the latter is this country's burgeoning underground economy. Cynicism is, of course, corrosive and unchecked can destroy not only the state but the balance of the social fabric as well.

These five characterizations of the state provide a framework for sorting through one's own perspective. There may be other structures that are more useful, but the essential point is that anyone engaged in research concerning a dominant institution needs to have a conceptual framework that can provide a broader context for the meaning of their work. Without a conceptual or philosophical framework, the scholars run a greater risk of conducting isolated or disjointed research and failing to understand the broader implications of their work.

It is difficult enough to think through one's own view of the state let alone try to reach some conclusion about the mood and perspective of the American people. In his chapter, "An Ungovernable Nation," in *The End of the American Era*, Andrew Hacker asserts, "America was founded on the premise that legitimacy inheres only in private activity" (1970, pp. 126–27). If that tradition survives today, the state has little hope for legitimacy in its present form. On the other hand, Harris argues at the conclusion of *Freedom Spent* that many Americans welcome a dominant, freedom-suppressing central state:

> Freedom can be a heavy burden, because it demands the kind of mental and moral exertion that many people are not equal to. They want to be told what to do, and they seek leaders who will command them, who will provide them with the dependence and security of childhood. They are the timid men Jefferson spoke of who prefer the calm of despotism to the boisterous sea of liberty. The number of such people in this country cannot even be guessed at, but there must be a lot of them to have brought our nation to its turning point—where the people allow their government to behave as though they exist for its sake. (1976, pp. 439–40)

The assessment of American views on the role of the state is complicated by the existence of what political scientists Lloyd Free and Hadley Cantril have termed the "operational spectrum" versus the "ideological spectrum" (Free and Cantril 1967). Simply put, Congressman Jones's ideological spectrum may call for a reduction in the defense budget, and on an abstract level the congressman speaks as an opponent of federal deficits. When the Pentagon designates the large Air Force base in his district for closing, however, Jones's operational spectrum comes into play. The congressman is no longer dealing with the abstract and is likely to do everything he can to reverse the decision. Hence, what a number of popular articles have termed "America's shift to the right" is very difficult to assess. Political attitudes clearly represent a moving target. How far the scholar goes in attempting to understand and reconcile his or her views with the populace is beyond the scope and competence of this chapter. It would be refreshing simply to see evidence of understanding of the importance of knowing one's own view.

CONCLUSION

The title of this chapter conveys some promise of linking marketing, the state, and legitimacy. It is hoped that the concept of legitimacy has been made clear and that a useful structure within which to view the state has been devised. Ironically, the role of marketing may be the murkiest of the three elements. This lack of clarity may be attributable to the reluctance to step back and establish a perspective on marketing. It should be noted immediately that this is *not* a call for the reincarnation of the old science vs. art debate; nor is it an invitation to broaden, extend, truncate, shrink, or otherwise fold, spindle, or mutilate the definition of marketing. (The field seems already to have consumed an inordinate amount of time engaged in definitional exercises.) If marketing is viewed as an institution, would any of the five propositions suggested above be helpful in understanding it? Any number of questions could be raised. For example, Nisbet points to a loss of sense of community and a decline in authority as threats to the system. Has marketing, with its emphasis on self, contributed to this condition?

The question also needs to be posed concerning the nature and role of the central state. How can or should marketing scholars study and/or serve the state? What lessons are to be learned from marketing's longstanding relationship with the institution of business?

In sum, before marketing scholars rush to embrace the practices and goals of a variety of federal agencies, perhaps there is a need to reflect on what marketing is, what it has to offer major institutions, and the character and nature of those institutions.

REFERENCES

Brogan, D. W. (1944), *The American Character*, New York: Alfred A. Knopf.

Chamberlain, Neil W. (1973), *The Limits of Corporate Responsibility*, New York: Basic Books.

Dahl, Robert A. (1963), *Modern Political Analysis*, Englewood Cliffs, N.J.: Prentice-Hall.

Dahl, Robert A. (1970), *After the Revolution?*, New Haven: Yale University Press.

Epstein, Edwin M. (1969), *The Corporation in American Politics*, Englewood Cliffs, N.J.: Prentice-Hall.

Fine, Sidney (1956), *Laissez Faire and the General Welfare State*, Ann Arbor, Mich.: Ann Arbor Paperbacks.

Free, Lloyd J. and Hadley Cantril (1967), *The Political Beliefs of Americans*, New Brunswick, N.J.: Rutgers University Press.

Greenberg, Edward S. (1974), *Serving the Few*, New York: John Wiley.

Hacker, Andrew (1970), *The End of the American Era*, New York: Antheneum.

Harman, Willis W. (1976), *An Incomplete Guide to the Future*, San Francisco: San Francisco Book.

Harris, Louis (1979), "Confidence in Most Institutions Down," *ABC News-Harris Survey*.

Harris, Richard (1976), *Freedom Spent*, Boston: Little, Brown.

Lasch, Christopher (1979), *The Culture of Narcissism*, New York: W. W. Norton.

Lindblom, Charles E. (1977), *Politics and Markets*, New York: Basic Books.

MacIver, R. M. (1929), *The Modern State*, London: Oxford University Press.

Nisbet, Robert (1975), *Twilight of Authority*, New York: Oxford University Press.

Nossiter, Bernard D. (1978), *Britian—A Future That Works*, Boston: Houghton Mifflin.

Potter, David M. (1954), *People of Plenty*, Chicago: University of Chicago Press.

Revel, Jean-François (1971), *Without Marx or Jesus*, New York: Delta.

Sturdivant, Frederick D. et al. (1970), *Managerial Analysis in Marketing*, Glenview, Ill.: Scott, Foresman.

2

GOVERNMENT MARKETING: AN INQUIRY INTO THEORY, PROCESS, AND PERSPECTIVE

Michael P. Mokwa

As marketing has formally extended the boundaries of its discipline to encompass the public and third sectors, tools and techniques of market programming and research and the impediments to their implementation have been the overwhelming concerns. Less effort has been expended to understand societal and public problems, political or social ideology, and the dynamics of policy processes. Valid definitions and characterizations of most sociopolitical markets and public products are lacking. Thus relatively few public and third sector decision makers have actively embraced marketing, and their educators have neither researched nor studied it.

The growth of selective applications of marketing tools and ideas throughout the nonbusiness sectors has generated much curiosity along with mixed, but encouraging results. A good foundation has been built, but more architecture is needed. A change in orientation is an appropriate step.

In the past, many marketing advocates have been guilty of committing a sin against their cherished doctrine, the "marketing concept" that dictates "know thy consumer!" A selling approach focused on the values and norms of the marketing discipline has guided much of the development and promotion of marketing knowledge, a real product, to the public and third sector markets. More intensive interest in the perceived problems, needs, and expectations of the consumer is vital to enhance product design, delivery, and diffusion. As government marketing is systematically introduced, public sector needs and problems present a conducive, complex market encouraging a higher consciousness and continued developmental effort.

The political system is and will continue to be severely strained. Public problems are increasing in complexity. Solutions are more difficult and less determinant. Government productivity is questioned. The demands of citizens, "government consumers," are expanding, and their expectations are rising. Yet the conflicting ideology of cutback is being endorsed, mandated in the voting booths, thus reducing resources for many public programs. Credibility and legitimacy are challenged explicitly with vigor and frequency, implicitly with alienation and apathy. Simple patchwork solutions built on symbolic benefits are not the answer; more responsive and effective public policy is. The need within government across all levels and most areas of programming is a more responsive and effective policy development process, itself not a simple challenge.

A public policy role for marketing is difficult to articulate and implement. Marketing is certainly no panacea; nor is it a simple recipe for reform. However, it can be a more conscious and precise dimension of the policy process, and it can positively affect responsiveness and encourage effectiveness. Construction, communication, and adoption of an appropriate perspective and concept of government marketing is a provocative challenge. Sociopolitical reality must be integrated with generic marketing thought. Both would be enriched.

This chapter outlines some fundamental concepts, a few important issues, and directions for elaboration and development. First there is a brief overview of selected public sector marketing literature and indicators of practice; next, an exchange perspective of marketing and related policy process implications are presented. Finally, key dimensions of government marketing contexts are described.

PUBLIC SECTOR MARKETING—AN EVOLUTION

Scholarship should be a catalyst as fields of knowledge coverge. The state of public sector marketing is currently difficult to determine accurately. The field involves many unrelated applications and a disjointed literature dispersed through different disciplines, primarily marketing, public administration, and policy sciences. Assuming—maybe somewhat dangerously— that scholarship is leading or only reasonably lagging practice, study of the literature melding marketing and government can uncover patterns of development and deficiency.

Lack of an appropriate definition of the boundaries and terrain of the public sector complicate this task. Government problem solving has not followed a well-identified course. Complicated organizational and financial arrangements blur the boundaries' distinguishing sectors. Categorization of policy contents and processes are equally murky. Therefore, many conventional generalizations and taxonomies about government are risky bases for scholarship. Likewise, stereotypes of marketing are tenuous.

The nature, powers, and proper domain of marketing have been debated excessively. Intradisciplinary consensus has been built upon connotative acceptance of voluntary exchange as a core construct and expansive boundaries of practice (Hunt 1976). The invariant nature of marketing in all organizations' policy processes is a tenable theoretical position. However, pragmatic questions temper pervasive promises. A problem in interrelating theoretical and practical paradigms is evident, particularly to the policy researcher or policy maker (for example, Arndt 1979). In conclusion, it is difficult to isolate properly inclusive boundaries for government marketing, and valid exploration of its nature requires significant perspective.

The Marketing Movement

Government marketing should not be confused with conventional "public policy" research in marketing that has been limited to regulatory issues, nor with viewing the government as a market, a buyer of goods and services. Government marketing views public sector jurisdictions and organizations as marketers or "sellers"—developers of benefits who must communicate, valuate, and deliver those benefits to complex citizen/consumer markets. Yet it should be noted that regulatory policy can be studied by analyzing the government as a marketer (compare Mokwa, Enis, and Kangun 1979) and that "buying can be marketing too" (Kotler and Levy 1973).

An extensive nonbusiness marketing literature review and interpretation has recently been presented by Lovelock and Weinberg (1978), and an expansive bibliography has been compiled by Rothschild (1977). A selected overview limited to capturing the foundations and portraying the state of the art within government marketing is presented here.

Kotler and Levy (1969) forcefully demonstrated that all organizations face marketing decisions. They concluded that organizations do not choose whether to practice marketing, only how to practice it. Argumentative controversy was stimulated; scholarship was also stimulated (for example, Kotler and Zaltman 1971; Zaltman, Kotler, and Kaufman 1972; Sheth and Wright 1974). The scholarship prevailed. New domains and directions were opened formally within the marketing discipline. However, some irony exists. Nearly 20 years earlier, Wiebe (1951) had presented provocative ideas and examples of merchandising public issues using marketing communications strategies. Forty years earlier, Breyer (1931) had devoted a chapter in his marketing textbook to studying public utilities as a market commodity. Other pioneering examples undoubtedly exist. Therefore, years before the formal broadening of marketing's boundaries, practitioners and scholars recognized some of its pervasive characteristics.

The idea of "social marketing" as a framework for planned change advanced the decision parameters of marketing. Many adventures into fields such as the arts, family planning, health services, higher education, and public transit advanced marketing into new domains creating their own fragmented literatures. While implications for government marketing can be found, sociopolitical contexts and issues are seldom treated explicitly. Consumer research and market-mix semantics are the common themes; a certain sterility is projected in much of this literature. Lack of depth and very limited scope are characteristic. This holds for most of the public sector marketing literature.

The best-developed, most insightful works focusing specifically on government marketing include: an argument that the marketing concept is not a valid premise for most public organizations (Etgar and Ratchford 1975); a contrast of public and private marketing dynamics and implications for public sector adoption (Lovelock and Weinberg 1975); description of marketing mania in New York City and its detrimental impact (Shanklin 1975); an overview of the marketing problems faced by different types of agencies (Kotler 1975); an outline of the inhibiting effects of agency policy processes (Houston and Homans 1977); demonstration models of market research as an input to public programming (Ritchie and LaBreque 1975; D. Brown, Schary, and Becker 1978); discussion of market planning for community development (Blakely, Schutz, and Harvey 1977); an integration of marketing and program planning, budgeting, and review processes (S. Brown, Ostrom, and Schlacter 1978); advocacy for organizing the marketing function in public agencies (Claxton, Kinnear, and Ritchie 1978); and, currently the best-developed presentation, a reconceptualization of the problems of marketing communications strategies for public products and issues (Rothschild 1979).

Continuity and direction are limited throughout this literature. Substantive and management problems are seldom distinguished. Few presentations formulate frameworks or theories. Notably, a strategic perspective based upon knowledge of an agency's mission and competencies, comprehension of their market, and an integrated marketing policy process is missing. Finally, the literature is presented almost exclusively in marketing or business publications. Therefore, is the marketing movement an intrusion or an evolution?

A Public Productivity Base

Marketing has been almost totally ignored in the public policy and administrative literatures. No mention is made of it in any of the leading basic texts. The only published articles have been by Blakely, Schutz, and Harvey (1977), Brown, Schary, and Becker (1978), and Rosener (1977), who have contrasted citizen involvement techniques and managerial marketing. The policy fields of energy conservation and public transit have received limited attention (compare Lovelock and Weinberg 1978). Mokwa (1978) presented the first paper on marketing at a national American Society for Public Administration convention. It was a simple advocation for public administrators to become aware of marketing and included a description of marketing principles. The following year the extensive ASPA national convention program included one marketing session: Divita and Dyer (1979) called for a marketing response to a citizen consumerism movement; Mokwa and Enis (1979) described public sector marketing myths and myopic behaviors; Stafford and Lyons (1979) discussed public sector market research. Despite the limited and simple nature of this literature, an interesting trend suggests that there may be a public policy evolution in the direction of marketing.

The basis of marketing in government is curiously related to the productivity and evaluation literatures. About the same time that Kotler and Levy argued for broadening marketing, government researchers began to adopt an evaluative orientation. The classic criteria of efficiency slowly eroded as the fundamental measure guiding administrative behavior, being replaced by an emphasis first on productivity and then on citizen-evaluated performance. The evolution is a movement from an internal to an external orientation, but it has been slow and difficult. Interestingly, the drive has surfaced from the local levels of government, where accountability is tied more directly to performance and where distribution of performance is concentrated. An overview of this evolution, including a representative literature sample, is depicted in Figure 2.1.

The concept of public productivity measurement initially straddled the boundary between the jurisdiction of agency and its "clientele"—the citizenry (compare Hatry and Fisk 1971). Explicit measurement of substantive policy outcomes and their impact on citizens was a crucial step beyond the traditional orientation of the public organization. Inclusion of citizen feedback mechanisms (for example, Hatry and Webb 1973), development of evaluation theories, criteria, and studies (for example, Ostrom 1974; Lineberry and Welsh 1974; Katz et al. 1975), and, finally, involvement of citizens in policy formulation (for example, Hayes 1976; Susskind 1976) provided the foundation for exploring government marketing.

Melching (1976) reported on a pioneering workshop sponsored by the National Center for Productivity which studied the uses of marketing management and citizen involvement as a means of improving productivity in the public sector. Based on an analysis of workshop presentations and commentaries, he concluded:

> Unfortunately, government bureaucracies—in spite of the efforts of many public managers—too often become preoccupied with internal processes . . . part of the productivity problem is our need to develop a more effective orientation . . . toward citizen-government interactions and the citizen as a consumer . . . marketing and citizen involvement present high priority targets for the improved design and delivery of

FIGURE 2.1

**The Evolution of Government Marketing:
A Public Productivity Basis**

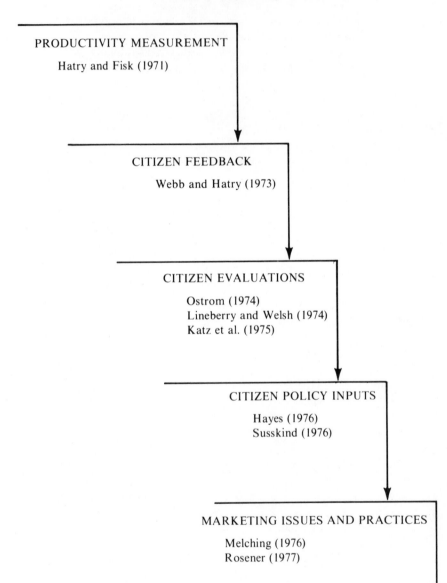

PRODUCTIVITY MEASUREMENT

Hatry and Fisk (1971)

CITIZEN FEEDBACK

Webb and Hatry (1973)

CITIZEN EVALUATIONS

Ostrom (1974)
Lineberry and Welsh (1974)
Katz et al. (1975)

CITIZEN POLICY INPUTS

Hayes (1976)
Susskind (1976)

MARKETING ISSUES AND PRACTICES

Melching (1976)
Rosener (1977)

public services . . . to become most useful, the concepts and tools need to be further developed and tested. (iii)

Thus, the public sector basis for marketing has evolved from a concern for productivity and recognition of the citizen as a government consumer. Techniques of market research and formative evaluation appear to be significant points of leverage for introducing marketing into government organizations. Yet, public decision makers should become more aware of the total scope of marketing thought and process.

MARKETING THOUGHT AND PROCESS—A PERSPECTIVE

The roots of marketing as a distinctive field of study were the problems of distribution and communication that confronted businesses as the market system grew in complexity and sophistication at the beginning of the twentieth century. Traditional economic theories and teachings were perceived not to explain adequately the dynamics of the "new" market system and its environment. Above all, economic principles did not provide the practical problem-solving guidelines that managers of commerce desired.

The evolution of the market system has continued, characterized by change, turbulence, complexity, increasing specialization, and sophistication. Marketing thought has been intricately involved, sometimes leading, sometimes following, and similarly characterized by change, turbulence, and some sophistication. Today the boundaries of marketing are no longer limited to commercial activity. Marketing is maturing into a social science with applied and some "pure" dimensions; it also maintains its practical, artistic perspective of strategic problem solving and managerial programming.

Problems of distribution and communication currently plague the public sector. These are compounded by citizen discontent and administrative frustration. Comprehension of marketing as a perspective for problem solving, a management technology, and a bank of theories and principles can provide direction for the government policy maker as it has for the business manager. Public problems may be less clearly understood, the values different, and the impacts more extensive, but the processes of marketing are similar. This is to advocate not that government adopt business principles and practices, but that generic marketing thought be developed for government and implemented.

A Generic Perspective

Marketing has many definitions. The best describe marketing as human activity directed at satisfying needs and desires through exchange processes rather than through direct coercion, supplication, or self-production (Kotler 1980). At the societal system level, marketing can be identified as the resource development, allocation, and accommodation processes that generate the quality of life. At the management level, marketing involves the configuration, symbolization, facilitation, and valuation of purposive, voluntary exchanges that are mutually accommodating and potentially satisfying. In Table 2.1 the basic elements of marketing are compared with fundamental conditions found in market systems.

Marketing as an exchange process can be characterized by five invariant elements: (1) there must be a minimum of two parties; (2) each party has unsatisfied needs producing a tension for satisfaction; (3) each party has an offering that could be of value—value deriving from its capacity to satisfy; (4) each party is capable of communication and of delivering their offering; (5) each party has relative freedom of choice to accept or reject the offer. When these conditions are present, there is the potential for marketing exchange (compare Kotler 1972).

Marketing can be studied using these basic elements to depict its fundamental structure, as presented in Figure 2.2. But the real conditions of marketing are more complex, and exchange involves dynamic cognitive and behavioral processes. For example, norms of exchange specialization distinguish the roles and related responsibilities of the marketer/seller and the buyer/consumer as portrayed in the figure. The marketer is more closely associated with the initiation and "management" of exchange, while the consumer is seen as a respondent. Complexity and dynamics pervade the marketing process.

TABLE 2.1

A Comparison Between Marketing Exchange Elements and Conditions

Marketing Elements	Marketing Conditions
Two parties	An environment
	Multiple relevant public
	Multiple participants
Needs	Desires
	Expectations and intentions
	Instrumental problems
Offerings of value	Products (benefit bundles)
	Costs/payments
	Distinctive capabilities
Communication and delivery capabilities	Markets
	Communication and distribution systems
	Marketing management programs (mixes)
Relative freedom of choice	Competition
	Complex choice dynamics
	Evaluation and control

FIGURE 2.2

A Simple Marketing Exchange Structure

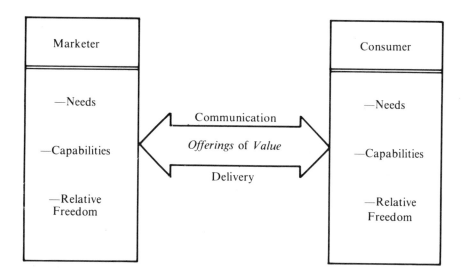

The Nature of Markets

Marketing exchange processes actually exist within ecological and human environments that (1) significantly influence, (2) can be influenced, but (3) cannot be controlled by the marketer or consumer. Likewise, many identifiable groups, relevant publics, can influence or potentially affect an exchange without being a direct participant. For example, regulators establish public service advertising rules; positive or negative media publicity affects the military recruiting process or a new coin in the currency system. Often multiple parties are directly involved in an exchange. Federal officials set military recruiting policies; a paid advertisement outlining the benefits of military life is presented on national television; local recruiters speak at high school assemblies; a youth and his or her parents decide together whether enlistment is appropriate.

"Needs" seldom propel the decision-making and behavioral processes in this affluent, socially influenced culture. Needs are strongly tempered by personal and social expectations. Implicitly, they become *desires* or *wants* anchored in symbolism and expression. To understand basic needs or survey demographic conditions is not sufficient to develop and execute exchanges effectively. There are welfare recipients demanding swimming pools in public housing projects, and there are elderly citizens rejecting welfare assistance and going hungry.

Complex bundles of benefits are constructed into products potentially to meet and satisfy consumers' functional and symbolic expectations and desires. The two dollar bill has shape, weight, and composition, but above all it has an *image*. A mass transit program provides transportation, but is it reliable and convenient, and does it serve meals? Therefore, appropriate product development is often a more critical threshold than communication or delivery; however, all must be interrelated for success, and a correct value must be determined.

Value is related to the consumer's perceptions or expectations of a product's ability to satisfy. If the consumer calculates the benefits to be greater than the costs, the exchange can be executed—product traded for payment. Cost and payment include both direct and indirect economic and psychological concerns. In noncommercial markets, this process is quite complicated. What is the cost to the service person of two years of military commitment—"especially the haircuts?" A dollar is paid for a lottery ticket, but how does the patron feel when he or she loses? Taxes are paid directly but the benefits are diffused throughout society.

All the parties in a market possess or can develop distinctive capabilities that strongly affect the ability to enter into exchanges. The most appropriately developed products are preferred. The one dollar bill entrenched in tradition is used rather than two dollar bills or one dollar Anthony coins. Only those with the desire, authority, and ability to absorb the costs enter an exchange. To take advantage of a $1,000 solar energy incentive an individual may have to spend $2,000 and incur aesthetic loss to his or her property.

An important condition is the evolution of "markets." Markets are the bounded domains and patterned systems of exchange potential. As they coalesce, complex communication and distribution systems are established. Desires and values converge. Comparative frames of reference are generated. A market can be a geographic area such as a municipal public service district, a specific location like the downtown post office, or a demographic characterization such as senior citizens. Markets can be identified by products, national parks, or benefits, recreation. They can be defined more abstractedly by identifying social, psychological, or behavioral characteristics. There are people who go to national parks frequently; those who go infrequently; and those who never go at all. The parks sell recreation, beauty, or a cheap place to spend a night while traveling to some consumers; to others, ecology and preservation are the products. The characteristics, attitudes, and behaviors that distinguish consumer groups can be used to form the market boundary or to identify submarkets referred to as segments.

Competition is a vital element of every market. It affects consumer choice, management decisions, and the nature of market boundaries. It can be direct or indirect, overt or covert. The Postal Service competes directly and overtly with national express delivery services. It competes less overtly and directly with telecommunication services; yet, these strongly influence the nature of its market. Mass transit programs compete with the well-established preferences in and patterns of personal transportation. Welfare programs sometimes compete at cross-purposes with work incentive programs. Black markets covertly pay cash for welfare vouchers. Therefore competition must be considered carefully with a creative comprehension of its effect on choice.

Marketing Management

Market complexity, change, and specialization dictate the need for conscious marketing management to direct and coordinate the elements of exchange. Traditionally, managerial marketing emphasized decisions about products, prices, promotion, and distribution policies based on consumer-oriented market research. Now a more comprehensive strategic perspective is developing (compare Enis and Mokwa 1979).

The objective of managerial marketing is to build effectively balanced demand relationships that satisfy consumers and the organizational mission simultaneously. To reach objectives, demand may require stimulation, such as encouraging more youths to enlist in the military; it may need conversion, such as switching people from private transportation to mass transit; or it may require extinction or de-emphasis, such as cigarette smoking in public places (Kotler 1973). The demand management tasks are different, and market strategies need to be distinctive, but marketing management processes are systematically similar. An outline and description of marketing management functions is presented in Table 2.2.

The marketing management process can be conceived as a decision system driven by the problems of: (1) analyzing and comprehending the market and its environment; (2) distinctly "matching" the organization with the most appropriate market segments and "positioning" this potential relationship in the competitive market space; (3) programming the elements of the market relationship; (4) implementing the plans and programs and effecting exchange transactions; and (5) formatively evaluating the decision process and exchange outcomes and impacts. Each management problem has a distinctive character and involves different analytical techniques—market research and planning in the initial phases and market auditing in control phases. The decision cycle starting with the dynamics of the market, and recycling with feedback from marketing evaluation provides an important heuristic for conceiving of marketing as a matching process. The decision cycle should be continuous. A responsive organization knows itself and its market; marketing relationships are continually changing: new desires and expectations interact with new objectives and competencies.

TABLE 2.2

Marketing Management Functions

Function	Description
Market analysis and intelligence (seeking)	The definition and characterization of a market and its environment, and identification of market potential.
Strategic market positioning (matching)	The analysis of market response potential in relation to organizational goals, resources, competencies, and environmental constraints, and designation of a desired strategic market position.
Market programming (mix decisions)	The design and valuation (pricing) of specific offerings (product/services) and of communications (promotion) and distribution (delivery) systems.
Consummating (transaction behavior)	The implementation of market programs and execution of exchange (transaction) episodes.
Marketing control (auditing)	The monitoring and evaluation of marketing decisions and actions and of market outcomes and impacts, and development of corrective decisions and actions.

Source: Adapted from Ben M. Enis and Michael P. Mokwa, "The Marketing Management Matrix: A Taxonomy for Strategy Comprehension," in ed. O. C. Ferrell, Stephen W. Brown, and Charles W. Lamb, Jr. Conceptual and Theoretical Developments in Marketing, Chicago: American Marketing Association, 1979.

Relative Freedom of Choice

To conclude this general overview of marketing, relative freedom of choice as an invariant exchange element warrants inspection. Consumer choice is complex, as demonstrated earlier. The free nature of choice is not easy to determine in many situations. Social pressure from a spouse or peer, a very persuasive advertisement, limited knowledge about a product or exchange conditions, limited choice alternatives—each of these can influence or reduce the relative freedom of choice. Yet the extent of free choice can be viewed more positively. An individual's vision to conceive the total situation, desire to assume decision responsibility, and ability to act on an environment thoughtfully all can affect the perception of freedom. For example, there is not much choice whether or not to pay federal taxes. But the dynamics of the annual transaction with the IRS allow many choices, particularly concerning when and how payment is made. The IRS has tremendous decision scope to manage responsively and effectively—an inquiry service producing valid answers, comprehensible forms, the use of advertising to build a positive image or to encourage early returns, a quick refund as a benefit for an early return. Clearly, marketing is a generic process with expansive public sector potential.

Conclusion

Government policy makers and administrators typically perceive marketing very narrowly, equating it with business practices, communication or distribution decisions, consumer research techniques, or serving every whim of consumer/citizens. This perception has stifled the adoption of marketing in the public sector. The purpose of the previous overview was to indicate the fundamental nature of marketing, to suggest its scope, and to provide some simple highlights of its application in government problem solving. The continued development of government marketing must be based on both the specific problems and contexts confronted by public decision makers and a valid theory of generic marketing, particularly its policy dimensions (Bagozzi 1974, 1975).

In marketing, the systematic study of actual policy-making behavior is perhaps the most underdeveloped area. Managerial marketing is characterized by many normative principles and robust analytical frameworks. Proscriptive research, intelligence, and planning are more heavily emphasized than operational and evaluative policy dimensions. Organizational issues have been ignored. A rich bank of isolated cases and examples are used selectively to support or reject principles and to demonstrate the utility of frameworks. Detailed, objective policy studies empirically exploring or "testing" theory are seldom reported. Thus questions about accuracy and reliability of many policy prescriptions are valid. This is a vital area for future research. Lack of an empirically based policy "science" literature inhibits knowledge transfer by reinforcing skepticism. Nevertheless, the positive heuristic value of marketing frameworks for the creative, skilled decision maker is now firmly established.

GOVERNMENT MARKETING—DISTINCTIVE CONTEXTS

Noncommercial marketing scholarship and practice has been conditioned extensively by its commercial heritage rather than by a generic perspective. An underlying premise has been the spectacular success of business marketing: the competitive dynamics of markets, profit criteria for evaluation, and adoption of rational entrepreneurial management technologies are the focal elements. From this premise, stereotypic models of business contexts and practices have been formulated and are used as bases for generalizations and a frame of reference—an implicit "ideal" type—in comparative analysis. Tendencies have evolved to (1) conceive of entire sectors or industries homogeneously, (2) isolate surrogate or surface dimensions for comparisons, and (3) overstate and overgeneralize.

A fundamental overstatement is the success of businesses and related connotations of failure in noncommercial sectors. Rates of new product failures and small business bankruptcies portray a different situation. The broadest generalizations are the comparative stereotypes of sectors. Differences *within* sectors are often more compelling than those distinguishing between sectors. The political characteristics of large corporations approximate those of many government organizations. Small social service agencies frequently operate much like small businesses. Government/business partnerships cross traditional boundaries.

All businesses are not alike, nor are they all successful. All government agencies and jurisdictions are not alike; success and effectiveness are not prevasive, nor is failure. Finally, most business and government organizations do not operate by the norms and principles preached in textbooks; textbook stereotyping is very misleading. The ideal of competitive markets, the validity of profit criteria, and the extent of rational management are questionable dimensions of business reality. Continued anchoring of noncommercial marketing in business stereotypes will inhibit its maturity. Better elaboration of government contexts and integration with generic marketing thought are necessary.

Many Government Contexts

The government is neither small nor homogeneous. The expansive scope of its activities can be perceived by scanning a budget or even a budget abstract—usually a somewhat startling experience. Conceiving the patterns of government action is a more rigorous task; comprehending the changing contexts may be a political art.

An important ideology of government has been to use structure to encourage balanced power. While effective execution of this is questionable, federal, state, and local jurisdictions are entrenched and new hybrids are evolving at regional levels. Likewise, problem-solving and policy patterns involve executive, legislative, and judicial interactions. It is easy for marketing advocates trained in the commercial sector to view structural arrangements naively or implicitly. For example, attention is usually limited to federal issues. State and local, or "service integration," problems are ignored or poorly factored into government marketing studies. These areas do involve crucial problems and often provide the most accessible and willing environments for marketing analysis.

The diffuse areas of government policy and activity are very important but well beyond simple or brief discussion. After all, government does more than make and enforce laws! As a protector, arbiter, and allocator of both social and economic values, its involvement or potential involvement is nearly pervasive even in a system that fears concentration of power and attempts to limit it severely.

One way to outline the policy domain is to use conventional content criteria elaborating each field, from agriculture and arts to zoos. More abstract categorization would identify functional activities: protection, regulation, distribution, redistribution, "support" operations (compare Lowi 1964). Another could isolate product/market attributes such as the essential levels of sociopolitical benefits; divisibility of consumption; direct compensatory potential; extent of voluntary compliance and choice; differentiation of market characteristics (including values); augmented sociopolitical benefits; cost diffusion or transfers; efficacy of commercial market dynamics or alternatives (compare Shanklin 1975; Spratlen, Chapter 3 in this volume). Regardless of the taxonomy, the scope of problems and contexts is very broad and, of course, related to the traditions and environments of each policy field, government function, and product/market domain. The marketing problems and strategies of protecting the "arts," for example, are different than those of distributing or redistributing the arts. Structural interactions among Congress, the National Endowment for the Arts, and each state arts council complicate the tasks. However, marketing could be incorporated more precisely into these tasks.

Policy Development

Symbolism and substance, mandates that are too vague or too narrow, interaction with and interference by multiple constituencies, public review and regulation related to accountability and social responsibility, poor measures of effectiveness, difficulty in determining demand, and service-oriented products—these are among the characteristics of policy contexts and processes used to differentiate between the public and private sectors. However, these appear to characterize more accurately the convergence of public and private contexts and processes, rather than their differences (compare Murray 1975). There *are* critical differences; but these are not the surface distinctions magnified when contrasting sector stereotypes (compare Rainey, Backoff, and Levine 1976).

Problem solving is the core of all policy. Simply, put, it is the developmental movement from concepts to decisions—action or nonaction. Ideology, problems, technologies, structures, performance indicators, and "system slack" are appropriate differentiating criteria for comprehending and distinguishing policy contexts and processes. At the ideological level, government is clearly different from commerce; for example, commerce can be selective in the problems it chooses to approach and explicitly limited and exclusionary in the strategies it chooses to enact. Government thus confronts the most pervasive, undifferentiated problems that typically possess the most experimental or indeterminant technological solutions. Needless to say, government has tended to formulate policy patterns that avoid risk, maintain contexts, and adapt to situations incrementally. Government policy processes are considered more reactive and bureaucrative than the contrasting commercial "ideal type" portrayed by a proactive search for opportunities and by responsive strategies. Indeed, serious investigation of the commercial response to social responsibility pressures or the automotive and energy industries struggle with survival would dilute the ideal type.

In conclusion, government policy processes are poorly understood, but so are business policy processes. Policy should be conceived as a system with content and process dimensions that move ideas *developmentally* toward actions. Stages such as agenda setting, issue analysis, design, adoption, implementation, evaluation, and termination can be outlined and can guide study and practice (compare Anderson 1975; Jones 1970). In government, structure and mandates reinforce divisions between stages; however, there is no definitive "policy cycle." To paraphrase May and Wildavsky (1978) liberally, no simple predetermined policy system in which all policies inevitably develop. As the policy space becomes increasingly crowded, it is apparent that policies—processes and contents—are more difficult to isolate, define, and outline. Past policies become part of the environment generating new problems, and the techniques of designing a solution are at odds with the finesse required to implement it.

A more valid perspective on policy development would enhance government marketing practice and thought and, more generally, enrich all marketing thought. The policy science orientation of public sector research could provide valuable direction and insights.

CONCLUSION—KNOWLEDGE AND PRACTICE

Marketing is a perspective and a technology. In this chapter both dimensions have been explored, probing for the foundations and the developmental problems of generating government marketing consciousness and precision. To date, marketing is comprehended poorly and often misunderstood throughout the public sector. Its contribution has been minimal and inhibited. Marketing advocates must learn more about sociopolitical contexts and processes. Naive stereotypes about government and about business must be rejected and replaced with better policy research based on a generic concept of marketing.

Government decision makers and scholars must also think and behave beyond myths about marketing and myopia about the nature of their problems and contexts. Viewing citizens as consumers and marketing as an invariant process of exchange are the foundations. Implementing this ideology will not be easy, but the evolution from productivity concerns to effectiveness and responsiveness issues is establishing the direction. More extensive use of proscriptive and evaluative consumer studies, formative policy evaluations, incremental program efforts, and education are clearly the best points of leverage to develop government marketing practice.

Adequate theory is necessary to lead, refine, and serve as a communication media. Lack of interdisciplinary bases and effort characterize the current state of scholarship and appear to produce and reinforce tendencies to stereotype and to deal with surface concerns. This situation must be changed. Interdisciplinary interaction and involvement in the field could dramatically enhance theory and perspective. There are many directions: richer theories of policy development; more focus on the conflict dimensions of exchange; better elaboration of the dynamics of product/market evolutions; models of effectiveness that are empirically based and represent realities; and, of course, pragmatic insights for the public policy maker and administrator. Government marketing is an interesting challenge and an important issue.

REFERENCES

Anderson, James E. (1975), *Public Policy-Making*, New York: Praeger.

Arndt, Johan (1979), "Toward a Concept of Domesticated Markets," *Journal of Marketing* 43 (Fall); 69–75.

Bagozzi, Richard P. (1974), "Marketing as an Organized Behavioral System of Exchange," *Journal of Marketing* 38 (October); 77–81.

———— (1975), "Marketing as Exchange," *Journal of Marketing* 39 (October); 32–39.

Blakely, Edward J., Howard Schutz and Peter Harvey (1977), "Public Marketing: A Suggested Policy Planning Paradigm for Community Development in the City," *Social Indicators Research* 4; 164–84.

Breyer, Ralph F. (1931), *Commodity Marketing*, New York: McGraw-Hill.

Brown, Daniel J., Philip B. Schary and Boris W. Becker (1978), "Marketing Down the Road: The Role of Marketing Analysis in Transportation Planning," in Subhash C. Jain, ed., *1978 Educators' Proceedings*, pp. 359–62, Chicago: American Marketing Association.

Brown, Stephen W., Lonnie L. Ostrom and John L. Schlacter (1978), "PPB and the Marketing Contribution: Implications for the Management of Public Enterprise," in ed. John W. Sutherland *Management Handbook for Public Administrators*, pp. 720–48, New York: Van Nostrand Reinhold.

Claxton, John D., Thomas C. Kinnear, and J. R. Brent Ritchie (1978), "Should Government Programs Have Marketing Managers," *Michigan Business Review* 30 (May); 10–16.

Divita, Salvatore and Robert F. Dyer (1979), "Public Sector Marketing: A Proactive Response to Citizen Dissatisfaction," Paper presented to the American Society for Public Administration National Convention, Baltimore, April.

Enis, Ben M. and Michael P. Mokwa (1979), "The Marketing Management Matrix: A Taxonomy for Strategy Comprehension," in ed. O. C. Ferrell, Stephen W.

Brown, and Charles W. Lamb, Jr. *Conceptual and Theoretical Developments in Marketing*, pp. 485–505, Chicago: American Marketing Association.

Etgar, Michael and Brian T. Ratchford (1975), "Marketing Management and Marketing Conflict in Non-Profit Organizations," *1974 Combined Proceedings*, pp. 258–261, Chicago: American Marketing Association.

Hatry, Harry P. and Donald M. Fisk (1971), *Improving Productivity Measurement in Local Government*, Washington D.C.: Commission on Productivity.

Hayes, Frederick O'R. (1976), "Interaction Between Government and Citizen," *National Center for Productivity Workshop*, Annapolis, MD: (July).

Houston, Franklin S. and Richard E. Homans (1977), "Public Agency Marketing: Pitfalls and Problems," *Business Topics*, (Summer), 36–40.

Hunt, Shelby D. (1976), "The Nature and Scope of Marketing," *Journal of Marketing*, 40 (July); 17–28.

Jones, Charles O. (1970), *An Introduction to the Study of Public Policy*, Belmont, CA: Wadsworth Publishing.

Katz, Daniel, Barbara A. Gutek, Robert L. Kahn and Eugenia Barton (1975), *Bureaucratic Encounters: A Pilot Study in the Evaluation of Government Services*, Ann Arbor, MI: Institute for Social Research.

Kotler, Philip (1972), "A Generic Concept of Marketing," *Journal of Marketing*, 36 (April), 46–54.

Kotler, Philip (1975), *Marketing for Nonprofit Organizations*, Englewood Cliffs, NJ: Prentice-Hall.

Kotler, Philip (1980), *Marketing Management Planning, Analysis and Control*, Englewood Cliffs, NJ: Prentice-Hall.

—— and Sidney J. Levy (1969), "Broadening the Concept of Marketing," *Journal of Marketing*, 33 (January), 10–15.

—— and Sidney Levy (1973), "Buying is Marketing Too," *Journal of Marketing*, 37, (January), 54–59.

Kotler, Philip and Gerald Zaltman (1971), "Social Marketing: An Approach to Planned Social Change," *Journal of Marketing*, 35 (July), 3–12.

Levy, Sidney J. and Gerald Zaltman (1975), *Marketing, Society and Conflict*, Englewood Cliffs, NJ: Prentice-Hall.

Lineberry, Robert L. and Robert E. Welsh, Jr. (1974), "Who Gets What: Measuring the Distribution of Urban Public Services," *Social Science Quarterly*, 54 (March), 700–12.

Lovelock, Christopher H. and Charles B. Weinberg (1975), "Contrasting Private and Public Sector Marketing," in ed. Ronald C. Curham *1974 Combined Proceedings*, pp. 242–47, Chicago: American Marketing Association.

—— (1978), "Public and Nonprofit Marketing Comes of Age," in *Review of Marketing 1978*, pp. 413–52, Chicago: American Marketing Association.

Lowi, Theodore J. (1964), "American Business, Public Policy, Case Studies and Political Theory," *World Politics* 16 (July); 667–715.

May, Judith V. and Aaron B. Wildavsky (1978), *The Policy Cycle*, Beverly Hills, Calif.: Sage.

Melching, Jerry (1976), *Governmental Effectiveness: Responding to Citizen Needs*, Columbus, Ohio: Melching Associates.

Mokwa, Michael P. (1978), "The Development of Marketing Thought and Technology in the Public Sector," Paper presented to the American Society for Public Administration National Convention, Phoenix, Ariz., April.

—— and Ben M. Enis (1979), "Moving Public Administration Beyond Marketing Myths and Myopia," Paper presented to the American Society for Public Administration National Convention, Baltimore, April.

—— and Norman Kangun (1979), "Consumer Policy Decisions: A Marketing Perspective," *Public Policy Issues in Marketing* 1; 34–47.

Murray, Michael A. (1975), "Comparing Public and Private Management: An Exploratory Essay," *Public Administration Review* 34 (July-August); 364–71.

Ostrom, Elinor (1974), "Exclusion, Choice and Divisibility: Factors Affecting the Measurement of Urban Agency Output and Impact," *Social Science Quarterly* 54 (March); 691–99.

Rainey, Hal G., Robert W. Backoff and Charles H. Levine (1976), "Comparing Public and Private Organizations," *Public Administration Review* 35 (March-April); 233–44.

Rathmell, John M. (1973), "Marketing by the Federal Government," *Business Topics* (Summer); 21–28.

Ritchie, J. R. Brent and Roger J. LaBreque (1975), "Marketing Research and Public Policy: A Functional Perspective," *Journal of Marketing* 39 (July); 12–19.

Rosener, Judy B. (1977), "Improving Productivity in the Public Sector: An Analysis of Two Tools—Marketing and Citizen Involvement," *Public Productivity Review* 2 (Spring-Summer); 3–11.

Rothschild, Michael L. (1977), *An Incomplete Bibliography of Works Relating to Marketing for Public Sector and Nonprofit Organizations*, no. 9-577-711, 2nd ed., Boston: ICCH.

—— (1979), "Marketing Communications in Nonbusiness Situations or Why Its So Hard to Sell Brotherhood Like Soap," *Journal of Marketing* 43 (Spring); 11–20.

Shanklin, William L. (1975), "New York City: A Portrait in Marketing Mania," *California Management Review* 18 (Winter); 34–40.

Sheth, Jagdish N. and Peter L. Wright (1974), *Marketing Analysis for Societal Problems*, Urbana: University of Illinois Press.

Stafford, James E. and H. E. Lyons (1979), "Community Research: A Public-Private Partnership," Paper presenter to the American Society for Public Administration National Convention, Baltimore, April.

Susskind, Lawrence E. (1976), "Citizen Involvement in the Design, Assessment and Delivery of Public Services," Paper presented to the National Center for Productivity Workshop, Annapolis, Md., July.

Webb, Kenneth and Harry P. Hatry (1973), *Obtaining Citizen Feedback: The Application of Citizen Surveys to Local Governments*, Washington, D.C.: Urban Institute.

Wiebe, G. D. (1951), "Merchandising Commodities and Citizenship on Television," *Public Opinion Quarterly* 15 (Winter); 679–91.

Zaltman, Gerald and Pol Jacobs (1977), "Social Marketing and a Consumer-Based Theory of Marketing," in Arch G. Woodside, Jagdish N. Sheth, and Peter D. Bennett (eds.) *Consumer and Industrial Buying Behavior*, 399–408, New York: North-Holland.

Zaltman, Gerald, Philip Kotler and Ira Kaufman (1972), *Creating Social Change*, New York: Holt, Rinehart and Winston.

3

GOVERNMENT GOODS AND SERVICES: CHARACTERISTICS AND CONCEPTS FOR MARKETING ANALYSIS

Thaddeus H. Spratlen

The production and consumption characteristics of public goods are generally recognized in economics, and they have received particular attention in welfare and public choice economics. However, analysis to date in public sector marketing has not generally reflected the established differences between private and public goods. Such differences in the context of market exchange relationships are explored in this chapter. Marketing concepts and perspectives are analyzed with an emphasis on developing a classification framework with particular theoretical and analytical usefulness for government marketing.

Most of the chapter is devoted to a discussion of classification frameworks for analyzing government goods and services. Marketing implications of the analysis are briefly summarized along with some conclusions that can be drawn from the analysis.

Before proceeding with the discussion of classification frameworks, it seems useful to distinguish between government marketing and marketing to the government. The latter is really a type of industrial marketing. Government units are composed of industrial buyers or customers. Conventional analysis in managerial marketing is generally applicable (Robertson 1979). Government marketing, that is, marketing by the government, is a type of public and nonprofit or social marketing. Programs, services, and other outputs of government units represent exchangeable values which have various forms of individual, collective, or other consumption, usage, and exchange attributes. They are or can be marketed as public sector products. Conventional analysis in marketing may need to be modified when it is used in government organizations. Some aspects of marketing may be inappropriate or inapplicable to government marketing. The issues of propriety or applicability remain to be explored fully in the development of government marketing.

It should also be noted that the question is still largely unaddressed as to whether, how, and to what extent government should engage in marketing. This analysis is confined to specific relationships involving a useful classification framework. It is implicitly assumed that such a framework would have at least benign, if not beneficial, uses in many areas of government operations.

THE CLASSIFICATION OF GOVERNMENT GOODS AND SERVICES

There are three broad frameworks of classification for government goods and services using industrial, functional, and product attribute or marketability criteria, each of which is outlined here. But the primary focus of this discussion is on a framework that emphasizes product attribute and marketability criteria.

A Classification by Industrial Groups

This type of classification is outlined in Table 3.1. It is of course the same as the official standard industrial classification of goods and services (U.S. Bureau of the Budget 1957).

For purposes of government marketing (or for marketing to the government as that may be relevant), the various categories can be approached conceptually in much the same manner as in consumer or industrial marketing. Differences arise primarily with respect to institutional arrangements and constraints. Thus a commissary store operates much like a membership discount or general merchandise store, except for Department of Defense regulations that stipulate policies or practices not encountered in conventional retail merchandising for equivalent product assortments. Incidentally, it has been noted that the federal commissary system is larger than the merchandising operations of several national chains (Haveman 1970, p. 8). In such situations there are few really fundamental differences with respect to government marketing. From an organizational buying perspective, government organizations can be approached in a conventional customer perspective as is done in commercial marketing.

A Classification by Government Function

The scope of government functions can be defined administratively with respect to the 20 categories of activities listed in Table 3.2. From

TABLE 3.1

Industrial Classification of Government Goods and Services

Major Industrial Divisions*	Major Group Title	Illustrative Subtitles and Product Service Groups
01–09	Agriculture, forestry, and fisheries	Agricultural, animal husbandry and horticultural services; experimental farms; fish hatcheries
10–14	Mining and metals	Exploration and development of mineral properties; quarries
15–17	Contract construction	Construction of highways, streets, and bridges; sewage and sanitary facilities and other structures
19, 24–25, 30–31	Manufactured durable goods	Semifinished and finished products; mechanical and chemical transformation into equipment, fixtures, furniture, etc.; military hardware
20–23, 26–29, 32–39	Manufactured nondurable goods	Processing food, beverages, fiber, and textiles; printing and publishing
40–49	Transportation, communication, electric, gas and sanitary services	Railroads, local suburban, and interurban transit; motor freight and warehousing; air, pipeline transportation services; electric and gas utilities, sanitary services
50–59	Wholesale and retail trade	Commissaries, warehousing operations; petroleum bulk stations; marketing of farm and other products
60–67	Finance, insurance, and real estate	Social insurance, banking and nonbank financial institutions; housing agencies
70–79	Personal, business, and recreation services	Parks, national and state reserves; sporting and recreational camps

TABLE 3.1 (continued)

Industrial Classification of Government Goods and Services

Major Industrial Divisions*	Major Group Title	Illustrative Subtitles and Product Service Groups
80	Medical and other health services	Hospitals, clinics, and health centers, medical research laboratories
81	Legal services	Legal aid, public defender services
82	Educational and library services	Schools, libraries
84	Museums, galleries, and gardens	Art galleries, botanical and zoological gardens
89	Miscellaneous services	Scientific research, engineering services

*These two-digit numbers should be preceded by 91, 92, or 93 to indicate federal, state, or local government, respectively.

Source: U.S. Bureau of the Budget, *Standard Industrial Classification Manual* (Washington, D.C.: Government Printing Office, 1957), pp. 215–17.

TABLE 3.2

Categories and Budgetary Importance of Government Administrative Functions, by Level of Government, in Selected Years (percentage)

Category	All Governments in U.S. 1976	Federal 1978 Estimate	State 1976	Local (City and County) 1976
1. Agricultural services[a]	N.A.	0.3	N.A.	N.A.
2. Education, training and employment	17.0	4.7	32.1	13.0
3. Energy resources	N.A.	1.7	N.A.	N.A.
4. Fire protection services (local only)	0.6	N.A.	N.A.	4.8*
5. Fiscal, financial operations, and control[b]	9.6	9.7	2.0	8.9
6. General government and administration	N.A.	0.9	N.A.	N.A.
7. Health and hospitals[c]	4.4	9.6	6.0	8.6
8. Housing; community and regional development[d]	N.A.	2.9	0.3	2.3*
9. Libraries	N.A.	2.9	0.3	2.3*
10. National defense and international affairs[e]	16.0	24.7	N.A.	N.A.
11. Natural resources and environment, including parks and recreation	3.3	2.6	2.1	3.9
12. Police protection and corrections	1.7	N.A.	2.2	8.4
13. Postal services	2.2	—	—	—
14. Public utilities	4.0	N.A.	3.6	16.1*
15. Sanitation and sewage services	1.3	N.A.	1.4	8.2*
16. Scientific/ technological research and development	N.A.	1.0	N.A.	N.A.
17. Social and welfare services[f]	22.4	33.7	16.8	11.1
18. Supply stores (alcoholic beverage stores)	N.A.	N.A.	1.0	0.3*
19. Transportation	4.8	3.5	9.8	8.0

TABLE 3.2 (continued)

Categories and Budgetary Importance of Government Administrative Functions, by Level of Government, in Selected Years (percentage)

Category	All Governments in U.S. 1976	Federal 1978 Estimate	State 1976	Local (City and County) 1976
20. Other functions and programs; unallocable expenditures[g]	12.7	5.3	22.7	5.4
Total	100.0	100.0	100.0	100.0

Note: Asterisk indicates city only. "N.A." indicates information not available.

Federal budget outlays do not include off-budget operations amounting to more than $10 billion, such as the Board of Governors of the Federal Reserve System, Federal Financing Bank, Postal Service fund, United States Railway Association, Rural Telephone Bank, and a few other less well-known federal entities (The Budget of the United States Government, 1980; p. 311) Washington, D.C.: Government Printing Office.

[a]Includes mainly research, advisory, and other technical assistance; excludes farm income stabilization since most of this is presumably not applicable to marketing-related activities.

[b]Includes revenue sharing at the federal level; net interest payments and other fiscal controls. Comparability between levels is distorted by lack of uniformity of reporting categories.

[c]Includes health care services; expenditures for research and education; training grants for health care work force; health and safety programs.

[d]Includes urban renewal, economic and industrial development; disaster relief and insurance; mortgage credit and theft insurance.

[e]Military and other defense expenditures; foreign economic, financial, and military assistance; conduct of foreign affairs; foreign information and exchange.

[f]Income security along with other social services (rehabilitation, counseling, etc.)

[g]Includes veteran's benefits and services (e.g., 4.1 percent of federal budget outlays); also the "not available" categories.

Source: U.S., Department of Commerce, Bureau of the Census, (1978). *Statistical Abstract of the United States* Washington, D.C.: Governmental Printing Office. *The Budget of the United States Government,* (1980). Washington, D.C.: Government Printing Office. Fiscal 1980.

a marketing point of view such a classification contains many overlapping product types and potential areas of marketing activities. Thus in its basic form such a classification would be used mainly for purposes of descriptive analysis and administrative convenience. Also it should be recognized that product and service marketing applications may be quite limited relative to total expenditures in a given program or administrative category. In the case of agriculture, for example, research, advisory and technical assistance account for only 13.2 percent of federal outlays in fiscal 1978. The remaining 86.8 percent was expended for income stabilization and other subsidy programs. As noted in greater detail by Sethi in Chapter 7 of this volume, income transfers as politically distributed benefits are less amenable to marketing methods and strategies than programs of direct product and service delivery.

A Classification by Benefits

A functional classification can be made more useful by associating it with various categories of benefits. The framework could be used to stress the idea that government goods and services have (or should have) some identifiable set of benefits associated with them. Then, if the operations and activities of government organizations are to be approached from a marketing perspective, one major focus would be to develop an optimal set of benefits associated with the purposes and programs of the organization. In this way market objectives, constituencies, priorities, and exchange results could be identified and, once identified, developed for appropriate marketing presentation.

Benefits could be categorized along the following lines:

1. Physiological (relating to biogenic or biological requirements and functions of people). Examples: medical care, family planning, and related health services.
2. Psychological (relating to the mental or psychic motivational, cognitive, and adaptive problems of people). Examples: counseling for alcoholism, drug abuse, adjustment to aging and related problems of individual and group behavior.
3. Ecological (relating to the physical environmental requirements of people). Examples: pollution abatement, wild life preserves, noise reduction programs, energy conservation, etc.
4. Economic (Relating to the resource-utilization tradeoffs, and cost requirements of meeting the material needs of people). Examples: job search services, industrial development, sheltered work programs for the disabled, etc.
5. Technical (Relating to the scientific and technological requirements of innovation, technical change and the impact of technology in society). Examples: fluoridation of water supplies, nuclear power plants safety, etc.
6. Social-Cultural (Relating to the education, religious, institutional, esthetic, value, and other patterned roles and relationships of people in a group setting). Examples: support for the performing arts, library services, schools, museums, etc.

The list of benefit categories could be refined and extended in many different ways to aid the process of benefit segmentation or the development of other marketing strategies.

A CLASSIFICATION BY PRODUCT ATTRIBUTES AND MARKETABILITY

Neither of the preceding classification frameworks has a strong conceptual or analytical basis for use in government marketing. For either, benefit criteria can be linked to well-established concepts of benefit segmentation in traditional marketing management practice. But this still does not provide particularly unique extensions or applications for government marketing once proper allowances are made for social or public benefits and externalities that should be contained within government marketing practices.

The concept of marketability is an essential part of the framework and so should be defined before it is applied. The physical possibility of marketing government goods and services is one meaning. Economic feasibility is another. Social and/or political desirability is a third. Of course, any combination of these three meanings could also be used. Generally both economic feasibility and social desirability are implied in the term *marketability* as used here.

The use of product attributes and marketability criteria involves an attempt to interpret government marketing so that a logical connection can be made between product attributes and customer as well as marketer responses to them. When properly refined, such a framework offers the foundation for developing marketing strategies or for application in other areas of marketing management in the public sector.

An outline of the framework is presented in Table 3.3. Several illustrations are provided in which government goods and services are rated with respect to being high, medium, or low on a given attribute. The content and importance of each category of attributes is discussed below.

Divisibility of Consumption

This criterion is one of the most important for distinguishing public from private goods and services. For the latter there is customarily a high degree of divisibility in consumption—so much so that the exclusion principle applies. An individual can consume, realize benefits, and exclude others from sharing directly in the consumption benefits. Just the reverse tends to be true of most government goods and services.

One manifestation of this attribute is that, when it occurs, public goods can be consumed by one individual without reducing their availability to others; alternatively, one more consumer can be added without increasing the cost of making the goods or services available. Examples that come readily to mind are fire protection, national security, contagious disease and air pollution control, highways, weather forecasting, and regulation of nuclear waste disposal. Such goods have a high degree of collectivity and

TABLE 3.3

Government Product Attributes and Marketability Criteria

Attributes/Criteria	Description and Rating of Relevant Product		
	High	Medium	Low
Divisibility of consumption	Postal services; surplus equipment; publications	Mass transit; routes, fares and services may be designed to serve particular groups of riders	Fire protection since it must be provided to all for personal and public safety
Extent of social merit	Public education and its contribution to personal development and public wealth	Alcoholic beverage monopoly in several states (e.g., prices are usually lower in nonmonopoly states)	Tobacco promotion and subsidies to aid farm and industry groups; state lotteries
Importance of voluntary compliance in acquisition and use	Public libraries; government savings bonds and other investment securities; social insurance	Burglary and fraud prevention (may involve cooperation and private property security arrangements)	Legal protection of private property and contract enforcement
Availability of private market alternatives	Housing and transportation; college education	Local home and property protection; mail and parcel delivery services	Water supply and utilities; weather forecasting; sanitary services

TABLE 3.3 (continued)

Government Product Attributes and Marketability Criteria

Attributes/Criteria	Description and Rating of Relevant Product		
	High	Medium	Low
Efficacy of money price alternatives	Housing and transportation; college education (exceptions occur in connection with equal opportunity or other welfare goals)	Local home and property protection; mail and parcel delivery services (mainly supplementary to public services which are provided by government)	Water supply and utilities; weather forecasting; sanitary services (must be provided on a need basis or for public health and safety)
Distribution of social benefits	Programs of rent subsidies and public housing (shelter environment, etc.)	Parks, recreation, and amenities; energy conservation; metrification	Government sale of alcoholic beverages

external effects associated with them. Geographic contiguity may also be of critical importance in their distribution and consumption. Private ownership and control are necessarily quite minimal; thus private marketability is quite limited (or nonexistent). That is, there tends to be a direct relationship between divisibility and private marketability. For example, government goods that do have a high degree of divisibility in consumption and marketability would include military hardware, surplus equipment, electric energy, stockpiled minerals, agricultural commodities, mass transit, postal services, and publications. Such goods and services can be marketed with a high degree of immediate transfer and adaptation of traditional marketing methods and techniques. But those on the low end of the divisibility continuum are less marketable in conventional exchange terms. Information about them or behavior in response to them, of course, can be marketed. Thus fire safety and the elimination of fire hazards at home or at work can be marketed even though protection as such is not. Also fire protection service delivery could be approached with a marketing and logistics emphasis. Maximizing the speed of response or optimal assignment of personnel and equipment could then be approached with marketing considerations in mind.

Extent of Social Merit

Most government products are presumed to contain a considerable degree of social merit. Their provision contributes recognizable and redeeming social benefits to some specified group of citizens or to the community or society at large. Efforts to redistribute income and wealth, assure standards of public health in restaurants, and provide security for the elderly are examples of government services with a high degree of social merit that would be generally recognized. Even those of dubious or disputable social merit (military hardware, nuclear power weapons and facilities, herbicides or other chemicals for biological warfare, tobacco products, and the like) can usually be associated with meritorious features and with specified benefits to market segments in the context of a particular nation's social, economic, or political interests. But such an interpretation would also extend to private goods. That is, even tobacco products and especially alcoholic beverages provide distinct social benefits to some, despite their acknowledged harmful effects.

There does not appear to be any consistent relationship between the extent of social merit in a government good and its marketability. A more compelling public welfare rationale to support marketing can be formulated for those goods which have a high degree of social merit. Disease or fire prevention and control, vehicle inspection services, and utilization of safety equipment are examples. But because value and/or behavior change may be involved in the consumption or usage process, marketing may be a relatively weak and inefficient tool or an auxiliary tool for influencing their consumption. Thus it should be recognized that government marketing, as with social marketing generally, may be used to reduce rather than enlarge consumption. Safety programs then would be marketed, in part, because they reduce the consumption of fire protection, hospital services, traffic control personnel, and related resources.

Importance of Voluntary Compliance

Government sanctions provide a strong basis for obtaining compliance with prescribed conduct in many areas of life. Responsiveness to the rules of law defines expected patterns of behavior and may reduce the applicability of marketing. In areas where government predominates and responsiveness to laws is strong, marketing is likely to have only limited usefulness in the operations of government. Examples where this occurs would include contract enforcement, police protection of private property, prevention of theft and restraint from personal assault on other persons.

As with divisibility it seems likely that a direct relationship generally prevails with marketability. Voluntary compliance in acquisition and consumption is high in such product areas as the use of census data and publications, patronage of mass transit and postal services, participation in government savings bond campaigns, patronage of restaurants, parks, and the like—and so is the potential for government marketing.

Availability of Private Market Alternatives

In many product areas there are government and private market alternatives. Education, health care, housing, and savings and investment instruments are familiar examples. There are likely to be greater opportunities for marketing in such areas than when private market alternatives are not present. Thus in national defense there is categorical differentiation from the private marketplace. Mercenaries excepted, national defense is not a private market offering. Of course, military hardware and related technology do provide government marketing opportunities that are widely exploited. Moreover, marketing techniques may be used in lobbying activities to gain support for particular defense programs and weapons systems, and the benefits of national security may also be marketed to the political advantage of certain groups. But it has long been recognized that government enterprise can also be detrimental to the functioning of the private marketplace (U.S., Congress 1933).

Generally, a direct relationship appears to exist between the marketability of government goods and the availability of private market alternatives. Whether government can be expected to market competitively with private enterprise would depend upon production and public policy as well as other considerations.

With respect to production, the type of cost structure is highly influential. A decreasing cost structure, for example, results in a situation in which private firms cannot compete profitably. In effect this describes potential or actual monopoly conditions. Pure examples would be weather forecasting and ocean lighthouse services. Within existing capacity or supply conditions, serving additional users does not increase unit costs. Economies of scale in production also occur in such operations and necessitate that contiguous areas be served by the same source of supply (Tullock 1970, p. 94).

Public policy concerns for equity, access, or other welfare goals may also dictate a government marketing option. Consumer and worker safety programs, city water and gas utilities, sanitary services, and "public power," along with the TVA at the federal level, illustrate such considerations.

Efficacy of Money Price Alternatives

Money price alternatives are commonplace in government marketing where a high degree of divisibility of consumption and voluntary compliance in use exist. Tolls for turnpikes or highway services, fares for parking and mass transit ridership, and charges for utility services come most readily to mind. But all such areas represent a very small proportion of government output. In the vast majority of instances (national security, most forms of education, and the like) few money price alternatives exist. Thus, in conventional terms at least, marketability and the efficacy of money price alternatives would be directly related. Consider the comparisons shown in Table 3.4. In terms of expenditures (by the value of output and other measures) an overwhelmingly large portion of government goods and services fall within the low (or no) money price alternative and low marketability. Since national defense, education, and social welfare services comprise over two-thirds of all government output, the availability of money price alternatives and marketing in conventional market exchange terms are generally limited to much less than one-third of all government operations. As previously noted, this does not apply to the government-as-organizational-buyer aspects of marketing.

Distribution of Social Benefits

The distribution of social benefits is somewhat related to social merit attributes. For example, the federal government accounts for over three-fifths of research expenditures in the U.S. economy. While a substantial amount is focused on applications to military and space technology or to the

TABLE 3.4

Money Price Alternatives and Marketability of Government Goods and Services

Extent/Criteria	Money Price Alternatives	Marketability
High	Education Public transit	
	Health care services Sanitation services Housing services	Agricultural services Public utilities
Medium	Space research and exploration Housing	
	Social insurance Welfare programs	Natural Resource Use
Low (or Nonexistent)	Most forms of government regulation and general administration Police protection	National defense International relations

operations of public institutions (highway departments, mass transit agencies, and so on), there are spillover benefits that extend well beyond the direct or immediate applications. For example, as an extension of space research and technology, the physically disabled have been provided with various prosthetic devices. An important role for marketing exists in expanding the adoption of technology from government-sponsored research and innovation. Much of this would fall within the category of marketing information and ideas for increasing the social benefits to be derived from a government program or administrative function.

MARKETING IMPLICATIONS

The characteristics and concepts presented here have many uses in government marketing. Generally, primary emphasis would be focused on those goods and services to which responses are not likely to be elicited by coercion or the use of the police powers of the state. In the latter instance, legal administration or the operation of some explicit threat system become more important than voluntary compliance through marketing. In such areas marketing can be a supplementary process for encouraging compliance. It may also be used to help reduce enforcement costs or the general operations of government.

It has been stressed that government goods and services which are low on many of the product and marketability attributes, offer rather limited opportunities for traditional marketing. But, recognizing their characteristics, it becomes systematic rather than arbitrary to place government operations outside the scope of marketing. Surely aspects of so-called free goods can be marketed. The collective aspects of their externalities or other attributes should simply be taken into account when applying marketing methods and strategies.

By using a product attribute and marketability approach, it becomes easier to understand why certain products are marketed (priced and sold in conventional or comparable exchange processes) and others are distributed politically or administratively through transfers, subsidies, or other arrangements with payments made from general or special revenue sources.

As suggested by Rathmell (1973), marketing analysis can also aid in the determination of which products can be provided most effectively through the marketing process, which ones through a public administration process, and which ones in some combination arrangement.

Additionally, improved management and utilization of resources expected from the use of marketing can be enhanced through a more systematic approach to analyzing government product attributes and the customer responses made to them. In addition to what has already been mentioned, the kind of framework presented can help to (1) identify areas of need for government goods and services; (2) improve communication between citizens as consumers and the government as marketer; and (3) encourage government units to become more responsive, constituent-oriented institutions.

CONCLUSIONS

Public goods have many characteristics that present challenging problems and tasks for government marketing. For purposes of theory and strategic marketing practice, the process can be enhanced through a more systematic conceptual and analytical framework. Product attribute and marketability criteria offer some instructive ways of analyzing and adapting market exchange concepts and techniques for use in government marketing. It has been emphasized here that a useful classification framework can be developed from such characteristics as divisibility in consumption, extent of social merit, importance of voluntary compliance, availability of private market alternatives, efficacy of money price alternatives, and distribution of social benefits. When applied in the analysis of particular goods and services, they should help to improve theory and practice in government marketing.

REFERENCES

Gaedeke, Ralph M., ed. (1977), *Marketing in Private and Public Nonprofit Organizations—Perspectives and Illustrations*, Santa Monica, Calif.: Goodyear.

Greenberg, Barnett and Danny Bellenger (1974), *The Classification of Consumer Goods: An Empirical Study*, Atlanta: School of Business Administration, Georgia State University.

Haveman, Robert H. (1970), *The Economics of the Public Sector*, New York: John Wiley.

Kotler, Philip (1975), *Marketing for Nonprofit Organizations*, Englewood Cliffs, N.J.: Prentice-Hall.

Lovelock, Christopher and Charles B. Weinberg, eds. (1978), *Readings in Public and Nonprofit Marketing*, Palo Alto, Ca.: Scientific Press.

Mushkin, Selma, ed. (1972), *Public Prices for Public Products*, Washington, D.C.: Urban Institute.

Phelps, Edmund S., ed. (1962), *Private Wants and Public Needs—Issues Surrounding the Size and Scope of Government Expenditure.* New York: W. W. Norton.

Rathmell, John M. (1973), "Marketing by the Federal Government," *MSU Business Topics* 21 (Summer): 21-28.

Robertson, Jack W. (1979), *Selling to the Federal Government.* New York: McGraw-Hill.

Smead, Elmer E. (1969), *Governmental Promotion and Regulation of Business*, New York: Appleton-Century-Crofts.

The Budget of the United States Government, (1980). 96th Cong., First Session. Washington, D.C.; Government Printing Office.

Torres, Juan de (1972), *Government Services in Major Metropolitan Areas: Functions, Costs, Efficiency*, New York: Conference Board.

Tullock, Gordon (1970), *Private Wants, Public Means—An Economic Analysis of the Desirable Scope of Government.* New York: Basic Books.

U.S., Bureau of the Budget (1957), *Standard Industrial Classification Manual.* Washington, D.C.: Government Printing Office.

U.S., Congress, House (1933), *Government Competition with Private Enterprise*: 72nd Cong., H. Rep. 1985, Washington, D.C.: Government Printing Office.

U.S., Department of Commerce, Bureau of the Census (1978), *Statistical Abstract of the United States.* Washington, D.C.: Government Printing Office.

4

AN INNOVATION ADOPTION PERSPECTIVE FOR MARKETING IN THE GOVERNMENT

Dale D. Achabal and Robert W. Backoff

Extending the application of marketing to the public sector was suggested by Kotler and Levy (1969) a decade ago, and this area has received some attention in the marketing literature (Rothschild 1977). A review of major public administration journals and proceedings reveals that, with few exceptions, the issue has been largely ignored (Kotler and Murray 1975; Rosener 1977; Brown, Ostrom, and Schlacter 1978). In light of the interest in broadening the application of marketing concepts, the question arises: Why have public sector managers and educators not been more receptive to the adoption of a marketing orientation? An innovation diffusion context lends insight into this dilemma. Since public sector managers perceive a marketing orientation and the changes implied by its use as something new to their organizations, it should be viewed as an innovation. Thus we can draw on existing innovation research in formulating a strategy to accelerate the adoption and utilization of marketing in the public sector.

The literature on the adoption of innovations by organizations emphasizes three sets of factors. The first stresses the characteristics of the potential adopters; the second isolates the attributes of the innovation itself as perceived by the potential adopter; and the third concerns the relationship between the organization and its operating environment. This chapter addresses these factors as they relate to the adoption of a marketing orientation in the public sector. Before turning to a discussion of these factors, we briefly review some general environmental constraints and opportunities affecting the transfer of marketing concepts to public agencies.

THE CHANGING ENVIRONMENT

Historical and Contemporary Constraints

Historically there have been several obstacles to the effective transfer of marketing ideas to government agencies, and these continue to exist. In general, public managers associate marketing with the provision of private goods and services and equate marketing activities more specifically as being represented by sales and advertising. This outlook stems from limited exposure to the marketing concept—a concept which also remains foreign to many managers in the private sector (Kotler 1972).

In this country, elected officials are given primary responsibility for the formulation of public policy, and they act as representatives of citizen interests. Administrative agencies historically have viewed their role as the implementation of predetermined policies and programs of the elected executive and legislative officials—politicians. An underlying belief that public agencies and administrators should not engage in efforts to mobilize citizen demand for public services has developed (Fried 1976). Further, many public administrators feel that surveying of citizen needs and use of citizen inputs should be the responsibility of elected officials, politicians, political parties, and special interest groups. Thus citizen demands and inputs are perceived to be registered through the political process, not through direct interaction between administrative agencies and their existing and potential clientele. Public administrators perceive their role as principally implementing, not formulating programs. Until recently the primary role of public agencies was to provide undifferentiated essential services (for example, police, fire, water, garbage) rather than social services (for example, health, welfare) (Jones and Kaufman 1974; Lineberry and Welch 1974; Levy, Meltsner, and Wildavsky 1974). The provision of essential services was publicly mandated to all citizens regardless of their actual or perceived need. This allowed the public agency little discretion with respect to providing services differentially to specific segments of the community. A more contemporary position recognizes that consumer needs vary even with respect to essential services and that this differential impact must be considered.

Organizationally, government agencies have restricted the employment of individuals with marketing skills to public information offices or as outside marketing consultants on a project-by-project basis; so a broad sustained internal marketing capability and orientation is rarely evident in a public sector agency. Further, given the limited employment opportunities for marketing specialists, public sector educators have generally had little incentive to offer courses dealing with marketing issues. Public administration scholars have not grasped the potential utility of marketing ideas for public management, largely as a result of their own education and training, which typically does not include an exposure to marketing concepts. Until recently few schools of public administration were closely associated with business schools but tended to be housed in political science departments or as separate schools of public administration (NASPAA 1978).

Facilitating Trends

Today several societal trends and specific changes in public sector policies and programs provide a more receptive atmosphere for the transfer of marketing ideas and practices. Three of the significant societal trends include (1) a greater emphasis on social needs, (2) a blurring between the public and private sectors, and (3) an increased rate of social change.

Societal Trends

Government today is being asked to meet many new social needs as well as to provide more of the traditional services. This has led to a proliferation of federally financed programs which are frequently delivered through an intergovernmental system at the state and local levels (Wright 1978). To control these intergovernmental service delivery programs, the federal government has instituted an extensive set of requirements for state and local agencies to follow. The requirements mandate that these agencies engage in the identification of citizen needs and conduct program effectiveness evaluations to receive initial and/or continuing funding.

Historically, many private and public sector managers drew sharp distinctions between the two sectors; today, however, there is a real blurring of such distinctions as we see an increase in the coordinated activities of government and private enterprise. Intermingling of governmental and private enterprise activities is observable in various "mixed" undertakings, such as the provision of government services by contract with private corporations (Smith 1975; Wamsley and Zald 1976). Mutual involvement is facilitating an increased interchange of ideas and practices of management between public and private managers.

Finally, rapid change in the operating environment of public agencies has necessitated a proactive and adaptive type of public management. One of the principal environmental changes concerns the increased interdependencies between the public agency and other public organizations, private enterprises, and clients. Given this high level of interdependence, management and operation of complex service delivery systems have the potential of generating many negative externalities. As a result, public managers must engage in longer-term planning, anticipate potential externalities, and adapt their programs and delivery systems more rapidly.

Changing Emphasis in the Management of Public Services

There have been a number of recent changes in the management of public services in the United States that suggest opportunities for the more extensive diffusion of marketing concepts in public agencies.

First, there has been a greater emphasis on citizen participation and input into public policy formulation and evaluation (Yin et al. 1973). The traditional policy-making activities of elected officials have been supplemented by direct involvement of citizen groups and neighborhood associations in the planning and approval of new programs. In addition, some federal requirements mandate citizen evaluation of existing services.

Second, newly institutionalized citizen participation roles have affected the orientations of public sector managers. They have had to place a much greater emphasis on citizen involvement in the planning and evaluation process to be more responsive to genuine client needs and preferences. Concomitantly, a new emphasis on equity in the treatment of clients and distribution of services has been evident. Therefore, when dealing with questions of program design, public administrators have changed their view of citizens from being "targets-to-impact" to "consumers-with-choices" (Clayton and Gilbert 1971).

Third, there has been a renewed emphasis on more efficient utilization of existing resources and a greater concern for assessing and improving productivity in public sector agencies. Recently a number of older, large U.S. cities have been faced with such rapidly declining resources that their very survival has been threatened, for example, New York City. These cities have failed to employ basic management concepts, which necessitate the careful design of program strategies that are consistent with current and projected resources.

As a result, an increasing number of public agencies are contracting on a competitive bid basis with private enterprises to provide selected services. This "privatization" of the provision of public services has established a quasi-price mechanism in the public sector. Greater use of private contracting allows a better identification of program service provision costs.

Last, new methods of management are being widely employed. Two of these methods clearly facilitate direct transfer of marketing concepts and methods to the public sector. As a result of federal requirements, state and local government agencies have begun to build in-house capability to undertake program evaluations and needs assessment surveys (Hatry, Winnie, and Fisk 1973; Kerr et al. 1980; and May 1980). Both programs are conceptually consistent with the need to undertake a strategic audit in the early stages of the strategic planning process.

THE INNOVATION DIFFUSION PERSPECTIVE OF GOVERNMENT MARKETING

We propose that a useful approach to understanding the opportunities and constraints on the transfer of marketing to the public sector is to conceive of these ideas as innovations and to draw upon the many studies of innovation, especially those done in the public sector for assistance. In studying organizational innovations, an innovation is usually defined as an idea, practice, or material artifact perceived as *new* by an adopting unit, which may be an individual or organization (Zaltman, Duncan and Holbeck 1973; Downs and Mohr 1978; Eveland, Rogers and Klepper 1977). We are particularly interested in the adoption of marketing concepts, strategies, and methods by public organizations. Why do we consider such ideas new for public organizations? Most general purpose government organizations currently do not use modern marketing ideas, and those that do use them do so in minor areas of operation. Thus attempts to transfer concepts, strategies, and methods of marketing to public sector organizations suggest that they will be perceived as new. As Robertson has suggested, one might conceptually distinguish the extent to which an innovation is perceived as new in terms of a perceived extent of behavioral change required. A discontinuous innovation (involving the establishment of both new products and behavior patterns) is perceived as having more disruptive effects than dynamically continuous (not generally altering behavior patterns), or continuous (least disruptive influence on established patterns) innovations (1967, 1971). In fact, it may be that public organizations do engage in marketing activities (as defined by the marketing profession) but do not realize it; if so, marketing ideas will still be perceived as new, that is, as innovations.

The literature on the adoption of innovations by collective structures such as organizations is not as well developed as that for individual choice behavior (Rogers and Shoemaker 1971). The literature on public organization adoption of innovations is even more sparse (Mohr 1969; Feller, Menzel and Engel 1974; Backoff 1974; Bingham 1976; Yin, et al. 1976, 1977; Feller, Menzel and Kozak 1976; Eveland, Rogers and Klepper 1977; Roessner 1977; Nelson and Yates 1978; Perry and Kraemer 1978; Agnew, Brown and Herr 1978). We can draw upon some general organizing concepts and frameworks and identify some critical variables that appear to facilitate or constrain the adoption of innovations in organizations generally and public organizations particularly. Several classes of factors have been widely utilized to organize the determinants of organizational innovation (Zaltman, Duncan and Holbeck 1973; U.S., Department of Housing and Urban Development 1976; Havelock 1969; Downs and Mohr 1978). Classes include the organizational and individual attributes of an adopting organization, the types and attributes of innovations adopted, and the relations between the adopting organization and innovation support systems (change agents, marketers) in its environment. The underlying theoretical argument implied by this framework is simply that the probability of organizational adoption and implementation of one or more innovations is dependent upon the type of innovations to be adopted, the characteristics of the adopting organization and its members, and the specific characteristics of the organization's task environment and its external exchanges with change agents or support systems promoting the innovations.

In the next sections we address these different classes of variables and present a short list of the more important determinants of public organization adoption of marketing. It will become apparent that opportunities are available for greater and more rapid adoption of marketing innovations by public organizations. As well, marketing professionals do face substantial barriers in marketing their ideas to general purpose government organizations.

The Target Population—The General Purpose Government Agency

General purpose government agencies are subunits of general purpose governments, including the city, county, state, and federal governments in the United States that serve particular jurisdictions and provide a wide range of services (for example, police, fire, sanitation, highways, and social services). Agencies within these systems are subject to control by elected legislative and executive officials and normally compete for revenue from a general fund supporting all government agencies. Use of the term *general purpose* is intended to distinguish them from special purpose governing bodies, such as local educational authorities (districts) and special districts that provide single service lines, raise revenue (frequently through tax levies), and use funds targeted only for that type of service provision. Election or appointment of leaders of these public organizations is normally distinguished from the process used for the general purpose government.

Why are these agencies of special importance to our discussion of transfer and adoption of marketing innovations? First, these agencies employ 70 percent of all government officials and utilize 80 to 90 percent of all government revenues (Wright 1978). Second, the existing literature on marketing in the public sector tends to ignore these agencies, despite their importance to the provision of public services (Gaedeke 1977). Third, these agencies are more likely to view "marketing" as foreign to their operations and thus perceive marketing as new for their agencies, that is, as innovations! Work with this type of public agency suggests that only modest diffusion and adoption of marketing has been evidenced among these agencies. Most diffusion seems to have taken place within special purpose organizations, such as educational and health agencies.

There are examples of successful adoption of innovations by general purpose governments and their agencies. Dayton, Ohio, is a city that uses marketing concepts and methods extensively (Dayton, City of 1977). The Dayton case is atypical in many ways; it has always been at the forefront of innovation within the larger cities of the United States. It is a commission-city manager form of government that is run more like a business firm with the commission as the board of directors and the city manager as chief executive officer. Only an hour's drive from Dayton is Columbus, Ohio, with a council-mayor form of government where few of the new marketing ideas are applied even though in many ways one could consider it a "progressive" city government. What accounts for differences in adoption? Drawing upon existing empirical studies of general purpose government agencies adoption of innovation, we highlight some of the differences.

Is there a real or felt need for the type of innovations marketing professionals could offer general purpose agencies at all levels of government? The diffusion and adoption of marketing innovations to these governmental agencies is extremely important at the present time. Most agencies are faced with demands for economizing in the provision of services or for "cutback management" (Levine 1978). At the same time they face shifting client populations, needs, and demands. In short, the problem agenda for these agencies seems to fit nicely with marketing concepts and methods.

Research on the adoption of innovations in public organizations suggests that a major impetus initiating the search for innovations is the identification of a problem or issue. Eveland, Rogers and Klepper (1977) call this first stage of the innovation adoption process *agenda-setting*. During this stage, the public organization's general problems are defined and commonly recognized. Many public organizations today perceive performance gaps related to resource scarcity and are searching for solutions for cutback management. Many of the strategies or tactics they employ are widely used marketing strategies and tactics (Levine 1978). For example, to offset a decline in resources an agency might attempt to diversify programs, clients, and constituents. Needs assessment and segmentation analysis would clearly benefit these organizations. Other strategies include educating the public about the agency's mission, mobilizing dependent clients, and experimenting with less costly service delivery systems. Activities similar to those employed in assembling a marketing mix can be utilized by a public agency to smooth decline due to financial cutbacks. These activities may include cutting low prestige programs, improved targeting on problems, shifting programs to other agencies, improving forecasting capacity to anticipate further cuts, and installing more rational choice techniques, such as zero-base budgeting and evaluation research. It would appear, then, that public organizations are facing a need to employ various strategies to manage demand for and supply of their services, strategies ranging from creating new demands to reducing demands (Kotler 1979).

Assuming public organizations have agendas with the types of problems that suggest a search for innovations, then a second stage in the adoption process is *matching* possible solutions to the identified problems

(Eveland, Rogers and Klepper 1977). The researchers found in studying the introduction of an innovative information-processing system that the extent of government agencies' professionalism related positively to both performance gap identification and matching the innovation to that problem. We expect, therefore, that marketing concepts and methods are more likely to be adopted by agencies with leadership and sub-units that have more *professionalism* (are more integrated into a professional community as a result of formal education, occupational specialty, and self-identification). A second factor that helps predict successful matching of the innovation with an agenda of a public organization is the *innovativeness* of the organization, or the propensity of the organization's members, particularly its leaders, to reach outside itself for new solutions. We conjecture that public organizations that are higher in innovativeness will be more prone to adopting marketing ideas.

Several other factors should be noted as contributing to the probability of innovation adoption by public agencies. A major factor appears to be the availability of *slack resources* (Feller, Menzel, and Engel 1974); public agencies with uncommitted resources may be more likely to adopt marketing. This variable's role may be greatly reduced in a period of cutback management. Another variable to consider is the basic commitment of a public organization's leadership to improved organizational performance and their willingness and ability to utilize output criteria to *assess their effectiveness* (Eveland, Rogers, and Klepper 1977). In such cases, needs assessment and evaluation research activities are likely to be employed and draw upon marketing skills. One negative factor that keeps turning up in public organization studies is the extent to which the public organization has inflexible union and civil service rules and regulations (Feller, Menzel, and Engel 1974). These agencies are less likely to have the ability to adopt and utilize new innovations.

Attributes of Marketing Innovations for Public Agencies

Rogers and Shoemaker (1971) have suggested five general characteristics by which any innovation may be described and have shown how individuals' perceptions of these characteristics may be utilized in predicting the rate of adoption. These characteristics are significant in evaluating alternative adoption strategies, since they may allow marketers to predict potential public agency administrators' reactions and perhaps modify certain of these reactions by the way marketing concepts, strategies, and methods are named and packaged. The five attributes are relative advantage, compatibility, complexity, trialability, and observability. It is the public agency administrator's perceptions of these attributes related to marketing—marketers' perceptions—that will affect the rate of adoption of marketing by public sector agencies.

As noted by Rogers and Shoemaker (1971), the relative advantage of a new idea may be emphasized by a crisis. The comparatively more rapid adoption of marketing in health care and the arts is a case in point. It can be argued that hospitals, museums, colleges, and other nonprofit organizations have been faced with recent funding crises that threatened their long-run survival and required improved operating efficiencies (Kotler 1979). For example, hospital administrators in numerous markets have experienced declining occupancies in many specialties and increasing regulation requiring certificates of need. This type of situation had not been widely faced by general purpose government agencies until the passage of Proposition 13-type legislation in California and other states. One significant exception on the federal level is the Department of Defense's (DOD) shift to an all-volunteer force (AVF). Reduction in enlistments forced the DOD to consider alternative approaches, including highly sophisticated research methods, market segmentation, and increased advertising to attain AVF manpower requirements.

Many aspects of marketing are highly compatible with the existing values, past experiences, and needs of public agencies; however, significant exceptions do exist. One problem is that marketers have attempted to introduce marketing concepts to the public sector as a "package." This approach has increased perceived complexity and reduced compatibility with the organization norm. While marketing scholars have criticized agencies that view marketing as being synonymous with advertising or sales, these elements may be more highly compatible with an agency's immediate needs. An explicit attempt to decompose marketing into its component parts might positively affect marketing's rate of total adoption in the public sector.

The marketing concept states that the fundamental objective of an organization should be customer satisfaction. This organizational philosophy is compatible with the general purpose government agency whose origin is based on the premise that essential services should be provided to all citizens. However, this ostensibly does not allow the public agency to provide services differentially to specific target populations. Hence an inherent incompatibility can exist with a central concept of marketing—market segmentation. This incompatibility may be reduced or eliminated through an assessment of a potential adopting agency's marketing needs.

For example, in a Midwestern metropolitan fire department faced with continuing budgetary problems, a needs assessment program was initiated which convinced the agency to utilize market segmentation as a way of improving organizational efficiency and effectiveness. The agency lacked sufficient equipment and manpower to service the current level of demand effectively. They analyzed the market and developed fire prevention and fire safety programs tailored toward the needs of specific user segments (for example, fire prevention in high-risk buildings and industrial areas) and were able to reduce the primary demand for their services. This strategy helped to alleviate the previous equipment and manpower shortages and improved the delivery of fire protection services to consumers in the metropolitan area. The agency has now adopted a position that recognizes that consumer needs vary even with respect to essential services and that this differential impact must be considered.

This example is also related to the fourth attribute affecting the rate of adoption of an innovation—trialability. Decomposing the "package" of marketing concepts allows public agencies to experiment with selected elements on a limited basis. Rogers and Shoemaker note that "new ideas that can be tried on the installment plan will generally be adopted more rapidly than innovations that are not divisible" (1971, p. 155). They point to evidence that relatively earlier adopters may perceive triability as more important than do later adopters since the more innovative adopters have no precedent to follow at the time they adopt.

Possibly the greatest barrier to the rapid adoption of marketing by general purpose government agencies is the inability, especially in the short run, for other agencies to observe the results of a marketing orientation. Alternatively, a hospital may achieve increased occupancy, or a college increased enrollment—both readily observable by competing hospitals and colleges. General purpose government agencies have multiple objectives, many of which are difficult to measure. Also, there tends to be less inter- and intra-agency consensus on objectives (Rainey, Backoff, and Levine 1976). The ease of other agencies observing the beneficial effects resulting from the use of a marketing orientation is severely restricted; however, public managers are beginning to examine marketing as a way of explaining and improving their services to their clients and publics.

RELATIONS BETWEEN AGENCY AND ENVIRONMENT AND INNOVATION ADOPTION

Research has suggested some factors characterizing the agency's relations with its environment that facilitate or limit innovation adoption. A very important factor that would seem to apply for the adoption of marketing methods is *accountability* to outside groups. Eveland, Rogers, and Klepper (1977) suggest that accountability is important during the third stage of the public organization innovation adoption process—the redefinition of the innovation in terms of applicability in form and use to the potential adopting organization. We conjecture that marketing innovations will be adopted more frequently by public agencies that are more accountable externally (to clients, funders, political superiors, and so forth). There can also be too much accountability such that innovation is limited; thus we suggest a need for further refinement of the range of accountability within which innovation would be most likely.

The second major determinant refers to the extent of *external system support* for the organization is its efforts to adopt the innovation. This factor is extremely important. One way of looking at this is from the perspective of the change agents (marketers) and the characteristics of the exchanges between the change agents and the target organization. Marketers interested in public sector issues find themselves at a point between traditional marketing tools and contexts to which they feel a primary responsibility and new tools, contexts, and demands. This often results in role conflict. Rogers and Shoemaker note that diffusion programs often fail because change agents are more innovation-minded than they are client-oriented (1971, p. 238).

In our role as change agents, we must have a sufficient understanding of the perceived needs of public sector agencies to ensure that we are presenting marketing in a manner compatible with the public manager's needs and values. We must actively market marketing concepts if we are to expect a reasonable chance that they will be adopted by the public sector. The diagnosis of the public manager's needs is one of the most important and difficult roles we must play in ensuring that a marketing orientation will be adopted in the management of the public sector. Visiting scholar positions available in many agencies as well as conferences can stimulate the necessary dialogue to speed this process. It is essential for marketers since most public agencies are in the early stages of adopting marketing innovations to communicate more effectively with the public organizations. One clear need is a set of terms that is both familiar to public managers and at the same time consistent with the terminology of the marketing profession. In Table 4.1 we propose a set of public sector terms that we believe meet these requirements. We use the idea of service delivery system in the table because marketing activities are usually centered around the planning and implementation of service delivery programs. One can substitute "agency" or "public organization" for service delivery system if one's focus is on the entire agency.

CONCLUSIONS

Marketing is multi-faceted. Its value is enhanced when those with the proper understanding and tools work with it. Marketing can be presented in a variety of ways; it is appreciated most by those who understand its subtleties. However, there is a price to use marketing.

This chapter has suggested a variety of issues that need to be addressed if we are to accelerate the adoption of marketing in the public sector. Our analysis of general purpose government agencies from an innovation adoption perspective suggests some useful strategies and tactics. First of all, target agencies should be identified that:

TABLE 4.1

A Comparison of Equivalent Basic Concepts and Terms for Private Sector Marketing Management and Public Sector Service Delivery System (Agency) Management

Marketing Management		Service Delivery System Management	
General Framework	Specific Concepts	General Framework	Specific Concepts

Assessing market opportunity	Environment
	  Macro Issues
	    Legal/political/regulatory
	    Sociocultural
	  Competitors
	  Markets
	  Customers
	Marketing systems
	  Objectives
	  Strategy
	  Implementation
	  Organization
	Current marketing policies and procedures
	  Product
	  Price
	  Channels/distribution
	  Communication/promotion
		Assessing service opportunity	Environment
			  Macro issues
			    Legal/political/regulatory
			    Sociocultural
			    Competitive cooperative
			    Citizenry within jurisdiction, target populations
			    Clientele
			Service delivery systems
			  Objectives/priorities
			  Strategy
			  Policy implementation
			  Organization
			Service delivery policies and procedures
			  Service programs
			  Payment (users/clients)
			  Provision/distribution
			  Communication/information

TABLE 4.1 (continued)

A Comparison of Equivalent Basic Concepts and Terms for Private Sector Marketing Management and Public Sector Service Delivery System (Agency) Management

General Framework	Marketing Management Specific Concepts	General Framework	Service Delivery System Management Specific Concepts
Planning	Setting corporate mission/objectives	Planning/policy formulation	Setting agency mission/objectives (city vs. agency)
	Develop marketing strategy		Design service delivery strategy
	Market identification		Needs assessement
	Define actual and potential market		Define risk population
	Define target markets		Define target population
	Positioning		Define service population
	Integrate market entry and mix strategy		Integrate program structure
	Formulate marketing tactics/programming		Formulate service delivery tactics/programming
	Establish sales targets		Establish utilization/provision levels
	Establish marketing budget		Establish service provision capacity constraints
	Determine marketing mix allocation		Determine resource allocation
	Determine pricing		Determine fees
Control	Marketing implementation	Implementation/ evaluation	Service provision
	Control of marketing activities		Control and monitoring of service delivery programs
	Evaluation: strategic audit		Program evaluation and impact assessment
	M.I.S. for control and evaluation		M.I.S. for monitoring and evaluation

- have a large federal program and are mandated to conduct needs assessments, program evaluations, and active citizen participation as requirements for ongoing funding;
- involve a significant degree of joint private-public interaction, including contracting with private firms for service delivery;
- currently provide, or have the potential to provide, differentiated services to segmented markets rather than undifferentiated, essential services;
- face a turbulent environment and rapidly changing client needs;
- have problem agendas which give high priority to cutback management strategies or have slack and/or discretionary resources; and
- have a high degree of professionalism—chief executive support for innovation and utilization of advanced management techniques for integrated planning and control (PPB, MBO, etc.).

Finally, we must market marketing concepts and methods by:

- stressing the broadened concept of marketing;
- stressing the public manager's role in agency demand management;
- considering decomposing the marketing "package" to decrease the perceived complexity and increase its trialability;
- initially stressing programs with the highest benefit-cost relationship, segmenting programs as potential adopters of a marketing orientation;
- communicating marketing to public managers utilizing public agency terminology;
- establishing on-going relationships with public agencies utilizing a collaborative, problem-solving approach; and
- actively communicating ideas in public management journals and conferences to generate increased professional public manager exposure to marketing concepts, strategies, and methods.

REFERENCES

Achabal, Dale D. and Mark I. Alpert (1976), "A Macro-Marketing Approach for Planning and Evaluation of Emergency Medical Services Delivery Systems," in *Marketing: 1776-1976 and Beyond*, ed. Kenneth L. Bernhardt, Chicago; American Marketing Association.

——— (1978), "Marketing and Preventive Health Care: The HMO Example," in *Marketing and Preventive Health Care: Interdisciplinary and Interorganizational Perspectives*, eds. Philip D. Cooper et al., Chicago; American Marketing Association.

Agnew, John, Lawrence Brown and J. Paul Herr (1978), "The Community Innovation Process," *Urban Affairs Quarterly* 14, no. 1: 3-30.

Backoff, Robert W. (1974). "*Organizational Innovation Theory: Integration, Evaluation, and Prescription*," Ph.D. dissertation, Indiana University.

Bingham, Richard (1976), *The Adoption of Innovation by Local Government*, Lexington, Mass.: D. C. Heath.

Brown, Stephen W., Lonnie L. Ostrom and John L. Schlacter (1978), "PPB and the Marketing Contribution: Implications for the Management of Public Enterprise," in *Management Handbook for Public Administrators*, ed. John W. Sutherland, New York: Van Nostrand Reinhold.

Claxton, John D., Thomas C. Kinnear and J. R. Brent Ritchie (1978), "Should Government Programs Have Marketing Managers?" *University of Michigan Business Review* 30 (May); 10–16.

Clayton, Ross and Ron Gilbert (1971), "Perspectives on Public Managers: Their Implications for Public-Service Delivery Systems," *Public Management* 51 (November); 8–13.

Daft, Richard L. and Selwyn W. Becker (1978), *Innovation in Organizations*, New York: Elsevier North-Holland.

Dayton, City of (1977), *1977 Program Strategies*, Dayton, Ohio: Office of Management and Budget.

Downs, George W. and Lawrence Mohr (1978), "Toward a Theory of Innovation," *Administration and Society* 10 no. 4: 379–408.

Eveland, John D., Everett Rogers and Constance Klepper (1977), *The Innovation Process in Public Organizations*, Ann Arbor; Department of Journalism, University of Michigan.

Feller, Irwin, Donald Menzel and Alfred Engel (1974), *Diffusion of Technology in State Mission-Oriented Agencies*, University Park; Center for the Study of Science Policy, Institute for Research on Human Resources, Pennsylvania State University.

Feller, Irwin, Donald Menzel and Lee A. Kozak (1976), *Diffusion of Innovation in Municipal Governments*, University Park; Center for the Study of Science Policy, Institute for Research on Human Resources, Pennsylvania State University.

Fried, Robert C. (1976), *Performance in American Bureaucracy*, chap. 3, Boston; Little, Brown.

Gaedeke, Ralph M., ed., (1977), *Marketing in Private and Public Nonprofit Organizations*, Santa Monica, Calif.: Goodyear.

Hatry, Harry P., Richard E. Winnie and Donald M. Fisk (1973), *Practical Program Evaluation for State and Local Government Officials*, Washington, D.C.: Urban Institute.

Havelock, Ronald (1969), *Planning for Innovation Through Dissemination and Utilization of Knowledge*, Ann Arbor; University of Michigan, Press.

Jones, Bryan D. and Clifford Kaufman (1974), "The Distribution of Urban Public Services," *Administration and Society* 6 (November); 337–60.

Kerr, John R. et al. (1980), "Program Planning and Evaluation: A Citizen-Oriented Approach," in *Government Marketing: Theory and Practice*, eds. Michael P. Mokwa and Steven E. Permut, New York: Praeger.

Kotler, Philip (1972), *Marketing Management*, Englewood Clifs, N.J.: Prentice-Hall, pp. 14–27.

——— (1975), *Marketing for Nonprofit Organizations*, Englewood Cliffs, N.J.: Prentice-Hall.

——— (1979), "Strategies for Introducing Marketing into Nonprofit Organizations," *Journal of Marketing* 43 (January); 37–44.

—— and Sidney J. Levy (1969), "Broadening the Concept of Marketing," *Journal of Marketing* 33 (July); 10–15.

Kotler, Philip and Michael Murray (1975), "Third Sector Management—The Role of Marketing," *Public Administration Review* (September–October); 467–72.

Levine, Charles H. (1978), "Organizational Decline and Cutback Management," *Public Administration Review* 38, no. 4 (July–August); 316–25.

Levy, Frank S., Arnold S. Meltsner and Aaron Wildavsky (1974), *Urban Outcomes*, Berkeley: University of California Press.

Lineberry, Robert L. and Robert E. Welch (1974), "Who Gets What: Measuring the Distribution of Urban Public Services," *Social Science Quarterly* 54 (March); 700–12.

Lovelock, Christopher H. and Charles B. Weinberg (1975), "Contrasting Private and Public Sector Marketing," in Ronald C. Curhan (ed.), *1974 Combined Proceedings*, pp. 242–47, Chicago; American Marketing Association.

May, Peter J. (1980), "Sample Surveys as Feedback Mechanisms for Guiding Decision Making at the Municipal Level," in *Government Marketing: Theory and Practice*, eds. Michael P. Mokwa and Steven E. Permut, New York: Praeger.

Menzel, Donald (1978), "Intergovernmental Support of Technological Innovation in Local Government," *Administration and Society* 10, no. 3: 317–34.

Mohr, Lawrence B. (1969), "Determinants of Innovation in Organizations," *American Political Science Review* 63; 111–26.

National Association of Schools of Public Affairs and Administration (1978), *1978 Directory of Programs in Public Affairs and Administration*, Washington, D.C.: NASPAA.

Nelson, Richard R. and Douglas Yates (1978), *Innovation and Implementation in Public Organizations*, Lexington, Mass.: Lexington Books.

Perry, James L. and Kenneth L. Kraemer (1978), *Diffusion and Adoption of Computer Applications Software in Local Governments*, Irvine; Public Policy Research Organization, University of California.

Rainey, H. G., Robert W. Backoff and Charles H. Levine (1976), "Comparing Public and Private Organizations," *Public Administration Review* 36 (March–April); 233–44.

Robertson, Thomas S. (1967), "The Process of Innovation and the Diffusion of Innovation," *Journal of Marketing* 31 (January); 14–19.

—— (1971), *Innovative Behavior and Communication*, New York: Holt, Rinehart and Winston.

Roessner, J. David (1977), "Incentives to Innovate in Public and Private Organizations," *Administration and Scoiety* 3, no. 3: 341–65.

Rogers, Everett M. and F. Floyd Shoemaker (1971), *Communication of Innovations*, New York: Free Press.

Rosener, Judy B. (1977), "Improving Productivity in the Public Sector: An Analysis of Two Tools—Marketing and Citizen Involvement," *Public Productivity Review* 2, no. 3 (Spring–Summer); 3–11.

Rothschild, Michael L. (1977), *An Incomplete Bibliography of Works Relating to Marketing for Public Sector and Nonprofit Organizations*, 2nd ed., #9-577-771, Boston: Intercollegiate Case Clearing House.

Smith, Bruce L. R., ed., (1975), *The New Political Economy: The Public Use of the Private Sector*, New York: John Wiley.

U.S., Department of Housing and Urban Development (1976), *Factors Involved in the Transfer of Innovations*, Washington, D.C.: Office of Policy Development and Research.

Wamsley, Gary L. and Mayer N. Zald (1976), *The Political Economy of Public Organizations*, chap. 1, Bloomington; Indiana University Press.

Wright, Deil S. (1978), *Understanding Intergovernmental Relations*, North Scituate, Mass.: Duxbury Press.

Yin, Robert K. (1977), "Production Efficiency Versus Bureaucratic Self-Interest: Two Innovative Processes?" *Policy Sciences* 8; 381–99.

——— et al. (1973), *Citizen Organizations: Increasing Client Control over Services*, Washington, D.C.: RAND.

——— et al. (1976), *A Review of Case Studies of Technological Innovations in State and Local Services*, Santa Monica, Calif.: RAND.

Zaltman, Gerald, Robert Duncan and Jonny Holbeck (1973), *Innovations and Organizations*, New York: John Wiley.

5

PROBLEMS APPLYING CONVENTIONAL WISDOM TO SOCIAL MARKETING PROGRAMS

Paul N. Bloom and William D. Novelli

The discovery that marketing has much to offer social change efforts has created considerable excitement within both the marketing profession and the community of social change (including social welfare) organizations. Marketers have found a challenging new set of problems upon which to test their theories and techniques. At the same time, social change organizations have found a promising new set of ideas and approaches to use in addressing difficult problems. Clearly social marketing has "arrived," with the future promising to bring an even closer union between marketing and social change endeavors.

Although much has been written about the promise of social marketing (Kotler 1975; Perry 1976; Blakely, Schutz, and Harvey 1977; Gaedeke 1977; Bogart 1978; Gutman 1978; Lovelock and Weinberg 1978), relatively little attention has been paid to how difficult it is to transfer the technology of marketing to the arena of social problem solving. The literature has given minimal coverage to the problems associated with using the same marketing approaches for "selling" offerings such as smoking cessation, charitable giving, and breast self-examination as have been used for selling toothpaste, soap, and automobiles. The chapter addresses this subject, providing a survey of the various problems that can arise in trying to use conventional marketing wisdom within social marketing programs. We hope that by identifying these problems we can give social change organizations a more realistic picture of the potential of modern marketing, so that marketing is neither oversold nor used inappropriately. While we strongly believe that marketing can help social change efforts, we also believe that social marketing must be done with caution.

It is important to clarify what we mean by "social marketing" before going any further. Social marketing is "the design, implementation, and control of programs seeking to increase the acceptability of a social idea or practice in a target group(s)" (Kotler 1975, p. 283). It is an endeavor that can be engaged in by profit-making organizations (for example, a liquor company program encouraging "responsible drinking") as well as by nonprofit and public organizations. It also is an endeavor that generally encourages people to do something that will be beneficial to others besides just themselves (Lovelock 1979). For example, responsible drinking, safe driving, and smoking cessation can all reduce health hazards or lower insurance premiums for others. In short, we are talking about the marketing of "social behaviors" (Lovelock 1979) by any organization to any target group.

The following discussion proceeds by identifying the problems social marketers tend to confront in applying conventional marketing wisdom in eight basic decision-making areas: market analysis, market segmentation, product strategy development, pricing strategy development, channel strategy development, communications strategy development, organizational design and planning, and evaluation. Although many of the problems we identify may face a broad spectrum of marketers, it is our belief that the discussed problems tend to affect social marketers with more regularity and severity.

MARKET ANALYSIS PROBLEMS

A basic tenet of marketing is that an organization builds its marketing program using research on the wants, needs, perceptions, attitudes, habits, and satisfaction levels of its markets. The good marketer is supposed to examine previous research on his or her consumers and, if necessary, conduct original consumer research in order to design maximally effective marketing strategies. Although profit-making marketers surely have difficulty accumulating valid, reliable, and relevant data about their consumers, the data-gathering problems facing the social marketer tend to be far more serious.

Social marketers typically find that they have less good-quality secondary data available about their consumers. The consumer research literature has not "broadened" sufficiently to be of much help. There are relatively fewer studies on health behavior, conservation behavior, safety behavior, helping behavior, and so forth. Moreover, available secondary studies tend to be limited in scope and often of poor quality. Many of these studies have been done by agencies with severe budget constraints. Convenience samples and simplistic analysis procedures therefore predominate.

Social marketers also have more difficulty obtaining valid, reliable measures of salient variables. In doing primary data collection, social marketers must ask people questions about topics such as smoking, sickness, sex, and charity—topics which touch people's most deep-seated fears, anxieties, and values. People tend to be more likely to give inaccurate, self-serving, or socially desirable answers to these types of questions than they are to questions about cake mixes, soft drinks, or cereals.

Often it is more difficulty to sort out the relative influence of identified determinants of consumer behavior. Social behaviors tend to be extremely complex and usually hinge on more than just one or two variables. The reasons patients drop out of antihypertensive drug therapy, for instance, may be related to an individual's sense of self-control, lack of family support, drug side effects, physician-patient miscommunication, or any combination of these and other factors. It is extremely difficult for respondents to sort out these contributing variables in their own minds and articulate them to a researcher so that they can be recorded and analyzed for marketing planning. Furthermore, asking physicians to untangle patient behavior is often no more enlightening than asking the patients themselves. For example, a recent study of physicians revealed that the reason patients were not on antihypertensive therapy was that they were not following the regimen that had been prescribed for them. This may be logical in a self-evident way, but it is not very helpful to the marketing planner.

Finally, social marketers typically have more difficulty getting consumer research studies funded, approved, and completed in a timely fashion. Social change organizations typically have very limited funds, and the intangible output of a research study is often more difficult to justify to donors or funding organizations than is the more tangible output of a new program or publication. Furthermore, if the federal government is involved in some way in the proposed research, lengthy delays often will occur while the questionnaire and research design are approved by (1) the agency doing the study, (2) its department, (3) the Office of Management and Budget, and (4) other parties. For example, the Office of Cancer Communications of the National Cancer Institute began the paperwork on a straightforward three-stage study of knowledge, attitudes, and reported behavior related to breast cancer in April 1977. Red tape has delayed the completion of the analysis of the full study until December 1979.

As a final comment on market analysis problems we must point out that the red tape that chokes and delays consumer studies can lead to some very unsound but highly original research tactics. One ploy is to conduct focus groups with fewer than nine respondents, thus getting around the letter, if not the spirit, of the clearance regulations concerning what constitutes a survey. However, this tactic, while it may provide some useful research hypotheses, can lead to misleading conclusions and poor planning because the focus groups are often not followed by larger-scale studies to evaluate the preliminary findings and assess the hypotheses. The misuse of qualitative research as a substitute for rather than a precursor to more definitive research appears to be a common problem among many social change organizations.

MARKET SEGMENTATION PROBLEMS

The process of dividing the market into homogeneous segments and then developing unique marketing programs for individual target segments (while perhaps ignoring certain segments) is fundamental to modern marketing. Market segmentation is generally viewed as being more productive than treating the entire market in an undifferentiated manner.

Although market segmentation is widely utilized and accepted by most profit-making and many nonprofit marketers (for example, universities and hospitals), social marketers find, first, that they face pressure against segmentation in general, and especially against segmentation that leads certain segments to be ignored. The notion of treating certain groups differently or with special attention while perhaps ignoring other groups completely is not consistent with the egalitarian and antidiscriminatory philosophies that pervade many social change organizations, particularly those within government. The social marketer is, therefore, frequently asked to avoid segmenting or to try to reach an unreasonably large number of segments (Lovelock and Weinberg 1975). If a marketing plan has only a few target markets identified, requests will be made to add to the list of targets until—with the limited funds that usually are available—only a very broad and very shallow marketing effort is authorized. This will produce a "shotgun" effect; the opposite of the "rifle" approach a marketer normally attempts to bring to bear.

Second, social marketers frequently do not have accurate behavioral data to use in identifying segments. The data collection problems described earlier impede segmentation by making it difficult to separate users from non-users. Utilizing self-reports on behaviors like breast self-examination and contraceptive usage can be very misleading, and it may be impossible to obtain other behavioral measures (for example, observational data).

Last, target segments most often consist of those consumers who are the most negatively predisposed to their offerings. Social marketers often segment on the basis of risk to the consumer. They will target their efforts at drivers who tend to avoid using seat belts, sexually active teenagers who tend to avoid using contraceptives, heavy smokers, and so on. This means that social marketers often face target markets with the strongest negative predispositions toward their offerings—the exact opposite of the situation faced by most commercial marketers.

PRODUCT STRATEGY PROBLEMS

Once the marketer has analyzed the market and determined target segments, he or she should then develop an offering that conforms closely to the desires of the target segments. Conventional marketers typically will adjust product characteristics, packaging, the product name, and the product concept to increase the likelihood of a "sale" to the target segments. However, social marketers tend to have less flexibility in shaping their products or offerings (Kotler 1975; Lovelock and Weinberg 1975). They often find themselves locked into marketing a given social behavior that cannot be modified or changed. This could occur because the government might approve of only one method of behavior. For example, social marketers may be able to market only one method of getting a home insured against floods or one method of getting a child immunized. On the other hand, they *may* be able to market several methods of quitting smoking, getting physically fit, or conserving energy.

In addition, social marketers often have more difficulty formulating product concepts; they frequently find that the "product" they are selling is a complex behavior which may, in some cases, have to be repeated over a considerable period of time. It therefore becomes difficult to formulate a simple, meaningful product concept around which a marketing and communications program can be built. Effective concepts like a "squeezably soft toilet paper" and an "extra thick and zesty spaghetti sauce" do not come readily to mind when thinking about marketing behaviors such as drug therapy maintenance or use of an in-home colon-rectal cancer detection test (the hemocult test). In addition, the problems associated with doing consumer research tend to hinder product concept development.

Because any activity in the product strategy area is difficult for social marketers, many ignore this aspect of marketing planning. Instead, they concentrate their efforts on developing advertising and promotion strategies for a product they have been told to sell. However, social marketers should recognize that although they may be unable to adjust the *performance* characteristics of their products, they may be able to adjust the *perceptual* characteristics of their products and achieve significant results. Through minimal amounts of product-testing research with consumers and some creative concept development, social marketers can gain confidence that the "signals" being transmitted by their products are favorable. They can also avoid making the type of product strategy mistake made by the Agency for International Development in a program designed to persuade Nicaraguan mothers to give their babies the proper treatment for diarrhea (a major cause of infant mortality). This program failed because nobody bothered to do any in-home product testing of the "Super Lemonade" (a rehydration solution) the program promoted. It was discovered at a later date that the solution was not administered in many cases because the mothers—who sampled it before giving it to their babies—thought it tasted bad. There was also an indication that some women may have had difficulty measuring the ingredients and concocting the solution.

PRICING STRATEGY PROBLEMS

Marketers of products and services find that the development of a pricing strategy involves primarily the determination of an appropriate (that is, goal-satisfying) monetary price to charge for an offering. On the other hand, social marketers find that the development of a pricing strategy primarily involves trying to reduce the monetary, psychic, energy, and time costs incurred by consumers when engaging in the desired social behavior.

Moreover, while marketers of products and services usually have considerable control over what it costs consumers to purchase their offerings, social marketers tend to have less control over consumer costs. The social marketer can do little about the amount of extra time it takes to engage in a behavior like car pooling or about the embarrassment one incurs when getting an examination for cervical cancer. In some cases, all the social marketer can do is try to make sure that consumers perceive the various costs accurately. In other cases, however, the social marketer may at least be able to cut some red tape or eliminate other inconveniences—in effect, lower the price. This last strategy is being employed in the Food Stamp Program of New York State. They have made it easier to get enrolled and have eliminated the necessity of putting up any money with your stamps in the retail stores.

CHANNELS STRATEGY PROBLEMS

Developing a channels strategy usually gets an organization involved with (1) selecting appropriate intermediaries through which to distribute its products or offerings, and (2) formulating ways to control these intermediaries to make sure they behave in a supportive manner. Social marketers typically must distribute the idea of engaging in a social behavior and/or a place to engage in the social behavior rather than a tangible product. However, they find that, relative to more conventional marketers they have more difficulty utilizing and controlling desired intermediaries.

Social marketers often find that they cannot convince desired intermediaries, such as doctors or the television news media, to pass along and support an idea; nor can they control effectively what these intermediaries might say if they choose to cooperate. Control over clinics, community centers, government field offices, and other places where a social behavior might be performed or encouraged is also frequently lacking. Unfortunately, social marketers usually cannot provide financial incentives to desired intermediaries to get cooperation, as a business marketer would do, and they generally cannot afford to build their own distribution channels. To achieve a smoothly functioning distribution system of largely volunteers, social marketers must rely primarily on the attractiveness of their offerings, the creativity of their appeals for assistance, and the quality of their intermediary training programs.

The problems associated with establishing, utilizing, and controlling distribution channels produce a major difference between social and conventional forms of marketing. The following two examples illustrate how serious these problems can be:

1. The Federal Flood Insurance program has had difficulty getting insurance companies' agents to add flood insurance to their product line. The agents have seen this insurance as being hard to learn about, hard to sell (with government forms and regulations to worry about), and low in profitability.

2. A program designed to motivate physicians to teach their patients smoking-quitting skills ran up against the problem that, although the physicians wanted to cooperate, they did not know how to be teachers. It therefore became necessary to teach physicians how to teach patients, a task which was complicated by the inclination of many physicians to be "know-it-alls" and not want to be taught anything.

COMMUNICATIONS STRATEGY PROBLEMS

Marketers use several approaches to communicate with their target markets, including advertising, public relations, sales promotion, personal contact, and atmospherics. Social marketers, however, often find that their communications options are somewhat limited. As discussed in the previous section, social marketers sometimes find channels for their ideas unavailable or difficult to control.

For instance they usually find paid advertising impossible to use. This problem may arise because of advertising's cost or because of media fears of offending certain advertisers or audiences by carrying messages about controversial social issues. In addition, many voluntary organizations may see paid advertising as impossible to use because they fear the effects on all-voluntary organizations. If the American Cancer Society pays for an anti-smoking campaign, then the media might ask the American Lung Association and others to pay for their campaigns also. Furthermore, government agencies may see paid advertising as impossible to use because they fear criticism about wasting taxpayer money and having the media overly populated with government-sponsored advertisements. Questions could arise as to who controls the media if the government became the largest total advertiser.

An inability to use paid advertising restricts many social marketers to the use of public service announcements. Since the competition for PSA time and space in heated, social marketers often find they cannot control the reach and frequency of their messages among their target segments. Audience coverage, therefore, becomes much more uncertain.

Social marketers face several other communications problems as well. Often they face pressure not to use certain types of appeals in their messages (Houston and Homans 1977; Lovelock and Weinberg 1975). Funding organizations and other influential parties may not want to see a social change organization "cheapened" by the use of hard-sell, fear, or humor appeals. The use of hard-sell and fear appeals may also be unwise when target audiences are strongly predisposed against a social behavior. These appeals could backfire and solidify a person's feelings against behaviors such as using seat belts, stopping smoking, or drinking responsibly. In general, an audience reaction of "they can't tell me how to run my life" is much more likely to confront a social marketer than a more conventional marketer.

Social marketers also often have difficulty explaining desired behaviors within the confines of a short message. Complex behaviors like "drug abuse prevention" cannot be explained effectively in a few words. In fact, experts in the drug abuse field find this behavior hard to explain with a word limit. As a consequence, many social marketing messages must use the old standby, "For more information, please call or write . . ."

Finally, it can be difficult to conduct meaningful pretests of messages. Given the problems social marketers tend to have with selecting appeals and communicating desired behaviors, it would seem essential for careful pretesting to be done on social messages. However, pretests of social messages run up against the same funding and measurement problems discussed earlier. For example, in a recent test of a message on the need to take mental patients out of institutions and accept them into our communities, few respondents gave expected (but socially unacceptable) comments such as "I don't like the message," "These people are dangerous and unpredictable," or "I don't want them in my neighborhood."

Pretesting is also made less meaningful by the lack of any norms or standards against which newly tested social messages can be compared. Clearly, it would be instructive to the social marketer to know how his or her message performed compared to previously tested messages on measures of comprehension, recall, believability, personal relevance, and so forth. Fortunately, social marketers working in the health area can now get comparison data on pretest performances by using the newly established Health Message Testing Service. This system, funded and administered by the National High Blood Pressure Education Program of the National Heart, Lung, and Blood Institute and by the Office of Cancer Communications of the National Cancer Institute, has now tested more than 25 television and radio messages with samples of up to 300 individuals. The system invites randomly selected subjects from specified target audiences to view "pilot" television programs that have health messages and other commercials appearing within them. The system is also currently planning to develop a print testing capability (Novelli 1978).

ORGANIZATIONAL DESIGN AND PLANNING PROBLEMS

The well-managed marketing organization has a marketing person in a key position at the top of the organization chart and numerous well-trained marketing individuals throughout the organization. This organization will have a marketing plan developed annually, with policies set up to make sure the plan is implemented and monitored. However, most social change organizations do not operate in this way, and, typically, social marketers must function in organizations where marketing activities are poorly understood, weakly appreciated, and inappropriately located. Social change organizations have a tendency to adopt marketing in small doses. The management may decide to try out some of this "new stuff" called marketing by hiring a few employees or consultants with marketing backgrounds. These marketers are generally assigned to work with Public Affairs or Public Information Offices because management generally equates marketing with communications or promotion. The results the marketers can achieve in these positions are quite limited, since they have little influence over program development and administration and must restrict themselves primarily to telling people about the features of the program. Thus, social marketers are often programmed for mediocre performance from the very beginning. They cannot convince management to give marketing the prominence it needs to prosper, and they cannot earn their way to prominence through outstanding performance. This dilemma may continue to confront social marketers as long as social change organizations are dominated by physicians, lawyers, scientists, law enforcement specialists, social workers, and others who often feel uncomfortable and unfamiliar with marketing.

Another problem social marketers frequently face is that they must function in organizations where plans (if any are developed) are treated as "archival" rather than "action" documents. Social change organizations, particularly those in government, do not feel the direct competitive pressures that the business world feels. Employees do not lose their jobs or gain promotions according to how well the organization does. Consequently, the need to plan or to follow a plan is not perceived as strongly. This attitude, of course, can seriously impede the social marketing effort.

EVALUATION PROBLEMS

Evaluating the effectiveness of a marketing program is difficult for all marketers. One must first determine valid measures of effectiveness and then develop a research design that is capable of isolating the role a marketing program has had in effecting change in these measures. Naturally, social marketers face the same problems in doing evaluation studies as they face in doing market analysis studies. They have serious problems with measurement and with getting support and approval for the research. In addition, social marketers find, first, that they frequently face difficulties trying to define effectiveness measures. Unlike business firms, which may have quantitative objectives stated in terms of profitability, sales, or market share, social change organizations may merely have vaguely stated mission or goal statements from which measures of effectiveness are difficult to derive (Houston and Homans 1977). Even after lengthy discussions with management, social marketers often have problems selecting performance indicators to monitor how well they are doing.

Second, social marketers often find it impossible to estimate the contribution their marketing program has made toward the achievement of certain objectives. Assuming that effectiveness measures can be identified for the social marketer, there is frequently little chance that a causal relationship can be demonstrated between the marketing program and those measures. One can rarely isolate the role that a single program has played among numerous interacting efforts and forces. For example, how could the American Cancer Society determine its contribution to the recent decline in the teenage smoking rate? Could it separate out its role from that of either the National Cancer Institute or the jogging fad among young people? Unfortunately, evaluation problems like these can often be answered only by educated guesses. The research expenses required to solve these kinds of evaluation problems would be prohibitive. About all social marketers generally can do is evaluate their impact on submeasures of effectiveness, such as attitudes, knowledge, and awareness, and even this can be highly problematical and expensive to achieve.

CONCLUSION

The relationship between social marketing and conventional commercial marketing may be somewhat like the relationship between football and rugby. The two marketing "games" have much in common and require similar training, but each has its own set of rules, constraints, and required skills. The good player of one "game" may not necessarily be a good player of the other. In this chapter we have attempted to document why we feel social marketing is the more difficult "game" to play or master. Indeed, social marketing is more like a continuous battle or struggle than a game. Although it may be interesting and rewarding, it requires hard work, perseverance, and considerable analytic and creative skills.

REFERENCES

Blakely, Edward J., Howard Schutz and Peter Harvey (1977), "Public Marketing: Policy Planning for Community Development in the City," *Social Indicators Research* 4: 163–84.

Bogart, Leo (1978), "The Marketing of Public Goods," in *Marketing in Nonprofit Organizations*, ed., Patrick J. Montana, pp. 62–73, New York: Amacom.

Gaedeke, Ralph M., ed. (1977). *Marketing in Private and Public Nonprofit Organizations*, Santa Monica, Calif.: Goodyear.

Gutman, Evelyn (1978), "Effective Marketing of a Cancer Screening Program," in *Marketing in Nonprofit Organizations*, ed., Patrick J. Montana, pp. 143–47, New York: Amacom.

Houston, Franklin S. and Richard E. Homans (1977), "Public Agency Marketing: Pitfalls and Problems," *MSU Business Topics* 25 (Summer): 36–40.

Kotler, Philip (1975), *Marketing for Nonprofit Organizations*, Englewood Cliffs, N.J.: Prentice-Hall.

Lovelock, Christopher H. (1979), "Theoretical Contributions from Services and Nonbusiness Marketing," Working paper 79–16, Harvard Business School.

—— and Charles B. Weinberg (1975), "Contrasting Private and Public Sector Marketing," in *1974 Combined Proceedings*, pp. 242–47, Chicago: American Marketing Association.

——, eds. (1978), *Readings in Public and Nonprofit Marketing*, Palo Alto, Calif: Scientific Press.

Novelli, William D. (1978), "Health Messages: Milk Duds, Sunburns and Other Consumer Perspectives," Working paper, Porter, Novelli and Associates, Inc., Washington, D.C.

Perry, Donald L. (1976), *Social Marketing Strategies: Conservation Issues and Analysis*, Santa Monica, Calif.: Goodyear.

II

EXPLORING GOVERNMENT PROGRAMS

INTRODUCTION TO PART II

Military manpower . . . food stamps . . . mail delivery . . . Amtrak . . . solar energy incentives . . . NASA technology . . . New York City . . . consumer education . . . trade regulation. The range of public sector products and markets is expansive and growing, despite pressures to shrink government involvement. The nature of government products and markets is complex and dynamic. Diffuse, fragmented values are common, varying levels of demand and support are characteristic, and change is inevitable!

A public program is an expression of political values, an allocation and distribution of specific, limited public resources. It is government in action: problems are salient; political processes are real; services are designed and delivered; citizens interact with bureaucracy; observers probe for indications of success or its absence; and decisions are made to continue, modify, expand, and terminate. As such, public programs are an excellent field laboratory in which to explore, study, and learn—often to experiment and always to evaluate.

The chapters of Part II present constructive analyses of field studies involving important government programs. The chapters demonstrate the application of fundamental marketing theories and methods in public program design, implementation, and formative evaluation. Analytical marketing frameworks (and related vocabulary) are used to conceptualize, compare, and critique a wide range of government program policies. The purpose of this section is exploratory. The skeptical and tentative use of marketing in most federal programs is a theme surfacing throughout the chapters. It is contrasted with the enthusiastic adoption and maturing of a marketing orientation in a few public programs. Consequently, the need to continue exploratory and experimental efforts to increase our understanding of government marketing methods and contexts is reinforced. The insights and conclusions presented throughout this section provide encouragement and guidelines for scholarship and practice.

A significant social experiment, an All-Volunteer Military Force (AVF), emerged in the early 1970s. It generated perhaps the most intense conscious strategic marketing effort at the federal level. The AVF concept, goals, and "accession/retention" program have been subjected to continuous public and political scrutiny, frequently producing controversy and debate. In the first chapter of this section, A. J. Martin discusses the nature and role of "Marketing and Manning the Military." The author carefully describes the complex sociopolitical environment of the AVF and outlines the dynamics and difficulties of formulating, implementing, and controlling an expansive government marketing strategy. From a diffusion perspective of marketing methods, the AVF is particularly important because it is the federal government's most extensive investment in conscious marketing. The successes and especially the problems and failures tend to be magnified and become powerful political instruments inhibiting or supporting the policy development role of marketing in government.

Like the AVF, the National Food Stamp Program is important, expansive, and frequently controversial. Unlike the AVF, the food stamp program has not formally adopted a comprehensive marketing orientation. In Chapter 7, "Marketing the National Food Stamp Program: Can a Public Welfare Program Be Run Like a Business?" Prakash Sethi poses a challenging question emanating from the perspective that associates marketing with the private sector. The author suggests that the food stamp program bears a remarkable resemblance to a national program for a commercial product. Using a marketing management framework, the food stamp program is analyzed and critically evaluated. Noting the distinction between commercial and government contexts, Sethi concludes that the program, particularly its efficiency, could be significantly improved by adoption of a marketing consciousness.

Comparative studies of marketing programs offer an opportunity for simultaneously transferring and enriching theory and practice. In "An International Perspective on Public Sector Marketing," Chapter 8, Christopher Lovelock compares the marketing efforts of national public agencies in Britain, Canada, and the United States, investigating three program areas—postal operations, passenger rail services, and energy conservation. Interesting opportunities are identified for sharing marketing analyses, methods, and strategies across national boundaries. Ironically, the United States is seen to be lagging in the application of marketing expertise by federal public agencies, despite its long tradition of commercial marketing expertise. The author suggests that the political structure of the United States constrains effective use of marketing by public sector organizations.

"Comparative Public Sector Marketing: Contrasting Two Canadian Programs" continues the comparative and international themes. In Chapter 9 J. A. Barnhill and Stanley Shapiro study two very different public programs, Canada's Northern Native Cooperative System and Canada Post. The extent of marketing development within these programs is found to be a critical factor influencing their responsiveness and effectiveness. The authors argue that marketing is a catalyst for changing restrictive and passive policy orientations. They suggest that this may be marketing's major contribution to the public sector.

Elaborating an issue discussed previously in this section, energy policy, Chris Allen investigates the "Causes of Mass Consumption—Related Societal Problems and the Role of Marketing in Fostering Solutions" in Chapter 10. The author demonstrates the need to understand the attitudes and life styles of consumers when formulating public policy. Basic flaws in government-sponsored energy programs are a result of inaccurate and inadequate attitudinal and behavioral profiles of citizen consumers, according to the author. An alternative profile formulated through consumer research is proposed, and a strategic approach to marketing communications based upon the research is advocated.

Energy policy is also the focus when George Tesar explores "The Role of Marketing in the Introduction of Consumer Products by Government" in Chapter 11. The author contends that government agencies' involvement in commercial consumer and industrial markets is growing. Increasingly government is choosing to introduce products through or into the "free" market system rather than through coercive mandates. Frequently these ventures are poorly managed from a marketing perspective and produce marginal or unsuccessful results. A new product introduction/demonstration framework is used to analyze and discuss the market entry of the Electric Hybrid Vehicle by the Department of Energy. This framework provides a coherent approach for studying actual market dynamics under field test conditions, thus increasing the potential for success.

Conducting consumer and market research or formulating new product introduction/demonstration projects, however, does not ensure the success or effectiveness of government programs. Often the substantive problems confronted are extremely complex, and the arsenal of solutions is inadequate or experimental. Sometimes the political process shrouds managerial logic. In Chapter 12, Claude Martin, Jr. describes "The Situation Confronting Introduction of the Anthony Dollar."

The Anthony dollar, while technically a direct substitute for the heavier and larger Eisenhower dollar, was proposed and designed to become an integral element of the currency mixture through active, high velocity circulation. A marketing study undertaken by the author for the Federal

Reserve System concerning introduction of the coin is reported and discussed. The study highlighted problems and opportunities that the federal government would confront in introducting the Anthony dollar. Given the unsuccessful introduction of the Anthony dollar and the previous failure of the two dollar bill, the chapter raises the question, "Why is marketing research frequently ignored when government programs are formulated and enacted?"

6

MARKETING AND MANNING THE MILITARY

A. J. Martin

As the United States entered the 1970s, a bold and innovative approach to manning the nation's armed forces became a reality. The All-Volunteer Force (AVF), America's most extensive attempt to meet its peacetime military manpower requirements without the compulsion and coercion of conscription, has been in operation since the end of 1972. The active force alone has recruited over 2 million individuals since the end of the draft. Reserve force recruits bring the overall total close to 3 million. In moving from draft dependence to total market dependence, the Department of Defense (DOD) has assumed the role of a marketer to the youth of the nation. The AVF is a large-scale, often controversial test of the application of marketing theory and practice to a national public policy issue.

This chapter describes the voluntary manning of the armed forces from a marketing perspective. It then proceeds to identify government marketing peculiarities, constraints, and issues illustrated by the DOD experience. Finally, it recognizes the challenge of the decade of the 1980s, with its declining youth population, to the success of marketing's application to the AVF. This discussion does not try to make a case for or against the volunteer force. Rather, it attempts to treat marketing's role in support of it.

MILITARY MANNING—A MARKETING PERSPECTIVE

The DOD, in its military personnel procurement process, lost a powerful and persuasive force for focusing attention on military service as use of the draft ceased. In its place, the military services turned to the tools of private sector marketing to stimulate the supply of volunteers.

The volunteer force has drawn extensively on marketing theory, practice, and expertise. Market research has been employed to explicate the enlistment decision process and to plan and evaluate recruiting and advertising activities. Promotional strategy management has been evaluated by marketing professionals as at least on a par with private sector practice. Theories concerning the relative contribution of advertising and a sales force when marketing an intangible, high-risk, once-purchased product have influenced the structure of the recruiting effort. Respected marketing organizations, such as advertising agencies, research houses, and consulting firms, as well as individual academic consultants, have been called upon.

The volunteer force today is supported by a varied "product" line, a national "distribution" system, a nationwide recruiting sales force, a large-scale advertising and promotional campaign, and a sophisticated buyer qualification system to enforce enlistment standards that act much like a pricing mechanism in influencing the supply of volunteers. A central market information system, a "corporate" market research program, and an institutional advertising program support the individual military service recruiting programs. In fiscal year 1980, the $825 million recruiting program is designed to accomplish over 650,000 active and reserve force enlistment transactions in the form of enlistment contracts.

This analogy to private sector marketing has value in analyzing how the tools developed in the private sector are used to meeting this specific public management challenge. The enlistment of an individual into the military is a voluntary transaction. It is a transaction in which the prospective enlistee is being asked to promise to provide certain things to the service of his or her choice. He incurs costs. He gives up, to a degree, discretion over what he will be doing, where he will be doing it, and when he will be doing it. He offers his time, energy, brainpower, physical capacity, and so forth. In effect, he offers himself as a manpower resource. The enlistment qualification standards (mental, physical, moral, and educational) create barriers to entry. They constrict and expand the supply of qualified prospects and are directly influenced by market conditions. Further, the enlistee incurs opportunity costs, the lost benefits of foregoing other uses of this time and capabilities. In still another sense, he may incur social costs in that he will wear a uniform and cut his hair or beard in a way that easily identifies him as a serviceman. He may incur a cost in coping with the possible disapproval of his peers. The potential enlistee does therefore incur costs; or, put another way, he pays a *price*.

On the other hand, the enlistee is the recipient of benefits through this act of enlistment. All of the many need-satisfying attributes of military service are available to the enlistee. If the experience of serving in the military has the capability of satisfying an unfilled need for the prospective enlistee, then it has utility for him. The marketing man would say that the set of need-satisfying attributes perceived as having utility (or value) to the potential enlistee is the *product* in this transaction.

On the other side of this transaction is the military, usually represented by a recruiter. The recruiter's job is to provide decision information to the potential enlistee (the buyer) to aid him in making a decision that is good for him as well as for the military. The military can be viewed as both supplying need-satisfying attributes and receiving in return through this voluntary transaction a manpower resource capable of contributing to the DOD mission. Obviously, accomplishment of the defense mission places necessary limits on recruiting. Just as a corporation must be profit-directed, this voluntary military manning program must attract the numbers and quality of people necessary to meet the requirements of military jobs.

The military recruiting program, exclusive of the examining function, is essentially a promotional effort consisting of over 21,000 recruiter salesmen (costing about $560 million including overhead, personnel, and support) and about $125 million in advertising.

The cost per accession is related to market image and relative propensity to enlist. The Air Force, as evidenced by DOD market surveys, enjoys the highest enlistment propensity among today's enlistment-age youth; whereas the Marine Corps has the most difficult market task, relatively, in terms of expressed propensity. Recruiting for the reserve force is a much more localized activity, somewhat less dependent on recruiting and advertising, and somewhat more dependent on personal feedback (word-of-mouth) from reservists in their local community.

A basic assumption underlying the military recruiting program is that the long-term future of the volunteer force depends in large measure on the ability of the services to provide information that enables the enlistment prospect to make a sound and informed choice regarding military service. The DOD has long been aware that the most effective and persuasive means of conveying information about enlistment opportunities is face-to-face communication between prospect and recruiter. However, given the relatively small number of recruiters and the very large number of prospective enlistees (about 4 million 18-year-olds in 1979), a truly effective communication effort, without heavy reliance on the mass media, becomes a physical and economic impossibility.

Because the decision to enlist for military service for several years is such an important one, it was obvious that recruiting advertising could not be the prime factor in the communication of enlistment information. This is the role of the recruiter who can respond credibly to a broad range of prospect inquiries and aid the prospect in the enlistment decision. Therefore, the role of recruiting advertising was determined to be recruiter support aimed at creating awareness of service opportunities, affecting attitudes toward enlistment, and providing prospect leads to recruiters through national inquiry mechanisms and local recruiting station inquiries.

Recruiting advertising is perhaps the most often criticized and least understood function in the military personnel procurement process. Advertising in any arena is often suspect and sometimes maligned—principally because it is so difficult to demonstrate its impact. This is especially true of the recruiting effort, which is so highly dependent on personal selling to "close the sale."

Notwithstanding the difficulty of quantifying advertising impact with precision, the services have exerted sustained and concentrated efforts to answer the question, "What do we get for our advertising dollar?" They have relied principally on the measurement of direct responses (coupons, cards, toll-free telephone attitudes toward military service). In addition, some experimental advertising research has been completed, and more extensive field experiments are being developed to measure advertising impact on enlistments and improve DOD ability to size advertising budgets.

MILITARY MANNING—ILLUSTRATIONS FOR GOVERNMENT MARKETERS

The application of marketing theory and practice to the AVF affords a case study which can illustrate many of the characteristics, peculiarities, constraints, and problems that may be encountered by other government marketers. Six of the many possible issues are discussed as examples to demonstrate translation of marketing to the government setting.

First, the field of marketing too often carries a "pejorative halo." The words *marketing, advertising,* and *selling* are viewed by many in government, especially economists, to be associated with a second-class, nonresearch-based, nonquantitative, soft discipline.

The government marketer, therefore, may be required to develop a second, more situationally acceptable, vocabulary. In volunteer force marketing, product becomes offering; promotion is communication; price becomes barriers or standards; sales are accessions; the buyer is a potential enlistee; and product demand is termed *supply.*

Negative views toward marketing and advertising are not always without justification in the private sector. The government marketer, since he normally is not within the purview of such regulatory agencies as the Federal Trade Commission, has a special responsibility to be above reproach in the use of marketing tools.

In August 1979, the FTC chairman wrote to the heads of all government agencies that use advertising on the subject of this special responsibility. The latter included the following:

> In recent months, the FTC has received complaints that government advertising is inaccurate, misleading, or even occasionally deceptive. Although these complaints are not verified, I am concerned that they may ultimately undermine public confidence in the integrity of communications between the public and the government. I therefore want to alert you personally to this potential problem, and offer the

services of our advertising review staff should you wish to consult with them regarding any of your advertising campaigns.

Many public and private organizations routinely implement their own internal review procedures to ensure that their advertising is true. FTC staff members also routinely review commercial advertising for truthfulness and accuracy. If you wish to enlist our staff's assistance, either to help review your own advertisements or establish your own internal review procedures, FTC staff members would be happy to assist you in any way.

I am taking the liberty of raising this issue because I strongly believe that we in government have an obligation to monitor our own advertising as scrupulously as we review the advertising in the private sector. There is a special reason for this. In the commercial marketplace, we can count on consumers to maintain a healthy skepticism toward product claims because they understand that the purpose of advertising is to encourage sales for a profit. But citizens expect that their government will deal honestly with them, without expectations of gain or profit. To merit their trust, we must hold our own advertising to standards of integrity at least as stringent as we hold private advertisers. Indeed, government may ultimately be held to an even higher standard of "fiduciary" responsibility toward the public, and must thus aspire to standards of absolute accuracy and fair dealing in its advertising. (Internal document)

The moral appears to be that government marketing is such a sensitive issue that it has the potential to attract regulation and regulators, even when there is no legal mandate for such oversight.

Second, programming and budgeting for a marketing effort in government place unusual demands on the public marketing manager. "How much is enough?" is always a difficult question to answer with confidence, but it is much more challenging with no "bottom line" against which to ratio marketing effort. Program and budget review is further complicated when the product is itself a class; and competitive effort is difficult, if not impossible, to gauge.

Budget sizing decisions become easy targets that are very difficult to defend against competent and cost-conscious congressional staffs; so there is an increased need for well-researched and empirically based cost-effectiveness relationships for long-term government marketing programs.

The DOD has found it necessary to become increasingly research-oriented in recruiting and advertising. No government marketing program, no matter what the initial legislative support, can avoid for long the necessity of building and defending its requests for public resources on empirical evidence that demonstrates accomplishment of program objectives for taxpayer dollars expended. DOD experience argues that early and sophisticated evaluation be built into government marketing programs, particularly at their inception. After-the-fact attempts to relate cost to results have been a very poor substitute for well-planned and analytically sound market evaluation.

Third, the taxpayer deserves at least the same quality marketing management as the stockholder of a major private sector firm. Unfortunately, though, inability to staff adequately with marketing professionals can lead to overdependence on contractors in government marketing.

In-house staffing in DOD for the particularly specialized marketing functions has been the focus of criticism in management audits of volunteer force marketing. In DOD these problems have been caused by reductions in overhead personnel staffs (a shrinking bureaucracy) as well as by overly mechanistic personnel systems. The latter lack flexibility, are not familiar with and do not understand marketing functions, and undergrade and therefore underpay marketing personnel.

Viewed from the private sector, marketing jobs in government have limited attractiveness. The job titles are foreign. Washington is not New York or Chicago in terms of advertising and marketing business activity. Job prospects question the transferability of experience back to the private sector. Top-level (Federal Senior Executive Service) salaries are not comparable to senior private sector marketing salaries and have not kept pace with inflation. There is always the question of whether a government marketing effort will last in the face of politically driven policy changes (What if the draft were to be reinstated?). These and other factors tend to influence the best potential government marketing managers away from government employment.

Fourth, product changes are relatively difficult to accomplish for government marketers. A true marketing perspective, as opposed to the tendency simply to sell an existing product, is difficult to foster in government. The requirements of the public organization tend to be emphasized over what private sector practitioners would call a consumer orientation.

To marketing theorists and practitioners, a critical issue is the nature of the government managerial process itself. In DOD, an argument could be made that given the need, at the end of the draft era, to implement rapidly a system to recruit over 400,000 active force enlistees per year, the recruiting effort could only be a selling effort, at least initially. Necessarily, promotion of the existing product was stressed. There was no time, no market research tradition, and no in-house marketing expertise to permit a consumer-oriented, product-development approach to the recruiting challenge. The military services have been tremendously successful in implementing that selling program. The issue now, however, is different: Has DOD moved enough toward a true marketing perspective to allow for the necessary product adjustments to ensure competitiveness of the active and reserve forces in the "baby bust" decade of the 1980s?

Fifth, government marketers will find it difficult to adapt to changing market conditions. In defense, which boasts a highly sophisticated and effective planning, programming, and budgeting system, there is an eighteen-month time lag between initial planning estimates and ultimate appropriation of resources by the Congress—if Congress passes an appropriation bill prior to the start of a given fiscal year!

Congressional decisions substantively and time-wise are difficult to forecast. The checks-and-balances system was not designed to be highly efficient. Separate and highly uncertain authorizing legislation, independent of money bills, to change product offerings are often required (for example, enlistment bonus program authority).

An analysis of current DOD recruiting market difficulties would support the hypothesis that the AVF marketing program is out of phase with the business cycle. In 1974–75, when unemployment was high and recruiting was relatively easier, DOD and the Congress began reducing resources for recruiting and post-service educational benefits (GI Bill). Enlistment standards were raised, and the ratio of military to civilian entry-level wages began to decline. As the economy turned around, youth unemployment declined, propensity to enlist dropped, and recruiting results showed declines in high-quality enlistees. Many of these difficulties can only be lessened by a relatively slow process of legislative changes.

It may be necessary to avoid reductions in resources in public marketing programs that are sensitive to fluctuation in the business cycle. Erring on the high side in terms of public marketing resources (including costly attributes of the product) may be necessary in such programs when market conditions are temporarily favorable.

Sixth, a fundamental issue for those interested in exploring and developing government marketing is the question of appropriateness of applying marketing tools in government settings. The national debate on the sustainability of the volunteer force in the face of the declining youth population of the 1980s and the recent recruiting market tightening have raised questions about the ability of a marketing approach to maintain military strength levels. Alternatives to the present approach are being seriously considered in Congress.

Some critics of the voluntary system for manning the military are also critical of a so-called marketplace approach. This argument was made in congressional testimony on February 14, 1979, before the Subcommittee on Military Personnel of the House Armed Services Committee by Professor Charles C. Moskos of Northwestern University. He argued, "The market system is not the way to recruit an AVF nor is it the way to strengthen a service institution." The appropriateness of a market approach that attempts to meet the needs of prospective enlistees and their influencers was questioned. He implied that valued (by the prospective enlistee) attributes of military service, such as job training, opportunities to better one's life, and good benefits for self and family, are somehow inappropriate motivations for enlistment. He further suggested that attempts to match such attributes of military service with the needs of prospective enlistees are somehow inconsistent or undermine a relatively more highly valued (by people other than the prospective enlistee) concept of service to country.

The emphasis on the promotion or selling of the benefits of military service has often been criticized. DOD youth market studies indicate that service to country is, in general, a valued attribute of military service. However, patriotism is less valued than those other attributes of service listed above. The same research indicates essentially no difference in patriotism between young people who express a positive likelihood of enlistment and those who do not. It also shows that patriotism, though not typically salient in the minds of our young people, is related to their perception of the threat to the nation. DOD has no evidence to suggest that service members who are principally attracted by other than patriotic motives are any less effective in their performance of duty as soldiers, sailors, airmen, and marines. Additionally, research, dating back to the pre-Vietnam draft era (internal documents 1964), indicates about the same relative level of importance for patriotic motivation among service members.

MARKETING'S FUTURE MILITARY MANNING CHALLENGE

DOD strategy for sustaining the volunteer force in the next decade involves reducing demand for new enlistees, particularly the limited-supply high-quality prospects. This aims to permit maintenance of recent high-quality market share by the services and DOD as a whole.

The assumption is that competitiveness can be maintained. Currently, however, DOD's market share is declining. As noted, the product has eroded somewhat in that post-service educational benefits have been reduced while availability of other federal educational funds have increased with no associated service obligation. Entry salaries have declined compared with civilian opportunities. Youth enrollment in CETA public service programs has increased, and the youth unemployment rate is down.

A complicating factor is maintenance of reserve and National Guard unit strength. Recruiting for these units, which involve local, hometown, and part-time service, is a new experience for DOD. Before the volunteer force, young people sought out reserve service to avoid being drafted into active forces. As ability to recruit for the reserve forces improves, competition with the active force has the potential of becoming an increasingly serious problem. To avoid this problem, DOD must develop imaginative approaches to reserve recruiting and training to open reserve service to those who are now employed in the civilian sector. Today an individual with no previous military training is almost forced to quit his or her job in order to take initial reserve training. If we can solve this problem we can continue to draw on the baby boom youth during their twenties.

DOD must turn to a product-development, more marketing-oriented approach if it is to sustain its competitiveness in the youth market in the 1980s. For example, market segmentation opportunities must be evaluated and appropriate strategies implemented for both active and reserve recruiting. Full-time active service must be made more attractive in terms of the needs of high-quality potential recruits. DOD is now conducting an extensive in-market "new product" test in which shorter enlistments and enhanced educational benefits are being evaluated experimentally for the active force.

Market data is also being used to focus attention on ways to expand the market for reserve service. Reserve force enlistment incentives have been implemented, initial training requirements have been made more flexible, and shorter terms of enlistment have been instituted. All are in consonance with market research findings.

Higher than expected first-term enlisted attrition rates in both active and reserve forces are evidence of dissatisfaction associated with "product" use and have obvious implications over time for the effectiveness of recruiting and advertising. DOD is attempting to reduce attrition rates through improved quality of life and personnel management practices.

The future success of marketing's application to manning the military will depend on DOD's ability to adapt its enlistment offering to the needs of its changing market. This process is constrained by the needs of the military services in accomplishing their assigned missions; required legislative changes to alter enlistment bonuses, military pay, educational benefits, and other attributes of military service; and the lead time involved in changing defense plans, programs, and budgets.

As the United States enters the 1980s, the volunteer force will continue to face complex managerial problems. The adverse demographic trend appears certain to increase costs and aggravate the challenge to voluntary manning. The effectiveness of DOD's marketing management will be a central and major determinant of whether the United States' armed forces continue to be manned on a voluntary basis in peacetime. As the voluntary system receives the constant scrutiny and regular reassessment it deserves, the appropriateness of the market approach will surely remain an emotional ingredient in the national debate.

Explorations and developments in government marketing should not overlook the successes and mistakes embodied in this nation's pioneering attempt to do what has never before been done by any nation—man a military force, active and reserve, consisting of nearly 3 million people, on a voluntary, free market basis.

7

MARKETING THE NATIONAL FOOD STAMP PROGRAM: CAN A PUBLIC WELFARE PROGRAM BE RUN LIKE A BUSINESS?

S. Prakash Sethi

In the last decade experts have argued, and with some logic, that nonprofit institutions and the public sector could serve their constituencies and clients better and provide improved services more efficiently and at lower cost if they were to use the principles and practices that have been developed and used to such tremendous advantage in the private sector. In a sense, this is a variation on the theme of improving government efficiency by making government run more like a business. An extensive survey of recent marketing literature (for example, Gaedeke 1977; Henion 1976; Kotler 1979; Lovelock 1977; Montana 1978; Lovelock and Weinberg 1978) reveals two important findings: (1) if the number of publications is any indication, it would appear that the shepherds are becoming increasingly convinced of the potency of this idea and its deliverance potential; and (2) there is growing concern that the flocks are not yet accepting the concepts and that a great deal more missionary work is needed.

THE PROBLEM IN PERSPECTIVE

In its scope and magnitude, the administration of the food stamp program is akin to running a large business with little of the private sector's

The author is grateful to Mrs. Nancy Snyder, former deputy administrator for the Family Nutrition Program, USDA Food and Nutrition Service, and Mr. Al Ulvog, director of planning, research, and evaluation, Office of the Inspector General, USDA, for their assistance and cooperation in the preparation of this presentation. The analysis and conclusions are the author's alone, however, and not those of the USDA.

homogeneity of goals, clarity of performance criteria, and flexibility of management tools—including systems of rewards and penalties for individual executives. The consequence is that program management is invariably more complex, less efficient, and more vulnerable to misdirection. For example, just as organizations select and reach out to target consumers, the food stamp program identifies potential recipients according to eligibility standards, develops communication programs to increase the proportion of recipients in the eligible population (outreach), and distributes stamps in the most suitable denominations. Potential recipients are then serviced through local networks of distribution outlets. The administrative efficiency of the program is maintained by management and operator training programs; performance reporting systems for quality control; and an independent audit and enforcement system designed to weed out ineligibles, prevent fraud and abuse among both recipients and program operators, and maintain program integrity.

However, these resemblances between the marketing of a product in the private sector and marketing of a service in the public sector are at best superficial and at worst misleading. There are several fundamental structural and operational differences between the private and the public sectors.

In the first place, managers in the public sector do not always have a unified set of goals with clearly defined priorities, nor do they play an important role in the development of such goals. In the private sector, program goals and strategies are developed within the organization, and top management is an integral part of the decision making. Management has a great deal of freedom and flexibility to develop and implement strategy. On the other hand, federal programs are generally developed in Congress and the White House, with goals designed to satisfy various constituencies. The outcome is often equal emphasis on conflicting goals.

Secondly, in the private sector, managers have an effective constituency—stockholders and directors—that rewards efficiency in the delivery system, while maintaining promised or contracted levels of service to other constituent groups. Increases in service levels and efficiencies in the delivery system are tied together in the overall goals of the organization and are complementary.

For public sector programs, Congress and the White House theoretically represent all segments of the population. In reality, however, the representation of various groups is greatly influenced by the effectiveness of organized lobbying. Thus in the public sector the manager is accountable to a multiplicity of constituent groups, with the users (recipients of services) perhaps having the strongest influence on goals and policies, and the cost bearers (the taxpayers, indirectly through Congress) having the least influence.

Third, managers in the public sector are measured by a different set of performance criteria than are managers in the private sector. Quite often the stated criteria for measuring performance are different than the practiced criteria, that is, political rationality has a higher priority than economic rationality.

Public sector programs are invariably subjected to scrutiny designed not to measure efficiency but to ensure that the vested interests of various groups are adequately protected. Adequacy of delivery is measured not in terms of the cost of delivery compared to benefits delivered but in terms of meeting the requirements of system processes—adequate hearings and public comment, due process, compliance with department rules, and so on. Thus, when tradeoffs must be made, they are made in favor of satisfying the "process" requirements of the system rather than achieving input- or output-related efficiencies.

Finally, public sector managers have little freedom to change elements of the system if they are dissatisfied. Much of the system's decision-making structure and process is legally mandated and externally imposed. The system therefore often works quite independently of its managers, who must accommodate themselves to the system's inherent logic or illogic.

My analysis leads me to conclude that large public sector programs are not completely amenable to the application of private sector organizational principles and practices. The dominant rationality for the public sector programs is political. Economic rationality, which aims at minimizing costs, is relegated to a secondary position.

But once a consensus as to goals and strategies has been achieved among competing constituent groups, the marketing concept can play an important role within the domain of operational tactics by improving the efficiency of the delivery system and thereby maximizing total return to various constituencies. Before this can be accomplished, though, significant changes in the structure of the system are needed to balance the influence of competing groups in setting goals and objectives, to provide managers with a cohesive set of goals against which the performance can be measured, to increase management discretion and authority to institute changes in various elements of the system and effect program efficiencies, and to develop a system of incentives and penalties that reward not merely process compliance but improvement in results.

THE FOOD STAMP PROGRAM

The food stamp program is the largest single program in dollars operated by the Department of Agriculture. With fiscal year 1979 appropriation of $5.8 billion, it represents over one-third of the department's budget. The FY 1980 budget is estimated to be in the $7 billion range. In FY 1978, the program covered over 16 million participants and 5.4 million households—1 out of 13 Americans and 1 out of 14 households. By February 1979, the number of food stamp recipients had increased to 18.6

million. In terms of those theoretically eligible, the program reached about 50 percent of the population in FY 1978. Program management involved over 2,700 federal employees, or 3.4 percent of the department's workforce. If the value of distributed food stamps were equated with annual sales in the private sector, the national food stamp program would compare favorably with such industrial and consumer product giants as Proctor & Gamble, Dow Chemical, and Eastment Kodak. It would rank among the top 30 companies in *Fortune's* list of the top 500 industrial corporations. In terms of numbers of customers or clients served, it could be compared with large national retail chains like Sears, Roebuck and Penneys.

Historical Background

The food stamp program was begun in 1939 as a pilot project to help the needy. Participation in the program had reached about 4 million people when it was suspended on March 1, 1943, due to the increased demand for food and increased employment opportunities during World War II. At President Kennedy's instigation the program was revived as a pilot in eight counties in 1961 to improve the availability of food to the needy throughout the United States. The Food Stamp Act of 1964 made the program permanent and available to any county wishing to participate. By September 1966, 331 food stamp projects were active in 40 states and the District of Columbia, with 1.2 million participants. There was a rapid increase in the program when legislation set uniform standards for participating counties making more people eligible. Between May 1969 and February 1971 there was a twofold increase—from 3.2 million to 6.9 million—in the number of people receiving food stamps. Again in 1973, food stamp legislation mandated a nationwide food stamp program unless a state could show that participation of a particular area would be impossible or impractical.

At the peak of operation during a period of high unemployment, 19.3 million persons participated in the program. During this period, recipients were required to pay for a portion of the total value of the stamps they received. The cost to the recipient was based on a variety of factors— household income, household size, and locational considerations that might increase the cost of housing and utilities.

A major revision of the food stamp program was mandated under the Food and Agriculture Act of September 29, 1977 (7 USC 2011, Food Stamp Act of 1977, Public Law 95-113). Among the many changes, the new act eliminated the requirement that recipients purchase the stamps. This reform was expected to extend the benefits to those people, especially the elderly, who were otherwise eligible but did not participate because of the purchase requirement. The act standardized certain deductions for housing and related costs, thereby simplifying certification procedures for establishing eligibility standards and benefit levels. These changes were intended to improve efficiency by reducing errors in verifying eligibility and determining benefit levels, and reducing trafficking and fraud. Another requirement of the new act was that all able-bodied people actively seek work.

An added factor is the Food and Nutrition Service (FNS) regulations for quality control standards for maintaining program efficiency and recovering benefits already paid to ineligibles. These regulations are generally quite weak and offer state administrative agencies little incentive to attempt to recover funds paid out to ineligible recipients because of unintentional errors or fraud.

The elimination of the purchase requirement went into effect on January 1, 1979, with states having to convert their caseload to the new requirement by June 30, 1979. At this point, it is impossible to project the impact of this provision of the program. Preliminary estimates had indicated that the new act would increase benefits for about 5 million people, about 3 million would find their benefits reduced, and another 1.3 million would be dropped altogether.

Program Administration

State public welfare agencies are responsible for day-to-day administration of the program. This includes determination and certification of eligible recipient households; issuance of Authorizations to Participate (ATPs), which permit recipients to acquire food stamps; periodic recertification or decertification of recipients to take into account changes in income levels or other factors; outreach; provisions for hearings and conducting investigations; and all other activities related to program operation in accordance with the act and FNS regulations.

These public welfare agencies are the agents for the large federal Aid to Families with Dependent Children (AFDC) program administered by the Department of Health, Education and Welfare (HEW). They also operate the Medicaid program and in many instances state and local general assistance programs. They see their first responsibility as accountability to HEW and perceive the "contract" with USDA for food stamps as an add-on to already overburdened state systems. Differing eligibility criteria and operating guidelines among the programs intensify the dichotomy, particularly when the client populations served overlap approximately 45 percent nationally.

The Washington office of FNS, USDA, is responsible for formulating and administering the current and long-range policies of the Food Stamp Program authorized by the Food Stamp Act of 1977. Seven regional offices act as liaison between Washington and the state welfare commissioners and other officials and state agencies. Their staffs provide direction in implementing and coordinating FNS policies; give technical and training assistance to state agencies to ensure compliance with policies and procedures; approve firms to accept food stamps from participants; authorize and oversee firms through field staff located throughout the country; monitor state performance through quality control and efficiency and effectiveness reviews; direct corrective action in states where program deficiencies are noted; and approve state plans of operation, amendments, manuals, and operating procedures. Regional offices also make recommendations for designation of areas to receive emergency food stamps and monitor issuance and use of those stamps at disaster locations.

PROGRAM ANALYSIS WITHIN A MARKETING FRAMEWORK

Mission Analysis

In terms of mission analysis, three points stand out.

First, the underlying rationale of the program is that of entitlement, namely, any household that meets the income criterion is entitled to the benefits provided in the program. The only requirement is that an able-bodied person must register and look for work. However, given the relative lack of employable skills among food stamp recipients and high unemployment rates, this requirement has been largely ineffective in securing employment for the registrants. Instead, it has meant additional paperwork—and the resultant costs—to satisfy the procedural requirements of the new act.

Second the primary emphasis is on raising the nutritional level of low-income households. However, there is nothing in the act that relates distribution of food stamps to achievable or measurable increases in nutritional levels. In other words, performance criteria in this instance are output-related. The focus is on the number of households receiving food stamps rather than approaches to raising nutritional levels. To date, no studies statistically relate availability of food stamps to measurable changes in nutritional levels among households receiving food stamps. Nor does the new act mandate determination of any direct association between food stamp disbursements and increases in nutritional levels as a measure of the effectiveness of the program.

Third, the declaration of policy emphasizes only the interests of the recipients. It makes no mention of the interests of those who pay for the program—although for the first time in the history of the food stamp program, the 1977 act puts a cap or limit on total appropriations of $5.85 billion for FY 1978 and $6.19 billion for FY 1979. Attempts are already underway to remove this ceiling.

Outreach or Maximizing Market Share

At present, the program reaches an average of 42 percent of the people who might be eligible for benefits. The size of pool is estimated on the basis of the proportion of low-income families in the population. A variety of factors may account for the gap between those who are potentially eligible and those who are currently in the program. These include possible errors in the estimate of eligible population size; the gap between those who are theoretically eligible and those who can be effectively reached; lack of effort on the part of some states or state agencies in promoting the program; and reluctance or ignorance on the part of some eligible recipients to apply for the program.

The Food Stamp Act of 1977 deletes the wording of the previous law requiring states to "insure the participation of eligible households." According to the Senate Report on *Food and Agriculture Act 95-180* (May 16, 1977), "the phrase 'to insure participation' contained in the current Act is not used because of the unintended burden it placed on States in effectively administering the provision." This language contributed to a 1974 court decision forcing USDA to issue specific and binding outreach instructions to the states. Congress did not intend that outreach efforts be decreased, however: "Low-income families should be informed about how the 'new' Food Stamp Program would work and about their duties and responsibilities under the new program." (*House Report on Food and Agriculture Act 95-464*, June 24, 1977). Accordingly, Congress modified the outreach language and expanded the notice requirements. The new law requires states to inform low-income people, including those receiving public assistance, unemployment compensation, and Supplementary Security Income, about the availability of food stamps and associated requirements.

Advocacy groups seeking to broaden the scope of the program have emphasized the low outreach figures as an indication that FNS is not fulfilling its mandate and have played an effective role in forcing FNS to expand outreach efforts with relative disregard for the ultimate cost of such a policy.

In marketing terms, the outreach program has two characteristics that should be noted. First, the apparent reward system for the program manager—at the state and local level—is based on increasing market share without regard to cost. The pressures to increase outreach levels have the effect of giving less attention to weeding out applicants who should not be in the program.

Second, since the federal government pays 100 percent of the costs of food stamps and 50 percent of all administrative costs, the system is akin to the third-party payment prevalent in Medicaid and similar insurance programs. Under this arrangement, the federal government or some other governmental agency pays the cost of medical care on behalf of the recipient to the provider of the service—in this case, the physician. Since neither the doctor nor the patient have to share any costs or stand to benefit from any cost savings there is little incentive to control costs or improve performance relative to costs.

Market Segmentation: Identifying Types of Recipients

In marketing a product in the private sector, prudent policies dictate identifying different classes of customers in terms of ease, cost, or risk of selling. Similarly, in distributing food stamps an attempt is made to evaluate different applicants in terms of eligibility for participation in the program. This is called the certification process.

In the food stamp process as depicted in Figure 7.1, a household makes application at the local welfare office, obtains its coupons through a coupon issuance office, and purchases food at grocery stores. The stamps are then redeemed and destroyed.

Applicant

Participation in the food stamp program is on a household basis. Households apply for assistance at local welfare offices. When an identifiable food stamp application has been made, it is processed within 30 days of date of receipt; then applicants are provided an opportunity to obtain food stamps.

Welfare Office

As a means of food stamp program accessibility, the program is operated through local welfare offices across the country. Within this module, the principal activity is that of determining household eligibility and certifying applicant households.

Household eligibility is determined by applying certain financial and nonfinancial criteria. One important financial criterion is an income test based on the nonfarm income poverty guidelines established by the Office of Management and Budget (OMB). The OMB guidelines are adjusted annually each July 1 by the change between the average Consumer Price Index (CPI) for the 50 states and the District of Columbia for the preceding calendar year and the CPI for March of the current year. Using these guidelines, three deductions are allowed for determining income eligibility: standard deduction, earned income deduction, and excess shelter and dependent care deduction. All these deductions are standardized to the extent possible based on a predetermined formula.

Applicant households must also meet an assets test. Assets cannot exceed $1,750, except that households of two or more where at least one

FIGURE 7.1

The Life of a Food Coupon

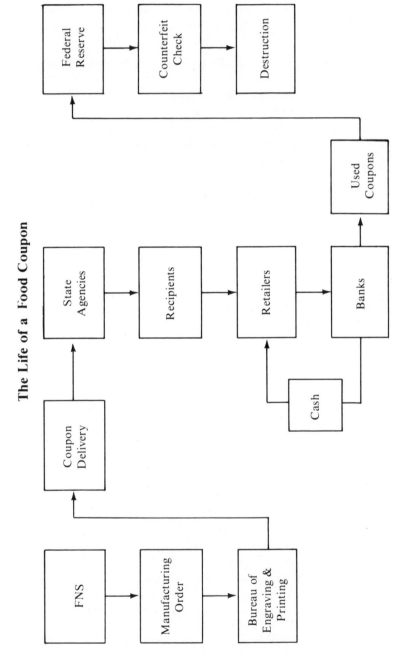

Source: Adapted by the author.

member is 60 or older are allowed assets of $3,000. Items not considered assets for food stamp purposes include homes and surrounding property, household goods and personal effects, licensed vehicles used primarily for income-producing purposes, and the cash value of life insurance policies and pension funds. The ownership of a car with a blue book value of less than $4,500 is also excluded. Households that put their money, possessions, or property in someone else's name in order to qualify for food stamps are ineligible for a period of up to one year.

When household eligibility is determined and the household otherwise complies with program standards, including appropriate cooperation during eligibility determination, it is certified as eligible and issued food coupons.

The certification process, however, is highly susceptible to inefficiency and abuse. In a large number of states, poorly paid and poorly trained caseworkers must often contend with complex regulations that force them into situations where they must interpret information provided by applicants who regard them as adversaries. In inner cities, where a majority of food stamp recipients reside, a caseworker often operates in a depressing work environment, and the threat of physical violence lurks below the surface. There have also been instances of harassment of recipients. To protect the privacy of the recipients from overzealous state employees, both the law and FNS regulations have built a number of procedures into the certification process that are often perceived as working against accurate determination of the level of benefits. In determining eligibility level, the caseworker cannot do any independent checking but must accept references provided by the applicant for verification of information. Applicants are not required to provide their Social Security numbers to enable the agency to use computer matching of recipient names with those of municipal employees, public employees, or private employer payrolls. Nor can the federal government currently use the computer data collected by various state agencies. In studies recently conducted in Florida by the auditors of the Inspector General's office of the U.S. Department of Agriculture, computer matching of income data between food stamp recipients and employees on the municipal and public school payrolls showed that as many as 30 percent of those receiving food stamps may have lied about their income. The USDA is planning to seek changes in the Food Stamp Act that, among other things, would require applicants to furnish Social Security numbers on applications and state agencies to undertake computer matching as a measure of quality control.

The Product—Food Stamps

Food stamps are made available in denominations of $1, $5, and $10. As an element of outreach, advocates of food stamp recipient groups have lobbied for easier availability of stamps. This has taken many forms, including establishment of more offices open for longer hours. Some groups have demanded that a nationwide standard be established where a case-worker would be made available for every 250 eligible households. Other measures include immediate replacement of food stamps when a recipient reports them stolen and relaxation of verification standards of the information supplied by the applicant on the basis of which food stamp allotment is determined.

An important element in this approach is the expectation on the part of recipients as to their rights and obligations. Recipients are viewed as passive, with little obligation to make some effort to apply for and receive stamps. Instead, the emphasis is placed on their right to receive stamps. with the major burden shifted to the provider agencies to maximize availability without regard to cost.

The state agency of each participating state is responsible for the issuance of coupons to eligible households. The agency may assign the responsibility for coupon issuance to other establishments such as banks, savings and loan associations, credit unions, the postal service, community action agencies, and migrant service agencies. Assignment of the issuance function to other parties, however, does not relieve the agency of its responsibility to ensure that assigned duties are carried out in accordance with established regulations. The state agency may issue food coupons through (1) a household issuance record (HIR) card system; (2) an authorization to participate (ATP) system; or (3) a direct coupon mail-out system.

One of the significant sources of losses in the program is the unauthorized use of ATP cards that are reported stolen or lost. At present, the preventive system is largely ineffective as a deterrent. It takes literally weeks, if not months, before anyone knows that an ATP card reported lost in the mail was actually redeemed. So there is no way to trace the user of an unauthorized ATP card and, even worse, to enforce recovery of funds. For all practical purposes, the losses must be written off as unrecoverable.

After the eligible household obtains its food coupons, it may purchase food at authorized food stores.

Promotion

The new act requires that state agencies inform low-income households about the availability, eligibility requirements, and benefits of the food stamp program. FNS regulations provide specific rules for the state agencies as to the expenditure levels and type of information activities the agencies must undertake to expand outreach and meet the requirements of the new act. Assistance to applicants also includes provision of bilingual personnel and printed materials, where necessary, to explain the program and the procedure for filling applications.

USDA must also develop nutrition education materials to help people with low reading levels understand the relationship between diet and health and how to buy and prepare nutritious, economical meals. State agencies must prominently display in all food stamp and public assistance offices posters supplied by USDA listing foods that contain substantial amounts of recommended daily allowances of vitamins, minerals, and proteins for children and adults; menus that combine such food into meals; details on eligibility for other programs administered by USDA that provide nutrition benefits; and general information on the relationship between diet and health. Pamphlets with this information for home use are also available at food stamp and public assistance offices.

No corresponding requirements or incentives exist for the FNS to publicize cost efficiencies or losses due to fraud, abuse, and mismanagement. In the private sector, cost savings are translated into higher profits for the firm, greater rewards for the manager, and lower prices for the consumer. Thus everybody gains from efficiencies. A public service program is akin to monopoly pricing in the private sector. Since USDA is the only source of food stamps and benefits are legislatively determined, the recipient does not gain anything by assisting the supplier in improving efficiency. The program manager is not personally rewarded for efficient management but may even be penalized if cost-cutting efforts antagonize powerful vested interest groups. At the same time, program managers are publicly chastized for program inefficiencies or cost overruns over which they may have little control and for which they may have little support from political leaders.

Program managers are thus quite reluctant to promote efficiency in the delivery system or to publicize program deficiencies. Even where information is released, it is often couched in language designed to obfuscate rather than illuminate, with the result that the critical variables are downplayed or understated. For example, losses of millions of dollars of program funds due to payment of benefits to ineligible recipients are innocuously termed "error rates."

Distribution Channels

Recipients use the food coupons like cash to purchase food in authorized retail stores. Only those stores, at least half of whose sales are staple foods, are authorized to accept food stamps. Authorized nonprofit food-buying organizations, such as coops, can accept payment for food orders prior to delivery.

Commercial banks redeem coupons from authorized retail food stores, meal services, and wholesale food concerns. Coupons submitted for redemption must be endorsed and accompanied by a properly filled out and signed redemption certificate. Redeemed coupons are canceled by the bank receiving them and are then forwarded to the Federal Reserve Bank.

Ninety-one FNS field offices located in various states are responsible for certification of retail stores. The certification process has been beset with a host of problems, including difficulties in verifying stores applying for certification, especially in the inner-city areas. Because of the sheer numbers of stores (about 300,000), it is extremely difficult to institute effective checks against stores accepting stamps for ineligible products, such as alcoholic beverages, or for cash at discounted value. Even when fraud is involved, the store may have no incentive to ensure adequate compliance with food stamp regulations because it may increase costs in terms of slowdown at the checkout counters, staff training, and potential loss of business. There is a greater propensity for misdealing and trafficking in stamps among small or marginally profitable stores than among large stores, and there is a concentration of both small and marginally profitable stores in the inner-city areas. The result is that, in large cities like Chicago and New York, food stamps are used to buy almost anything, especially in low-income areas with a concentration of food stamp recipients.

STRATEGIC PLANNING—PROGRAM ADMINISTRATION

The administrative system is somewhat akin to the private sector situation in which a manufacturer sells products through independent retailers and also provides part of their marketing and promotional expenses; however, in the first place, a manufacturer has a great deal of flexibility in selecting and maintaining distribution outlets on the basis of their performance, and secondly, a manufacturer can use a variety of incentives to spur performance at these outlets. FNS, on the other hand, must deal with the agencies designated by a state. These agencies perform various other functions and are subject to a multiplicity of often conflicting pressures, thereby making them less responsive to FNS needs. The performance incentives available to FNS are also largely procedural and punitive in character, that is, FNS may withhold administrative funds if state agencies do not improve performance.

From its inception, the food stamp program has been plagued with a high rate of error resulting in payment of benefits to ineligibles and to many others at a level higher than permissible by law. The loss of funds from these errors has been variously estimated to range between 5 and 15 percent for different states, with certain large city programs incurring losses as high as 30 percent. Efforts at recovery by the FNS and the states have been inadequate and actual restitution minimal compared with the magnitude of the problem and the size of losses.

The incidence of proven fraud (convictions) has been quite low—about 2 percent of total disbursements; however, it would be erroneous to conclude that the magnitude of actual fraud is small. According to a report by the inspector general, USDA, to the Senate Committee on Appropriations dated April 25, 1979, program losses resulting from actual fraud convictions are currently estimated to be less than $8 million a year. However, if every error attributable to an individual recipient was considered probable fraud, program losses would exceed $400 million per year.

The high error rate is due partially to misreporting of income, household size, and other related factors. The recipient error rate is 60.6 percent for all overissued error cases. (Errors due to underreporting of income are estimated to account for about half the losses in the program.) States are hampered in the verification process by cumbersome procedures, inexperienced caseworkers, allocation of inadequate financial and manpower resources, and failure to follow through.

The FNS regulations under the new act pertaining to verification of income and other information will aggravate an already severe problem. They discourage independent verification of income or household size unless this information appears questionable to the caseworker, and then only through contacts supplied by the applicant. In addition, the regulations do not specify what constitutes "questionable" and how a caseworker might determine it.

The elimination of purchase requirements provides an added incentive to the unscrupulous. Assuming the costs and risks of detection and apprehension to be similar under the old and the new program, the elimination of the "cash investment" increases the payoff from deliberate misreporting. Fraud problems are thus likely to be exacerbated under the new program, as appears to be borne out in early reports from major cities. With the conversion to the new regulations and the elimination of purchase requirements, there has been a significant increase in the number of ATP cards reported lost or stolen. At the same time, the number of cards returned each month because of death, change of address, and so forth has shown a precipitous decline. In New York City, for example, where an estimated 10 percent of ATP cards were previously returned undelivered, the rate has now declined to 2 percent.

New FNS regulations require that states send an individual notice of adverse action to each household receiving a reduction or termination of benefits because of the new rules. A household that requests a fair hearing within ten days of receipt of the notice can allege that the benefits were computed incorrectly or that the new law was being misapplied, thereby continuing benefits at the old rate pending the outcome of the hearing. A number of new procedural requirements would make these regulations quite onerous in terms of time and labor and therefore expensive for the states. In the likely event that a substantial number of households request hearings, the states' capacity to conduct hearings would be overwhelmed, thereby continuing payment of improper benefits to a large number of households for a considerable period of time. Since the states do not gain any monetary advantage from expediting the hearings, total losses to the program from this failure could be significant. An added factor in the FNS requirement that states notify people who had received unauthorized benefits in the past is that states will not terminate current or future benefits for failure to pay past claims or even agree on a payment schedule. Furthermore, if two demand letters are unanswered, the state agency may terminate further action by declaring the claim to be uncollectable. In the past it has been nearly impossible to collect overpaid benefits from such households. The new regulations are likely to aggravate the situation even further.

The new act provides for the USDA to reimburse state agencies 50 percent of all administrative costs involved in the operation of the food stamp program. USDA is also authorized to pay not less than 75 percent of the costs of state food stamp program investigations and prosecutions. Two measures are provided to ensure efficient management of the program: (1) increased reimbursement from 50 to 60 percent, provided the error rate according to the quality control program is less than 5 percent; and (2) establishment of elaborate work rules and reporting requirements and withholding of funds if states fail to comply.

Cost sharing provides no incentive for the various agencies to improve their operations, since savings do not revert to them. At the operational level they are likely to be viewed as cost cutting and therefore adverse to the employment of people who would be directly involved in improving operations. There are no penalties to the firstline supervisors for poor performance or rewards for superior performance.

Increasing cost sharing from 50 to 60 percent, subject to an error rate under 5 percent, is not an adequate incentive either. A uniform 5 percent rate ignores the problems of areas where a high error rate may be beyond the control of state agencies. In cases where current error rate is well above 10 percent and is unlikely to come down appreciably, there is little incentive to improve management or cut costs. Withholding administrative funds may also be a potentially ineffective tool. Politically it may be very unpalatable to apply, and it may be quite time-consuming because of potential legal challenges on procedural and substantive grounds which the states could use to delay enforcement.

SUMMARY AND CONCLUSIONS

The major distinctions between a private and a public sector program should now be apparent. The political considerations inherent in the goal-setting and structural constraints externally imposed on the program administrators make public sector programs qualitatively different despite their superficial similarity to private sector programs. We do not maintain that political considerations and structural constraints are unnecessary or undesirable. On the contrary, since a public welfare program is an income transfer program, it is understandable that the beneficiaries would want to limit the discretion of program managers to affect their benefits adversely. However, once these constraints are accepted, it is still possible to improve program efficiency by using the marketing concept. In conclusion, I propose the following considerations and recommendations.

1. One major requisite is a change in "mind set" on the part of all involved in the administration of the program. Perceiving the agency mission as a "social contract" that balances the needs of recipients and taxpayers need mean no conflict between competence and compassion. I would recommend the cap on annual appropriations for the program. The department should earmark this appropriation to the states in proportion to the population potentially eligible to participate in the program and the projected outreach targets. These targets should be widely publicized among the recipient groups and their spokespersons, with emphasis on the fact that any diversion of resources to those ineligible for benefits will reduce those otherwise available to the eligible. This should enlist the support of legitimate recipients in ferreting out fraudulent claimants and also in putting pressure at the state and local level for improving program efficiency.

2. The situation with regard to ATP cards is not dissimilar to the use of credit cards in the private sector. Credit card systems like VISA and Master Charge have on-line systems that provide instant verification for the authorized use of their credit cards. Given the total number of ATP cards outstanding, a similar on-line system should be quite feasible as well as cost-effective. Moreoever, since there are in existence a number of national tie-lien networks used by the private sector credit card companies and the thousands of banks issuing such cards, it might be possible for an ATP verification system to be tacked onto one of these systems.

3. A radical change in the communication effort is called for if public sector programs are to develop a constituency that supports efforts at minimizing waste due to fraud, abuse, or other factors. Instead of downplaying inefficiencies, waste, and abuse, the ideal strategy would be to publicize the harm to society in general and to taxpayers in particular that occurs because a given program is managed in a manner contrary to its intended purposes and costs more than it should. One of the first tasks of public sector program managers should be to develop a constituency tht could counter the influence of beneficiary groups at the policy and strategy stages of program development.

4. One way to correct trafficking in stamps would be to consolidate the distribution system by reducing the number of smaller, low-volume stores accepting food stamps. Critics of this proposal may well argue that such a proposal would force a large number of minority-owned firms in inner-city areas out of business and would also cause inconvenience to a great many recipients. But experience in the private sector has also shown that large stores tend to offer a greater variety of goods at comparatively lower prices. Consolidation should allow otherwise marginal stores to become bigger, exploit relative economies of scale, and become more profitable, while at the same time benefitting consumers through lower prices and increased variety and quality of goods offered.

5. The program should provide far greater flexibility in establishing variable criteria for benefits and operational performance for different states and regions based on local conditions. Experiments should be made with block grants of food stamps to various state administrative units based on estimated levels of outreach among eligible households. The grants should not be adjusted upward except for errors in estimating the size of the market. In case the states err in distributing food stamps to ineligible households, they must make up the losses from their own budgets, which is tantamount to capping at the local level.

6. Instead of paying a fixed percentage of all administrative costs, a "standard work unit" for case processing should be developed. This would be an artificial unit based on optimal time required for processing a simple application. Different complexity levels would be assigned multiple work units. The total caseload in a state can then be measured in terms of "standard work units" and states paid on the basis of processing these units. State agencies would decide how to use these funds. Any savings from improved operations would go to the state; spending over the optimal amounts would be absorbed by the state.

7. Since certain errors are endemic to any large-scale operation, they should be recognized as a necessary cost of operation. A zero error rate is impossible to achieve, but with the establishment of standard work units and optimal workloads tolerable error rates for various regions could be established. During a transition period of, say, three years, states could be paid 50 percent of all savings realized through a reduction in the error rate until the rate reaches the optimal level. After the transition period, states should be required to bear all losses attributed to an error rate above the optimal.

8. In addition to cost sharing, states should be allowed to keep part of recovered funds for their own use, preferably in paying their 25 percent share of such costs. Since successive recoveries are increasingly difficult, sharing of recovered funds should be based on a formula that pays states a smaller percentage of initial recoveries, with percentages increasing for successive recoveries.

REFERENCES

Gaedeke, R. M. (1977), *Marketing in Private and Public Nonprofit Organizations: Perspectives and Illustrations*, Santa Monica, Calif.: Goodyear.

Henion, Karl E. (1976), *Ecological Marketing*, Columbus, Ohio: Grid.

Kotler, Philip (1979), "Strategies for Introducing Marketing into Nonprofit Organizations," *Journal of Marketing* (January): 37–44.

———— and Sidney J. Levy, (1969), "Broadening the Concept of Marketing," *Journal of Marketing* 33 (January): 10–15.

Lovelock, Christopher H., ed. (1977), *Nonbusiness Marketing Cases*, no. 8-378-001, Boston: Intercollegiate Case Clearing House.
—— and Charles B. Weinberg (1978), "Public and Non-profit Marketing Comes of Age," in *Review of Marketing 1978*, eds., Gerald Zaltman and T. Bonoma, pp. 413–52, Chicago: American Marketing Association.
Montana, Patrick J., ed., (1978), *Marketing in Nonprofit Organizations*, New York: AMACOM.

8

AN INTERNATIONAL PERSPECTIVE ON PUBLIC SECTOR MARKETING

Christopher H. Lovelock

As the use of marketing matures in the public sector, it makes increasing sense for managers of public agencies to study the approaches used by comparable organizations in other jurisdictions and to seek out answers to common problems. This chapter will focus on comparative analyses of marketing by three kinds of national public agencies, thus raising the question, How comparable are similar agencies in other countries? To provide insights, three different program areas in three countries—Canada, the United Kingdom, and the United States—will be analyzed and compared.

The three areas of activity selected are postal operations, passenger rail services, and energy conservation programs. These activities are national undertakings in virtually all industrialized countries. The first two are services, offered for sale in exchange for money (though customer revenues may not be enough to cover full costs). The third falls into the category of "social behavior marketing," wherein an agency seeks to encourage adoption of new behaviors offering social benefits (Lovelock 1979). Table 8.1 lists the nine agencies studied.

Information for this chapter was obtained, in part, from interviews with managers in each of the nine organizations studied and from a wide range of public documents that they made available. The author is most grateful for their cooperation but assumes responsibility for the views expressed and conclusions reached. This paper has also benefited from helpful comments on earlier drafts by Professors Charles B. Weinberg of the University of British Columbia and Michael P. Mokwa of Arizona State University.

TABLE 8.1

The Nine Agencies Studied

Service	United States	United Kingdom	Canada
Post office services	U.S. Postal Service	Post Office	Canada Post
Passenger rail services	National Railroad Passenger Corp. (Amtrak)	British Rail	VIA Rail Canada
Energy conservation	U.S. Department of Energy	Department of Energy	Energy, Mines, and Resources Canada

Source: Compiled by the author.

THREE DIFFERENT NATIONAL MARKETS

It is important to be aware of significant geographic, population, income, and political characteristics of the three countries before reviewing marketing programs conducted by the different agencies. Important information is summarized in Table 8.2 and discussed in more depth below.

Population and Geography

The United States is the largest of the three countries in population, having almost four times as many people as the United Kingdom and over nine times the population of Canada. But Canada has about 6 percent more land area than the United States and more than 40 times that of the United Kingdom. Despite the resulting major disparities in average population density, around three-quarters of the population in each country are urban residents; Canada and the United States simply have far more empty space between their cities. Most of Canada's population is squeezed into a long, narrow belt averaging only 50 miles wide across the entire 4,500 mile width of the country, a fact that has important implications for transportation and communications.

Both the United States and Canada combine remarkable climatic and topographical variety. The United Kingdom by contrast, has a temperate climate, and its countryside presents relatively few significant natural barriers to land travel or other forms of communication.

Economic Comparison

Although the United States has the world's largest economy, when expressed on a per capita basis the figures for the United States and Canada

TABLE 8.2

Comparative Background Information

Feature	United States	United Kingdom	Canada
Population in early 1979 (millions)	217	56	23
Land area (thousands of square miles)	3,615	94	3,852
Population density (per square mile)	60	594	60
Percent of population in urban areas	74	78	76
GNP in 1978 (billions of U.S. dollars)	1,799	217	185
GNP per capita (U.S. dollars)	8,329	3,875	8,043
Government structure	Federal	Central	Federal
Government form	President and Congress	Parliament	Parliament

Source: Compiled by the author.

appear very similar, approximately double the British level. This complicates cost comparisons, since the "same" cost in each country may represent significantly different proportions of the average citizen's disposable income. Fluctuating exchange rates further confuse such comparisons.

Government Structure

Two structural characteristics of government have important implications for the management of public enterprises: the division of powers between national and lower levels of government, and between the executive and legislative branches.

In Canada and the United States there is a significant division of powers between the federal and state or provincial governments and a further division between the state or province and various types of local governments. Britain, by contrast, is a centrally governed country with no intermediate level of legislative authority between the national parliament and local governments.

The United Kingdom and Canada also share a governmental form that distinguishes them from the United States. Both have a parliamentary system in which the executive and legislative branches of government are, for all practical purposes, combined. The U.S. Constitution, by contrast, explicitly seeks a division of powers between the two branches through a calculated system of checks and balances.

Summary

Britain, Canada, and the United States are all advanced Western, industrial democracies. Nevertheless, significant differences in geography, population, economy, and governmental structure have led to differences in the political values, institutions, and traditions of each country. Any discussion of the marketing efforts of their post offices, passenger rail corporations, and energy departments must recognize the extent to which the factors discussed above shape the nature of the marketing task and either constrain or facilitate it.

POSTAL SERVICES

Postal service was among the first organized activities of government. It was essential to the effective management of military campaigns and to continued contact with distantly located administrative centers. Only later did the mails assume major importance for commercial activity and personal correspondence. As a result, postal services in most developed countries are enveloped in a sense of tradition that influences management today.

There is a long history of cooperation and interchange of ideas among the national postal services of the world. For instance, the concept of a flat-rate, inexpensive, domestic postal fee—prepaid through the use of postage stamps—was a marketing innovation that has spread around the world since Britain first introduced the Penny Post in 1840.

The past decade has seen important changes in the management of postal services in all three countries. In 1969, the British Post Office became the first postal service to exchange its government department status for that of an independent public corporation, a change that was also proposed in the United States and Canada. The United States went part way in 1971, replacing the Post Office Department by the United States Postal Service, an independent agency of the executive branch of the federal government. Canada Post remains a government department, although there has been talk for many years of transforming it into an independent Crown Corporation, and a study was made recently of the most appropriate organizational form (Canada Post 1978). Table 8.3 summarizes key information concerning the three agencies.

Prior to the 1970s, marketing was virtually unheard of as a management function in postal services. The following criticisms made by consul-

TABLE 8.3
Postal Service: Comparative Statistics

Item	U.S. Postal Service[a]	British Post Office[b]	Canada Post[c]
Base price of first-class letter (U.S. cents), January 1, 1980	15.0	20.0 (1st class) 16.0 (2nd class)	15.3
No. of items mailed annually (millions)	99,829	10,137	6,056
Items mailed annually per capita	460	181	275
Total employees	663,067	172,122	53,053
No. of items mailed per employee (thousands)	150,556	58,894	114,150
Total post offices and sub-offices	39,733	22,793	8,230
Post offices per 100,000 persons	18	41	36
Corporate structure	Independent government agency	Public corporation	Government department
Year of separation from government	1971	1969	N.A.
Mail service profit (loss) (millions of U.S. dollars)	1,423[d]	66	(437)
Mail service operating expenses (millions of U.S. dollars)	17,529	2,893	1,435
Paid media advertising expenditures (millions of U.S. dollars)	10.4	10.4	3.3
Other businesses operated by the agency	Money orders, retail service on passports, and U.S. Savings Bonds	Telecommunications, data processing, banking (GIRO), retailing of many government services, including National Savings.	Money orders

a Year ending September 30, 1979.
b Year ending March 31, 1979 (statistics are for postal business only).
c Year ending March 31, 1979.
d Operating revenues less operating expenses (excludes govern-

Note: All figures have been converted to U.S. dollars at the following rates: £1 = $2.00, $1 Cdn = $0.90.
Source: 1979 Annual reports of each agency and personal communications.

tants reviewing Canada Post in 1969 could well have been applied at that time to other national postal systems:

> Officers in the [Post Office] Department lack the marketing orientation essential for an efficient service. They see the market as users of mail rather than of communications, transportation and banking services. The services that the Department is permitted to provide under the Post Office Act have been interpreted precisely and have been offered in an administrative and unimaginative manner. . . .

> Employees who serve customers lack the discretion necessary to deal with them: the rate system is not sufficiently flexible; the need to spread delivery of unaddressed mail over seven days hinders customer use of this service; retailing facilities leave something to be desired from the point of view of hours, lobby layout, and graphic design; promotion and community relations policies reflect a lack of customer orientation; and communication with large customers is presently inadequate (Barnhill 1975, p. 293).

Since then, the U.S., British, and Canadian postal services have made significant progress in some areas. Marketing organizations have been established, new services (products) have been developed and introduced based on analysis of customer needs, and programs for the various products have increasingly been subject to the rigor and discipline of formal marketing plans. But progress has been uneven, and the scope of marketing-related activities has not always extended across the full range of the marketing mix—product development, pricing, distribution systems, and communication efforts—as a look at each of these will show.

The Postal Product Line

The U.S. Postal Service is the largest of the three postal operations, reflecting not only the size of the U.S. population but also a higher number of items mailed annually per capita. This is accounted for in part by the widespread use of direct mail advertising in the United States. In recent years, Britain and Canada have aggressively sought to encourage development of the direct mail advertising industry as a means of building mail volume.

Britain's Post Office differs from its U.S. and Canadian counterparts in that it is responsible for providing a much more extensive range of services. In addition to its postal business, the Post Office also runs a large banking operation, the National Girobank, plus the nation's telecommunications services (although responsibility for these is soon to be transferred to a new public corporation). Even within the postal sphere, however, the Post Office offers a broader product line than USPS or Canada Post does. It has been aggressive in developing new types of services tailored to the needs of specific market segments (usually corporate mailers). These tend to be high-value-added products, such as different types of express package delivery services. Some of these are national in scope; others are limited to specific geographic areas.

New services directed at the general public include some intended for rural residents. Borrowing a concept that originated in Switzerland, the British Post Office has introduced Post Buses. In rural areas where conventional public transportation is limited or nonexistent, the vans used for mail delivery and pick-up have been replaced by eight-to-ten seat minibuses. Although schedules are limited, the post buses have proved popular. In mid-1979 some 160 were operating in different parts of the United Kingdom. Another innovation in certain outlying areas is that postmen deliver not only mail but newspapers, prescriptions, and groceries, too.

The U.S. Postal Service and Canada Post have been slower to innovate. Nevertheless, both have introduced several new services. While most have been generated internally or developed in response to customer requests, some refinements have resulted from studying services developed elsewhere. For instance, USPS's Express Mail copied certain forms, policies, and procedures from Data Post, an express delivery service in Britain. But unlike Data Post, which is restricted to contracts with large mailers, Express Mail is available at selected major post offices to all mailers. The British Post Office has been monitoring the USPS experience and is now thinking of introducing an over-the-counter variant of Data Post.

Another successful USPS service, undertaken jointly with Western Union, has been Mailgram, whereby WU accepts and transmits a message electronically and USPS delivers a hard copy to the addressee. A new effort by the Postal Service to develop an electronic mail service, called E-COM, is being opposed vigorously by other communications companies but is expected to win limited government approval.

On the other hand, an innovation venture undertaken by USPS in the early 1970s was quickly squelched by special interests. In 1973, USPS developed a range of postal-related products and retail services, such as packaging materials, scales, postage stamp dispensers, and photocopying services, which were designed for sale in all post offices. They were intended to make postal service more convenient for the individual mailer and to contribute to both the efficiency and the profitability of the postal system. In 1973-74, a number of retail postal boutiques were opened in the lobbies of 28 large post offices across the nation. In addition to selling the products noted, these boutiques also distributed philatelic items and other items already made available in large post offices, such as food stamps, migratory bird permits, passport applications, and IRS publications.

But representatives of small business interests, primarily stationers, exerted pressure on Congress to terminate what they perceived as "unfair competition" by a public agency (Permanent Select Committee on Small Business 1974, Committee on Post Office and Civil Service 1975). Although no proof was ever offered to substantiate the committees' claims, the boutiques were removed, and sale of most of the postal-related goods was discontinued. Photocopying services were restored after a public outcry, and packaging items continue to be offered as a local option in some post offices.

The scope of services offered by Canada Post is similar to that of USPS. A number of new products have been developed in recent years, including Telepost (a Canadian derivative of Mailgram) and various types of package services directed at the needs of large mailers. However, the agency's unsettled labor relations, which some observers blame on its government department status, have done serious damage to the quality of the postal product. This has made it hard for Canada Post to compete in the parcels and packages business, where it has no monopoly protection.

On the other hand, all three postal services have enjoyed considerable success expanding their philatelic services. These have proved popular with collectors and offer a high contribution.

Pricing Policy

First class mail rates in Britain are significantly higher than those in the United States or Canada, despite the lower level of personal incomes. During the early 1970s government pressure forced the British Post Office (and other nationlized industries) to hold down prices in an effort to control inflation. The net result was huge deficits, especially in postal operations. Later these restrictions were relaxed and postal prices rose sharply. Mail volumes declined in response but then recovered.

Postal pricing policies in Britain are noteworthy on several counts. While subject to government review, pricing decisions are the responsibility of the Marketing Department, which recognizes these decisions as a key element of marketing strategy. The Post Office is required by the government to set overall prices at levels that will ensure that total postal income meets total expenditure plus a target return of 2 percent on turnover. But the general approach adopted is to gear prices to individual services so that, while all services meet at least their direct costs, the contribution they make individually to overhead and profits varies in accordance with marketing and other considerations.

As a public corporation, the Post Office has far more control over its pricing decisions than does Canada Post or USPS. The flexibility that it enjoys has allowed it to relate prices to the realities of the market place and to compete vigorously for contract business from large corporate mailers. Other features of interest include the availability of both first and second class letter mail options (offering next working day and fourth working day delivery, respectively) and the absence of discounts for nonprofit organizations.

At Canada Post, as in Britain, pricing studies and recommendations are the responsibility of the Marketing Unit. But the agency's status as a government department requires that the price be the same to all Canadians within each service category, despite very real differences in the cost of serving different markets. Rate changes for first and second class mail must be approved by Parliament.

At USPS, pricing decisions are the responsibility of the Finance Department, not Marketing, and are thus closely tied to cost considerations rather than marketing ones. USPS has been hampered in its ability to change prices because any such move must be approved by the Postal Rate Commission, an independent regulatory agency. When USPS wishes to change its rates it must submit an application to the PRC, which then hears testimony from interested parties, including both competitors and mail users. Rate hearings, from the date of first filing to a final decision, typically take ten months—a long time horizon for management, particularly in an era of rapid inflation. USPS is prohibited from cross-subsidizing services from one class of mail to another (although it may do so within a class). Hearings before the PRC have for the most part attempted to determine whether USPS has properly attributed institutional costs among the different classes of mail. United Parcel Service, a major competitor, has been active in arguing that fourth class parcel mail should be assigned a higher share of institutional costs, thus driving up parcel mail prices and providing United Parcel Service with a price umbrella.

USPS offers substantially reduced bulk rates to nonprofit organizations, a service for which it receives a government subsidy. The two-cents-per-item discount offered to large mailers as an inducement to presort their first class mail is a discount of a different nature. This is a relatively recent innovation, designed to reduce postal processing costs. It has been widely promoted through advertising and personal selling, and USPS claims it has been fairly successful.

Distribution

Britain and Canada have twice as many retail post offices per head of population as does the United States. In Britain, postal outlets serve as a virtual supermarket for government services. Counter clerks in large offices deal with more than 110 different kinds of transactions. In addition to postal business, they also handle such services as sale of licenses for vehicles, dogs, and other purposes; payment of pensions and family income supplements; provision of Girobank and National Savings Bank services; and sale of savings certificates and government securities. Nonpostal services are handled on a contractual basis for both central and local government departments; the Post Office receives a flat 4 percent commission, and such sales now account for some 60 percent of over-the-counter volume. New services and contracts are being actively sought, and post offices in certain large cities recently began selling transit passes. In 1979, the Post Office began an experiment whereby foreign exchange services were introduced in 14 large post offices. By contrast, the range of nonpostal services offered by U.S. and Canadian postal outlets is quite limited.

Both Britain and Canada have renovated numerous retail post offices with a view to providing a more attractive environment for customers and employees. USPS has started a trial refurbishment program, but most U.S. post offices, while sometimes impressive externally, remain drab and unattractive inside. Although USPS has placed a number of automatic post offices in freestanding locations such as shopping center parking lots, operating problems with the automatic vending machinery have discouraged expansion of this program.

In the United States, attempts to save money by closing rural post offices have, in general, been blocked by Congress. This raises the question of whether more extensive use, on the British model, could be made of retail post offices in the United States and Canada. But the USPS and Canada Post product lines are limited to mail and related services; their only non-mail service is postal money orders, and sales of these are declining steadily. Federal-citizen contacts for other services are relatively few. Whether state or provincial and local governments could sufficiently overcome their suspicions of federal government operations to let post office outlets distribute some of their services is an open question.

Communication Efforts

Given the size of each of the three agencies and the fact that they attempt to serve virtually the entire populations of their respective countries, the paid media advertising budgets employed by each are exceedingly modest. The ratio of advertising expenditures to operating revenues amounts to 0.06 percent for USPS, 0.36 percent for the British Post Office, and 0.25 percent for Canada Post. A distinctive feature of Canadian communication efforts is that all messages must be prepared in both official languages, English and French.

USPS is able to take advantage of public service announcements for messages of a noncompetitive nature, such as encouraging mailers to mail early in the day or use zip codes. Prior to postal reorganization, this was the only type of advertising used. The use of paid media advertising by USPS is a controversial issue. Some congressmen apparently view such expenditures as an inappropriate use of "postal ratepayers' dollars."

All three agencies have developed sales forces to promote the use of postal services among corporate and institutional mailers, but the sales department at USPS headquarters does not have the line relationship to customer service representatives in the field that is enjoyed by their British and Canadian counterparts. The net result at USPS is relatively more emphasis on reactive customer service efforts as opposed to proactive new business development.

Appraisal

Britain's Post Office clearly handles a much broader range of responsibilities than does USPS or Canada Post. Even if one disregards the telecommunications side of its business, it is still striking to see the extent to which the Post Office has been able to maximize use of its retail outlets and find ways of using its rural delivery and transportation services for new purposes.

The Post Office is also noteworthy because it has made a profit on its postal business each year since 1976-77. Unlike USPS and Canada Post, it receives no government subsidies. High postal charges and a small, densely populated country are two factors in Britain's favor. On the other hand, mail volumes per capita and labor productivity are relatively low.

Applying the tools of marketing analysis and planning leads an organization to focus on the needs of its largest and potentially most profitable customers. But doing so may generate criticism for a public agency. For instance, in Britain a government review committee concluded that postal marketing efforts focused too closely on "very large customers" and argued that more attention needed to be devoted to smaller users and the general public (Carter 1977). Recent actions by the Post Office have displayed more concern for customer relations, including an informative corporate advertising campaign directed at the general public in 1978-79.

In all three countries, the postal service and the local post office are probably the most visible manifestation of the federal or central government in the community. Good service is taken for granted, but failures in the service are readily seized upon as evidence of poor management and a bad product. A British study revealed the atmosphere in which postal executives work when it commented, "The Post Office record . . . deserves responsible criticism, but not the exercise of our national habit of condemning all things British as though they were the worst in the world" (Carter 1977).

PASSENGER RAIL SERVICES

Like postal service, passenger rail service is sold to customers at a price. And like the mails, passenger rail travel is also shrouded in tradition and nostalgia. But the resemblance ends there. Governmental involvement in running and administering the mails goes back for centuries, along with the tradition of a jealously guarded letter mail monopoly. By contrast, passenger rail travel is a relative newcomer to the public sector, as a result of the de jure or de facto nationalization of privately owned services operated by independent railroad companies.

Table 8.4 summarizes information concerning passenger rail services in the United States, Britain, and Canada. The combination of historical development patterns, government policies, and geographic dispersion of major population centers in the three countries has produced three very different rail passenger services. It should be noted that 55 percent of British Rail's annual passenger mileage is accounted for by commuter services, which tends to make the average trip distance appear relatively short as well as inflate the average number of journeys made per capita.

The Three Corporations

Great Britain's four private railway companies emerged from World War II in bad condition and were nationalized in 1947. The British Railways Board is a holding company for a variety of different businesses and divisions. It includes the passenger and freight rail services of British Rail, a container-carrying company (Freightliner, Ltd.), a shipping line (Sealink UK Ltd.), eleven harbors, British Rail Hovercraft Ltd., 29 major hotels, a station and on-train catering operation (Travellers-Fare), a locomotive and rolling stock construction company, an international consulting firm (Transmark), and a North American passenger sales operation (BritRail Travel International, Inc.). Rail passenger revenues, including contractual payments by government, accounted for approximately half the BRB's consolidated income of $5 billion in 1978–79.

By contrast, the National Railroad Passenger Corporation (better known by its trade name, Amtrak) and VIA Rail Canada, Inc. (a name carefully chosen to be bilingual) are much younger and smaller organizations. Amtrak was formed in 1971 as a semi-public corporation to take over the intercity passenger rail services previously operated by 13 private railroad companies. (Other railroads have since transferred their passenger services to Amtrak). VIA became an independent Crown Corporation in 1978, charged with the responsibility of taking over intercity passenger rail services previously operated by the privately owned CP Rail and the government-owned CN Rail.

The Rail Product

British Rail, unlike Amtrak and VIA, has responsibility for almost all the variables that create or interfere with the passenger rail trip product. It owns the track in addition to the stations and the rolling stock; it is

TABLE 8.4

Passenger Rail Services

Item	Amtrak (U.S.)	British Rail	VIA Rail Canada
Created	1971	1947	1977[a]
No. of premerger railroads	13	4	2
Passenger route mileage	26,000	8,497	15,000
Percent on-time performance[b]	62	91	N.A.
Total journeys made per year (millions)	19	724	6
Total passenger miles per year (millions)	4,029	19,100	1,700
Average journey length (miles)	212	26	310
Average no. of journeys annually per capita	0.1	12.9	0.22
Average passenger miles annually per capita	19	341	68
Total passenger revenues (millions of U.S. dollars)	313	1,544	120
Average revenue per passenger mile (U.S. cents)	7.8	8.1	7.1
Annual government contract payment for passenger services (millions of U.S. dollars)	0	955	239
Operating surplus (deficit) after contract payments (millions of U.S. dollars)	(582)	83[c]	N.A.
Paid advertising expenditures in 1979 (millions of U.S. dollars)	8.5	15	2.3
Other activities	Mail Package Express	Freight ferries, Hovercraft Hotels, Property Engineering, Consulting, Advertising	None

[a] Originally formed as a subsidiary of the Canadian National Railway in 1977, VIA became a Crown Corporation in 1978. VIA figures exclude commuters.

[b] Defined by British Rail as not more than five minutes late; defined by ICC (for Amtrak) as within five minutes of schedule for each 100 miles traveled, subject to a maximum of 30 minutes for routes exceeding 600 miles.

[c] Includes freight business.

Source: Annual reports of each agency (FY 1978 for Amtrak and VIA, FY 1979 for British Rail) and personal communications.

responsible for freight as well as passenger operations; and virtually all personnel whose behavior might have even a remote bearing on passenger service performance—from freight train crews to security officers—are its own employees. Amtrak and VIA lack this degree of control. Although Amtrak has acquired and is modernizing track in the Northeast Corridor (Boston-New York-Washington), elsewhere its trains operate over often poor-quality track owned by the railroads and are subject to freight train interference. VIA runs over CN and CP tracks that are in fairly good condition and relies on these companies' operating personnel to run the trains.

British Rail operates three types of services—a national network of fast "Intercity" trains, commuter services into London and a few other major cities, and slower feeder and connector services. BR's commuter services are politically sensitive and of less consistent quality than the Intercity services; they tend to give the entire system a more negative image than it deserves. Amtrak and VIA have minimal involvement in short-distance commuter services and carry the bulk of their passengers on corridor services for distances of 100–500 miles. They also provide once-daily services over routes up to 3,000 miles long, during which trips most of the passenger complement turns over several times, although tourists may travel the entire distance as a form of scenic "land cruise."

Since the mid-1960s, British Rail has made major progress in upgrading its Intercity product. Mainline electrification and introduction of 125 mph diesel trains have greatly increased average train speeds and helped win an increased market share for rail, despite construction of parallel motorways (Keen 1979). On some routes, rail's market share exceeds 70 percent, but speed is not the only product attribute on which BR management has been working. The chairman, Sir Peter Parker, believes that "marketing a railway requires meticulous attention to detail . . . everything from the smile on the guard's [brakeman's] face to the cleanliness of the lavatories goes to make up the sales package" (Lester 1978). Parker is working to instill a marketing consciousness throughout the system and formally credits marketing for the system's success in boosting passenger traffic (British Railways Board 1979).

Amtrak and VIA similarly are conscious of the need for internal marketing and are working toward this end, but they have somewhat less control at present. They are also working to upgrade their equipment and (in Amtrak's case) some of the roadbed. On short and intermediate routes, Amtrak has new Amfleet passenger cars and French-built Turbotrains and is refurbishing the 12-year-old Metroliner cars. But strikes by the manufacturer have delayed delivery of its long-distance "Superliner" cars by over a year, thus forcing continued reliance on equipment 20 to 40 years old. VIA has inherited equipment dating mostly from the mid-1950s, but this had been better maintained than comparable U.S. equipment; new LRC (light, rapid, comfortable) cars are on order.

When Amtrak first initiated service, it had minimal control over the equipment; so it focused attention on two product-related variables that it could control—cleanliness and on-board amenities, notably meal services. All three railways perceive the importance of meals as an adjunct to enjoyable rail travel and subsidize meal prices to stimulate ticket purchase.

Distribution

British Rail's route structure is dense, and there has been little change in the BR network since the early 1960s. VIA is in a period of consolidation as it seeks to rationalize the former CP and CN passenger services, several of which parallel each other across the lengthy transcontinental routes, although serving different cities en route. Amtrak inherited a sharply pruned passenger route system in 1971 and subsequently expanded it at Congressional urging. Critics charge that certain routes reflect political rather than market priorities; certainly some governors and congressmen have fought vigorously to retain or reintroduce rail service in their states.

In early 1979, the government proposed a 43 percent cut in the size of the Amtrak route network to eliminate many lightly used services. But in mid-year, when fuel shortages developed and the price of gasoline rose sharply, Amtrak enjoyed a big increase in patronage. The cuts actually made in fall 1979 were limited to about 20 percent—mostly on routes which Amtrak may not have been sorry to lose because of limited market potential and often poor-quality track.

Pricing

When Amtrak initiated service in 1971, it immediately revamped the inflexible pricing structure it had inherited and cut many fares. VIA's early moves centered on development of a new "Fare for All Plan," including many discount prices to replace the previous CN and CP fares. As these actions prove, passenger rail services freed of the regulation imposed on their private predecessors have more control over the pricing element of the marketing mix than over either product or distribution and can thus act faster in making changes (although in the case of VIA all pricing changes require the approval of the Ministry of Transport, which is particularly concerned with the impact of rail pricing on bus competition).

Traditionally, the world's railways have adopted a conservative approach to pricing, computing standard rates according to distance traveled, with premiums for first class service and discounts for certain categories of passengers (principally children). Until 1968, British Rail had such a system, accompanied by an inconsistent jumble of promotional fares that were hard to administer. That year the old system was abolished and replaced by a new approach that related base fares on each route to quality of product, strength of market demand, and nature of competitive activity (Ford 1977). A series of four different structures tailored to the demand curves of different market segments was built around these base rates. The intention was to discourage trading down by those able to pay the relatively costly standard fares, yet to maximize travel, especially during low-demand periods of the day or week, among more price-sensitive groups. A relatively recent pricing innovation at British Rail is the promotion of Railcards, available to senior citizens and students for $14 per year; these entitle the owner to travel anywhere on the system for half the regular fare. Another version, the Family Railcard, costs $20, and requires one adult to pay the standard fare while allowing a second adult and up to four children to travel any distance for a flat fare of $1 each—a clear attempt to appeal to families who might otherwise travel by car. Subsequent BR research indicates a substantial increase in revenues as well as in the number of journeys made. It has also found that Railcards, especially the senior citizen's version, are often given as presents.

VIA's new pricing structure is also highly segmented, allowing discounts for off-season round trips and travel by groups, elderly people, and children. All three rail services now accept credit cards for payment; although common practice in North America, this is an innovation at British Rail. Each of the three also offers system-wide passes, although BR only sells these overseas. BR also sells regional passes, which are available to domestic customers.

Advertising and Promotion

British Rail's advertising budget in 1978–79 was about $15 million, and it has been running three separate campaigns—one to promote its Intercity services, a second to reach commuters and other rail users in London and Southeast England, and a third targeted at the general public and designed to influence opinion in favor of the railway system. A promotion with Kellogg's (allowing sharply discounted fares for accompanied children in return for cereal box tops) proved highly successful in 1977 and was copied by Amtrak the following year. The Amtrak promotion was promptly criticized by consumer groups for including sugar-coated cereals! BR has since moved on to joint promotion with soap powder manufacturers.

Recently, BR introduced a Great Rail Club for children aged 5 to 15. For an annual fee of $4, members receive badges, T-shirts, four issues of the club magazine, and discount vouchers. The objective is to promote rail travel among young people. BR hopes for 200,000 members.

Annual advertising expenditures at Amtrak in 1979 were reduced by Congress from $10 million to about $8.5 million. Amtrak's marketing management sees advertising expenditures as highly cost-effective and would like to spend significantly more, having found that rail travel demand is highly responsive to advertising. This is not surprising, given its very low market share and high potential for trial. But, in annual budget reviews, Congress has thus far limited Amtrak's advertising expenditures. In 1978-79, advertising used the slogan "We've been working on the Railroad" to dramatize the corporation's efforts to improve service. These ads featured Amtrak personnel who had been selected for outstanding performance, thus seeking to boost employee morale, too. With Amtrak's reservation lines swamped in the aftermath of the gasoline shortages of mid-1979, print advertising switched to factual information on services, fares, and travel times under the headline "These Days It's Easier to Ride Us Than to Reach Us."

VIA moved quickly after its formation to develop an aggressive advertising and promotional campaign ("Serious Marketing Gets VIA on Tracks" 1979). In addition to introducing the new corporation, advertising has successfully promoted connecting services and package tours by rail. The 1979 advertising budget was about $2.3 million. VIA is also developing a new reservations system called RESERVIA. In 1981, this system will be connected with Air Canada's RESERVEC II, making Canada the first country in the world with a nationwide intermodal reservations capability. Eventually it may be possible to use any RESERVIA terminal to make reservations for rail, air, rent-a-car, hotel, and (it is hoped) major ferry services.

Appraisal

British Rail, Amtrak, and VIA are very different organizations in many respects. BR is a mature public corporation, operating a wide array of services in addition to intercity passenger rail transportation. It enjoys a contractual relationship with the government rather than begging for subsidies to cover its deficits. Amtrak, although displaying greater marketing expertise (which it has had to develop from scratch in its eight-year existence) is bedeviled by a poor product which it does not fully control. Its future—even the size of its advertising budget—is largely in the hands of politicians, many of whom remain deeply distrustful of the public corporation concept. VIA has some similarities to Amtrak but has learned from the latter's misfortunes (Roberts 1979). Like BR, it has a contractual relationship with government. It has inherited a better product from CN and CP than Amtrak did from most of the U.S. railroads and has the advantage of greater ridership; on a per capita basis, two and a half times more people in Canada ride trains than in the United States. Finally, VIA's marketing management team was built on the solid foundation of the passenger staff of CN Rail, which was probably the most marketing-oriented of all North American railroads during the 1960s and early 1970s.

ENERGY CONSERVATION

Unlike postal and rail services, energy conservation is a more abstract "product," and a difficult one to market. Individuals may perceive the costs of practicing conserving behavior as outweighing the resulting personal benefits. Yet the economic and political benefits of energy conservation for the larger society grow ever more apparent.

Yergin (1979) identifies three types of conservation. First is out-and-out *curtailment*, when supplies are interrupted and energy saving is forced upon people. Second is *overhaul*, representing truly dramatic changes in the way people live and work. The third is *adjustment*, entailing changes both in capital stock, such as purchase of home insulation and use of more energy-efficient appliances, and also in behavior, such as setting thermostats at more efficient levels, driving more slowly, and turning off unnecessary lights.

It is in this third category of conservation that marketing strategies by government agencies offer major leverage. As in postal marketing, energy conservation programs must be directed at almost the entire population, although some segments are more important than others. The marketing tools available to government agencies are basically *communication* (urging people to save energy and providing specific information and advice on how to do so) and *pricing* (using the mechanism of increased taxes to raise energy prices and thus discourage demand and offering economic incentives such as grants and tax legislation to encourage energy-saving capital investments).

Nonmarketing tools include *legislation* to change (1) product standards (ranging from buildings to autos to appliances) to make them more energy efficient; and (2) behavior (such as reducing highway speed limits and requiring operators of public buildings to adjust their thermostats). Even here, effective communications and financial penalties, a form of pricing, for noncompliance may be necessary program ingredients.

Before the crisis resulting from the Arab oil embargo of 1973-74, there had been limited recognition of the need for energy conservation; only minimal action had been undertaken at a national level in any of the three countries. The embargo and the subsequent quadrupling of oil prices by oil-exporting nations provided a major stimulus to governmental efforts to encourage conservation. But the actions taken in the three countries varied significantly. We'll look at each country separately—beginning with the United Kingdom, which was the first to initiate a national program—and then offer a brief comparative appraisal of conservation marketing efforts.

United Kingdom

The British government responded quickly to the energy crisis of 1973-74. It set up a Department of Energy in 1974 and instituted a 12-point energy conservation program that same year. Directed at both individual and industrial users, it included incentives, legal compulsion, economic pricing of energy, and a major communications campaign.

The communications campaign, firmly based on consumer research findings, began in January 1975 and has continued in modified form in subsequent years. Built around the slogan, "Save It," the program seeks to secure both immediate reductions in energy use and the longer-term changes in public attitudes and habits needed to secure continuing economies. The Department of Energy works closely with the Central Office of Information, a government agency that plays a coordinating role for all government advertising and publicity in Britain. The budget for 1978–79 was approximately $4.5 million.

Paid media advertising efforts have been supplemented by exhibitions, syndicated articles, booklets, and instructional films made available free by industry. There have also been publicity campaigns by the nationalized coal, gas, and electricity authorities and by the tightly regulated oil industry. Prices of all energy sources have been raised sharply. The increase in gasoline prices reflects not only rising costs but also sharp increases in excise taxes to discourage consumption.

The U.K. Department of Energy has worked closely with other government departments, the fuel supply industry, and manufacturers and distributors of insulation materials to ensure a coordinated policy and a coherent set of messages. In addition to consumer research, retail audits have been used to monitor movements of insulating materials through retail outlets as a measure of the effectiveness of communications efforts (Phillips and Nelson 1976).

As Britain moves toward complete energy self-sufficiency, reflecting its major coal deposits and North Sea oil and gas, the conservation marketing task is becoming harder. Communications messages now focus on the financial costs of energy waste, with advertising suggesting that waste is "disgusting" and that conservation saves money. The slogan has been adapted to "Don't Waste it—Save It!"

Current policy emphasizes provision of information and promotion of specific advisory services and incentives. For instance, industrial advertising now promotes the availability of small government grants ($150) toward the cost of hiring energy consultants from an approved list to undertake one-day audits of plants and offices and identify opportunities for energy savings. The Department of Energy offers a quick, free advice service by telephone on any energy-related problem. Finally, the Department of Industry provides grants for energy-saving modernization programs in company plants.

Canada

Although Canada was not seriously affected by the 1973–74 oil embargo, the government moved promptly to reduce energy waste. Federal responsibility for energy conservation efforts has rested with the Conservation and Renewable Energy Branch of Energy, Mines, and Resources Canada.

In recent years, federal communication efforts have been budgeted at around $2.7 million (U.S.) annually. Virtually every element in the marketing communication mix has been used, including paid media advertising, publications, public relations, and various other promotional efforts involving third parties. The program is reviewed annually, with each year's campaign seeking to build on the base created by those of previous years (Hutton 1979).

As in the United Kindom, efforts are directed at both industrial and domestic users, with major emphasis on self-help and practical advice. In an effort to prevent Canadians from developing the negative perceptions of energy conservation encountered among many Americans, who often view it as threatening to their comfort, independence, and economic security, communications attempt to create a positive image. The slogan, initially, "If You're Not Part of the Solution, You're Part of the Problem," has shifted to "Energy Conservation—Be Part of the Solution."

Innovative features of the Canadian program include the Energy Bus Program, which makes on-site energy audits for businesses, and an extremely popular 30-minute TV film, "The Hottest Show on Earth." This film uses a mixture of animation, comedy, drama, and popular science to dramatize the importance of a potentially boring subject—home insulation—and to motivate people to take action on installing or reinstalling insulation. The government offers to pay the first $450 (U.S.) of insulation costs.

Publication of a series of short books on conservation is another Canadian innovation. One of these is "The Car Mileage Book," a free 106-page pocket book on how to buy, drive, and maintain a car to save energy and money. Within nine months of its first publication in September 1977, more than 2.4 million had been distributed through the mails, Gulf service stations, and provincial motor license bureaus. Two other major oil companies promoted availability of the book through bill stuffers to all credit card holders.

A distinctive characteristic of Canada's information efforts is their bilingual quality. All advertising is produced separately in both English and French, but one message is not necessarily a direct translation of the other. Consumer research by the Conservation Branch has shown that English-speaking Canadians respond better to rational appeals, whereas French-Canadians are more likely to respond to a relatively more emotional appeal. The key French slogan can be translated as "Energy Conservation—Let's All Do Our Part." A program known as "Ener$ave" in English becomes "Ener$age", literally "Energy-Wise" in French.

Reflecting the federal-provincial division of responsibilities, the Conservation Branch works closely with provincial energy departments and commissions. It delegates certain functions, such as operation of the Energy Buses, to the provinces. In general, the federal and provincial agencies seem to have succeeded in working together toward a common goal. There is also close coordination between the branch and selected citizen groups in disseminating communications and implementing conservation programs.

Unlike Britain, Canada did not make significant early efforts to curtail demand by raising energy prices. In December 1979, however, the proposed federal budget presented to Parliament by the minority Conservative government included a provision to increase federal taxes on gasoline by 16 cents per gallon. This and other items in the budget became contentious political issues for an already weak government; the House of Commons voted down the budget, and the government was obliged to resign.

United States

In the view of some observers, the oil shortage of the winter of 1973–74 was seen by many Americans as *the* energy crisis, something that had happened rather than a portent of things to come. Politics delayed the formation of a cabinet-level Department of Energy (DOE) in the Federal Government until 1977. Prior to that time, responsibility for conservation efforts was spread across many different offices. An agency known as the Federal Energy Administration (FEA) employed several people with titles such as "energy conservation marketing specialist," but political pressures confined its consumer marketing efforts to public service advertising involving such vague messages as "Don't be Fuelish."

On the other hand, FEA was quick to initiate consumer research studies. A series of regularly conducted national surveys provided important insights into how American consumers felt about energy conservation, the extent to which they practiced it, and the reasons why they resisted it (Milstein 1977). But the agency showed little inclination to use these research findings to mount a forceful communication campaign.

Unfortunately, the situation did not improve significantly with the formation of the U.S. Department of Energy (which absorbed most of the FEA staff). Poor organization compounded by constant reorganization and jealously guarded empires within the federal bureaucracy led to a lack of coordination and clear direction. Conservation was seen as threatening by many regional interests, especially energy-rich states or those which felt economically and politically threatened by federally imposed changes. This situation served to intensify lobbying efforts to emasculate the DOE, and made it almost impossible for the department to develop and implement bold conservation programs.

Finally, in 1978, the Department's Consumer Motivation Branch (CMB) initiated a program with well-defined strategy and objectives. Consumer research played an integral part of both program formulation and evaluation. As reported by Hutton (1979):

> The overall objective of the CMB is to encourage private sector groups (e.g., financial institutions, retailers, etc.) to work voluntarily with the DOE to test and evaluate approaches which the private sector can later implement to motivate consumers to become most efficient users of energy. While the ultimate target of CMB activities is the consumer, it is the private sector which is the focus of CMB actions and the mechanism through which objectives will be achieved. (p. 13).

Efforts by the CMB have centered on regional test marketing of programs to encourage customers to consider the energy costs of major appliances when purchasing them, and cooperative programs have been undertaken with local retailers. During 1979, a $2 million paid-advertising program, dubbed "Project Payback," was tested in six cities.

The Iranian crisis and oil price increases of 1979 gave new impetus to the need for a strong energy conservation program in the United States. Energy prices, especially gasoline, rose sharply but still remained far below those prevailing in most industrialized countries outside North America. Suggestions were made that a 50 cent per gallon tax be imposed to raise gasoline prices and discourage consumption, but the federal government appeared unwilling to adopt such a measure. Meanwhile, incentive programs to encourage conservation remained minimal.

In September 1979, it was reported that the DOE and several congressmen were urging development of a $50–95 million conservation advertising program similar to the Canadian effort. However, this proposal was reportedly stirring opposition within the government "from critics who contend that a costly ad campaign would waste taxpayer money" (Schmitt 1979). But in November, the DOE launched a month-long "Low Cost/No Cost" campaign in six New England states, designed to help households reduce home energy consumption by as much as 25 percent. A small booklet, which contained eleven inexpensive recommendations for saving energy in the home, was mailed to all households in the region. The mailing included a free plastic controller to reduce hot water flow from showers. Complementing the mailing was a month-long advertising campaign using TV, radio, and newspapers. The cost of the program, estimated at $3 million, was shared jointly by DOE and the private sector. DOE news releases stated that results from the program would be used to decide early in 1980 whether to expand the program nationwide (U.S., Department of Energy 1979).

Appraisal

The Energy Departments in Britain and Canada have made major efforts to market both the concept and the practice of energy conservation to their national populations, although it is difficult to assess precisely how much the communication programs have contributed to nationwide energy savings.

Implementation strategies and message content in the two countries reflect their differing situations. But, in both cases, an aggressive ongoing program, modified over time in response to consumer research, is now institutionalized.

Energy conservation policy in the United Kingdom has relied to a large extent on the voluntary response of both corporate and domestic consumers to a combination of higher prices, practical advice, information, and exhortation. More recently, investment incentives have been introduced and publicized. The approach has been to persuade people of the *need* to save energy and to demonstrate specifically *how* to do so. Research findings have indicated that people were generally ignorant of such basic approaches as home insulation.

The Canadian strategy has been broadly similar. Its communication program is highly regarded among those responsible for conservation efforts in other countries and has been suggested by some as a model for U.S. efforts.

By contrast, U.S. efforts during the 1970s appear feeble, disorganized, and thwarted by politics. Many organizations, including state and local agencies, utilities, and oil companies, have provided advice and exhortation on conservation. But there has been no federal leadership to coordinate these disparate efforts and build a strong, integrated program.

Many legislators and federal officials still feel that governments should not spend public money on paid media advertising. As a result, DOE communications efforts have been confined at the national level to bland public service advertisements. However, "Project Payback" and "Low Cost/No Cost" regional campaigns suggest that DOE may be moving to adopt a more active posture that will include acceptance of the need for professionally developed paid communications programs on a national basis.

INSIGHTS AND IMPLICATIONS

What can be learned from these comparative profiles? What insights do they provide that might be useful to marketing managers in the public sector or to appointed and elected government officials concerned about obtaining effective performances from government agencies and public corporations? In the balance of this chapter, insights concerning public sector marketing are identified and key implications are discussed.

Marketing Expertise Is Transferable

There are many instances of international exchange of marketing concepts and practices between public agencies. For instance, a British Rail subsidiary, Transmark, has consulted to Amtrak; USPS adapted certain forms and procedures from the British Post Office when developing its Express Mail product; VIA Rail Canada executives monitor passenger rail marketing efforts in other countries and periodically exchange information with their counterparts in other national rail systems; the British Post Office has studied the private sector Bell System's marketing practices in the United States and also monitored marketing developments at USPS; and Britain, Canada, and the United States have shared insights from their energy conservation marketing and research programs at meetings of the 15-nation International Energy Agency. The Canadians, in particular, find that U.S. consumer research provides helpful inputs. Marketing managers in public agencies have much to learn and little to lose from sharing insights and experiences with their counterparts from other countries. The "not invented here" syndrome should be avoided; there is no shame in borrowing. But it is essential that borrowed concepts be carefully evaluated in the context of the home country's market environment and then suitably adapted. It is also important to recognize that constraints may inhibit management's ability to develop a marketing program for an agency to be as effective as its foreign counterparts'.

Service Must be Provided to Uneconomic Segments

Unlike most private firms, public sector marketers cannot ignore small, unprofitable, or geographically dispersed market segments. Thus, national passenger rail corporations in all three countries are expected to maintain uneconomic routes for social reasons; and postal agencies must deliver to outlying rural areas and maintain retail post offices in thinly populated locations.

In most instances, it is unrealistic to set such market service requirements and then expect a public agency to operate in the black. However, a sense of market discipline is restored if (as has happened with British Rail and VIA Rail Canada) the government enters into an annual contract with the agency to buy those services that are inherently uneconomic and that the agency cannot expect to operate at break-even or better. This provides more explicit focus on certain market segments or particular services in the agency's product line than a policy of subsidizing the agency to the extent of the annual deficit.

Public Agencies May Lack Control Over Their Product

Many public agencies and corporations are not in full control of their product. Eight years after its formation, Amtrak is still trying to modernize the automated fleet of rolling stock it inherited, is still forced to operate over poorly maintained track owned by private railroads, and is subject to frequent interference with its schedules by other companies' freight trains. The implication for management, consumers, and legislators is that one shouldn't expect miracles from marketing. Funds may be needed for long-term capital improvement. It may be years before their benefits become apparent. Other problems requiring time for resolution include organizational restructuring, revisions of labor agreements, and changes in consumer habits and expectations.

Governments May Constrain Pricing Policies

Governments have often tried to influence or even dictate public agencies' pricing policies (usually downwards) for social, economic, or purely political reasons. In the early 1970s the British government deliberately held down postal rates and rail fares in an attempt to restrain inflation. Eventually it found that financing the huge deficits incurred by these agencies was itself inflationary and allowed prices for these services to rise to more realistic levels. Many policy makers in Canada and the United States have urged that energy prices be raised sharply through the imposition of new federal taxes, as a means of discouraging consumption. But it has not proved politically possible to pass the necessary legislation.

Holding down prices results in a consumer surplus for those market segments that could and would pay more. One alternative is to develop pricing policies that increase revenues from less price-sensitive segments, while keeping prices within affordable bounds for those who are unable or unwilling to pay more. Doing this requires that management have good understanding of the demand curves of different segments. An alternative is to raise prices for all segments and offer direct subsidies to consumers with lower disposable incomes.

Politicians May Object to Paid Media Advertising

Public agencies in the United States are more likely than those in Canada or the United Kingdom to find elected officials resisting the use of paid media advertising. The U.S. Department of Energy has been obliged to limit most of its communication efforts to public service announcements (PSAs) and public relations. Neither of these are as effective as paid media advertising because the marketer lacks control over the format, scheduling, and placement of the messages. The content of PSAs tends to be bland and inoffensive, since hardhitting, controversial messages that might offend another advertiser (or an editor's political sensibilities) are unlikely to be broadcast or published. Moreover, the marketer has no guarantees that the content of publicity releases in the media will correspond to what was originally desired. Even where paid advertising is allowed, unrealistic constraints may be placed on the advertising budget, as has happened with Amtrak and USPS, thus blunting the effectiveness of communications efforts and making it difficult to use a segmentation strategy.

There is a clear need to educate both public managers and elected or appointed officials about the role that carefully developed and targeted communications campaigns play in helping public services and programs achieve their objectives. The limitations of PSAs and public relations efforts need to be made clear. Finally, it is essential to educate those who control financial appropriations to appreciate the concept of advertising as an investment and to recognize the importance of not usurping managerial prerogatives.

Political Involvement Harms Long-Range Planning

Political involvement in the affairs of public agencies is often motivated by short-term political expediency, being exercised through such activities as budget reviews, public hearings, and attempts to change or delay the thrust of past legislation. This may make it very difficult for an agency to develop and adhere to a long-term strategic marketing plan.

Public agencies need to sell governments and individual legislators on the importance of developing and implementing long-range plans. In turn, governments must be prepared (1) to grant public agencies greater independence from the political arena, (2) to encourage and support long-range public planning (including marketing plans), and (3) to award multiple-year financing for product and market research and development.

Sustained Government Commitment Is Needed

National social change programs such as energy conservation are likely to entail unpopular departures from current practices. Both individuals and organizations may feel threatened. Popular antipathy often born of ignorance or lack of perceived benefits may lead legislative bodies to seek to delay or dilute carefully prepared programs. This may encourage consumers who oppose the changes, and even many fence-sitters, to refuse to comply with the behavior changes that are being advocated.

Public agencies cannot rely on communications alone to bring about voluntary change. Economic incentives, mandatory changes, or both (backed by enforcement in selected instances) may be necessary to obtain the desired cooperation. Sustained government commitment may be essential to maintaining the momentum of such social change programs.

Government Ambivalence May Reflect Political Realities

Governments are most likely to display ambivalence and lack of commitment to public agency programs in situations where the executive branch of government (the president) is in a weak position relative to the legislative branch (Congress); or there is a weak coalition or minority government in a parliamentary structure, lacking consensus on a specific policy issue.

Both situations strengthen the hand of dissident groups within the legislative body, thereby encouraging politically expedient compromises, especially where unpopular programs or agencies are concerned. The lack of progress in energy conservation programs in the United States is partly due to such problems. There was a general political consensus in Britain during the minority Labour government of Prime Minister Callaghan that energy conservation was highly desirable. But political expediency may have been behind the decision to return the speed limit to 70 mph. Canada's minority Conservative government fell in December 1979 as a result of a vote on the national budget which included a controversial proposal to increase the gasoline tax by 16 cents. The impact of these problems can be reduced, though not eliminated, by designing mechanisms that provide for less dependence by public agencies on short-term financing decisions by government and frequent use of facilitating legislation.

Public Sector Marketing Is More Complex in Federal Nations

The presence of both federal and state or provincial governments complicates the marketing of public programs by adding an extra layer of government within whose jurisdiction many program components may fall. To implement energy conservation programs may require changes in numerous state or provincial laws and affect local public agencies responsible for communicating changes to residents of the state or province in question.

There is a danger that, without carefully planned cooperation, agencies at the two levels of government may find themselves pulling in contrary directions and confusing their constituent markets in the process. On the other hand, the presence of this intermediary level of government offers federal agencies the opportunity to enhance their own marketing efforts through a policy of careful coordination. This can result in two sets of mutually reinforcing programs being directed at the market—one closely tailored to regional concerns and the other reflecting a national perspective.

U.S. Public Agencies Face More Outside Interference

Efforts by public agencies to develop new markets and introduce new products are more likely to meet resistance from special interest groups in the United States than in Britain or Canada. Amtrak, USPS, and energy conservation programs all have had their marketing efforts sharply criticized by lobbies and private firms, and sometimes they have been eviscerated or blocked altogether at the legislative level.

There is a clear need for U.S. agencies to adopt a more aggressive stance and fight for greater independence. Greater insulation between Congress and these agencies might reduce the incidence of such interference.

CONCLUSIONS

Comparisons of performance between similar agencies in different countries may be complicated by factors outside management's immediate control. Operating costs of public services reflect variations in population density, geography, climate, and wage rates. Direct price comparisons are distorted by shifting exchange rates and by differences in disposable incomes and relative purchasing power. Other financial comparisons may be obscured by different accounting procedures. Political and regulatory constraints, as well as labor agreements, not only affect costs but may also inhibit short-term efforts to improve the revenue base by adding or modifying services or making selective price changes.

Despite this caveat, an important conclusion remains: significant opportunities do exist for sharing marketing analyses, techniques, and strategies across national boundaries. A cross-national comparison of similar public agencies' performance in different countries may also provide valuable insights into the extent to which political structures and processes facilitate or impede effective marketing efforts by a particular agency.

In the aggregate, U.S. public agencies appear to be relatively less successful marketers than their British and Canadian counterparts. This is ironic given the long tradition of marketing expertise in the U.S. private sector, but it demonstrates that the political traditions and governmental structure of the United States are not particularly conducive to effective public management.

REFERENCES

Barnhill, J. Allison (1975), "Developing a Marketing Orientation: A Case Study of the Canada Post Office," in *Marketing Combinations to the Firm and Society*, ed. R. C. Curhan, pp. 293–98, Chicago: American Marketing Association.

British Railways Board (1979), *Annual Report and Accounts 1978*, London: British Railway Board.

Canada Post (1978), *Considerations Which Affect the Choice of Organization Structure for the Canada Post Office*, CB 32-34/1978, Hull, Que.: Supply and Services Canada.

———(1979), *Annual Report 1979*, Hull, Que.: Supply and Services Canada.

Carter, C. F. (1977), *Report of the Post Office Review Committee*, Cmnd. 6850, London: Her Majesty's Stationery Office.

Ford, Roger (1977), "Pricing a Ticket to Ride," *Modern Railways* (August): 302–5.

Hutton, R. Bruce (1979), "Overview of 'The Energy Crisis and Consumer Conservation: Current Research and Action Programs' Workshop," in *Advances in Consumer Research*, ed. W. L. Wilkie, Vol. 6, pp. 12–14. Ann Arbor, Mich.: Association for Consumer Research.

Keen, P. A. (1979), "Inter-City Market Is a Moving Target," *Railway Gazette International* (May): 407–11.

Lester, Tom (1978), "Peter Parker Takes the Strain," *Marketing* (London) (December): 19–20.

Lovelock, Christopher H. (1979), "Theoretical Contributions from Services and Nonbusiness Marketing," in *Conceptual and Theoretical Developments in Marketing*, eds. S. W. Brown, Q. C. Ferrell, and C. W. Lamb, Chicago: American Marketing Association.

Milstein, Jeffrey S. (1977), "Attitudes, Knowledge, and Behavior of American Consumers Regarding Energy Conservation with Some Implications for Governmental Action," in *Advances in Consumer Research*, ed. W. D. Perreault, Vol. 4, Atlanta, Ga.: Association for Consumer Research.

National Railroad Passenger Corporation (1979), *Amtrak 1978 Annual Report*, Washington, D.C.: Amtrak.

Phillips, Nicolas and Elizabeth Nelson (1976), "Energy Savings in Private Households: An Integrated Research Program," *Journal of the Market Research Society* (October): 180–200.

Roberts, Robert (1979), "VIA Gets a Better Start than Amtrak," *Modern Railroad* (October): 72–74.

Schmitt, Richard B. (1979), "An Advertising Blitz Urging Conservation of Energy is Mulled," *Wall Street Journal*, September 14.

"Serious Marketing Gets VIA on Tracks" (1979), *Marketing* (Toronto) (January 1): 4.

United Kingdom, Post Office (1979), *Report and Accounts 1978–79*, London: Her Majesty's Stationery Office.

U.S., Committee on Post Office and Civil Service (1975) *Report on Postal Service Sales of Postal Related Items*, Committee Print no. 93–26, Washington, D.C.: Government Printing Office.

U.S., Congress, House, Permanent Select Committee on Small Business (1974), *The Effects of the Postal Service's Policies on Small Business*, H. Rep. 93–1468, Washington, D.C.: Government Printing Office.

U.S., Department of Energy, (1979) "Low-Cost/No-Cost Program Sponsored by Energy Department and New England Council" and "Fact Sheet: Low-Cost/No-Cost Program," News releases from Office of Public Affairs, Region 1, Boston, November 8.

United States Postal Service (1980), *Annual Report of the Postmaster-General, Fiscal 1979*, Washington, D.C.: United States Postal Service.

VIA Rail Canada Inc. (1979), *Annual Report 1978*, Montreal, Quebec: VIA Rail Canada Inc.

Yergin, Daniel (1979), "Conservation: The Key Energy Source," in *Energy Future: Report of the Energy Project at the Harvard Business School*, eds. R. Stobaugh and D. Yergin, pp. 136–82, New York: Random House.

9

COMPARATIVE PUBLIC SECTOR MARKETING: CONTRASTING TWO CANADIAN PROGRAMS

J. A. Barnhill and Stanley J. Shapiro

Public sector marketing, like its private sector equivalent, varies greatly in its degree of acceptance and implementation. Wide variations can be brought into focus by examining different types of marketing programs undertaken by different departments of government. Two departments of the government of Canada have been chosen to illustrate existing extremes. One department, Indian Affairs and Northern Development, has limited its marketing involvement to the indirect encouragement of northern native cooperatives through the financial support of consulting studies, sporadic advertising, and strengthening of the distribution system used to move products to and from the native people of Canada. The other department, the Canada Post Office, has developed a large and sophisticated marketing program.

The marketing activities of these two organizations—the northern native cooperative system and the Canada Post Office—are discussed in this chapter. After reviewing the differences that exist between the two organizations in both marketing development and practice, the implications of this paired comparison are explored.

MARKETING UNDERDEVELOPMENT—THE NORTHERN NATIVE COOPERATIVE SYSTEM

The first native cooperative was started in northern Canada 20 years ago. Today, more than 50 such cooperatives are to be found, predominantly in small communities, across the 1.5 million square miles of the Northwest Territories and Nouveau Quebec. All but five of these cooperatives are north of 60° latitude. To provide the necessary linkages to "southern Canadian" and other markets, two cooperative federations and a government-owned distribution and marketing company, similar in many respects to a cooperative, have been established. These "second-level" marketing intermediaries or extension organizations augment the marketing and distribution activities of the individual cooperatives.

At the "primary" or first level, that of the individual cooperative, marketing considerations have little or no role to play in evaluating the arts and crafts made by native artisans. These products have become a major source of income for the members of each cooperative. Consequently, strong social and economic pressures dictate that whatever is produced—regardless of its quality—should be purchased, stored, and then transported to other institutions (notably the federations and the cooperative) for wider distribution and ultimate sale. The same factors often influence not only the initial willingness to purchase but also the price actually paid for Eskimo arts and crafts.

Such noneconomic considerations generate serious problems as products move through the various channels of distribution toward the ultimate consumer. Since the second-level marketing intermediaries are either reluctant or unable to return items to producers or their local cooperatives, lower-quality or overpriced products tend to accumulate. Consequently, many thousands of dollars are tied up in slow moving or "dead" inventory. Capital efficiency and profitability are diminished, goodwill and credibility are lost, and both suppliers and customers become disillusioned with the system.

Individual cooperatives also attempt to provide the native people with consumer goods and a few services. Primary emphasis is on furnishing the food, clothing, housing, and other products required for physical survival. Geography and climate combine to inhibit transportation and the storage of goods so timing and problems of physical distribution dominate the entire process. The cooperatives have generally proven to be substandard retailers. Store facilities are not maintained well. Much of the merchandise is stale, rotting goods that "the people" do not want or need. Prices are approximately 10 percent higher than one finds at Hudson's Bay Company outlets and higher still in those Northwest Territories communities where there is no competition. Credit practices are irregular, often exploitative, and a serious problem in most cooperative stores.

The Role of Second-Level Marketing Intermediaries

How well developed is marketing in the three second-level extension organizations? Both marketing development and marketing practice are significantly more advanced than one finds in the individual cooperatives. But, in comparison with most North American wholesale, distribution, and marketing institutions of comparable size and scope, the extension organizations remain relatively underdeveloped. The relevant marketing similarities and differences between these organizations—the Canadian Arctic Cooperative Federation Limited (CACFL), La Fédération des Coopératives du Nouveau Quebec (FCNQ), and the Canadian Arctic Producers Limited (CAP)—are highlighted in Table 9.1.

Both federations order, assemble, expedite, and account for goods— mainly food, clothing, and household furniture—flowing to the northern cooperatives. The federations also perform most of the functions of merchant middlemen for native-produced goods moving from the cooperatives to markets outside of northern Canada. In addition, the five CACFL retail outlets operating in the Northwest Territories offer a relatively complete selection of northern native products. CAP passively accepts, wholesales, and promotes northern native cooperative products—especially carvings, prints, crafts, and garments—as well as stationery produced in southern Canada with a northern native motif.

The three organizations provide very little advice about product line development. A member cooperative or a native artisan seeking assistance in various aspects of arts and crafts production will receive some guidance. However, that assistance is more likely to be provided by a government employee or someone on the staff of a local cooperative.

The extension organizations make no conscious effort at market segmentation or target marketing. The concepts as such are unknown, and no such practices are followed under another name. In effect, the CACFL's Northern Images stores are mainly oriented toward local tourists and the general retail trade of the Northwest Territories. The FCNQ and the CAP have an end-market orientation toward art galleries in particular and retailers generally. No real program of export market development has been undertaken by the extension organization. Of the three organizations, the FCNQ has become the most progressive, aiming major sales promotions at selected larger metropolitan centers in Canada and the United States.

The four main alternative channels of distribution for northern native products are shown in Figure 9.1, with illustrative prices for an Eskimo carving noted in brackets. The channel used most commonly for distributing such products involves no less than three middlemen and so results in a price to the consumer 4.5 times that of the most integrated direct-to-consumer channel (A), 2.25 times that of the channel (B) with only one intermediary retailer, such as the Hudson's Bay Company, and 1.5 times the price to the ultimate consumer for a channel (C) with two intermediaries.

Promotion, albeit variable in quality and quantity, is the major marketing function undertaken by these second-level organizations. The CACFL uses local retail advertising, publicity, and point-of-purchase promotion at its Northern Images stores. Institutional advertising for these stores has occasionally been provided by the government of the Northwest Territories. The FCNQ has a reasonably strong personal selling force. Sales

TABLE 9.1

Nature of Marketing Development in Northern Native Cooperative System

Marketing Functions	State of Development		
	CACFL*	FCNQ*	CAP*
Functional orientation	Physical distribution and retailing	Physical distribution	Physical distribution/ marketing
Product line offering	Orders, assembles, and expedites goods flowing to northern coops; provides retail outlets for relatively complete selection of northern native products	Merchant middleman for wide range of products flowing to and from individual northern native cooperatives	Passively accepts, wholesales, and promotes northern native cooperative products, especially arts, crafts, garments, and stationery
Product line development	Some advice offered to producer cooperatives	Advice and training provided to producer cooperatives	Advice, by exception, offered/responded to producer cooperatives
Target marketing	Little; mainly oriented toward local tourists and general retail trade	Little; mainly oriented toward galleries and retailers generally; little export development	Little; mainly oriented toward galleries and retailers generally; sporadic and limited export development

TABLE 9.1 (continued)

Nature of Marketing Development in Northern Native Cooperative System

Marketing Functions	State of Development		
	CACFL*	FCNQ*	CAP*
Pricing	According to schedule of mark-ups on cost	Predominantly cost plus with some market adjustments	Primarily based on schedule of mark-ups on cost
Promotion	Local retail advertising, publicity, and point-of-purchase promotion; occasional institutional advertising	Personal selling and sales promotion, e.g., trade shows, directed solely to distributive institutions	Occasional consumer advertising; personal selling and sales promotion limited and overly passive
Market information	No market research; limited market intelligence	No market research; some market intelligence	No market research; some market intelligence
Management	Solid retail store and physical distribution management; little other marketing management capability	Solid physical distribution management; little other marketing management capability	Variable wholesaling management; little other or weak marketing management

*CACFL—Canadian Arctic Cooperatives Federation Limited; FCNQ—La Fédération des Cooperatives du Nouveau Quebec; CAP—Canadian Arctic Producers Limited.

Source: Compiled by the authors.

FIGURE 9.1

Alternative Channels of Distribution and Price Structures

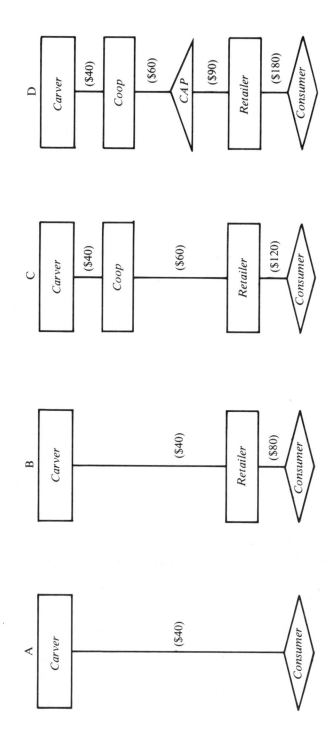

promotion varies greatly from year to year with the most ambitious efforts involving well-developed displays presented at appropriate trade shows. CAP's promotion has consisted mainly of showroom order taking along with a limited program of on-the-road personal selling, selective sales promotion and occasional institutional advertising.

No systematic market research study of any type has been undertaken by these three extension organizations. Market-related information available to the cooperative system consists almost entirely of the market intelligence gleaned by sales people reporting on their experience in the market place.

The Government Position—Benign Marketing Neglect

Despite the millions of dollars it has spent on subsidizing the system of northern native cooperatives, Canada's Department of Indian Affairs and Northern Development has done little or nothing to provide these cooperatives with marketing "know how." A modest degree of management counseling is provided by government officials and consultants. Governmental agencies have also furnished support services and financial aid when gluts of soap stone carvings, Indian art, or fur garments have occurred. However, the Canadian government—generally through inaction and/or the withholding of funds—has repeatedly rejected proposals that it underwrite market research studies or help establish an integrated distribution network.

The cooperative system and in particular the extension organizations are apparently expected to provide whatever degree of marketing expertise is necessary for the viability of that system. The prevailing governmental policy of benign marketing neglect is surprising, especially in light of the tendency of the relevant department to underwrite and, in large part, direct most other aspects of Eskimo and Indian life. Serving as a facilitating marketing force is, it seems, one role Indian Affairs and Northern Development is unwilling to accept.

MARKETING IN THE CANADA POST OFFICE

The appointment on July 7, 1968, of a new postmaster general was widely hailed as especially appropriate given the range of problems (labor unrest, mounting deficits, fluctuating service standards, and poor public relations) confronting the Canada Post Office. The new postmaster general was viewed as a "problem solver," a "doer," a man with a business background who would make changes, for instance, bring in new management, develop a new organization, guarantee employees an opportunity to make meaningful contributions, and, more generally, provide the CPO with a new sense of purpose.

By September 1968, this new postmaster general had directed the CPO to retain outside consultants to work with Post Office employees in carrying out a detailed evaluation of every aspect of postal operations. One of the resulting investigations dealt specifically and at great length with marketing issues. That study, *The Post Office in the Market Place*, launched the first stage of marketing development in the CPO and made four major conceptual contributions (Mintzberg et al. 1960):

1. The Post Office was presented as a marketing system consisting of an input subsystem, process subsystems, and an output subsystem;
2. The concept of market segmentation, both by customer and by content, was introduced;
3. Marketing strategies reflecting a consumer orientation, clearly formulated marketing objectives, and a series of operating premises were formulated; and
4. The influence of environmental restraints, notably competition, technological developments, and socioeconomic trends, were discussed at length.

In addition, the Marketing Task Force made specific recommendations as to the nature of the marketing information system that was deemed necessary and the type of marketing organization being recommended. A detailed study of Parcel Post was presented as an illustration of how marketing might be adapted to an existing CPO program.

Another of the commissioned baseline studies reported the lack of a marketing orientation. The consultants wrote:

> Officers in the Department lack the marketing orientation essential for an efficient service. They see the market as users of mail rather than of communications, transportation and banking services. The services that the Post Office is permitted to provide under the Post Office Act have been interpreted precisely and have been offered in an administrative and unimaginative manner. (CPO 1969)

The Establishment Stage (Mid-1968 to Mid-1971)

While the report of the Marketing Task Force introduced several new and useful concepts, marketing executives subsequently hired from the "outside" still had to operationalize what had been recommended in fairly general terms. By May 1970, the following statement of CPO marketing policy had been formulated and approved:

> It is the policy of the Canada Post Office to become marketing oriented, through development of a marketing capability and organization, comparable to the best examples in private industry. In our view, the

Post Office exists to serve the people of Canada, in pursuit of their social and economic objectives. Marketing orientation therefore means an organized concern for the needs of our customers, and a recognition that we exist to serve them. Services must be planned, and priced so as to meet the greatest degree of customer need, while achieving a much more satisfactory financial result. The aim is to bring every service provided by the Post Office as close as possible to financial self-sufficiency, thereby relieving the burden on all other services, and on the tax-paying public.

As an extension of this policy statement, six basic marketing objectives were formulated, each one corresponding to a principal area of Post Office marketing activity. Briefly, the objectives were:

1. Maintain a direct and continuous channel of communication with major customers to ensure servicing of their total needs in the most profitable way and to provide essential customer contact.
2. Maintain a comprehensive appreciation of all factors having a significant effect on present or future market conditions, including customer needs, competition, technological changes, mailing and distribution patterns, and business trends.
3. Investigate, evaluate, and develop product and pricing changes or new service concepts that may enhance profitability of existing services or identify new lines of profitable endeavor for the Canada Post Office.
4. Simplify and refine methods of doing business to the mutual advantage of both customers and the Post Office.
5. Develop a selling capability that will ensure achievement of full market potential for each product and service of the Canada Post Office.
6. Improve and maintain Post Office public offices to the best contemporary standards of appearance and decor and recruit, train, and motivate counter sales and service staffs to serve customers in the most efficient and friendly way.

Based on the direction provided by these objectives, an analysis of 11 major marketing problems and 8 major marketing opportunities was conducted. A marketing plan that included specific market and product strategies for such areas as electronic communications, direct marketing, parcel sales, and premium mail evolved from this analysis. Since market planning required information on products, markets, customers, and competitive conditions, a marketing research program was launched in 1971. The research program was introduced with two objectives in mind: (1) to provide a substantive base for analyzing market conditions, public attitudes, the image of the Post Office, and the manner in which business uses the mail, and (2) to reveal specific user needs, suggestions, ideas, and concepts regarding the market.

Concern for the future and its impact on the CPO was reflected in the commissioning of an environmental forecast. The resulting report, released in March 1971, explored the likely impact of environmental change on the CPO and its marketing activities. Particular attention was paid in this report to socioeconomic trends, apparent changes in life styles, and expected technological breakthroughs.

The new marketing organization was being established at a time when the CPO as a whole was moving toward a decentralized structure. The organization reflected a mix of the functional, that is, Philatelic and Retail and Postal Rates and Classification, and market or user-oriented sections, such as Service Development and Customer Sales and Service. Later in 1971, a marketing organization was developed for Ontario's pilot autonomous region and directors appointed for the four previously mentioned sections of the Headquarters Branch. Marketing personnel throughout the CPO organization were expected to use a newly established Marketing Council as a vehicle for integrating their efforts and exchanging information.

The Growth Stage (Mid-1971 to Mid-1974)

A "commercial" orientation was a fundamental part of CPO marketing management philosophy throughout its second or growth stage. Seeking profits for the CPO, still viewed as an organization likely to become a Crown Corporation, was an objective consistent with that commercial orientation. An on-going commitment was also made to the formulation of market-oriented policies, objectives, and goals. Assured Mail was introduced as a "brave attempt to set standards for service." This program was oriented toward first-in, first-out service rather than the random mail handling—occasionally involving last-in, first-out postal service—that took place previously.

Development of the postal code was another major effort by the CPO to set and meet service standards. Marketing and Operations worked together in developing, implementing, and modifying the postal code. Indeed, marketing was then being viewed by the CPO, according to the former assistant deputy postmaster general of marketing, as an "extension of Operations" whose role was "to sell the code" and provide market intelligence through postal user conferences and its sales representatives.

CPO marketing personnel were also devoting considerable resources to planning and strategy formulation. Four new services were launched to improve the CPO's competitive capability and to meet marketing objectives.

Postpak

The CPO responded to a declining parcel volume by developing and evaluating a new form of Parcel Post Service. The results suggested that the

CPO was capable of competitively distributing consolidated parcels weighing up to 66 pounds, the traditional limit for fourth class mail packages. (Once the consolidated packages reached their destination point, individual items would be distributed by the recipient.)

In 1971, Postpak service was established in five major centers (Halifax, Montreal, Toronto, Winnipeg, and Regina) with a limited number (approximately 60) of destinations, mostly catalogue sales offices operated by Eatons and Simpson Sears. Competitive pricing and the absence of paperwork for users (such as the weigh bills required by "common carriers") were strategic aspects of Postpak expected to generate a growing demand. Consequently, this new service went "national" in 1972. Nevertheless, the Postpak launch was not without its problems. The program received markedly different degrees of organizational support in the various regions of an increasingly decentralized CPO.

Telepost

Telepost was launched in late 1972 with telecommunications companies providing the "hardware" and the CPO its extensive delivery service. Telepost initially required senders to have Telex machines. However, this service was subsequently expanded to over-the-counter and "phone-in" services at Canadian National/Canadian Pacific (CN/CP) offices. Telepost strategy was based on competitive pricing (that is, less than night letter), use of special envelopes, targetted promotion, and a selective distribution network.

Telepost also generated a certain degree of conflict within the CPO organization, even though this service had been reasonably well received in the marketplace. Once again, contributing difficulties included organizational confusion as to objectives, internal communication problems, and varying degrees of regional acceptance.

Certified Mail

In late 1972–early 1973, test market results suggested that Certified Mail be launched to meet the need of government, law firms, and financial institutions for a signature-acknowledgement receipt type of service that did not involve the hand-to-hand delivery associated with Registered Mail. Nevertheless, the expected shift in demand from Registered Mail did not occur initially. The major barriers proved to be legal stipulations and statutes which stated that official notice and other legal documents could only be delivered by Registered Mail. With the gradual modification of such provisions, Certified Mail has grown steadily in popularity. Because Certified Mail was considered an "appropriate" new service throughout the CPO, it obtained the desired degree of internal cooperation and regional support without undue difficulty.

Philatelic

The philatelic program of the Retail Marketing Branch also achieved considerable success. Until 1973, the philatelic program was a responsibility of the Financial Administration Branch. Consequently, there was no philatelic marketing organization and no orientation to the stamp collector market. In early 1973, however, a decision was made to develop a market-oriented philatelic program. The CPO joined in a world-wide survey of philatelic markets and stamp collector behavior. Analysis of survey results led to four major philatelic marketing strategies being implemented. By 1975, the philatelic program was a success. Revenues were up more than 500 percent from $2.5 million in Fiscal year 1973 to $13.5 million in fiscal year 1975. Not only had a source of high contribution revenue been exploited, but new markets had been developed, public needs were being better satisfied, and higher standards for postage products had been established.

Other marketing initiatives between 1971 and 1975 merit some mention. A study of electronic mail was undertaken, and Phase I (involving 13 case studies of major mail users) of the CPO's Business Market Analysis was completed. A formal management information service was developed. In addition, the first market demand model for Canadian postal products (MADAM) became operational in 1974. MADAM was developed to measure the likely impact of economic changes and strategic CPO decisions on postal volumes and revenues.

CPO marketing executives continued to demonstrate a keen interest in the future. A second environmental forecast has been produced by January of 1972. An overall review of economic, social, business, and technological trends was provided. In addition, special studies were made of specific environmental factors such as the shortened work week, general labor force attitudes and characteristics, electronic funds transfer systems, centralized credit transfer systems, direct mail advertising, and transportation. A management "Delphi" study on the future of the CPO was also conducted during the summer of 1973.

This period was one of increasing organizational stress within CPO-Marketing. Difficulties were experienced with the decentralized organization, the production (operations) orientation of the CPO, and the federal bureaucracy of which the Post Office was a part. The organizational environment was perceived by some marketing executives as inhibiting the development of a truly market-oriented Postal Service. By 1974, the CPO marketing organization at Headquarters had a mix of four functional-service components: Postage and Retail, Marketing Services, Sales and Customer Services; and Service Development and Mail Classification.

The Maturity Stage (Mid-1974 to 1979)

By late 1974, CPO-Marketing had become less oriented to external conditions and more oriented to internal conditions, particularly the financial performance of the CPO. In early 1976, for example, the importance of profitable marketing (and operations) was emphasized in an address by the new assistant deputy postmaster general for marketing in which he stated, "The job of Marketing can be summarized in six words, to improve the net financial position." However, the marketing concept was not lost during this period of maturation. During a 1977 review of CPO-Marketing, the deputy postmaster general asserted:

> Canada Post Office owes its very existence to only one purpose . . . to satisfy market needs for the transfer of communications and goods. We must be market-oriented. If we are not market-oriented in our thinking and planning, we are categorically denying our purpose for being.

Such statements notwithstanding, both formal market research and periodic meetings with customers revealed that real or perceived service failures—most notably unreliability and inconsistency of service—were regarded as the most serious CPO deficiency. More specifically, strife-ridden labor-management relations, the unrealized expectations associated with mechanization, and other operational dislocations had to be solved if CPO-Marketing was to gain credibility with its customers and compete successfully in the marketplace.

The increasing internal and financial orientation of CPO-Marketing was clearly reflected in marketing objectives for the period 1975-77, which included: specified revenue and volume targets; a required degree of postal code acceptance and mail standardization; selective new services (for example, Courierpost and Urban Parcel Delivery); effective communications with customers, customer association, and other influential groups; and an understanding of and commitment to the marketing role and objectives by all employees of the organization, both front-line and managerial. These aims were to be achieved by various strategic endeavors, the principal ones being productivity selling and revenue generation.

Productivity Selling

In July 1975, the marketing branch of the Manitoba Postal District formulated the new concept of productivity selling as follows: "A concise definition of Productivity Selling is practically impossible as it covers such a wide range of activities, and can take so many varying approaches. The objective, however, is clear: THAT PLANT EFFICIENCY IS MAXI-MIZED BY THE MAILING PROCEDURES OF THE CUSTOMER."(internal document). The CPO sales force was expected to convince major mail users that by adopting productivity-maximizing procedures in their plants they would benefit from "better mail service." Customer resistance to productivity selling was expected by the CPO since, in many cases, the benefits associated with this program were perceived as properly part of "normal" postal service, tended to be intangible and hard to document, and would require additional activities to be carried out and their costs borne by the customer. Such resistance was to be overcome by "aggressive and continuing sales effort."

Revenue Generation

In an effort to improve its revenues, the CPO undertook to increase both postal rates and the volume of mail handled. The marketing plan for 1975–76 to 1979–80 postulated increased revenues of 7 to 8 percent for each of the five years covered by that plan. Subsequently, rate increases were scheduled, the secretary of state started to pay a subsidy that covered the full costs of handling second class mail (newspapers, magazines, and other items of social or cultural value), and the volume of certain classes of mail increased in response to a sustained promotional effort.

Corporate marketing strategies for 1975–76 to 1979–80 included:

Expanding sales of existing services;
Complementing existing services with feasible new services;
Pricing all services competitively and in proper relation to each other; and
Encouraging customers to "trade up" to services that are more profitable to
  the CPO

These general strategies, in turn, were translated into specific market and product line strategies in the correspondence and communications market.

This final period began with CPO-Marketing suffering from considerable organizational turmoil. In early 1974, the first assistant deputy postmaster general for marketing (ADPMG-Marketing) went on full-time French-language training for a year. After an 18-month period of "acting" replacements, Mr. Larry Sperling, formerly of IBM and Consumers Distributing, was appointed ADPMG-Marketing in October 1975.

The organization Mr. Sperling inherited was not in the best of health. An internal "climate" report had severely criticized the Marketing Branch to the point of suggesting that CPO-Marketing be abandoned. What had prompted such severe criticism? The most likely explanation is the way new products and services had been launched. In its zeal to introduce Postpak, Telepost, and Assured Mail, CPO-Marketing had failed to coordinate effectively with the operating units of the CPO organization. On the other hand, a decentralized organization and a production bias made efforts at communication and coordination far more difficult than is usually the case.

Given these and other adverse organizational conditions, the new

ADPMG-Marketing moved quickly to rectify the situation. Primary attention was devoted to supporting effective individuals and contributing components. A major effort was made to develop credibility for CPO-Marketing with other parts of the postal organization, especially Operations. There was initially some modest shifts in the organizational structure, with more major organizational changes subsequently. The present structure is depicted in Figure 9.2.

An effort was made next to develop roles for marketing appropriate to the expected performance of the entire organization. One of the roles involved CPO-Marketing being supportive of financial and operational aims, for instance, through productivity selling, revenue generation, and the promotion of the postal code, and of standards and related procedures facilitating mechanization. A more traditional marketing role demonstrated the "marketing concept" in action. Useful linkages were to be provided between major mail users (and their associations) and the operating units of the CPO organization. A third role involved leadership in the CPO's overall planning process. Marketing studies and strategies were expected to serve as the point of departure for overall departmental planning. As much as possible, emphasis was placed on total "organizational marketing," not merely marketing by a branch at headquarters or by a limited number of district and regional marketing specialists.

COMPARING MARKETING DEVELOPMENT AND PRACTICE

Two very different forms of Canadian public sector marketing have been outlined in some detail. Comparisons between the two systems reveal them as being at the two ends of a public sector marketing spectrum. Such a comparison, focusing both on awareness of marketing as a discipline or formal body of thought and on the marketing practices of both the northern native cooperative system and the CPO, follows. A more detailed comparison, touching upon environmental conditions, organizational concerns, and management practices as well—is presented in Table 9.2.

The Northern Native Cooperative System

Despite sales of $30 million in 1978, the northern native cooperative system has demonstrated little or no awareness of formal marketing thought. The Department of Indian Affairs and Northern Development, which has provided financial support to the cooperative system, is reluctant to provide marketing expertise and has not become directly involved in the movement of goods either to or from individual native cooperatives.

The extension organizations are the most advanced marketing practi-

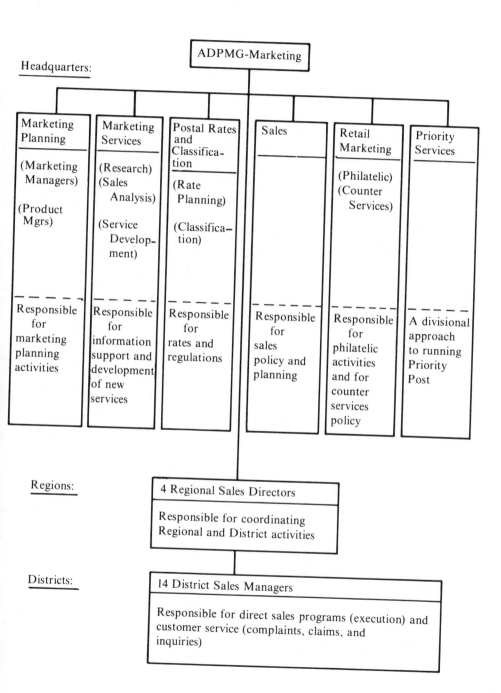

FIGURE 9.2

Areas of CPO-Marketing Responsibility, Circa 1979

Headquarters:

ADPMG-Marketing

Marketing Planning	Marketing Services	Postal Rates and Classification	Sales	Retail Marketing	Priority Services
(Marketing Managers) (Product Mgrs)	(Research) (Sales Analysis) (Service Development)	(Rate Planning) (Classification)		(Philatelic) (Counter Services)	
Responsible for marketing planning activities	Responsible for information support and development of new services	Responsible for rates and regulations	Responsible for sales policy and planning	Responsible for philatelic activities and for counter services policy	A divisional approach to running Priority Post

Regions:

4 Regional Sales Directors

Responsible for coordinating Regional and District activities

Districts:

14 District Sales Managers

Responsible for direct sales programs (execution) and customer service (complaints, claims, and inquiries)

tioners in the system. However, their approach is oriented predominantly to the distribution of goods to and from native cooperatives. Although some attention has been devoted to selling, sales promotion, retail advertising, and merchandising, action in these areas has generally been taken without any prior exposure or references to the relevant literature.

Formal ignorance of marketing notwithstanding, the two functional levels of the northern native cooperative system employ marketing practices with varying degrees of completeness and proficiency. Within the two federations, distribution practices are quite advanced, especially in light of the existing environmental inhibitors—notably climate, geography, transportation, communication, economic, and sociocultural conditions. The remaining marketing practices of the two federations, however, leave much to be desired. Sales, sales promotion, and advertising are limited both in scope and degree of development. Although some information on market likes and dislikes is gathered as a by-product of day-to-day operations, formal marketing research is nonexistent, and a relatively rigid form of cost-plus pricing is employed.

Canadian Arctic Producers, charged with the fundamental responsibility for the marketing and distribution of northern native products, has achieved a modest degree of financial success. However, this success has been generated by a demand pull for Eskimo arts and crafts rather than by progressive CAP marketing practices. CAP has undertaken no market research, and its market intelligence, marketing planning, sales and promotional efforts have been relatively modest. Only one new product has been developed in the last decade. Individual cooperatives and their member artists receive little or no feedback from the marketplace.

Formal marketing thought has had even less of an impact at the level of the individual cooperative. A policy of providing customers with what they want—a common-sense version of the "marketing concept"—sometimes governs retail store operations. By contrast, the "marketing" and distribution of arts, crafts, garments, and other items made by northern natives is a completely production-oriented process. Individual northern native cooperatives carry out a number of basic marketing functions in the course of their day-to-day activities, but buying, selling, pricing, transportation, storage, financing, insuring, and the like are performed in a perfunctory manner.

Marketing in the Post Office

In contrast to the northern native cooperatives marketing programs, CPO marketing has demonstrated a familiarity with contemporary marketing thought. The Marketing Task Force submitted a report in August of 1969 which urged adoption of the marketing concept, spoke of postal marketing systems, and introduced such notions as market segmentation and marketing intelligence. The marketing executives from the "outside" who subsequently joined the CPO utilized a "textbook approach" to marketing planning which, in turn, led to considerable importance being assigned to both marketing research and environmental monitoring. Product-market thinking subsequently became prominent. Product development efforts were undertaken with due regard for both competition (existing and potential) and pending technological breakthroughs. A sophisticated simulation model (MADAM) was introduced as a method of forecasting the likely impact on demand of changes either in postal rates or the aggregate level of economic activity. In sum, CPO-Marketing appears to have been as sophisticated in its marketing thought as most profit-oriented organizations of similar size.

CPO-Marketing also acted, throughout the decade in question, in a manner consistent with its demonstrated degree of familiarity with advanced marketing thought. The "marketing concept" became the cornerstone of the CPO's entire marketing effort. Marketing plans were prepared, market-oriented objectives formulated, market research studies launched and postal user conferences held. Products and programs were developed (or modified) in response to changing conditions in the market place. Mail markets were segmented and a distinct marketing strategy then generated for each major segment.

This historical review suggests a considerable degree of sophistication in marketing practice and thought. Admittedly, CPO-Marketing encountered a series of internal problems that hindered the introduction of new products and caused a shift in emphasis toward revenue generation and, more specifically, to "productivity selling." However, the ability to shift emphasis successfully while also gaining recognition as the CPO's principal change agent must itself be considered as prima facie evidence of a relatively sophisticated marketing capability.

IMPLICATIONS AND CONCLUSIONS

The preceding descriptions of the marketing activities of the Canada Post Office and the northern native cooperative system are informative in their own right. As comparatively summarized in Table 9.2, they also serve as useful additions to the limited amount of existing literature on public sector marketing, particularly in Canada. What does this chapter, however, add to previously discovered differences between public and private sector marketing, or to the existing typology of identified differences within the public sector (compare Lovelock and Weinberg 1975)?

The following considerations are advanced as important aspects of public sector marketing that have not been stressed in other discussions:

TABLE 9.2

A Comparative Analysis of Marketing Programs

Marketing Elements	Northern Native Cooperative System	Canada Post Office
General state	Underdeveloped	Developed
Organization		
Purpose	Socioeconomic development	Effective marketing of CPO
Aims	Aid native cooperatives/people	Quality and profit; performance-oriented services
Strategies	Through cooperative and government programs	Service and market-based
Structure	Ill-defined; loose	Well-defined; functional
Marketing mix		
Product/Service	Limited; little development	Development; expanding
Price	Production-based, cost-plus	Competitive; political
Promotion	Limited sales promotion	Sales-oriented; sporadic advertising
Distribution	Major orientation; strong capability	Inconsistent; competitive
Marketing functions		
Buying	Variable by coop; solid by federations	Tender-based
Selling	Variable; passive	Progressive
Storage	Variable; tends to be adequate	Quality facilities; variable handling
Transportation	Noncooperative private or government	Regular; scheduled
Risk	High; covered by government and federations	Limited
Financing	Government-based; native money	Tightening
Information	None	Quality program/ performance
Management	Overall; major weakness	Competent
Planning	Nonexistent	Regular; solid
Directing	Some	Well-directed
Analyzing	None	Variable
Decision making	Intuitive; underdeveloped	Variable
Controlling	Variable	Competent

Source: Compiled by the authors.

The government agency as marketing benefactor. The preceding discussion has been somewhat critical of the Department of Indian Affairs and Northern Development for its failure to do anything to improve the marketing activities of the northern cooperatives. The authors could have contrasted this "benign neglect" with the very active role undertaken by Canada's Department of the Secretary of State to strengthen, through the financing of special marketing studies, the marketing know how of the various artistic, cultural, and publishing communities that department serves. A number of other Canadian agencies have commissioned marketing studies designed to make it easier for client organizations, many in the private-for-profit segment of the economy, to market their goods and/or services. This role of government as marketing benefactor deserves more attention than it has received to date.

The labor-intensive nature of public sector marketing. Most government marketing is service marketing. Consequently, it must be recognized that a heavy direct labor component denies service marketing many of the economies of scale associated with consumer goods marketing. This fact becomes increasingly significant in a period of inflation. If its only costs had been direct labor costs, the Canada Post Office would still have operated in 1977–78 at a deficit. When labor costs are both high and, to a large extent, variable, one must be certain that efforts at public sector marketing will improve and not aggravate the overall financial picture. What constitutes sound marketing behavior is also influenced by such a cost structure. That the Canada Post Office used its marketing capability to encourage customer action consistent with efforts at postal mechanization seems entirely appropriate, the marketing concept and its customer orientation notwithstanding. The implications associated with high labor costs in many other forms of public sector marketing thus emerges as another area requiring intensive exploration.

A reluctance to be held to "hard and fast" performance standards. The absence of a profit-and-loss statement introducing the discipline of the "bottom line" is a well-recognized feature of governmental and third sector marketing. These two Canadian marketing programs, however, suggest a marked reluctance to accept organizational performance standards as a substitute for bottom-line accountability. Instead, the argument is advanced that "we are doing the best we can given the very difficult environmental conditions that govern our activities. Consequently, neither performance deficiencies nor failure to achieve targetted objectives—be these marketing or organizational objectives—should be held against us if that environment becomes even more turbulent." The authors are reluctant to conclude from these two programs that a determination to be judged on intent and effort rather than performance is a common feature of public sector marketing. However, placing the possibility on record seems in order so that it can at least be considered by those reporting on other public sector marketing efforts.

The public sector marketing unit as primary change agent. Whether the problem be the weight of bureaucratic inertia or the pressures associated with meeting day-to-day problems, change does not come easily to public sector organizations, especially in a period of budgetary stringency or when labor problems have seriously crippled the system's ability to deliver the already existing range of services. The experience of the Canada Post Office suggests that a customer or "public" marketing organization that monitors the environment and carefully watches prospective competitors can provide better service to the public. More generally, one of the most significant contributions that marketing can make to the entire not-for-profit sector may be the constant pressure marketing exerts for change in organizations otherwise preoccupied with traditional bureaucratic ends and means.

REFERENCES

Barnhill, J. A. (1975), "Developing a Marketing Orientation—A Case Study of the Canada Post Office," in *1974 Combined Proceedings*, ed. Ronald C. Curhan, pp. 293-98, Chicago: American Marketing Association.

—— (1979), "Marketing Developments of the Native Cooperatives," Paper presented at the Conference on Marketing's Contribution to Developing Nations, Copenhagen, School of Economics and Business Administration.

Canada Post Office Department (1969), "*A Blueprint for Change*," unpublished study done by Kates, Peat, Marwick and Co., Ottawa.

Lovelock, Christopher H. and Charles B. Weinberg (1975), "Contrasting Private and Public Sector Marketing," in *1974 Combined Proceedings*, ed. Ronald C. Curhan, pp. 242-47, Chicago: American Marketing Association.

Mintzberg, Henry et al. (1969). *The Post Office in the Market Place—Report of the Marketing Task Force*, Montreal: Stanley J. Shapiro.

Shapiro, Stanley J. and J. A. Barnhill (1980), "The Post Office in the Market Place— A Ten Year Retrospective," in *Macro-Marketing: A Canadian Perspective*, eds. Donald N. Thompson et al., Chicago: American Marketing Association.

10

CAUSES OF MASS CONSUMPTION–RELATED SOCIETAL PROBLEMS AND THE ROLE OF MARKETING IN FOSTERING SOLUTIONS

Chris T. Allen

Most major ecological problems confronting economically advanced nations are related to mass consumption. The problems of air and water pollution, solid waste disposal, and energy conservation have become so troublesome that they raise significant questions regarding the role of the market versus the government in ecologically threatened societies. Barry Commoner has posed the question, "Is the conventional marketplace economy fundamentally incompatible with the integrity of the environment?" (1972, p. 253). The answer likely is a resounding "yes" in political and economic systems which couple relative freedom in the marketplace with self-indulgent consumers.

This chapter will seek to outline the more salient underlying causes of major societal problems such as the energy predicament. The goal here is to advance the type of understanding that will be required if policy decisions are to be made that will effect solutions to this mass consumption–related variety of societal problem. The arguments developed in this chapter are employed in identifying the flaws in the present solutions that are evolving in response to the nation's energy problem. In its final section, the discussion highlights the role that marketing expertise can play in generating solutions to the problem of promoting energy conservation. While much of this paper is devoted to consideration of the energy problem, it should be emphasized that the underlying causes of this problem are at the root of a more general group of ecological problems that would encompass specific issues such as air and water pollution and solid waste disposal.

THE ROOTS OF THE MASS CONSUMPTION-RELATED SOCIETAL PROBLEM

Until recently, ever increasing production and the resultant consumption have been cherished as appropriate economic goals in Western societies. The success of the U.S. economy especially has been measured by the amount of output from the factors of production. Part of this output is extracted from the earth's reserves of raw materials, and part of it is deposited into the earth's reservoirs of pollution. If there were infinite reserves from which resources could be drawn and into which pollutants could be deposited, then output would undeniably be a most appropriate measure of economic success.

Several significant and provocative works have evolved in recent years that have generally argued for the de-emphasis of economic growth as a single measure of economic success (for example, Commoner 1972, Meadows et al. 1972). While each of these works is based on the notion that there are natural limits to economic growth, one of the earliest and perhaps most eloquent statements of the argument was advanced by Kenneth Boulding (1966), who argued that the earth must be viewed as a closed system with finite natural resources. Given a closed system viewpoint, growth in economic output is not only less desirable, but it is regarded as something to be minimized rather than maximized. The essential measure of success in the closed economy is not production and consumption at all but the nature, quality, and complexity of the total capital stock, including the state of the human bodies and minds in the system. Adopting a closed system viewpoint one might even argue that simple production and consumption increases are negative and to be avoided. While most economists have not gone so far as to condemn economic growth, it is clear that the closed system perspective advanced by Boulding and others has led to a diminished emphasis on economic growth as the single measure of economic success.

It is the notion of "natural limits to growth" which in part has raised the issue of a potential incompatibility between mass consumption economies and the environment, with a societal problem such as the energy predicament reflective of a natural limit being approached. However, upon closer examination, the potential incompatibility problem runs much deeper than a question of natural limits being imposed on unchecked economic growth. Given the adoption of a perspective which assumes that natural resources are not absolutely infinite, the issue of potential incompatibility between mass consumption and environment finds its roots in what might be considered a basic flaw which has evolved in the national character in nations such as the United States. American society, through the teachings and dicta of institutions, such as business, government, and even the church, has fostered a society of individuals devoted to maximizing their own (or their family's) well-being. Nowhere has this drive for self-satisfaction been more highly developed than in the area of economic goods and services. The individual consumer is taught to maximize his or her well-being without consideration of other consumers or the ecosphere. Those who practice and promote the drive to satiate individual needs have simply failed to recognize the negative public consequences of their actions—consequences which involve environmental deterioration and rapid resource depletion.

It is important to recognize that the self-interest motive that lies at the root of many ecological problems is propagated and crystallized by a variety of institutions. Whisenhunt (1974) argues that the predominant religions in Western cultures play an important role in legitimizing misuse of the environment. Christianity teaches that man is God's highest creation and that mankind was created separate from nature. Nature and the environment were created for mankind's use. If they become spoiled in the process, so be it.

The capitalist system has long been a target of those critical of the high level of material indulgence in American culture (Potter 1954). In evaluating the U.S. business system and its products, Feldman (1971) has concluded: "There has been a failure to recognize that these products, which are marketing outputs designed for individual satisfaction, are simultaneously inputs to a larger environmental system and as such may affect the well-being of society" (p. 55).

To complement the product assortment of the marketer, consumer advertising is developed as a persevering series of invitations and charges to the individual to take care of himself and his immediate family. What's more, the modern-day consumer movement disseminates a very similar message. As Hirsch (1976) has observed:

> The same ethos, albeit propagated for different motives, pervades what is in some respects the antimarket—the consumer movement of Ralph Nader and his followers in the United States and other countries. The individual is urged to secure maximum value for money for himself or herself. The approach is to the individual as maximizing consumer, rather than cooperating citizen. (p. 82)

This is not to say that looking after one's own self-interest does not have virtue; rather, placing more and more emphasis on self-interests simply produces less emphasis on social responsibilities and obligations. Clearly, in terms of the environment and its relationship to mass consumption, emphasis on individual need satisfaction has had negative consequences at the societal level.

Problems of environmental deterioration and resource depletion can be traced to a resource base that is essentially finite and a national character typified by self-indulgence, and they have spurred doubts regarding the prospects of coexistence between marketplace economies and the environment. The self-indulgence component of the problems becomes more malevolent in a society that places more and more importance on consumption. In this regard, Nicosia and Mayer (1976) have argued that consumption activities have become the means whereby individuals can realistically pursue the value of getting ahead in American society. Once the value of getting ahead, or "success through individual achievement," could be sought through production and the work environment. However, increased job specialization, larger organizations, and pervasive labor unions have reduced opportunities for the individual worker to distinguish himself in the work environment, with a resultant deflection of the success ethic into consumption activities.

The self-indulgent, consumption-oriented individual has certainly contributed to the remarkable success of the American economy, but given a resource base that is essentially finite the self-indulgent, materialistic feature of the American character has become something of a liability. This blossoming character flaw could be viewed as the force that possibly produces and certainly perpetuates the mass consumption–related breed of societal problem. The following sections utilize the notion that self-indulgence through consumption has been developed and nurtured by the major institutions of American society in order to identify pitfalls in the solutions that have evolved in response to the energy predicament and to propose solutions to the energy conservation problem that call for an expanded application of marketing expertise.

PITFALLS OF EVOLVING SOLUTIONS TO THE ENERGY CONSERVATION PROBLEM

The American consumer does not take energy conservation seriously. The primary devices that have been advocated for advancing energy conservation in the United States have evolved at the federal level. Inevitably these devices are analyzed and evaluated by federal legislative bodies. Since the demands of conservation could well run counter to the individual's propensity for self-indulgence, most consumers do not see it as their role to help foster energy conservation. In his analysis of data collected for the Federal Energy Administration, Milstein (1977) points out that approximately two-thirds of the American public blames the energy problem on either politicians or big business. This attitude leaves individuals' consciences clear as they maintain high levels of consumption in the face of the energy problem and produces the call for a federal energy policy to supply the solution to the energy predicament. The best examples of mechanisms for fostering conservation of energy offered by the federal government include a variety of schemes providing monetary incentives for reduced energy use (for example, tax rebates for installing insulation) and disincentives for heavy energy use (the gas guzzler tax). The problems associated with these devices are easily recognized.

It is probably unfortunate that the pursuit of solutions to the energy problem has been forced into the polarized political arena of the U.S. Congress. The price incentive/disincentive variety of solution seems especially susceptible to the type of infighting and resultant inaction that follows when specialized interest groups face off over an issue. To be effective in encouraging conservation, monetary incentives/disincentives would have to be sizable. From their examination of the potential impact of the price mechanism in reducing consumption of gasoline, Willenborg and Pitts (1977) concluded:

> Policy-makers are not likely to be successful in reducing consumption by using the price mechanism, at least not through small or gradual increases. The relative short-term inelasticity of demand for gasoline, as found in the study, would imply that only a dramatic increase—perhaps 100%—would be effective. (p. 31)

Such dramatic energy taxes would certainly create political furor. Furthermore, as Milstein (1977) notes, the use of higher prices as an incentive to conserve energy has another built-in limitation:

> Many people will be able to afford all the energy they want no matter how high the prices are likely to go. Those who will not be able to afford enough energy will not only sacrifice unfairly, they will probably resent the oil companies and utilities for raising their prices, the government for allowing the prices to rise, and the well-to-do for being able to afford the extra expense. (p. 319)

Thus, not only is it highly unlikely that price incentive/disincentive programs will evolve from the political process with magnitudes that will have a significant impact on energy conservation, but also the heaviest energy-using segments of the population are potentially least susceptible to this type of conservation program.

There is a more serious long-term liability inherent in this form of government energy conservation policy when one recalls the self-indulgent, materialistic nature of the American consumer. Paying the individual consumer to conserve energy feeds on his or her self-indulgent tendencies and accordingly may produce results in the short term, but doing so only reinforces the individual's self-indulgent character, which in fact lies at the root of ecological problems such as the energy predicament. Indeed, the whole notion of the federal government taking major responsibility for developing an energy policy to "solve" the energy problem is supportive of the self-indulgent nature of the individual consumer. The incentive/disincentive type of program will cultivate and sustain the attitude that conservation should be subsidized. The individual consumer can then justifiably sit back and wait for the government to subsidize all forms of energy conservation. The major part of energy conservation comes down to what the individual consumer does, and policy makers and other social change agents must foster attitudes that confront and oppose the self-serving tendencies of the American consumer if conservation is to have a significant and permanent effect on the energy predicament. More effort needs to be directed toward taking responsibility for energy conservation out of the hands of the federal government and placing it into the hands of the American consumer. It is in this area of shifting the responsibility for conservation that the marketing discipline, through present expertise and expanded research in the future, can have an enlarged role.

A ROLE FOR MARKETING EXPERTISE IN FOSTERING ENERGY CONSERVATION

Energy conservation is primarily a function of the way individuals purchase and use products in their daily lives. Stimulating socially conscious consumption (SCC) in the energy area will require at least a partial erosion of the self-indulgent nature of the American consumer. To create strategies for stimulating SCC, attitudinal components that reflect this self-indulgence must be identified. To date there exists only limited empirical evidence regarding the potential dispositional determinants of SCC, and present evidence is strictly correlational in nature. However, relationships between two attitudinal components, issue-specific concern and perceived consumer effectiveness, and proxy measures of SCC have been established. *Issue-specific concern* is defined as an individual's attitude of concern regarding a specific ecological problem; *perceived consumer effectiveness* is defined as the individual's perception of the effectiveness of individuals in contributing to the alleviation of the severity of societal problems through their own consumption behavior. Marketing strategies can be developed around each of these two constructs for purposes of advancing conservation.

Webster (1975) has observed that as a starting point the socially conscious consumer must be aware of the salient societal problem. However, because of individuals' predispositions to be self-serving, awareness often is not reflected in legitimate concern regarding a specific issue. In explaining the American consumer's hesitancy to conserve energy, Milstein (1977) notes that, although the majority of the public is aware of the energy issue, individuals remain skeptical and cynical regarding the nature and seriousness of the problem. Two studies (Kassarjian 1971; Kinnear and Taylor 1973), although performed in the context of societal issues other than energy, have demonstrated the relationship between issue specific concern and societally conscious consumption.

Even where the individual is aware of and legitimately concerned about a societal issue, he may not see the problem as related to his consumption activities. Here again, the self-indulgence aspect of the American consumer's character is germane. The individual has been instructed for decades, by a variety of sources, that his consumption is his own private affair. The link between excesses in consumption and ecological problems has been ignored. The individual's perceived effectiveness as a consumer is then a second dispositional component related to the phenomenon of the self-indulgent American consumer. Results from two empirical studies (Kinnear, Taylor and Ahmed 1974; Webster 1975) have demonstrated a strong correlational link between perceived consumer effectiveness and societally conscious consumption.

Using these two attitudinal components as a starting point, marketing strategies for fostering energy conservation can be developed. Given the present, limited state of knowledge regarding the phenomenon of societally conscious consumption, the strategies suggested below demand empirical evaluation in terms of their efficacy in affecting the cognitive precursors of energy-conscious consumption and in stimulating conservation. The objective of these strategies is long-term attitude change; accordingly; they are potentially most salient to the public policy maker, consumer group, trade association, or any social change agent with a fundamental motive of fostering energy conservation. Since the strategies are basically oriented toward creating primary demand for more energy-efficient products, they are less relevant to the individual firm.

Motivating energy conservation will entail generating communication strategies to influence both issue specific concern and perceived consumer effectiveness. Energy is an extraordinarily complicated problem area, with different sources (for example, government vs. private industry) often offering contradictory information about the problem. Given the complexity of the problem and the apparent contradictions that develop in communications about it, the self-indulgent consumer can usually find a counterargument or identify with a particular source that will allow him to reject the seriousness of the energy issue with a free conscience. To break through individuals' defense mechanisms, simple messages lending themselves to repetition without wearout and emphasizing the grave nature of the energy problem must be developed for mass market dissemination. Probably the most important characteristic of these messages is that they be acceptable to all parties with an interest in energy. Ideally the messages would be presented to the American public by a variety of sources to include private industry, public policy makers, and consumer groups. The public policy maker (the Department of Energy) would have to initiate the process by developing appropriate communications in conjunction with parties such as trade associations and consumer groups. The policy maker could further stimulate the communications process by airing the messages and offering partial subsidation to other groups for their sponsorship of the messages.

Given the self-indulgent character of the American consumer, true issue-specific concern will not develop as long as contradictory or confusing information about the energy problem is being presented to the American public.

Beyond concern for the energy problem, the consumer must be convinced that it is his or her responsibility to take individual action in response to the problem. American consumers must be persuaded that they can be effective in helping alleviate the severity of the energy problem. This will entail changing individuals' perceptions of the impact of their consumption. It will be a difficult task, but the possible pay-outs are enormous in that perceived consumer effectiveness potentially underlies a wide variety of consumption and product utilization behaviors.

To furnish the foundation for modifying perceived consumer effectiveness, individuals must be given basic information that demonstrates how changes in their behavior can significantly influence the amount of energy they use. Regarding the consumption of products, energy efficiency information display programs for automobiles and major appliances mandate that this type of information be supplied to the consumer. Consumers should also be regularly provided with information detailing how much energy they and other consumers are using. For example, this type of information is furnished by the utility meter, which shows the consumer how much energy is being used and details the future cost of continued utilization at the same rate. At present there exists limited empirical evidence (Milstein 1977) to indicate that feedback of behavioral performance in and of itself is an effective means of stimulating conservation.

The public policy maker is becoming more active in the area of providing energy information to consumers. Given this information base, communication strategies could be employed to influence individuals' perceptions of the degree of responsibility they must bear for alleviating the severity of the energy problem through their consumption behavior. For this purpose, strategies based on self-perception theory (Bem 1972) are likely to be more potent than conventional persuasive approaches. A self-perception strategy would attempt to modify the individual's view of himself. The individual needs to perceive himself as a person who takes action on important issues. One self-perception–based strategy that could be adapted for mass market utilization is labeling (Swinyard and Ray 1977). The limited empirical evidence comparing self-perception and persuasive strategies shows that self-perception is significantly more influential, especially when persistence of effects over time is the criterion (Miller, Brickman and Bolen 1975). As suggested for the attitudinal component, issue-specific concern, the efficacy of communications designed to change individuals' perceptions of their effectiveness as consumers would be enhanced by a variety of groups or sources sponsoring and delivering the messages.

The policy maker would be likely to benefit from expanded use of segmentation research in building communications designed to stimulate conservation. As practiced in the private sector, segmentation strategies entail identification of groups in the marketplace. Some of these groups will be pursued as the firm's target markets; others will be ignored because they lack potential. Rothschild (1979) has observed that for many of the problems faced by policy makers all members of society must comply if a given problem is to be solved. That is, the policy maker cannot afford to ignore certain groups in seeking solutions to major social problems. This typifies the situation faced by policy makers in the Department of Energy. For example, DOE has been charged with implementing a consumer education/persuasion program to stimulate widespread use of energy efficiency labels that are due to appear on 13 categories of major home appliances (McNeill and Wilkie 1978). Segmentation research should be beneficial to this problem, even though DOE is not faced with a situation where it will seek to tap the potential of certain segments while ignoring others.

It is likely that different groups in American society will vary in terms of their a priori receptivity to the Energy Efficiency Labeling Program (EELP). Segmentation research regarding the EELP could be oriented toward identifying groups both positively and negatively predisposed toward such a program. By focusing on groups with negative evaluations of the program and attempting to uncover the reasons for the negativity, the policy maker would have an important input for developing communication strategies designed to alter the negative attitudes. Allen and Dillon (1979) report the results of an exploratory study which examined the differential segment receptivity that is likely to exist in the case of the EELP. Two of the three segments identified were essentially negative in their evaluations of the forthcoming EELP. By examining the attitudes, political beliefs, and demographics of the three groups, explanations for the negative evaluations were supplied. These explanations would certainly benefit a communications strategist faced with the task of promoting widespread acceptance of the EELP.

CONCLUSION

The present discussion has suggested that the goal of energy conservation is most appropriately pursued through communication programs that seek, in the long term, to change consumers' attitudes. Communication strategies have been proposed with this purpose in mind, consistent with the notion put forth by Kotler and Zaltman (1971) that marketing skills can have an expanded role in addressing major social problems. Clearly more research is needed in the area of identifying and validating attitudinal constructs that are related to the consumer's self-indulgent nature and

underlie socially conscious consumption actions such as energy conservation. Empirical evaluations are needed regarding the efficacy of communication programs as devices for both modifying these attitudinal constructs and
stimulating energy-conscious behavior, and the marketing discipline certainly can play an active role in these research efforts. However, this
discussion goes a step beyond the idea that marketing skills are applicable in
solving major societal problems such as the energy predicament. Marketing
skills can be useful in developing mechanisms to address directly the cause of
problems such as the energy predicament. Marketers possess the type of
expertise that must be directly brought to bear on the mass consumption–related societal problem if permanent solutions to these problems are to be
found and a free market economic system maintained.

REFERENCES

Allen, C. and W. Dillon (1979), "On Receptivity to Information Furnished by the
Public Policymaker: The Case of Energy." In *Educators' Conference Proceedings*, edited by Niel Beckwith, et al. pp. 550–556. Chicago: American Marketing Association.

Bem, D. (1972), "Self-Perception Theory," in *Advances in Experimental Social
Psychology*, ed. L. Berkowitz, pp. 1–62, New York: Academic Press.

Boulding, Kenneth (1966), "The Economics of the Coming Spaceship Earth," in
Environmental Quality in a Growing Economy, ed. H. Jarret, pp. 3–14,
Baltimore: Johns Hopkins University Press.

Commoner, Barry (1972), *The Closing Circle*, New York: Bantam.

Feldman, Laurence P. (1971), "Societal Adaptation: A New Challenge for Marketing," *Journal of Marketing* 35 (July): 54–60.

Hirsch, Fred (1976), *Social Limits to Growth*, Cambridge: Harvard University Press.

Kassarjian, Harold H. (1971), "Incorporating Ecology into Marketing Strategy: The
Case of Air Pollution," *Journal of Marketing* 36 (July): 61–5.

Kinnear, Thomas and James Taylor (1973), "The Effect of Ecological Concern on
Brand Perceptions," *Journal of Marketing Research* 10 (May): 191–97.

—— and S. Ahmed (1974), "Ecologically Concerned Consumers: Who Are They?"
Journal of Marketing 38 (April): 20–24.

Kotler, Philip and Gerald Zaltman (1971), "Social Marketing: An Approach to
Planned Social Change," *Journal of Marketing* 35 (July): 3–12.

McNeill, Dennis and William Wilkie (1978), "Public Policy and Consumer Information: An Experiment on the Impacts of New Energy Labels," Center for
Consumer Research Working Paper Series, no. 12, Gainesville, FL.: University of Florida.

Meadows, D. et al. (1972), *The Limits to Growth*, London: Earth Island.

Miller, R., P. Brickman and D. Bolen (1975), "Attribution Versus Persuasion as a
Means for Modifying Behavior," *Journal of Personality and Social Psychology* 31 (March): 430–41.

Milstein, Jeffrey (1977), "Attitudes, Knowledge and Behavior of American Consumers Regarding Energy Conservation with Some Implications for Governmental

Action," in *Advances in Consumer Research*, ed. W. Perrault, Jr., vol. 4, pp. 315-21, Ann Arbor, MI.: Association for Consumer Research.

Nicosia, Francesco M. and R. Mayer (1976), "Toward a Sociology of Consumption," *Journal of Consumer Research* 3 (September): 65-75.

Potter, D. (1954), *People of Plenty*, Chicago: University of Chicago Press.

Rothschild, Michael (1979), "Marketing Communications in Nonbusiness Situations or Why It's So Hard to Sell Brotherhood Like Soap," *Journal of Marketing* 43 (Spring): 11-21.

Swinyard, William and Michael Ray (1977), "Advertising-Selling Interactions: An Attribution Theory Experiment," *Journal of Marketing Research* 14 (November): 509-17.

Webster, Fredrick (1975), "Determining the Characteristics of the Socially Conscious Consumer," *Journal of Consumer Research* 2 (December): 188-96.

Whisenhunt, D. (1974), *The Environment and the American Experience*, New York: Kennikat Press.

Willenborg, John F. and Robert E. Pitts (1977), "Gasoline Prices: Their Effect on Consumer Behavior and Attitudes," *Journal of Marketing* 41 (January): 24-31.

11

THE ROLE OF MARKETING IN THE INTRODUCTION OF CONSUMER PRODUCTS BY GOVERNMENT

George Tesar

Opportunities for involvement by governmental units in the design, development, marketing, and control of industrial and consumer products is growing. Virtually every governmental unit is interested in directly communicating with a variety of publics regarding its role, objectives, and performance. The National Aeronautics and Space Administration (NASA), the Department of Energy (DOE), and the Environmental Protection Agency (EPA), among others, are all interested in diffusing new technologies into industrial and consumer markets. The Food and Drug Administration (FDA) and the Department of Health, Education and Welfare (HEW) are interested in the development of standards and regulations for industrial and consumer products. Almost every department and agency is interested in developing and introducing socially relevant programs (Hayden, Tesar and Simon 1978).

Although many programs can be introduced through direct legislative action, there is a need to introduce some socially significant government programs through the free market system directly. As a result, a number of governmental units have become interested in applying marketing tools that traditionally were used by industrial and consumer firms. The diffusion of new technologies by NASA is a case in point.

The energy crisis of the autumn and winter of 1973 underscored the need for developing and applying governmental marketing tools. The energy crisis forced top public policy makers to realize that economic, social, and political stability is dependent on reliable and continuous development, planning, and management of energy and energy-related technologies. It became obvious that governmental units must be instrumental in developing energy sources, reducing energy consumption, and minimizing the dependency on foreign sources of energy (Shonfield 1976).

The need to apply marketing concepts to the energy crisis was further underscored by two fundamental facts. First, rapidly increasing costs of energy had an unprecedented impact on consumers' day-to-day life styles. Second, shortages of energy and petrochemically based raw materials stimulated manufacturers to reexamine their product lines and manufacturing processes.

In response to the energy crisis, consumers were asked to change their driving patterns drastically, adjust their daily habits inside their homes, and conserve energy in general. The majority of consumers were suspicious of these demands (U.S., Comptroller General 1977). They did not clearly understand the implications of these requests. Consequently, public policy makers have had to find new communication techniques to inform the public effectively regarding the importance of the energy crisis both to domestic and foreign policies.

Shortages of energy and petrochemically based raw materials have forced manufacturers of industrial and consumer products to reexamine their entire product development and market introduction strategies. Manufacturers have been compelled to introduce only products that will help their customers to modify individual consumption patterns within the context of the energy crisis. Therefore, manufacturers themselves have had to develop a sound understanding of the energy crisis and the changing needs of their customers ("The Implications of Energy on Marketing" 1978).

The objective of this chapter is to explore the basic issues that influence the need for developing and applying governmental marketing in the current economic, social, and political climate, specifically, the principal marketing tools used by government during the energy crisis, and finally, the effectiveness of the approach used by DOE in the introduction of electric and hybrid vehicles (EHV) in the United States.

ATTITUDINAL CHANGES RELATED TO ENERGY CONSUMPTION

There is an assumption which suggests that society does not fully understand the broad domestic and international dynamics of energy dependency and consumption (Rustow 1977). Specific consumer groups do not clearly understand the role that energy plays in foreign policy; they fail to understand that the reduction of energy consumption is essential in the successful maintenance of sound U.S. economic relationships with the rest of the world.

This fundamental lack of understanding of the relationship between foreign policy and energy consumption is supported by a number of recent domestic social and political trends which tend to be counterproductive in the development of a national energy policy. They are (1) a movement toward consumption equity, (2) an emphasis on nondestructive public policy, and (3) a tendency to guarantee equitable treatment for all constituents. The combination of these trends indicates a greater emphasis among individuals in the society on the enhancement of personal consumption and personal satisfaction at the expense of others.

The move toward consumption equity is inherent in the regulatory framework of the United States. Recently, movement toward consumer, environmental, and health and safety protection have been characteristic of the equity trend, which is reflected in the regulation of the 1960s and 1970s. The implicit goal of this wave of regulation is better distribution of wealth and improvements in the social and economic environment by regulating business more closely (Hayden, Tesar and Simon 1978).

The second trend, nondestructive public policy, is concerned with the implementation of public policy programs necessary to stimulate economic and social progress. This trend tends to decentralize decision making. It relies on local administrative units to demonstrate how a particular decision would influence economic and social activities in a particular geographic area. Interests of small groups often receive preferential treatment over the majority. This action often can result in economic and social dysfunctioning (Schultze 1977).

The tendency to guarantee equitable treatment for all constituents is deeply imbedded in the political fiber of U.S. society. Representatives of various constituencies are discouraged from developing and implementing public policy programs that are inconsistent with the objectives and interests of a given constituency. Consequently, this tendency reduces the effectiveness of public policy programs and often reduces propensity for change.

When the above attitudinal changes are superimposed on the energy crisis and examined within the context of the perceived role of the government as protecting the standard of living of the entire society, it becomes clear that public policymaking will have to find new and more effective ways to economic and social choices to society. Therefore, within the context of economic and social realities, governmental units will have to develop strategies to communicate and market these choices to society.

NEED FOR DEVELOPMENT OF APPROPRIATE MARKETING TOOLS

Marketing of socially relevant choices by governmental units requires a systematic reexamination of the general philosophy of marketing. Government marketing differs both in nature and in scope from conventional profit-oriented marketing. Conventional profit-oriented marketing focuses on the development, pricing, promotion, and distribution of products and services to individual customers at a profit. Government marketing also can differ from "social marketing," which focuses on offering public goods, services, and ideas to specific segments of society (Kotler and Zaltman 1971).

Government marketing is perceived by top public policy makers as a relatively narrow effort formulated to design, implement, and control socially relevant programs to maintain and improve the standard of living through maximization of domestic and foreign policy objectives.

Within the framework of public policy, government marketing is constrained. Individual governmental units cannot directly promote or advertise products or services in commercial markets; they can only communicate with groups in a descriptive and informative manner. They cannot develop products or services for direct commercial sale at a profit. They cannot operate a formal distribution system unless they have a special charter, as is the case with the U.S. Post Office. Government units also cannot develop pricing strategies for products and services outside of the direct or indirect taxation process.

An increasing number of policymakers suggest that it is the responsibility of government to stimulate socially relevant programs within the context of the above constraints. These same policy makers generally agree on three objectives as a basis for governmental marketing: (1) the need to promote systematically public policy issues—a form of public relations; (2) the need to research and identify economically based societal needs and consumption issues—a form of marketing research; and (3) the need to develop fundamental concepts characteristic of government-based economic objectives—a form of applied marketing.

Fragments of each component of governmental marketing are emerging independently in various governmental units. These fragments are not integrated into an overall framework because the individual governmental units often single out a specific marketing tool or approach and rely on it exclusively. Commercial demonstrations, for example, have been identified as a marketing approach that is often used to introduce new technologies into commercial markets, and the approach has become a principal component of governmental marketing today.

DEMONSTRATION PROJECTS AS A MARKETING TOOL

The demonstration concept focuses on two objectives: (1) to identify opportunities to accelerate commercial application of new technologies; and at the same time, to provide federal assistance for participation in demonstration projects; and (2) to enter into cooperative agreements with nongovernmental entities to demonstrate the technical feasibility and economic potential of energy-related technologies on a prototype or full-scale basis.

The basic objective of commercial demonstration projects is to stimulate diffusion of technical innovation including: (1) generating new information to aid potential adopters in deciding whether or not to adopt a new technological innovation; (2) generating significant levels of awareness among the relevant publics and providing them with opportunities to examine the usefulness and applicability of a technical innovation; and (3) stimulating those environmental changes necessary for widespread adoption by the majority of publics.

When the demonstration approach is introduced as part of governmental marketing, a number of basic problems become apparent. Conceptually, there appear to be two types of demonstrations, each with a different set of objectives. One type of demonstration effort is a test to determine whether or not the development of a new socially relevant technology is feasible and adequate in a controlled environment. This type of demonstration is concerned with the resolution of problems on a small scale so that these problems will not be present in a large-scale application.

Another type of demonstration is designed to illustrate the feasibility of a specific technology to potential users, investors, regulators, and the general public. This type of demonstration is particularly relevant when the support of diverse groups is essential in the success of the new technology. The first type of demonstration is labeled a *technical demonstration* and the second a *commercial demonstration* (Tesar and Cavusgil 1978).

In the context of conventional marketing, a technical demonstration is normally perceived as the engineering or pilot plant prototype—a phase in the product or process development cycle. The major objective is to demonstrate the technical feasibility of a new product or process. Technical demonstration is the responsibility of the initiator or innovator of the research effort and is considered to be one of the steps leading to the commercialization or market introduction of the innovation.

Commercial demonstration is associated with the operational prototype in the product or process development cycle. The operational prototype is frequently the result of the product development cycle. The operational prototype incorporates the new technology ready for commercial application. With the introduction of an operational prototype, all the technical problems are assumed to have been solved. The primary objective of commercial demonstration is to overcome market and environmental barriers and to enhance consumer acceptance of the innovation. It is considered the last step in the product or process development cycle.

In the application of demonstrations in government marketing the differences between technical demonstration and commercial demonstration have not been clearly stated. It appears that the demonstrations are treated as if they had common sets of characteristics: (1) both types of demonstrations are supported by federal funds; (2) in both demonstrations the private sector is actively involved; (3) both demonstrations are attempting to stimulate technological changes through development of concepts, products, and processes; and (4) both demonstrations are focusing on operations in the real world environment.

An examination of past demonstration projects helps to explain the underlying confusion over the differences. Traditionally, public funds were allocated only for research and development, the only exception being national defense. New technologies were developed under the management of specific governmental units; the market introduction of the new technologies and the investment decisions related to the new technologies were delegated to the private sector. The importance of the energy issue in the United States today led public policy makers away from this approach. In the case of DOE, it was perceived that a bridging mechanism was needed to maintain development of energy alternatives in a high state of readiness and to facilitate the implementation of energy technology alternatives before conventional market incentives are present (Tesar and Cavusgil 1978).

Most of the demonstration projects sponsored in the past can be classified as technical demonstrations. A RAND Corporation study indicates that, out of 24 demonstrations studied, seven resulted in significant diffusion of technology, while five demonstrations failed completely (Johnson, Merrow and Baer 1975). The common factors that contributed to successful execution of demonstration projects were: (1) all technical problems were resolved and the latest technology was well under control; (2) the private sector shared the costs and risks with the federal government—demonstrations funded entirely by the federal government produced little or no diffusion; (3) projects were initiated by private firms or local public agencies; (4) a strong industrial system for commercialization existed—diffusion generally is faster if the market and the distribution environment is conducive to the introduction of the new technology; (5) all components needed for commercialization participated, including potential manufacturers, distributors, consumers, and regulators; (6) tight time constraints were absent; and (7) political pressures from proponents and opponents of the new technology were absent (Johnson, Merrow, and Baer 1975).

These experiences clearly indicate that the success of a commercial demonstration effort is dependent on whether the new technology already exists and can be directly applied in commercial markets. The experiences also suggest that there is a significant difference between technical and commercial demonstration. Both can be incorporated in the government marketing effort; however, it is important to realize that the objectives of each are different. This difference is apparent when they are examined within the context of industrial and consumer marketing efforts. In a narrow sense the technical demonstration can be compared to the research and development effort as it is applied to the product or process development effort; the commercial demonstration can be compared to the development of marketing strategy including the test marketing effort.

THE ELECTRIC AND HYBRID VEHICLE
DEMONSTRATION PROJECT

On September 17, 1976, Congress approved the Electric and Hybrid Vehicle Research, Development, and Demonstration Act (P.L. 94–413) over the president's veto. The act directed Energy Research and Development Administration (ERDA) to advance electric and hybrid vehicle (EHV) technology and establish a rigorous schedule for in-use demonstrations. ERDA was also authorized to provide loan guarantee and planning grant incentives to encourage small business to participate in the research, development, and demonstration of EHV technology. Under Public Law 95–91, the Department of Energy Organization Act, DOE assumed the responsibility for the development and commercialization effort of EHV from ERDA.

Based on the results of studies conducted during the first year of the program, DOE recommended that Congress amend P.L. 94–413 to allow more flexible scheduling of procurement of vehicles allocated for the demonstration and to allow expansion of the loan guarantee program. Congress adopted these recommendations through specific provisions of the Department of Energy Act of 1978—Civilian Applications (P.L. 95–238). The existing DOE program reflects P.L. 94–413 as amended by Congress in 1978.

Congress approved introduction of 7,500 EHVs by 1984. The entire demonstration effort is to continue through fiscal year 1986. Participants in the demonstration will include consumers and organizations involved in the manufacture, distribution, and operation of EHVs. The legislation also indirectly included systematic stimulation of the EHV manufacturing industry.

More specifically, P.L. 94–413 as amended in 1978 provides for the following activities: research and development projects dealing with EHVs; promulgation of performance and safety standards for EHVs; demonstrations involving federal, state, and local governments, private individuals, and commercial and industrial organizations; a program of loan guarantees and small business planning grants; specific studies on barriers to the use of EHVs; and provisions for small business involvement.

The first objective of the demonstration project is to identify feasible missions within the capability of existing EHVs, life-cycle costs of EHVs, including battery replacement, market and environmental barriers, and infrastructure requirements. Second, the project hopes to provide various types of information: market pull stimulation of EHVs; factors affecting consumer acceptability of EHVs; requirements for research and development and specific product improvements; methods to overcome market and environmental barriers; public awareness information; and supporting infrastructure. The demonstration project's third objective is to stimulate strong commitment by participants and continuing interest in EHVs in colleges and universities.

To achieve the objectives of the demonstration project, DOE is responsible for the selection of a variety of local site operators to purchase, maintain, service, and control the vehicles. The site operators are responsible for providing their own management and sharing costs with DOE. They are also responsible for contributing to the development of market demand for EHVs in their local area. Site operators are obliged to support the infra-structure, assist in the development of a data base for DOE, and generate a strong public image for EHVs. Finally, it is the responsibility of the site operators to develop a good understanding of the market and environmental barriers for EHVs, including licensing problems, traffic control, insurance, and financial data.

The list of a site operator's responsibilities suggest that the assumed marketing strategy of DOE is to market EHVs through the site operators. DOE relies on the expertise of the site operators to develop a dynamic market segment for EHVs. Consequently, the marketing effort of the governmental unit is reduced to the planning and operational function only; the development and implementation of the actual marketing strategy is left to the site operator. A number of top public policy makers agree that this is the intent of government marketing today. They suggest that this will be the course that government marketing will take in the future.

In June 1978, five site operators for the DOE's demonstration project were selected. The number of site operators will increase in the future and will vary according to topographical and climatic locations throughout the United States to assure uniform integration of EHVs into the market.

GOVERNMENT MARKETING AND MARKET INTRODUCTION OF EHVs

When the objectives of the EHV demonstration project are examined within the context of government marketing as it is perceived by public policy makers today, it is evident that the overall concept of demonstrations is consistent with the basic government marketing framework. The demon-stration project is designed to provide market information needed to integrate EHVs successfully into the existing life styles of consumers. Information regarding consumers' life styles will be generated through the application of marketing research. Development of a sound competitive and distributive environment for EHVs will be accomplished through syste-matic development of marketing strategies. Finally, the demonstration project is charged with the development of an effective promotional and publicity program to diffuse information regarding market introduction and market acceptance of EHVs. This task will be accomplished through the development and application of promotional strategies and public relations.

Although a normative framework for government marketing suggests that multiple marketing tools and principles could be used to achieve the objective of the EHVs demonstration project, the operational framework does not explicitly recognize these tools or formulate specific strategies needed to realize the objective. In reality, formulation of the specific strategies is left to individual site operators who become a part of the demonstration project. Consequently, the success of the demonstration project depends greatly on individual site operators' ability to formulate marketing plans and develop marketing strategies for their demonstration sites as well as the EHVs.

Governmental units should not let individual site operators who participate in demonstration projects formulate marketing plans and develop marketing strategies. Governmental units should be more involved in these activities, primarily because the success of a demonstration projects depends on the implementation of integrated marketing strategies. Since the objectives of governmental units are fundamentally different from the objectives of individual site operators, the marketing plans and strategies should be clearly formulated by the governmental units and a thorough process of systematic implementation and control passed on to the individual site operators. Clearly more conceptual and theoretical development of governmental marketing is necessary before this can be successfully accomplished.

REFERENCES

Hayden, Bryan, George Tesar and William E. Simon (1978), *The Changing Nature of Business-Government Relations*, Washington, D.C.: Center for Strategic and International Studies, Georgetown University.

"The Implications of Energy on Marketing" (1978), *Nielsen Researcher*, no. 5: 2–11.

Johnson, L., E. Merrow and W. Baer (1975), *Analysis of Federally Funded Demonstration Projects*, RAND.

Kotler, Philip and Gerald Zaltman (1971), "Social Marketing: An Approach to Planned Social Change," *Journal of Marketing* 35 (July): 3–12.

Rustow, Dankwart A. (1977), "U.S.-Saudi Relations and the Oil Crisis of the 1980s," *Foreign Affairs* 55 (April): 494–516.

Schultze, Charles L. (1977), "The Public Use of Private Interest," *Harper's* (May): 43–62.

Shonfield, Andrew (1976), *International Economic Relations*, Beverly Hills, Calif.: Sage.

Tesar, George and S. Tamer Cavusgil (1978), "Market Introduction of Innovations by Governmental Agencies," Paper presented at the Annual Conference of the Product Development and Management Association, Boston, October 6.

U.S. Comptroller General (1977), *Report to the Congress, Convincing the Public to Buy the More Fuel-Efficient Cars: An Urgent National Need*, CED-77-107 (August 10). Washington, D.C.: Government Printing Office.

U.S., Department of Energy (1978), *Charpie Task Force Report; The Demonstration Project as a Procedure for Accelerating the Application of New Technology*, vol. 1 (February). Washington, D.C. Department of Energy.

12

THE SITUATION CONFRONTING INTRODUCTION OF THE ANTHONY DOLLAR

Claude R. Martin, Jr.

A major step in the reconfiguration of the nation's currency system took place on July 1, 1979, when the Susan B. Anthony one dollar coin was placed in circulation. Since that time the news media have reported that the coin appears to have been an initial marketing failure. While news accounts are not definitive evidence, they do provide a reasonable warning about market acceptance. A sampling of these news accounts shows the following:

> Susan B. Anthony doesn't get around much anymore . . . a poll of banks, department stores and coin collectors turned up only negative comments about the new coin. (*Detroit News* July 18, 1979)
>
> Is the Anthony dollar another Edsel? (*Detroit Free Press* August 17, 1979)
>
> Is the Anthony dollar a three dollar bill? . . . The dollar that nobody wants. . . . In Philadelphia, $8 million in uncirculated Anthony dollars. (*New York Times* September 2, 1979)
>
> Since July 20, demand has plummeted . . . most of the coins are mired in banks. (*Michigan Daily* September 15, 1979)
>
> The Federal Reserve Bank of Buffalo said that after the initial demand for the coin, orders from financial institutions have been "very, very low." (*Buffalo Evening News* August 20, 1979)
>
> Anthony dollar coin is a huge failure. It seems safe to conclude that the public has decided that it does not want the Susan B. Anthony dollar coin. (*Scranton Times* August 21, 1979)
>
> The feminists' triumph in getting a woman's likeness on an American coin has turned to ashes. The Susan B. Anthony dollar is a costly fiasco, rejected by merchants, bankers and the public alike. (*Jack Anderson*, September, 1979)

This chapter summarizes a key portion of the marketing research undertaken in advance of the coin's introduction that predicted many of the difficulties now being experienced. The objective is to illustrate how marketing research can be used in government to define marketing problems associated with the introduction of a new product—here, an addition to the coin and currency system. Unfortunately research alone is not enough; the strategic implementation of research was apparently not undertaken by the Bureau of the Mint. The bulk of the research findings appear to have been ignored. Frank DeLeo of the Mint commenting on the research said, "Claude [Martin] is living in a theoretical world" (*Michigan Daily* September 15, 1979). Stella Hackel, director of the Mint, said about the research, "That's his research project, period. It may or may not be valid" (*New York Times* September 2, 1979). The reaction of Mint Director Hackel to Jack Anderson was to complain that "the university had no business testing public acceptance of the coin."

Despite Hackel's comment, the research undertaken by the Graduate School of Business Administration of the University of Michigan was commissioned by the Federal Reserve System to study acceptance of the coin prior to its introduction. The focal point of the research was (1) to identify the major participants in the currency system who would be instrumental to that acceptance, and (2) to analyze the key problems and opportunities that the government faced in conjunction with the introduction of the coin.

ANTHONY DOLLAR—THE RATIONALE

Prior to examining the research it is necessary to understand the governmental reasoning behind the Anthony dollar. Technically the Anthony dollar is a substitute for the bulkier Eisenhower dollar coin. However, the intent of both the U.S. Bureau of the Mint and the Federal Reserve System was the have the coin become a more integral part of the circulating currency system.

> The current Eisenhower copper-nickel dollar does not circulate due primarily to its cumbersome weight and size . . . the Susan B. Anthony \$1 coin is only 9% greater in diameter than the quarter and only 43% heavier. Compared to the current Eisenhower coin, it is approximately 2/3 the diameter and 1/3 the weight.
>
> The current \$1 coin costs about 8¢ each to produce as compared to the new coin, which will be 3¢ each. This is a cost savings of greater than 60% per coin . . . based on production figures for the fiscal year 1978, the new coin would save \$4.5 million per year. (U.S., Congress, House, 1978)

While the above statement outlines some of the incentives for issuing the new coin, there are additional cost savings to various components of the federal government that far transcend the savings generated by substitution for the Eisenhower dollar. In 1979, there were estimated to be $3 billion in Federal Reserve one dollar notes in circulation. The demand for these notes has been increasing steadily—principally driven by inflationary pressure—to the point of production capacity of the Bureau of Printing and Engraving (U.S., Department of the Treasury, 1976) Without making changes in the physical quality of the note, the need for additional capital expenditures by the bureau was deemed to be imminent. As a result there was considerable congressional testimony stressing the practicality of a dollar coin replacing part or all of the paper dollar note circulation, now 60 percent of the total paper currency production (U.S., Congress, House, 1978). This substitution for the paper note and resultant economies was based on the fact that the one dollar note wears out in approximately 18 months and needs to be replaced, at a cost of 1.8¢ each. While the dollar coin costs more to initially manufacture, the life expectancy is 15 years. The direct substitution of the coin for the paper note would mean a production cost savings to the Treasury Department of 80 percent (U.S., Congress, House, 1978).

However, even production cost savings potential is outweighed by the prospect of more substantive distribution and handling savings by the Federal Reserve System. The Federal Reserve Bank of Chicago devised an estimated range of savings to the "Fed" from elimination of the one dollar note. Using 1976 data as a base, the estimated savings range from $17.9 million to $34.9 million. The lower estimate does not account for the new one dollar coin but only assumes a substitution of the present two dollar bill on a 100 percent basis for the one dollar note. In other words, a saving of $17.9 million by changing the lowest denomination of paper currency to the two dollar bill and having no new one dollar coin (*Dollar Coin Study* 1977). Obviously a system that would combine the one dollar Anthony coin and the two dollar note would effectuate savings somewhere within the $17.9 to $34.9 million range.

In its preliminary study for the new coin, the mint concluded that the two dollar bill reintroduction was a failure (U.S., Department of the Treasury 1976). This conclusion was reinforced by the circulation data of the Federal Reserve System and our preliminary in-depth interviews with major participants in the currency system. It was precisely this coupling of a distribution cost savings with the "ghost" of the two dollar bill failure that caused the Federal Reserve to commission the University of Michigan study of the new one dollar coin.

RESEARCH—PLAN, METHODOLOGY, AND DATA

Despite several "new product introductions" in the past several years (Kennedy half-dollar, Eisenhower dollar, and two dollar bill), there is little available basic research concerning user rates, perceptions, and attitudes toward the currency system. The need for a fundamental understanding of the key participants in the system was apparent if the Federal Reserve System was to undertake a marketing plan for the new coin.

The initial research step was to review secondary information concerning coin and currency, most of which furnished by the Federal Reserve or the Treasury Department. This was coupled with a series of in-depth interviews with top management of three major armored car services, the National Automatic Merchandising Association, the Bureau of the Mint, the Bureau of Printing and Engraving, and several major retailers. An understanding of the fundamental structure of the coin and currency distribution system as presented in Figure 12.1 was the outcome of these discussions.

First, there are the Bureau of the Mint and the Bureau of Printing and Engraving, the manufacturers coin and paper currency, respectively. The role of the Federal Reserve banks is to act as middlemen between those manufacturing facilities and the wholesaler/retailer in the system, the commercial banks. These banks provide coin and currency on demand to other financial institutions (savings and loan associations, credit unions, and so on), retailers, and consumers. Retailers and other financial institutions also act as additional middlemen between the consumer and supplier in the system. Interviews with these participants in the system brought out the fact that a basic "pull" rather than "push" strategy exists. In other words, the coin and currency are "pulled" through the system principally by consumer and retailer demands, rather than "pushed" onto the consumer and retailer by banks and the government.

The next step in the research was to conduct additional in-depth interviews with differing types of retailers and with commercial banks in order to identify more specifically the key decision makers in the system. Discussions reinforced the "pull" nature of the system and pointed to characterizing the monetary market as having many users but only a small number of decision makers. While the consumer is important in the system, the key decision on type of coin and currency to be used was identified as resting with certain types of retailers. The research to this point showed that retailers make certain assumptions about consumer preferences and develop their monetary supply mix accordingly. Perhaps the best illustration concerns demand for the two dollar note. Retailers reported they did not order the two dollar note from banks because they perceived the consumer, their customers, would not accept them. This was reinforced by the fact that the two dollar bill adds a degree of handling and storage inconvenience for the retailer.

Based upon the initial two layers of in-depth interviews, the research target for phase three was determined to be consumers and those retailers who are heavy users of coin and currency. Initial research showed that valid evaluation by consumers and retailers required the physical manipulation of

FIGURE 12.1

Flow of Currency

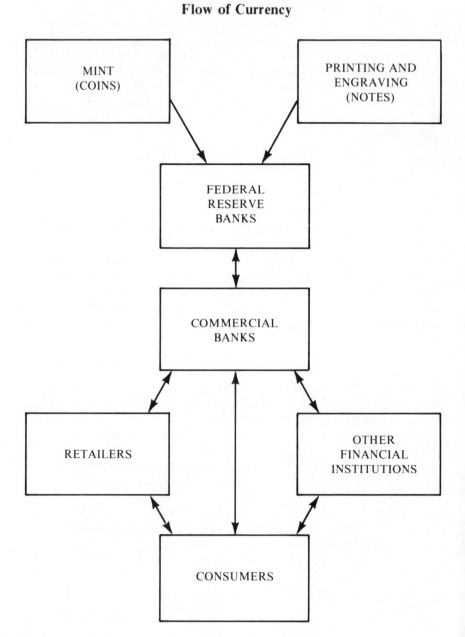

the coin. The budget commitment of the Federal Reserve and the limited availability of mockups of the coin forced the use of small groups of persons in the third phase. Thus, it was decided to use focus group interviews. The focus group technique involves "a loosely structured interview conducted by a trained moderator among a small group of respondents simultaneously" (Kinnear and Taylor 1979, p. 425).

In sum, preliminary research identified three key segments to acceptance of the coin: (1) large retailers, both grocery and other chains; (2) fast food merchants; and (3) consumers. These groups were the participants in focus group sessions held during October 1978, nine months before the anticipated introduction of the Susan B. Anthony dollar. The sessions were conducted by an experienced focus group moderator, with the author monitoring each session via closed-circuit television.

RESEARCH FINDINGS

During the preliminary phases of our research, the participants, particularly bankers, armored car operators, and retailers emphasized that retailers were the key to successful introduction of the new coin. They did not suggest that other groups were not important, but they did judge that retailers were the major decision maker in whether the coin was used extensively.

The results of the focus group interviews confirmed that retailers were the key. The overall evaluation of the focus group discussions defined consumers as users of money rather than key decision makers. Thus, there is an important strategic implication that any marketing by the Federal Reserve or the Mint should have been directed primarily toward decision makers, retailers, and secondarily toward users, consumers.

The basis for this overall evaluation of the relative roles of the retailer and consumer and the major findings concerning the problems and opportunities in marketing the new coin are detailed below.

Large Grocery Chains

Large chain grocery stores are classified as net receivers of five dollar bills and higher, and net users of two and one dollar bills as well as coins. In reality, little use is made of the two dollar bill. As net users of twos, ones, and coins, they make routine cash requests from local banks prior to daily preparation of their cash drawers. Limited volumes of currency and coin are kept in store safes, and the differences in net cash flow are maintained by armored car service. Even though certain days of the week are predictably high sales volume days, the cash requirements of large grocery chains are steady over time; thus, till preparation is usually a standardized procedure recognizing cash drawer, safe volume, and cash flow constraints.

Beyond till preparation, money is important in two other aspects. First, point-of-sale operations involve the transfer of limited amounts of cash between customer and cashier. Second, cash room operations involving sorting, counting, verifying, and wrapping of money consume many additional hours. Some of the larger chains have the benefit of modern sorting, counting, and wrapping machines, but many still employ manual cash room procedures. The substitution of the Anthony coin for the dollar bill would not interrupt the cash-ordering process or the transportation aspects (since "value" has not changed, and present specifications of the coin indicate volumes of like quantities of one dollar coins and one dollar bills are nearly equal). However, the cash drawer preparation would be significantly disrupted with rearrangement of most present drawer setups. Potential chaos among grocers would develop unless coin introduction is accompanied by additional action designed to provide cash drawer preparation instruction.

Efficiency found in point-of-sale procedures is threatened due to potential confusion of the dollar coin with the quarter, as well as the disruption of the change distribution procedures that are behaviorally set in most cashiers. Alteration of the money structure would require in-depth educating of cashiers and other sales personnel so that the fear of making errors is reduced, the chance of embarrassment removed, and claim of endangered profit margins eliminated. Cash room operations would be directly affected by the proposed monetary system. Since a new coin is involved, new or adjusted equipment would be needed to count, sort, and wrap the coin. The actual costs involved in capital outlay would be less for those grocery chains which do not possess modern counting machinery. Once again, pick-up service, if based on value or volume, should not increase due to the coin if inventories are held to their normal levels. It does seem reasonable to believe, however, that the additional weight of the Anthony coin over the dollar bill would eventually find its way into the fee charged by the armored car industry. Individual store safe capacities could also be a problem if the coin represents additions to cash inventory rather than substitution of the one dollar bill.

Finally, there is an overall lack of meaningful incentive on the part of most retailers to promote the use of the proposed monetary system. On the other hand, the new coin offers these retailers several opportunities. In the cash preparation and point-of-sale areas, the Anthony dollar when used in place of the dollar bill would eliminate the problems found in handling new bills (sticking together, rigidness). There is a strong potential for a decrease in transaction time once familiarity with the coin is established, since coins are easier to handle and disperse. Decreased transaction time means shorter customer lines, increased productivity (customers serviced per unit of time), and favorable customer reaction in the long run. Even though these savings are small when examined individually, in the aggregate the potential benefits become visible. In the cash room, manual counting of coins is quicker (stacking method) than currency, and the need for verifying is removed: both fully counteract the additional burden of wrapping the new dollar coin.

On a theoretical level, a new monetary system would offer a valuable promotional opportunity for government that could be strategically developed in many ways. Beyond a promotional framework, an opportunity for "image boosting" would be available. In the current political climate of Proposition 13 and other tax relief drives, the idea of government spending is a salient and emotional issue for most Americans. The government's drive to reduce the costs of producing currency and coin would be a highly visible campaign, one which could be used to the retailers' advantage. Any retailer able to establish a reputation for doing its part in trying to save tax dollars would be able to counteract some of the behavioral resistance of its customers.

Large Retail Chains

Large retail chains are somewhat more extensively distributed geographically than the large chain grocery stores. Companies such as Sears, K-Mart, and J.C. Penney are examples in this category. These organizations are a primary dispensor (user) of small currency and coin. The largest of these (such as Sears) employ sophisticated but expensive cash room machinery which enables fast, labor efficient cash-handling procedures. The rest are split between conventional cash room machinery and manual operations.

As with grocery chains, retail chains use cash (twos, ones, and coins) in cash drawer preparation, point-of-purchase procedures, and cash room operations. Generally, more credit transactions occur at the retail level than at groceries; however, the use of large bills and personal checks is becoming more widespread in both segments. The problems facing these large retailers are similar to those of grocery chains. The cash operations are nearly identical, although the nature of merchandise sold is different. In addition, the trend toward use of credit and larger bills has the potential of causing greater chaos in the retailer's cash drawer, suggesting conversion to newer cash register technology. Altering consumer spending habits and preferences is a monumental task unless approached uniformly. With respect to the Anthony dollar, if the seldom used fifty cent coin and the competing one dollar bill are continued in circulation, not only will cash drawer overcrowding become a problem but the breaking down of consumer preferences for the current system will be impossible. Storage capacity of retail safes is similar to groceries in that any general increase in total cash levels creates a shortage of space.

Retailers view coin conversion costs as a risk, since consumer acceptance of the coin is not guaranteed. Conversion would include cash drawer rearrangement, cash ordering changes, modification of cash room machinery, renegotiation of armored car contracts, and education of personnel. Businesses relying on manual cash room operations would probably be affected most in the long run; however, most new high-speed machinery in the field is designed to handle only the quarter and smaller, making equipment modification expensive. Conventional sorter-counters can usually process up to 400 coins per minute, and the coin wrapper an average of 15 rolls per minute. The price range of sorter-counters is $1,800 to $5,100; the average wrapper costs about $1,100. Conversion cost estimates are about 20 percent of original cost, with a time lag of six months. Conversion would be impossible if the fifty cent coin stays on the cash market, since conventional coin sorters can handle only six coins.

The retailers' major complaint is that no great advantage of the proposed monetary system is outwardly visible. This makes consumer acceptance a big "if." Tax dollar savings through government cost reductions seem too far removed from the immediacy of the typical consumer, and the disruption of learned preferences and behavior patterns would create confusion and negativism. The large retailer does not wish to become a target at which those negative reactions might be directed.

As with large chain grocery stores, large retailers have the opportunity of capitalizing on a salient consumer issue: reducing governmental costs. A customer would be uncomfortable using the dollar coin in place of the dollar bill at first; however, knowing that the coin costs less than half as much to produce as the current silver dollar and that its longevity makes it much more economical than the current dollar bill would quiet some vocal dissent. In cash room operations, cash handling would be simplified with the elimination of the tedious counting and verifying of one dollar bills. The definite shape and tightly controlled dimensions of any coin facilitate automatic handling, which is widely used by larger retailers. The coin would even precipitate an increase in automated operations industry-wide, since note-handling machines are slower and less efficient and experience a higher degree of outage or breakdown than coin-handling machines. In those retail establishments which still rely on manual operations, the increased use of coins might initiate purchase of automated equipment, initially increasing capital costs but in the long run saving labor dollars.

Fast Food Retailers

This large volume segment is made of businesses (primarily franchises) that feature limited menus and emphasize fast, dependable service at relatively low prices. Many names are familar in this area, especially in the hamburger market; however, the more aggressive competition has in recent years expanded into new areas such as roast beef, fish, chicken, pizza, and Mexican food.

Cash transactions in this segment are marked by frequent repetition and relatively low dollar amounts. Most fast food retailers are classified as net receivers of one dollar bills, but this can vary from one establishment to the next. As families opt more frequently for the convenience of a fast food meal, the picture of a net receiver of one dollar bills shifts to one of net dispenser.

As could be expected, fast food retailers are concerned with similar aspects of cash operations discussed in the large grocery chain segment. However, space restrictions are usually greater so that cash inventory levels are limited in scope, requiring daily (sometimes more frequent) pickups and deliveries of cash, and often allowing for skeleton cash room operations.

The key factor to cash handling in this segment is transaction time. Fast food businesses thrive on volume; cash window operations are engineered down to the most achievable level of time humanly necessary to carry out the cashier function. Interrupting this standardized operation would most likely interrupt current industry cost structures, unless any inconvenience factor is negligible. As net receivers of dollar bills (and potentially the same for the dollar coin), the fast food retailers would face increased cash room burdens, raising the possibility of large-scale conversion costs, equipment purchases, and manpower scarcity. However, retailers that find themselves closer to the net dispenser of dollar bill classification would not feel the effects of the new system as directly on cash room operations as on point-of-sale procedures. Addition of the Anthony dollar with no reciprocal removals of other denominations requires changes in cash drawer layout, adds weight and bulk to already congested safes, increases manpower requirements to roll coins for deposit, creates confusion on the part of employees, slows down transaction time (only during adoption period), and, most important, jeopardizes competitive positions if consumer reaction initiates changes in "brand loyalty" in the mass of fast food establishments.

The high sales volume of this segment provides an opportunity for rapid introduction of the new system. Moreover, the frequent promotions of these companies are another opportunity for a tie-in campaign to the Anthony dollar. In many cases this will be approachable on a national scale, making mass exposure of the monetary system potentially more attainable. Also, fast food retailers could be instrumental in quickly removing the dollar note from circulation once they decide to substitute coin for bills. The national organization structure is a strong factor which could be strategically employed to relay information continuously to the consumer at various stages in the promotional program.

This segment could realize benefits of decreased transaction time and easier cash handling, but none of these perceived benefits are considered substantial.

Consumers

Consumers were the largest segment in this analysis. Initially, we examined male and female consumers separately because of their traditionally contrasting purchasing behaviors; however, these distinctions proved to be insignificant in terms of segmentation. Female consumers normally use small currency and coin to pay for routine grocery purchases, meals outside the home, and a variety of other small value items. Generally, women carry $10 to $50, which they obtain from the bank or by cashing a check.

Among female consumers there is a fear of theft and a concern for availability. Women reported that these factors limit their personal cash consumption. Therefore, the total amount of cash is generally less than $50—in bills less than twenty dollar denominations. Women prefer old bills to new and are more likely to accumulate coins, despite their tendency to refrain from the use of the fifty cent coin. Women appear to be receptive to the concept of reduced government expenditures but are not eager to alter their spending behavior patterns drastically to effect any cost reduction program.

Male consumers do not vary significantly from the demand behavior outlined above; however, they are less likely to accumulate coins (except as collectors), despite their high frequency of coin use (phone, parking, tips, tolls, and so on). Men are most concerned with pocket bulging and wear, and they fear that changing the monetary system may add fuel to the inflationary fire. As with female consumers, the goal of reduced government spending registers positive responses with most male consumers, although that is partially muted by a dislike of government interference in their personal lives.

Consumers as a group show a strong and steady demand for small currency and coin. Any alteration in the monetary system would be felt immediately and deeply.

The basic problem in introducing the new monetary system to the consumer is the lack of perceived benefits. This indicates that there is no inherent product demand because there is satisfaction with the current system. The problem of attempting to alter consumer habits is serious because they perceive no need for the changes. Potential confusion with the quarter, general fear of the inflationary consequences of the proposed move, and the distrust of big government in individuals' lives are all factors threatening program success.

An additional consumer problem can be illustrated by examining their track record with the fifty cent coin and the two dollar bill; both are dismal failures in term of healthy market demand. Consumer behavior must be learned, and to the present no force has been strong enough to stimulate consumer acceptance of these two currency products.

The key opportunities and benefits for consumers are difficult to isolate. One possibility is that governmental cost savings are a politically salient issue to most consumers. Modifying the money consumers use does cause disruptions and reactions. Demonstrating that their sacrifice has purpose would at least make the program appear logical.

Reduction of government costs is perhaps a salient issue, but it is too far removed from the consumers' daily lives to be seen as a strong benefit to them. Therefore, direct benefits to the consumer must be developed, prioritized, and publicized. Convenience factors such as actual reduction of pocket change, ease of handling, and increased selection in automated purchases are possibilities.

Novelty itself may be a positive factor in the introductory period; however, this benefit will only aid in modifying consumer habits and preferences in the introductory stage. Once the novelty of the coin wears off, this opportunity will be lost.

SUMMARY AND CONCLUSIONS

The intent of this chapter was to outline the major problems and opportunities involved in introducing the Anthony dollar to the essential retailer and consumer sectors. This introduction presented a challenge for the strategic planners in the federal government and a background for future public policy decisions concerning the currency and coin system. Unfortunately, though, many dimensions of the challenge outlined here seem to have been ignored.

The regrettable point is that the cost savings to the government in both manufacturing and initial distribution are substantive. Government marketers needed to address the problem of consumer satisfaction with the present currency system and the attendant hesitancy to change. Retailers recognized this and have reacted strongly to government attempts to use a "push" strategy. The essence of effectively marketing the coin indicates a "pull" strategy. While there are some positive opportunities for certain retailers, the realistic perception that consumers are satisfied with the present system and are reluctant to change presents a real obstacle to a "pull" marketing strategy by the government. Viable benefits for both retailers and consumers must be developed more carefully, and then used to formulate strategic programs.

REFERENCES

Buffalo Evening News, August 20, 1979.
Chicago Sun Times, September 26, 1979.

Detroit Free Press, August 17, 1979.

Detroit News, July 18, 1979.

Dollar Coin Study (1977), Chicago: Federal Reserve Bank of Chicago, p. 2.

Kinnear, Thomas C. and James R. Taylor (1979), *Marketing Research; An Applied Approach*, p. 425, New York: McGraw-Hill.

Michigan Daily, September 15, 1979.

New York Times, September 2, 1979.

Scranton Times, August 21, 1979.

U.S., Congress, House, (1978), *Hearing Before the Subcommittee on Historic Preservation and Coinage on H.R. 12474*, 95th Cong. 2nd sess., May 17, Washington, D.C.: Government Printing Office, pp. 7–12.

U.S., Department of the Treasury (1976), *Small Dollar Coin*, Washington, D.C.: Marketing Division of The Bureau of the Mint.

III

USING MARKETING RESEARCH

INTRODUCTION TO PART III

Throughout the public sector, research activity is pervasive and data are plentiful; however, accurate and timely information for policy decisions is a scarce and valuable resource. Policy-anchored research is an investment requiring careful articulation of decision makers' information needs, values, and pressures. It involves tough calculations to set project priorities and critical monitoring to ensure execution and enhance utilization. Ultimately, the challenge is to aggregate and integrate projects into information systems supporting the policy process.

To suggest that marketing research can facilitate policy formulation, improve implementation, or enrich evaluation is an ambitious advocation. Yet government policies are proposed "in the public interest." Benefits are shaped and directly or indirectly channeled to citizen/consumers. Costs are diffused throughout the system, but paid by consumer/taxpayers. Public policy effectiveness thus can be found in the complex relationships built, nurtured, and maintained between citizens and their agents of government. The public interest can be conceptualized as a "market" where a diverse, fragmented consumer/citizenry demand and respond (consuming or ignoring) the individual and collective benefits offered by their government; a market in which substantial costs are generated and must be paid. As such, marketing research is a communication strategy (and methodology) for encouraging involvement of citizen consumers and formulation of more responsive policies.

Marketing research is a potentially powerful decision tool when managed correctly; it is a potentially powerful political weapon regardless of valid execution. There are significant questions concerning the role of valid market information in a policy system characterized by symbolic democracy, paternalistic programming, cooptive agency-client relationships, and complicated administrative webs of federalism. There are also caveats regarding policy makers' abilities to commission appropriate projects, design integrative information systems, and use information effectively, or regarding the abilities of consumer/citizens to articulate their values and demands accurately and evaluate their behaviors or policy proposals validly. Thus, marketing research is a risky investment, but the payoffs can be high.

Throughout this volume, marketing research is an important topic and is discussed frequently. Many chapters include descriptions of government marketing research efforts, typically as these relate to specific policy or program issues. In this section, marketing research, particularly the *use* of marketing research, is the central issue. Constructive analyses of public sector marketing research contexts, questions, methods, and utilization patterns are presented. The basic purpose of this section is to demonstrate the potential and problems of using marketing research strategies in the public policy process. The chapters are diverse and include discussions of municipal citizen survey programs, consumer research in federal regulatory agencies, sophisticated design issues inherent in federal programs, and "knowledge use" as a distinctive topic.

Municipal citizen sample surveys are a seemingly attractive yet provocative method for generating information about citizen/consumer's wants and values for use in local policy making. In Chapter 13, "Program Planning and Evaluation: A Citizen-Oriented Approach," John Kerr and his colleagues discuss a very successful program in Tallahasee, Florida. The program has received solid support from local policy makers, and the information it generates is used to make allocative and operating decisions. A "marketing information systems" orientation has been the cornerstone, rather than the quite typical research "project" orientation of many other citizen survey efforts. The result has been an atmosphere conducive to evolutionary development of the program and continuous reinforcement affirming the commitment of citizens and policy makers. The authors preview their current efforts to formulate an index of citizen satisfaction and estimate citizen utility functions. Both are significant methodological improvements over earlier survey designs. In conclusion, the program is proposed as a model for other municipalities.

A more critical evaluation of "Sample Surveys as Feedback Mechanisms for Guiding Municipal-Level Decision Making" is presented by Peter May in Chapter 14. In a thorough, insightful policy study of the experiences in five different programs—Dallas, Dayton, Nashville, St. Petersburg, and Walnut Creek—the author explores the lure of public market research, information needs of policy makers, and actual use of information generated in surveys. The direct informational impacts of these efforts were found to be quite limited, indicating problems justifying and legitimating surveys. However, political and symbolic impacts and an "insurance" function were found to produce strong secondary payoffs used by policy makers to justify survey expenditures. The political nature and the symbolic orientation of the public policy process is keenly portrayed in this chapter. It provides an important message for marketing advocates who are proponents of a more "rational" approach to policy and the powers of their techniques to create it.

"Estimating Population Parameters for the U.S. Postal Service: Methodological Issues in Developing and Using a New Sampling Frame" is the topic of Chapter 15. Muriel Converse, Steven Heeringa, and Maureen Kallick describe a marketing study conducted to obtain estimates of the volume of different types of mail sent by businesses, government agencies, and nonprofit organizations in the coterminous United States. A two-stage probability sample was designed with post offices as first stage and establishments as second stage units. The list of establishments was generated by postal carriers and supplemented by postal records and other sources. Sample establishments were asked to respond to two interviews and provide detailed data on their outgoing mail for one week. Sophisticated estimation techniques are applied, and possible sources of error and bias are outlined. The study indicates the problems inherent in designing and conducting valid research projects for expansive federal programs.

An area of federal policy in which marketing research has become increasingly significant is regulation. In Chapter 16, Kenneth Bernhardt outlines the scope of "Consumer Research in the Federal Government," particularly its role in regulatory activities. Starting with a detailed review of programs at the Federal Trade Commission, the author describes projects in 16 different agencies, indicating current work and future directions. An interesting discussion comparing public and private sector consumer research follows. The difficulty of public sector problem definition and the potentially extensive dissemination of government research results are among the distinguishing characteristics discussed. In conclusion, the author sees an accelerated need for policy makers to obtain information through market research, indicating dramatic increases in the scope and frequency of consumer studies throughout government.

In Chapter 17, Yoram Wind concurs that, as government increases its involvement in all aspects of marketing and management, public marketing research will expand. However, he is deeply concerned with the "Implications of Increased Government Regulations for the Quality and Relevance of Marketing Research," particularly for its primary purpose as an "objective" input for managerial decisions. The author suggests that government involvement has resulted in improved technical research quality but managerial relevance is fading as managers flinch at researching important questions with potential public policy implications. A prescription to continue technical improvements while preventing the loss of relevance and maintaining an appropriate cost-value balance is advocated.

Concluding this section on using marketing research, Rohit Deshpande and Gerald Zaltman introduce an important issue into the field of marketing in their elaboration of "The Characteristics of Knowledge: Corporate and Public Policy Insights," Chapter 18. Policy makers in all sectors indicate that coping with the explosion of knowledge is one of the most difficult tasks that they confront. The authors describe current research isolating the conceptual and instrumental dimensions of knowledge and factors affecting the use, misuse, and nonuse of social and policy science information. The quality of interaction between knowledge "producers and consumers" is a critically relevant factor influencing the transfer and use of knowledge. This conclusion paves the way for continued development and transfer of marketing knowledge within and between sectors. Simply, without a clear comprehension of the knowledge development, communication, and use processes, scholars and practitioners risk misunderstanding and irrelevancy, regardless of validity.

13

PROGRAM PLANNING AND EVALUATION: A CITIZEN-ORIENTED APPROACH

*John R. Kerr, James M. Stearns,
Roger R. McGrath, and Dean Block*

In light of citizen discontent manifested by taxpayer revolts, especially at the state and local levels, the time appears right for marketing to make greater contributions to the local public sector. Marketers purport to be in the business of meeting needs and satisfying target markets. Perhaps public administrators could be more effective if they better understood and applied marketing concepts and strategies. Past efforts to apply marketing skills in public administration have fallen short of expectations, and the problems of interfacing marketing with public administration are now receiving serious consideration. The ever-growing problem of making program planning and evaluation more effective will be discussed from a marketing information systems perspective in this chapter

INTERFACING MARKETING WITH PUBLIC ADMINISTRATION

The problems of interfacing marketing and public administration fall into two general categories: (1) marketing scholars' preoccupation with regulatory public policy rather than other government marketing issues and problems; and (2) the alienation of some public policy officials.

Ritchie and La Breque (1975) observed that concern with government regulation of trade practices has overshadowed and obscured marketing's past and potential contributions in other areas of public policy and administration. The authors point out that theoreticians and practitioners have been quick to report applications of marketing skills in nonprofit, social marketing, and regulatory public policy. Reports of utilization of marketing techniques in functional public policy were said to be meager. Functional policy decisions are "those that pertain to the nature and type of products or services provided by government (especially) local government directly to its citizens" (Ritchie and La Breque 1975). Reported results since 1975 do not indicate that this situation has changed markedly.

The local level of functional public policy is where a real paucity of contribution by marketing theoreticians and scholars is evident. Considering that the "typical" citizen is probably most directly affected by local policy, utilization of marketing skills is endemic to local public administration. However, the paucity cited is at least partially a result of and interrelated with the second problem area—the alienation of some public policy officials and administrators.

Dyer and Shimp (1977) and Hilger, Cundiff and Cunningham (1977) have addressed the problems of marketing research as an input to public policy decision making and attitude research for public marketers. The authors indicate that a superiority complex on the part of marketing people and resistance by public administrators have contributed to the problem. They cite the following comments by marketers to substantiate their point:

> The most severe disadvantage researchers must overcome is that public policy makers have neither the training nor experience in the use of research evidence.
> It appears that consumer research is often not appreciated by policy makers.
> For too long the public policy maker has been relying primarily on economists, lawyers, and journalists for information.
> It still will be up to the agencies and courts to decide what evidence and what research procedures to use, but at present they have only legal procedures, so they operate on the basis of fireside inductions.
> This . . . policy has not been advanced with even rudimentary supporting consumer evidence. (Dyer and Shimp 1977, p. 63)

Dyer and Shimp propose better communications and review and more and better information as possible solutions to the problem. Although they are primarily concerned with regulatory public policy, the solutions are relevant for functional public policy.

Understandably most local public administrators are somewhat reluctant to utilize marketing skills. The orientation of public administrators is equitable distribution of services in the face of myriad constraints and pressures. Many may know little of marketing information systems or market segmentation strategies. There does appear, however, to be potential for applications at the local level.

PROGRAM PLANNING AND EVALUATION—
CAN MARKETING HELP?

Local public administrators are frequently faced with answering the question, On what basis shall it be decided to allocate X dollars to activity A instead of activity B? The evolution of program budgeting into a program planning and budgetary system and current practices, such as zero-based budgeting, reflect the need to identify the basic purposes or objectives of a program, develop and evaluate the methods of achieving that objective, and evaluate the success of the selected alternatives in accomplishing their purposes.

In most cases, the criteria used to evaluate local public programs are concerned with efficiency rather than effectiveness. Most of the criteria in use focus on the program itself, usually in terms of cost, rather than the program's impact in terms of its original objectives. "What is needed for evaluation is criteria that come as close as possible to reflecting the basic, underlying objectives of the government—the effects upon people. These criteria should be expressed in any unit that is appropriate" (Hatry 1970). The criteria used in profit-making marketing strategy are straightforward: sales, market share, repeat purchases, and consumer satisfaction. However, Hatry (1970) laments the inadequacy of the approaches to criteria selection used by government. Often, public administrators allow tradition or expediency to govern criteria decisions. Thus, the focus of selection results in a cost orientation; rarely is a citizen- or a market-oriented approach taken (Stearns, Kerr and McGrath 1979).

Some public administrators do not perceive their mission from a marketing standpoint, while others recognize the resemblance. Yet most public administrators have had problems identifying different perceptions of public products (constituent attitudes) as well as acknowledging bona fide constituent concerns (consumer satisfaction) and using this information as criteria for program planning and evaluation.

While no one group is at fault, it appears that government marketing proponents could do a better job marketing both their ideas and research methods rather than blaming failures on public administrators. The authors provide testimony that theoreticians and practitioners from both marketing and public administration can work together for mutual benefit.

The purpose of this chapter is to present a framework, based on a marketing information systems concept, that is adaptable to the local government situation. The authors intend to describe how this framework has aided the City of Tallahassee, Florida, in program planning and evaluation. Past applications as well as current undertakings will be presented to provide the reader with a feel for the possibilities when the enlightened public administrator and the creative marketing researcher combine efforts and skills.

MARKETING INFORMATION SYSTEMS

One of the primary functions of marketing is to act as a liaison linking organizations and individuals into mutually beneficial exchange relationships. To accomplish this function, organizations must gather, disburse, and control information to serve their market segments more efficiently and effectively. Internally, information must be controlled to reach the appropriate decision authority centers, often under the rubric of the management information system. Externally, the organization must communicate with its task environment (customers, clients, consumer groups, government). This is referred to as promotion activity and includes media advertising, public relations/publicity, personal selling, and sales promotion.

Most important for organizations is their ability to sense the surrounding environment and adapt to it (compare Hodge and Anthony 1979). To do this, organizations must have sensors that gather information and relay it back to the organization. Often marketing research is the primary means for accomplishing this, but other information sources are available, such as suppliers, competitors, salesmen, external data from government, associations, and consumer groups (Nickels 1976, p. 45).

These three flows of information—from the organization to the environment, from the environment to the organization, and dissemination within the organization—make up the marketing information system. Figure 13.1 summarizes these information flows.

The achievements of the American private sector are directly traceable to the sector's exploitation and utilization of marketing information systems. The successes experienced in American consumer goods marketing are the result of marketing organizations continuously monitoring consumer needs and wants as well as effectively communicating how their product mixes meet those needs and wants.

Successes of government marketing have also been reported. Particularly, advances in the use of promotion for local governments in improving their marketing practices have been fairly common (compare Lovelock and Weinberg 1978). Also, local governments have been attempting to improve their monitoring capabilities through greater utilization of survey research for program planning and evaluation (Webb and Hatry 1973; Stipak 1979). But recent citizen discontent and its manifestations indicate that government may not be sensitive enough to shifts in its environment. Another American institution, the railroads, were once guilty of similar insensitivity. Unless government institutions wish a similar fate, they must establish effective marketing information systems and improve on more and different flows of information into the organization.

The local public administrator is subjected to many information sources that emanate from groups with vested interests. These groups may or may not reflect the needs and desires of the "market." Therefore, a more

FIGURE 13.1

The Three Flows of a Marketing Information System

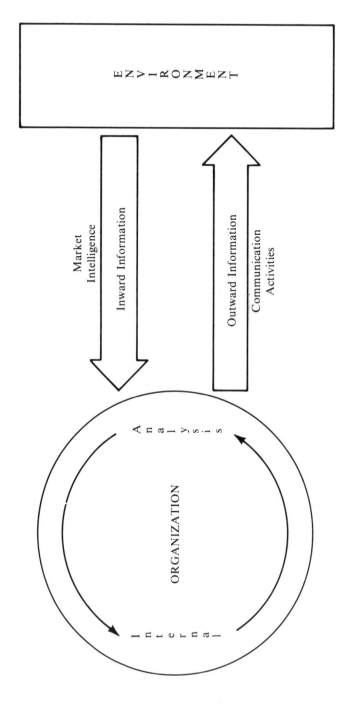

objective, ongoing information source is needed to preclude crises of confidence and improve resource allocation decision capability. Some advancements in monitoring capability have allowed one community to be citizen-oriented in its program and evaluation through the use of relatively simple marketing research techniques. By adapting a marketing information systems strategy, it will be shown, local governments can improve upon their ability to accomplish their mission—identifying and meeting the needs of their citizenry.

RESIDENT OPINION SURVEYS

Rationale

Reviews of current research indicate that cities have been relying on resident input for decision making (Kerr and Stearns 1978; Stipak 1979; Webb and Hatry 1973). This input becomes part of the information system from which public administrators can draw insights that are both internal and external to the organizations they manage. Specifically, local governments are providing or performing direct services; and public administrators, who use resident opinion surveys, are able to learn how the public they serve perceive the "public products" offered. Moreover, local governments need to ascertain the direction and intensity of resident attitudes toward various services, service levels, and alternative choices that public administrators might foresee, given certain budget constraints. Opinion statements that allow residents a range from strongly agree, agree, neither agree or disagree, disagree, to strongly disagree provide both attitude direction and intensity. Such Likert-type measurements have been widely used in marketing research, and the results become valuable input for marketing information systems.

During the past 10 to 15 years public administrators have put increased emphasis on improving program planning and evaluation. The emphasis has focused on improving technical management tools (program budgeting, system analysis) as well as ensuring responsive decision making through more intensive citizen participation. Often this is achieved through broadened citizen input since citizens, who for many reasons cannot attend public meetings or hearings, can have direct participation in the program planning and evaluation process.

Direct citizen participation is a key result of resident opinion surveys. These surveys often counterbalance the special interest groups that evolve through federal, state, or local mandates. Almost all governmental programs specify public hearings, published information and notices, and often specific efforts to accommodate special interest groups (for example, the elderly, handicapped, environmentalists). State sunshine laws and administrative procedures are established to increase direct citizen involvement. Often, the formation of special councils, boards, or committees results in a structure of broad representation from the community, whereby members from each potential interest group or organization are asked to serve on these councils, boards, or committees.

Some of these "broadly representative community groups" may, in time, develop a political rationale or existence beyond that intended. The interplay of personalities and emerging leadership may result in making a council an "interest group" of its own. Required hearings may attract only those with institutional interests to pursue. Broad community-wide needs can become lost or deemphasized when only small geographic areas or self-selected samples of interest groups and vocal minorities are heard.

Survey Uses

As described above, public administration's concern with functional public policy decision responsibility has resulted in resident opinion surveys to measure attitudes and perceptions of their constituent publics. The results of resident opinion surveys have been used for purposes that are both internal and external to the local government organization. The impact of these resident opinion surveys depends on the specific uses of the derived data for subsequent decision making.

Internally, resident input from surveys can be used to help measure the effectiveness of individual programs. Based on resident evaluations, the public administrator can suggest increases or decreases in budgets for any specific resident-related program. Moreover, a program that receives a mediocre evaluation can be designated for priority review. Another internal use of resident opinion data is to counter or support intraorganizational arguments for or against modifications or expansions of existing programs.

Externally, resident opinion survey results can be used as part of the information system by which local government obtains and disseminates information within the community. Survey results often can be used to confirm or deny information sources other than those used internally by local government organizations. While much externally derived information is political in nature, resident opinion data serve as a nonpolitical information source, particularly if an outside researcher conducts the resident opinion survey. Such data assist a local functional public administrator in assessing public sentiment on policy issues (for example, taxes, level of services). Moreover, resident opinion results provide public administrators with information that can be compared with information generated by special interest groups. In addition, resident opinion surveys tend to be viewed as vehicles for seeking out public opinion. In other words, resident opinion surveys improve information flows into the organization.

Survey Results

The City of Tallahassee, Florida, has conducted four annual resident opinion surveys beginning in 1976. The city manager and the director of the Office of Management and Budget initiated the request for a marketing researcher from the Florida State University to plan, conduct, and analyze resident input that could be used for several purposes. These public administrators wanted to upgrade as many city services as possible, but only after considering resident (user) attitudes and preferences. By conducting annual surveys they could note shifts in resident satisfaction or dissatisfaction regarding these services. Such longitudinal data would be helpful when considering departmental funding requests, departmental evaluations, and the ultimate allocation of funds to all program categories. In addition, the allocation of increased funds to specific services could be influenced by these longitudinal data. For example, in 1978 the Tallahassee city commissioners allocated several hundred thousand dollars in additional funds for traffic light synchronization and street maintenance. Both of these programs had been cited in the previous two resident opinion surveys as top priority items by Tallahassee residents.

In addition to budget priorities, the resident survey data have been compared with information obtained from special interest groups. In 1978 residents had an opportunity to indicate whether they thought fluoride should be added to the city's water supply. While special interest groups for both sides of this issue were making persistent inputs, the resident opinion survey provided nonpolitical input to the city manager and city commissioners.

The 1978 survey assisted the public administrators in assessing the issue of increased taxes and/or service charges and the levels of services performed or provided. Given the scenario that costs of providing these services exceeded revenues, residents were asked to indicate which, if any, services should be reduced. Nearly half of the residents wanted no decrease in funding for existing city services.

The 1979 resident opinion survey sought resident perceptions regarding whether city property taxes should be reduced even if this meant a cutback in some city services, other than electric, water, and gas. In addition, residents were asked whether they thought the price they pay for city government services is about the same as the quality of services received. Regarding the cutback in services, two out of ten respondents agreed, while half of the respondents disagreed. One out of three residents agreed that the price paid for city government services equates with the quality received; however, nearly four out of ten residents disagreed.

The use of survey research to monitor citizen sentiment is not unique to Tallahassee. However, the type of information sought and the use of the information in actual budgeting and policy decisions make Tallahassee a model for cities that wish to be sensitive to their citizens. As will be discussed, even more sophisticated attempts are being made to improve the monitoring system in Tallahassee.

AN INDEX OF CONSUMER SATISFACTION WITH LOCAL PUBLIC PRODUCTS

One of the key advantages of the annual resident opinion survey is its ability to sense change within the community. However, resident opinion surveys, while a significant improvement, have not advanced far beyond the Likert scale-type measures discussed. Marketing researchers have refined methods of conceptualizing and measuring consumer satisfaction or dissatisfaction. Recent efforts by Hunt (1977), Day (1979), and Day and Hunt (1979) have resulted in measures of satisfaction that provide administrators with valuable input for program evaluation in both the private and public sectors. These undertakings have evolved into an index of consumer satisfaction/ dissatisfaction with food products (Handy 1977). Currently, the authors are attempting to construct an index to monitor citizen satisfaction/dissatisfaction with public products (Stearns, Kerr and McGrath 1979).

The sequence of events to arrive at an index of satisfaction/dissatisfaction with public products is relatively simple. First, the salient attributes of public products must be identified using direct questioning. Alpert (1971) provides the rationale for direct questioning for attribute identification. Once the salient attributes are identified, a second survey is conducted asking respondents to express satisfaction levels on an ordinal scale with product attributes, individual products, and product groups—transportation or recreation would be examples of product groups. Through the use of optimal monotonic scaling and conjoint measurement, the researcher can arrive at one index number for satisfaction with all public products offered by the community.

This overall satisfaction index number, which would provide a composite for local government performance, can be broken down. First, importance weights and indices for product groups could be provided. In other words, not only would a satisfaction index for transportation be generated,. but the importance of particular products that make up that product group would be known. For example, if bus service and street maintenance are two "transportation" products, the administrator would have some feel for the importance (weight) of each in overall product group satisfaction.

In turn, each product could be decomposed by product attributes. Bus service may have a number of attributes, such as "being on time" and "courtesy of drivers." The index could indicate which attributes were most important for satisfaction with that product.

Such information would provide administrators with a much clearer picture of how goods and services are perceived by citizens and what the important attributes are. By conducting surveys periodically, comparisons can be made for shifts in citizen evaluations after resource allocations have been changed. Also, a decline in the satisfaction of a particular product group, product, or even attribute could serve as an early warning system to a city manager that something needs attention. After this problem area is attended to, the subsequent index would indicate if citizens perceived these efforts to be effective.

An index of this nature is currently being constructed in Tallahassee. When completed, it should provide city administrators with an even better monitoring device than the annual resident opinion survey. An annual index survey, supplemented by questions about whatever current issue is important (for example, fluoride), would be an important addition to the community monitoring system and provide a valuable flow of information about the "market" into appropriate decision authority centers of local government.

ESTIMATES OF CITIZEN UTILITY FUNCTIONS

Many communities are currently faced with reducing service levels or shifting resources among the services offered. In either case, local public administrators are once again faced with a decision for which little or no objective input from citizens is available. The decision maker needs some indication of the utility citizens hold for various services and funding levels to supplement the pressure exerted by special interest groups and factions within local government. The index of consumer satisfaction/dissatisfaction provides information about perceptions of performance, but what about tradeoffs that citizens would be willing to make to maintain or reduce tax levels? The use of conjoint measurement could aid the public administrator providing estimates of citizen utility functions.

The first widespread application of conjoint measurement in marketing research involved determining the importance of product attributes (compare Green and Wind 1975; Green and Srinivasan 1978) by asking consumers to rank order various combinations of levels of those attributes. A consumer of local public products is faced with a similar situation when asked to evaluate, say, three levels of expenditures versus three levels of four services offered by the community. By using the respondents' ranking of alternatives, the researcher can develop utility functions for services and expenditure levels, thereby giving the public administrator some idea as to which service should be cut, if any, when funding changes are to be made.

For example, if a community were interested in citizens' feelings about a reduction in funding (and therefore taxes) of 10 or 20 percent and possible combinations of service reduction that would accompany this funding change, the various combinations of possible alternatives could be ranked by citizens. In this way importance weights (conjoint part-worths) for the various alternatives could be derived, and the administrator would have an improved information source for funding changes. For example, one might expect more importance placed on police and fire protection than parks and recreation in some cities. Conjoint measurement may give some clues to tradeoffs citizens would be willing to accept through generation of part-worths. Obviously, this would be of great value for the administrator in justifying decisions and responding to the outcry for control of expenditures. As with the index, this information may serve to counterbalance pressure tactics by groups when decisions about funding cuts must be made.

CONCLUSIONS, IMPLICATIONS, AND INSIGHTS

Interfacing program planning and evaluation with marketing research concepts and techniques appears to be a feasible match when considering recent developments in local public administration. McCaffery and Bowman (1978) have chronicled the impact of citizen discontent on government agencies. The effects of this discontent, manifested by Proposition 13-type movements, have cascaded into all facets of administration thus emphasizing three key concerns: (1) the demands of constituents to participate in policy making; (2) the potential impact of not providing appropriate methods for participating; and (3) the hazards associated with the organization's failure to properly sense its environment. The inclusion of the marketing information system concept serves to minimize these problems by providing appropriate channels for constituent input.

Marketing information can be useful input when attempting to optimize the effectiveness and efficiency of the decision making associated with each phase of program planning and evaluation. The resident opinion survey is one example of how marketing information can facilitate these decisions. Resident opinion surveys can also be an integral part of the public administrator's assessment of resource allocation among competing programs in this era of resource scarcity.

The index of consumer satisfaction/dissatisfaction is a recent marketing research technique that can improve the monitoring system by providing a more precise and detailed longitudinal measure of constituent attitudes. Moreover, estimates of constituent utility functions for public products and funding levels could be a significant advancement in the decision making framework when the public administrator is faced with the problems of program cutbacks and elimination.

Several key insights regarding the interaction between the marketing researcher and the public administrator have become apparent. First, marketers must learn to "market marketing" to all levels of government. Unless marketing concepts are understood and focused at each level, marketing in government will only be marginally effective. Second, marketers must appreciate public administration problems. Public administrators must distribute services equitably rather than directing resources at the most profitable market segment(s).

Third, marketers must not sell what they cannot deliver. Many of the problems and much of the alienation of the past are results of overly optimistic promises by marketing people. Fourth, marketing experts should couch their suggestions in a framework that is relevant and understandable to the public administrator. Dazzling displays of statistical techniques and jargon are a sure way to estrange the practitioner, public or private. Fifth and last, marketers must report both successes and failures so that their valuable lessons can be shared by others. A real paucity of reporting is evident in government marketing and has restrained its development.

The joint efforts of some public administrators and marketing researchers have resulted in "opening the door" for future interaction between both groups. The primary objective of this chapter is to encourage interaction by providing examples of how marketing information systems and research techniques have aided public administrators who must wrestle with program planning and evaluation problems.

Problems dealing with program planning and evaluation are likely to intensify for public administrators in the future. While no single approach or technique is a panacea, the contributions evolving from the marketing discipline may serve to ease the burden.

REFERENCES

Alpert, Mark I. (1971), "Identification of Determinant Attributes: A Comparison of Methods," *Journal of Marketing Research* 8 (May): 184–91.

Altman, Stan (1979), "Performance Monitoring Systems for Public Managers," *Public Administration Review* 39 (January-February): 31–35.

Day, Ralph L., ed. (1979), *Consumer Satisfaction, Dissatisfaction and Complaining Behavior*, Bloomington: Division of Research, Indiana University.

—— and H. Keith Hunt eds., (1979), *Proceedings of the Annual Conference on Consumer Satisfaction/Dissatisfaction and Complaining Behavior*, Bloomington: Division of Research, Indiana University.

Dyer, Robert F. and Terence A. Shimp (1977), "Enhancing the Rate of Marketing Research in Public Policy Decision Making," *Journal of Marketing* 41 (January): 63–67.

Green, Paul E. and V. Srinivasan (1978), "Conjoint Analysis in Consumer Rsearch: Issues and Outlook," *Journal of Consumer Research* 5 (September): 103–23.

—— and Yoram Wind (1975), "New Ways to Measure Consumers' Judgments," *Harvard Business Review* 53 (July-August): 107–17.

Handy, Charles R. (1973), "Implications of the Index of Consumer Satisfaction for Public Policy Pertaining to Market Performance," in *Proceedings of Association of Consumer Research—1972*, ed. M. Venkatesan, pp. 738–41, Iowa City: Association of Consumer Research.

—— (1977), "Monitoring Consumer Satisfaction with Food Products," in *Con-*

ceptualization and Measurement of Consumer Satisfaction and Dissatisfaction, ed. H. Keith Hunt, pp. 215–39, Cambridge, Mass.: Marketing Science Institute.

Hatry, Harry P. (1970), "Measuring the Effectiveness of Nondefense Public Programs," *Operations Research* 18 (September-October): 772–84.

Hilger, Mary Tharp, Edward M. Cundiff and William H. Cunningham (1977), "Consumer Attitude Research: Help for the Public Marketer," in *Contemporary Marketing Thought*, eds. Barnett A. Greenberg and Danny N. Bellenger, p. 540, Chicago: American Marketing Association.

Hodge, B. J. and William P. Anthony (1979), *Organization Theory: An Environmental Approach*, Boston: Allyn and Bacon.

Hunt, H. Keith (1976), "CS/D: The Program Planning and Evaluation Perspective," in *Advances in Consumer Research*, ed. B. Anderson, pp. 259–60, Cincinnati: Association for Consumer Research.

—— (1977), *Conceptualization and Measurement of Consumer Satisfaction and Dissatisfaction*, Cambridge, Mass.: Marketing Science Institute.

Kerr, John R. and James M. Stearns (1978), "Not-for-Profit Marketing Management: The City of Tallahassee, Florida," in *Marketing Managment: Strategies and Cases*, eds., M. Wayne Delozier and Arch Woodside, pp. 814–31, Columbus, Ohio: Charles E. Merrill.

Lingoes, James C. and Martin Pfaff (1973), "The Index of Consumer Satisfaction: Methodology," in *Proceedings of Association of Consumer Research—1972*, ed., M. Venkatesan, pp. 689–712, Iowa City: Association of Consumer Research.

Lovelock, Christopher H. and Charles B. Weinberg (1978), "Public and Nonprofit Marketing Comes of Age," in *Review of Marketing 1978*, eds., Gerald Zaltman and Thomas Bonoma, pp. 413–52, Chicago: American Marketing Association.

McCaffery, Jerry and John H. Bowman (1978), "Participatory Democracy and Budgeting: The Effects of Proposition 13," *Public Administration Review* 38 (November-December): 530–38.

Nickels, William G. (1976), pp. 317–57, *Marketing Communications and Promotion*, Columbus, Ohio: Grid.

—— (1978), *Marketing Principles: A Broadened Concept of Marketing*, pp. 139–45, Englewood Cliffs, N.J.: Prentice-Hall.

Ritchie, J. R. Brent and Roger J. La Breque (1975), "Marketing Research and Public Policy: A Functional Perspective," *Journal of Marketing* 39 (July): 12–19.

Smith, Samuel V., Richard Brien and James E. Stafford (1968), *Readings in Marketing Information Systems: A New Era in Marketing Research*, Boston: Houghton Mifflin.

Stearns, James M., John R. Kerr and Roger R. McGrath (1979), "Advances of Marketing for Functional Public Policy Administration," in *Proceedings: Southern Marketing Association*, eds. Robert S. Franz, et al., Lafayette, L.A.: University of Southwestern Louisiana.

Stipak, Brian (1979), "Citizen Satisfaction with Urban Services: Potential Misuse as a Performance Indicator," *Public Administration Review* 39 (January-February): 46–52.

Webb, Kenneth and Henry P. Hatry (1973), *Obtaining Citizen Feedback: The Application of Citizen Surveys to Local Governments*, Washington, D.C.: Urban Institute.

14

SAMPLE SURVEYS AS FEEDBACK MECHANISMS FOR GUIDING MUNICIPAL-LEVEL DECISION MAKING

Peter J. May

Governmental officials are generally believed to make poor business-men. Public confidence in the abilities of officials—elected officials, their appointees, and administrators—to balance the satisfaction of diverse wants and effectively deliver services is low, particularly at the local level. The passage in June 1978 of California's Proposition 13, a statewide initiative that placed a limit on property taxes and reassessments, by a 65–35 percent margin has been attributed to voter frustration with governmental unre-sponsiveness and inefficiency, among other factors (Field 1978). Similarly, declines in approval rates of local tax and bond referenda are apparently closely linked to citizens' negative perceptions of governmental services. In short, officials are proposing programs which for a variety of reasons citizens are unwilling to "buy." Moreover, it is apparent that many citizens desire to exchange the services that they presently receive for less costly endeavors.

Within the growing literature on nonmarket functioning two themes recur in diagnoses of governmental unresponsiveness and inefficiency: (1) officials often have insufficient feedback concerning citizens' preferences and program functioning to balance wants and administer services properly; and (2) there is a lack of incentives for officials, particularly nonelected officials, to respond to people's dissatisfactions or inefficiencies in service provision (Wolf 1979). The first aspect to be addressed here is the "information

Financial support for this investigation was provided with a doctoral dissertation grant, No. 4-2814RG, from the Office of the Assistant Secretary for Policy Development and Research, HUD.

problem" as it relates to decisions regarding the levels and types of services that are publicly funded at the local level. The chapter discusses the limits of existing feedback and the appeal of periodic sample surveys as information mechanisms and then examines the difficulties of implementing and utilizing this type of "market research" to guide public decision making, drawing upon the experiences of officials in several cities. The final section provides preliminary conclusions regarding the value and functions of such feedback in local policy making.

INFORMATION FAILURES AND NEEDS

Politicians are well aware of the fact that images are at least as important as "true" conditions in enacting programs: citizen perceptions of a given condition (for example, crime in a downtown area) affect the legitimacy of governmental intervention; the economic feasibility of programs is dependent upon voters' willingness to approve taxes or users' willingness to pay fees; and political support for or resistance to programs is a function of beliefs concerning the distribution of benefits and costs. If officials are to develop and implement programs that are responsive to a diversity of needs, politically acceptable, and economically viable, they need "better" information than the often confusing mandate provided by elections every two or four years. Because of this need, referenda, public hearings, complaint processes, and informal gatherings are important feedback mechanisms. However, each of these provides officials with only a partial view of citizen perceptions and program impacts. It is possible to obtain the preferences of those individuals who are willing to participate in public hearings and the like, but it is difficult to ascertain how closely participants' and nonparticipants' views correspond. Similarly, through complaints about services officials can learn about perceptions of service deterioration, but they learn little about the relative effectiveness of various programs. As a consequence, even if officials wish to be responsive to various wants or service inefficiencies, the necessary information for them to do so rationally is often missing or difficult to interpret.

Officials' Muddled Views

The few studies of policy makers' awareness of citizen views that have been conducted to date suggest that policy makers misestimate the amount of support for major policy issues when generalizing from existing feedback. For example, in a study that addressed a range of municipal issues in an unidentified "large industrial American city," Siegel and Friesma (1965) found that community leaders tended to underestimate by some 20 percent citizen support for taxes and levels of satisfaction with services. Similarly, in comparing policy makers' expectations with survey findings in a San Francisco–area city, it is apparent that officials overestimate citizen desires for decreased taxes by some 30 percent but gauge reasonably well the levels of citizen satisfaction with services (May 1979).

Although these findings do not evidence gross misunderstandings and are limited to a few localities, they suggest that weaknesses do exist in the informational linkages between citizens, as both service demanders and cost-conscious taxpayers, and officials, as both elected representatives and service providers. Meltsner (1971, ch. 7) suggests that officials' uncertainties about citizen perceptions cause them to be cautious in their willingness to seek approval of new programs. Other studies show a substitution of professional norms as a basis for developing programs when officials are confused about people's needs (Levy, Meltsner and Wildavsky 1974). As a consequence of being cautious, officials often appear to be unresponsive.

Calling this situation a "crisis" in governance or urban service delivery would clearly be overly alarmist. When officials are aware of the wants and needs of various publics and how strongly those views are held, they often take actions that strike an acceptable balance between the satisfaction of the wants of some individuals and the costs imposed upon others. However, the weaknesses inherent in existing feedback—participation biases, insufficient flow of information, and the like—make it difficult for officials to assemble "mappings" of their organizational environment. It is not so much that information does not exist, as there are many sources of feedback at the local level, but that what does exist often cannot be interpreted as a useful basis for guiding decision making.

The Lure of Public Market Research

Because much of policy making and analysis involves tradeoffs at aggregate levels, measures that summarize the levels and distribution of program impacts, benefits, and needs are required to guide rational pro-grammatic and policy decisions. This need seems obvious to the analyst or politician who explicitly (or implicitly) assembles economically viable and politically acceptable program bundles. The analyst wants to know the relative effectiveness of existing programs, the benefits to be derived from planned programs, and the prevalence of various problems as input to policy analyses, program evaluations, or management processes. The elected offi-cial is more likely to be concerned with distributional consequences— "who gets what"—as well as the levels of satisfaction with or political support for different programs, if only to improve election possibilities. Thus, from the perspective of both the analyst and the elected official, aggregate-level feedback not readily obtainable from public hearings would seem to be desirable.

Certainly it is possible to take actions without such data or with inaccurate information. Implicit in the rational policy approach, however, is an assumption that "better" data can aid decision making. Thus a key issue is the quality (accuracy, or whatever standard one wishes to employ) of data that is required to improve decision making. Elected officials tend to want some latitude and thus tolerate a certain level of uncertainty in order to provide flexibility in shaping policies. Analysts tend to seek more precise assessments to perform their analytic tasks, but it is not clear how "good" such data need be.

Given the information problems discussed here, periodic sample surveys for assessing citizens' wants, needs, and perceptions of services are appealing aggregate-level feedback mechanisms for a number of reasons. Well-designed, well-implemented sample surveys minimize participation biases, making it possible to generalize findings to broader populations and to provide estimates of the relative prevalence of various perspectives. Second, citizen surveys (the term used here to refer to sample surveys of local populations) appear to be reasonable applications of market research techniques employed in assessing consumer wants and satisfactions in the private sector (Blakely, Schultz, and Harvey 1977; Wilson et al. 1976). Additional legitimization for citizen surveys is provided by the widespread use of opinion polls in election campaigns to explore citizens' attitudes and voting intentions. Because of this appeal, citizen surveys have been advocated by professional organizations such as the American Academy of Public Administration, International City Management Association, and National League of Cities and by respected research organizations such as the Urban Institute (Cates 1977; Hatry et al., 1977; Webb and Hatry 1973). Yet, as is often the case for public sector "innovations," citizen surveys have been extensively promoted before the quality or utility of survey data as input for local policy-making processes has been evaluated.

The Limits of Survey Feedback in the Public Sector

Certainly we should not expect citizen surveys to become cure-alls for policy making in the local context. They can be used to gather only certain kinds of information (that is, responses concerning those services or issues of which citizens are aware) on a periodic basis. Moreover, many cities do not have or are not capable of creating the analytic staffs required to monitor survey implementation and analysis. Perhaps the greatest constraint is the political environment in which program and policy decisions are made. In soliciting feedback, officials risk making themselves look "bad" in the eyes of the public, a consequence that is magnified in the public arena because of electoral accountability. Systematic feedback mechanisms also may be threatening to existing information sources—community leaders and organizations—as well as administrators who currently control information resources. Moreover, officials have few incentives to collect such information.

Recognizing these constraints, a number of questions remain concerning the role of public sector market research: Can "better" feedback concerning aggregate wants, needs, and program impacts improve local policy making? Are citizens able and willing to respond to such inquiries? Can "good" data regarding, for instance, the impacts and benefits of local programs be generated using survey methods? How readily will officials use such information to help guide decision making?

EXPERIENCES WITH CITIZEN SURVEYS

Sample survey techniques have been employed in this country at the local level to assess public sentiment for community issues or election issues for many years. However, only since the early 1970s have periodic surveys of citizen preferences and perceptions of services been employed. This type of survey, the subject of the present discussion, has been developed in very few cities to date, including Corvallis, Dallas, Dayton, Nashville, St. Petersburg, Sioux City, and a San Francisco-area city called Walnut Creek.

Because very few cities have sponsored periodic surveys to date, the basis for examining and generalizing implementation problems and levels of utilization is limited. Nevertheless, the five experiences that are currently discussed—Dallas, Dayton, Nashville, St. Petersburg, and Walnut Creek— provide a contrast in orientation and apparent rates of success that illustrates salient design, implementation, and utilization issues. The first four experiences are undertakings in cities of moderate size (235,000 to 813,000 population) involving several years of survey administration. The Walnut Creek effort differs in that it has been conducted only once to date and in a city of only some 50,000 population. It is included in the current examination because it provides an opportunity to explore developmental features in more depth than was possible in the other cities.

The Surveys

The five surveys are similar in content and overall design, although the relative emphasis of their different components varies (see Table 14.1). The Dayton, Nashville, and St. Petersburg efforts are primarily mechanisms for gathering programmatic information, such as levels of satisfaction with services. The Dallas and Walnut Creek surveys are broader in scope in that they also address preferences for taxing and spending. Each is administered on an in-person basis, except for Walnut Creek which is by telephone.

TABLE 14.1

Existing Citizen Surveys

City	Survey Years	Survey Contents	Sample Size
Dallas	1974 to present	Satisfaction with services/conditions	800 (odd years)
		Use of services	3,000 (even years)
		Spending preferences	
		Housing quality	
Dayton	1970 to present	Satisfaction with services/conditions	800
		Use of services	
Nashville	1974 –76	Satisfaction with services/conditions	1,000
		Use of services	
		Criminal victimization	
St. Petersburg	1973 to present	Satisfaction with service/conditions	500
		Use of services	
		Criminal victimization	
Walnut Creek	1977	Satisfaction with services/conditions	500
		Use of services	
		Budget/spending preferences	

Source: Compiled by author.

Annual city survey expenditures range from some $10,000 in Dayton and Walnut Creek to some $30,000 in Dallas (1977 dollars). Initial funding came from a variety of sources: Nashville and St. Petersburg received funds from the Department of Housing and Urban Development and the National Science Foundation through the Urban Institute; Dayton received funding from the Kettering Foundation; Dallas used HUD '701' planning assistance funds; and Walnut Creek used city funds. The efforts are sponsored by a budget and management unit or its equivalent in each city, with initial design and fieldwork being contracted for independently with local market research firms.

By academic standards for survey design and sample procedures, the efforts can be rated "good." The instruments have been well designed, sample procedures are good, and professional interviewing staffs have been employed. The corners that have been cut are primarily in questionnaire length (typically running 30 to 45 minutes), use of relatively small samples, and limiting the number of "call-back" attempts.

Willingness to Initiate Surveys

At first glance, the decision to develop a survey would appear to involve a balancing of informational needs against political risks and dollar outlays. Although it is difficult to separate rhetoric from reality, personal interviews with the individuals who supported survey development in each of the five cities studied suggest that officials believed, at least in retrospect, that feedback would enhance policy making. For example, a St. Petersburg official commented: "It is sickening to see the feedback that comes through politicians or through complaints. . . . I've been in business and I know the value of market research." The finance director in Nashville, under whose auspices their survey was conducted, remarked: "I made arbitrary decisions for many years and I felt uncomfortable about it. The survey sounded like something that might reveal things and provide support for decisions."

In addition, several political and bureaucratic factors appear to have influenced the development of each city's efforts. The rhetoric of improving citizen participation was offered by officials in several of the cities studied as a justification for surveys. Perhaps more important were the desires by the various officials who had advocated survey development in each city to "look good" among their peers. It is difficult to gauge how important this consideration was in the initial decisions, but it was certainly valued later on. One official remarked, in retrospect, that the survey effort had been "a real ego trip for me . . . researchers and other city officials were calling up asking about it . . . I liked the prestige and the Mayor liked the prestige." In addition to personal recognition, Dallas has received a national award for their effort from the International City Management Association, and St. Petersburg has received recognition in an external review of city operations.

Other factors also helped to minimize perceptions of risk in each city studied. Because surveys were but one of a series of managerial and budgetary improvements, they were viewed by some as "just another city hall project," to quote one department head. The availability of outside funding (in all but Walnut Creek) and expertise added credibility to the proposed undertakings as well as a hedge against claims that such efforts are "frills." Moreover, council-level attention and public awareness of survey efforts were minimal (if at all existent) since the surveys were initially internal to budget departments, outside funding was available, and the surveys constituted one of several reforms. Except for Walnut Creek, initial approval did not require public hearings or council debate; surveys more often than not were passed routinely as part of a larger package of expenditures.

Whether these are necessary conditions for surveys to be developed seems doubtful; they only foster a climate of receptivity for survey undertakings. Yet the fact that only a handful of cities have developed citizen surveys to date, despite extensive efforts to disseminate the "technology" by the

International City Management Association and the Urban Institute, is cause for skepticism. Interviews that I conducted with San Francisco–area city officials who have not undertaken such efforts substantiate existing reluctance to develop surveys. Only 2 of the 20 individuals interviewed expressed strong interest in initiating a survey and felt assured of council-level support for even modest funding of the effort. Even if outside funding were available, few felt "better" information or participatory opportunities were needed (4 out of the 20), although more thought such data could be useful as part of budget improvements. Even though these findings are limited to one area, they cast doubt upon the contention of citizen survey advocates that such efforts will become commonly used policy-making tools in future years.

Utilization, Misutilization, and Dysfunctions

In depicting the utilization of feedback it is useful to distinguish among several levels of usage:

Awareness. Users of survey information are aware that the survey addresses issues relevant to a decision.

Acknowledgement. Users of survey information correctly acknowledge survey results.

Influence. Information influences opinions concerning such matters as the existence of a problem or course of action to take.

Impact. A programmatic or policy change is instituted because of a finding.

Employing this categorization, the utilization of surveys in the cities studied is rated here according to subjective assessments of the frequency of each type of impact. Interviews with officials and a review of internal memoranda in each city provide the basis for the ratings.

As summarized in Table 14.2, the surveys undertaken in Dallas, Dayton, Nashville, St. Petersburg, and Walnut Creek have had relatively low levels of utilization. Only rarely have findings influenced policy or programmatic decisions. When they have had impacts, relatively minor issues were involved. The Dallas city manager has used findings to justify budget recommendations, and Walnut Creek officials believed survey results influenced budget cutback and revenue decisions. Yet the impacts in these two cities have not been extensive: officials are more likely to ignore results than to take actions based upon them. In the remaining three cities, administrators have been aware of survey findings since the results have formed one basis for setting departmental objectives and have been included in budgets. Yet rarely have survey data led to programmatic changes in these three cities. Considering the levels of utilization of findings to date, the

TABLE 14.2

Utilization of Survey Results

| City | Level of Utilization | | | |
	Awareness	Acknowledgement	Influence	Impact
Dallas	High	High	Occasional	Occasional
Dayton	Moderate	Moderate	Rare	Rare
Nashville	Low	Low	Rare	Rare
St. Petersburg	Moderate	Moderate	Rare	Rare
Walnut Creek	High	Moderate	Occasional	Rare

Source: Compiled by author.

Dallas experience serves to illustrate a relatively "successful" effort, and the Nashville experience illustrates an "unsuccessful" effort.

Dallas city administrators have been aware of survey results because findings are discussed in an annual formal review session and the city manager refers to them in justifying budget recommendations where appropriate. In some circumstances, such as increased staffing levels for animal control or increased levels of street maintenance, it seems likely that similar recommendations would have been made anyway since relatively high numbers of complaints had been received about those problems. In rarer cases, such as the council's decision to fund a variety of housing programs, the survey played a more instrumental role in influencing policy by identifying "problems" that previously had been overlooked or ignored. (Housing officials believe that without the survey findings as "leverage" no action would have been taken.) Yet, other than the city's housing department, which uses survey-based housing quality ratings in conjunction with demographic and attitudinal data as part of their planning efforts, departmental-level usage of survey results has been extremely limited. Several department heads with whom I spoke remarked that survey results cannot guide programmatic decisions (for example, the allocation of manpower) because findings are "too general" and cannot be disaggregated to the block level. Elected officials have been aware of findings, at least when released, but rarely have findings entered into policy debates. One council member remarked that he suspected "the same impact could be accomplished by reissuing last year's survey and calling it this year's."

In contrast to the "success" of the Dallas effort, an evaluation which is best applied in relation to the other experiences, Nashville's survey effort was dropped in 1976 because of lack of support for it within the city. The effort received much publicity among other localities and the general public with the dissemination of a booklet of summary findings. Yet, within administrative circles, results were rarely even acknowledged in decision making since the survey was developed and used primarily as a feedback device for the policy analysis unit of the finance department. Analysts occasionally used results to answer specific questions or to justify particular recommendations such as the development of an extensive sidewalk improvement program in the downtown area. However, it seems likely such decisions would have been made anyway. When a new finance director was appointed in 1976, he found little use of survey findings or support for the effort outside of the analysis unit so he dropped the operation. In retrospect he commented, "Polls are for politicians; I'm a businessman."

In addition to considering the level of utilization of findings, we should consider the legitimacy of various uses when assessing survey efforts. Officials may purposely misrepresent findings in order to fulfill such political ends as delaying decisions or grandstanding or suppress findings simply to avoid political embarrassment. While purposeful misutilization of findings does not appear to be pervasive in the cities investigated, several instances of unintentional misrepresentation are evident. For example, confusion of "social" and "statistical" significance was common in that differences in levels of satisfaction among sectors of a city or across time were implied to be socially important when sample errors did not permit attributing any difference. The impact of such misinterpretations, however, has been minimal in most decisions to date. Deliberate suppression of findings did not appear to be a problem, but the manner in which results have been reported (voluminous listings of results) and the lack of evaluative comments often have made it difficult for officials to identify "important" findings.

Survey results may also have dysfunctional impacts. The negative consequence of relying upon a limited number of measures in assessing performance—the "teaching to the test" phenomenon—as part of survey feedback is one possibility (Lawler 1976), but at present insufficient emphasis is placed upon surveys as part of management review to create such dysfunctions. More apparent was the shifting of officials' attention to those departments for which information was available and away from those units which were not included in survey questioning because they are not visible to the typical citizen (for example, planning, administration, legal departments).

Given previous research findings which show selective utilization of evaluation studies, research findings, and opinion poll results at other levels of government, the impacts of survey data described here should come as little surprise (Caplan, Morrison and Stambaugh 1975; Caplan and Barton 1976; Rich 1975). Survey feedback is but one source of information in the political arena; it does not enter a vacuum. While it may be "better" information in that it is statistically more representative, reliable, or valid than existing feedback, officials do not perceive its informational advantages because they are not concerned about data quality as such.

The Stumbling Blocks

Tentative conclusions concerning the factors that tend to foster and inhibit utilization of survey results can be drawn from these experiences. In each city the survey agenda, the availability of analytic expertise, and the quality of analysis appeared to play important roles in shaping the types and degrees of utilization. The consistency of my observations among the five cities studied suggests that idiosyncratic factors, with the possible exception of the singular influence of the Dallas city manager, did not play an important role in enhancing utilization.

Disjunctions between available feedback and the level of information that policy makers used in decision making were evident: administrators desired more disaggregated data than sample sizes permitted; spending preference questions that were included in Walnut Creek did not reflect those program decisions which officials addressed; and outcome measures such as citizen satisfaction could not be linked to programmatic decisions. Increasing the relevance and timing of survey feedback to the decisions officials make regarding program operations, budgets, and the like will enhance the value of survey feedback. However, this is difficult to achieve for a variety of reasons. First, it is hard to forecast which factors will be important some months before a decision, and decisions must often be made before results are available. Respondent inabilities to provide meaningful feedback form a second constraint. For example, it is possible to ask citizens about their spending preferences among major program categories—police and other services—but they are unable to express preferences at the more refined levels for which resource allocation decisions are actually made (for example, patrol vs. detective work). Third, the relevance of some measures such as citizen satisfaction with policy are extremely difficult to disentangle. Even if officials knew how to eliminate dissatisfaction, it is not clear that doing so is desirable since such actions often conflict with other goals.

A lack of analytic expertise has prevented the utilization of survey results after the release of the findings and has contributed to the misinterpretation of results. Recurring use of findings can be enhanced with the establishment of in-house analytic units, as was done in Dallas and St. Petersburg, but the credibility of findings as well as internal political support for survey operations is often jeopardized by such efforts. Because of the variety of capabilities at the local level, no single organization framework for structuring feedback is currently advocated. It is evident that most cities must contract for surveys if they are to be undertaken at all.

The reluctance of analysts to provide recommendations for programmatic or policy actions based upon survey results is another factor, related to the two discussed so far, inhibiting utilization. In some cases survey analysts chose not to make evaluative comments "as a political decision," to quote one official, since such commentary may have provoked confrontations with policy makers over their policy-making role and conflicts with administrators over the "correct" interpretation of results. The lack of evaluative comments constrains utilization since officials are incapable of translating survey results, which are "dumb data," into meaningful recommendations (Wildavsky 1977). At the heart of such translations are evaluative standards for guiding interpretation. Modest efforts can be made to develop such guidelines by asking officials to prejudge findings, but this is hard to accomplish since it involves making assessments of "social significance" without an adequate reality base.

In sum, it is possible to identify several factors that hinder survey utilization. The difficult part is overcoming the barriers presented by data limitations, a lack of analytic expertise, and inabilities to convert survey findings to meaningful information. In addition to these problems a paradox is presented if efforts are made to enhance utilization: many of the factors that foster effective utilization also act to make survey efforts unpalatable to local officials in particular. For example, internal expertise fosters ongoing analysis but jeopardizes the credibility of surveys. Increased relevance of survey results to policy decisions enhances the value of findings but threatens the decision-making latitude of officials. Thus the appropriate actions for even marginally improving informational uses of citizen surveys are not obvious.

CONCLUSIONS

Reassessing Citizen Surveys

While improvements in the effectiveness of survey data in guiding policy are possible, it seems unlikely they will enhance the impact of survey data appreciably, if for no other reason than findings are rarely "surprising" to local officials. Typically we should expect results to be used to justify particular actions or to verify the legitimacy of existing policies. On rarer occasions, surveys will indicate problems of one kind or another—dissatisfaction with a service, apparent underutilization of a program, or desires for changes in spending—for which officials may feel compelled to take action, but they will do so only if it is politically expedient.

Perhaps the best standard for assessing the value of survey information in local policy making is the "cost" of not having such feedback. In other words, if it were not available what errors in decision making would be made and what would be their consequences? When survey results are used simply to justify actions that would have been taken anyway, as seems to be most common to date, the "cost" of not having the feedback would at most be some delay in action. If the findings influence policies, the consequences of not having feedback depend upon the nature of the problem at hand. The feedback is of value if it helps avoid citizen hostility or wasted expenditures for unused programs. If findings unearth previously overlooked problems, they may be useful in drawing policy makers' attention to problems or in generating resources, but it would be of little direct consequence if feedback was not available in such situations. (Indeed, one may argue that "costs" are introduced in the latter case since officials must react to the previously overlooked problems.)

Even though surveys rarely have specific payoffs, there is evidence of more diffuse impacts. For example, officials' beliefs and assumptions are sometimes altered after several surveys, helping to clarify their understanding of "opinion climates." Similarly, the nature of questions asked by officials about programs sometimes shifts because of survey findings. In

Walnut Creek, officials switched from asking whether or not revenues could be raised to asking by how much, given findings that the current level of user fees was not a factor influencing nonutilization of services. Another subtle impact is the influence of survey processes upon officials' confidence. Many spoke of the comfort they received from "knowing where we stand." The difficulty with such appreciative impacts is that they do not provide visible payoffs that can be valued. How willing should citizens be to make officials happier with their decisions?

The Bottom Line

From the perspective of most elected officials, citizen surveys have failed to live up to their apparent promise as informational devices for guiding management and policy decisions, thereby making it difficult to justify expenditures for them. Perhaps this says more about the ways such surveys have been promoted to date than anything else; nevertheless it is clear that policy makers must be willing to justify such efforts in other than purely economic terms if they want to undertake them. The more subtle impacts of surveys as well as their occasional utility in protecting officials against gross misreading of citizens' sentiments make surveys *potentially* useful feedback mechanisms since they can have important payoffs that cannot be predicted. As such they are insurance mechanisms which must be valued against the risks of having an uncertain view of one's environment.

If future citizen surveys are similar in design and scope to those discussed here, clearly the feedback will be more useful for some purposes than others. Even if sample sizes are increased, it seems unlikely that the data will be of much value to administrators in helping decide such things as the allocation of manpower since they do not know much about the relationships between program inputs and service impacts. Survey findings have more potential in providing assessments of citizens' wants, the impacts of programs, and utilization of various services, but the policy implications of such data are rarely obvious. The most enduring impacts are more likely to result from the influence of surveys in shaping policy debates and sensitizing officials to the issues they face rather than guiding the decisions themselves.

REFERENCES

Blakely, E. J., H. Schultz and P. Harvey (1977), "Public Marketing: A Suggested Policy Planning Paradigm for Community Development in the City," *Social Indicators Research* 4 (May): 163–84.

Caplan, Nathan and Eugenia Barton (1976), *'Social Indicators 1973': A Study of the Relationship Between the Power of Information and Utilization by Federal Executives*, Ann Arbor: Institute for Social Research, University of Michigan.

Caplan, Nathan, Andrea Morrison and Russell J. Stambaugh (1975), *The Use of Social Science Knowledge in Policy Decisions at the National Level: A Report to Respondents*, Ann Arbor: Institute for Social Research, University of Michigan.

Cates, Camille (1977), "Using Citizen Surveys: Three Approaches," Unpublished report, Municipal Management Innovation Series, no. 15, International City Management Association, Washington, D.C.

Field, Mervin (1978), "Sending a Message: Californians Strike Back," *Public Opinion* 1 (July-August): 3–7.

Fukuhara, R. S. (1977), "Productivity Improvement in Cities," in *Municipal Yearbook 1977*, Washington, D.C.: International City Management Association, pp. 193–200.

Hatry, H. P. et al. (1977), *How Effective Are Your Community Services? Procedures for Monitoring the Effectiveness of Municipal Services*, Washington, D.C.: Urban Institute.

Lawler, Edward E. (1976), "Control Systems in Organizations," in *Handbook of Industrial and Organizational Psychology*, ed. M. D. Dunnette, Chicago: Rand McNally.

Levy, Frank S., Arnold J. Melstner and Aaron Wildavsky (1974), *Urban Outcomes: Schools, Streets, and Libraries*, Berkeley: University of California Press.

May, Peter J. (1979), "An Assessment of Sample Surveys as Feedback Mechanisms for Guiding Local Decision Making," Ph.D. dissertation, University of California, Berkeley.

Melsner, Arnold J. (1971), *The Politics of City Revenue*, Berkeley: University of California Press.

Rich, Robert F. (1975) "Selective Utilization of Social Science Related Information by Federal Policy-makers," *Inquiry* 12 (September): 239–45.

Siegel, Roberta S. and H. P. Friesma (1965), "Urban Community Leaders' Knowledge of Public Opinion," *Western Political Quarterly* 18 (December): 881–95.

Webb, Kenneth and Harry P. Hatry (1973), *Obtaining Citizen Feedback: The Application of Citizen Surveys to Local Governments*, Washington, D.C.: Urban Institute.

Wildavsky, Aaron (1977), "Policy Analysis Is What Information Systems Are Not," *New York Affairs* 4 (Spring): 10–23.

Wilson, R. et al. (1976), "Applications of Consumer Analysis in the Public Sector," Unpublished paper, SRI International, Menlo Park, California.

Wolf, Charles, Jr. (1979), "A Theory of Non-Market Failure," *Public Interest* 55 (Spring): 114–33.

15

ESTIMATING POPULATION PARAMETERS FOR THE U.S. POSTAL SERVICE: METHODOLOGICAL ISSUES IN DEVELOPING AND USING A NEW SAMPLING FRAME

Muriel Converse
Steven G. Heeringa
Maureen Kallick

In 1970, the U.S. Congress passed the Postal Service Reorganization Act, which changed the Post Office Department into the United States Postal Service (USPS), a quasi-governmental agency. In conjunction with this change, Congress ordered the Postal Service to evaluate the services it was providing in light of its customers' needs and to obtain a data base that would enable it to assess the impact of possible rate and classification changes on different groups of Postal Service users.

To meet the congressional requirement of the development of a substantial data base, a series of studies was designed by the Mail Classification Research Division, a newly established arm of the Rates and Classification Division of the Postal Service. Two of these studies were contracted to The University of Michigan Survey Research Center (SRC)—a Quantitative Description of the Household Mailstream; and a Quantitative Description

This project was conducted by the Survey Research Center, Institute for Social Research, University of Michigan. Many people contributed to the research design, but special credit must be given to Irene Hess, Head of Sampling Section, SRC, for the overall two-stage sample design, and to Robert Groves, who worked with her on the details of first-stage design.

of the Nonhousehold Mailstream. The first was conducted in 1977–78, and a final report submitted in 1978 (Kallick et al. 1977). The second, the subject of this paper, underwent a feasibility test in 1977, and the execution phase is currently in the field. Unfortunately there is little substantive data to report at this time, but the rather complex methodology of the study is of interest. A final report of the study was presented to the United States Postal Service in April 1980.

DATA REQUIREMENTS OF THE NONHOUSEHOLD MAILSTREAM STUDY

The contract with the Postal Service calls for national estimates of the quantity of mail sent by nonhouseholds, where nonhouseholds are defined to include all businesses (grouped into nine specified categories,* plus "all others"), units of government, and nonprofit organizations. Moreover, the mail sent by each of these nonhousehold groups is to be identified by type of contents, intended recipient, class and subclass, and cost-causing attributes such as weight and size.

Because the Postal Service requires levels of precision to be specified, probability sampling was necessary. And since the mail piece data must contain a combination of attributes known only to senders, nonhouseholds themselves had to be the respondent units. These two seemingly simple requirements imposed complex methodological problems. Consider, first, the sampling aspect. A probability sample can be drawn only if a sampling frame of the universe is available, and no available frame—a means of allowing every single nonhousehold establishment in the coterminous United States to have a known non-zero chance of selection into the sample—was known to exist. Therefore such a frame had to be constructed. Second, instrumentation had to be developed that would permit SRC interviewers entrance to the establishments' executives and make the potentially overwhelming job of cataloging every piece of outgoing mail manageable. The sampling considerations and the data collection design and instrumentation are discussed separately below.

SAMPLING CONSIDERATIONS

In order to draw a sample of establishments representative of non-household mailers of all sizes, industrial types, and geographic locations, a two-stage sample was designed. The first stage consists of a sample of post

---

*These are: department stores, mail order companies, telephone telegraph, other utilities, securities, mailing services, publishers, insurance companies, and banks.

offices grouped into primary sampling units (PSUs).* The second stage consists of a sample of establishments selected from the PSUs.

The First Stage Sample of Post Offices†

An important step in most survey sample designs is "stratifying" the elements in the universe. Stratification—which may be performed at each stage of the sample—involves the grouping of the elements in the universe into strata by known variation in those attributes which are highly correlated with variables to be measured in the study. Estimates derived from a stratified sample of a given size are expected to have smaller variances than estimates derived from a simple random sample of the same size. The gains in the precision of estimates achieved are related to the quality of stratification.

Stratification for the first-stage sample required grouping post offices in the manner suggested above. The Postal Service was able to identify each post office by geographic region and size measured by gross postal revenue. Unfortunately, no information was available to indicate how much of this revenue derives from nonhouseholds as opposed to households, how mail volume relates to postal revenue, or how establishments' use of mail varies within post offices. Consequently, gross postal revenue was used as the stratifying variable.

The Postal Service itself groups post offices into 11 cost accounting groups (CAGs) based on revenue. It was decided, therefore, to have the strata coincide, insofar as possible, with Postal Service CAG designations. Analysis indicated that offices within each of CAGs B to L were sufficiently different from offices in other CAGs to permit each of these to form a separate stratum. But 17 of the CAG A offices were so large that each became a separate stratum and was selected with certainty in the primary stage. Two other offices (one CAG A and one CAG B) had such a heavy concentration of certain types of mailers that they, at the request of the Postal Service, were treated as separate strata. In all, then, the universe of post offices was partitioned into 28 strata.

Selecting Offices Within Strata

For practical reasons, it was decided to select approximately 150 PSUs. The post offices selected had to be distributed in relation to the

---

*Although most PSUs consist of only one post office, eight consist of a cluster of several small post offices. Clustering post offices in these PSUs was necessary since very few establishments are served by each of the clustered offices and no one office would serve a sufficient number of establishments from which to draw a second-stage sample.

†For details of this phase of the study, see, *A Quantitative Description of the Current Nonhousehold Mailstream: Task 2 Report.*

universe of post offices with respect not only to size but also to geographic location. Starting with a desired total first-stage sample size of approximately 150, the number of offices to be selected from each stratum was determined. Then, to assure geographic balance, the number of offices to be selected from each geographic region was determined. Given the joint constraints of offices per stratum and offices per region, controlled selection was used to designate the distribution of PSUs by CAG stratum and postal region. Selection of PSUs within the CAG-region categories was made with probabilities proportional to 1976 gross postal revenue for each PSU. Maps showing the distribution of sample PSUs and of 1970 population depict a similarity between these distributions.

Division of Sample PSUs into Quarter-Samples

Although it would have been preferable to bring in all 150 sample PSUs on the first day of data collection, it was impossible to do all the preliminary work prior to the required start of field operations. Consequently, the sample of PSUs was divided into four quarter-samples, each in itself a legitimate probability sample balanced by post office size and geographic location. Data collection was scheduled to start with establishments in the first quarter-sample with remaining quarter-samples brought in as quickly as possible. As it turned out, the second quarter-sample was brought into the field in the beginning of the second calendar quarter of data collection, and the third and fourth quarter-samples in the beginning of the third calendar quarter.

The Establishment List

Once sample PSUs were selected, a list of nonhousehold establishments within those PSUs had to be developed. As stated earlier, the Postal Service required separate estimates for nine specific business categories as well as for "all other businesses," for government units, and for nonprofit agencies. A relatively small feasibility test indicated that the 11 groups of special interest generate over 50 percent of postal revenue but account for only about 20 percent of nonhousehold establishments in the United States (SRC Sampling Section and Postal Study Research Staff 1977). Because some of these groups are "rare cases" in terms of number of nonhouseholds and because the geographic distribution of specific types of households within postal areas was unknown, it was decided to obtain a listing of all nonhouseholds served by the first-stage post offices and to draw the sample from this list.

In order to draw the second-stage sample, each nonhousehold establishment located in the service area of sample post offices had to be identified by name, street address, industrial type, and size measured in terms of postage purchased in 1977. The obvious group to prepare the lists is, of course, postal carriers. They, better than any other group, are likely to know not only of the existence of nonhousehold establishments in the geographic areas of their routes (whether or not they deliver mail there) but also the industrial type of each.

Instrumentation was developed to enable carriers to record this information on sheets that could be used directly in keypunching. The carriers were given detailed instructions regarding both what to list and how to translate "what these establishments do" into specified industry-type groups. A description of the type of establishments that belong in each industry-type group, with numerous examples, was provided.

The one required piece of information that carriers were unlikely to know was postage purchased by the establishments they serve. Some of this information, however, could be obtained from post offices since they are required to keep records of meter, permit imprint, and second-class postage purchased from them. Copies of these records were obtained along with any other postage information they could provide. From all of these records, postage purchased in 1977 was calculated.

Probably the most time-consuming part of frame construction was merging postage records into carrier listings. In the feasibility test, a computer merge program was written and run on data collected from four cities. The results were disappointing. Less than 70 percent of the records could be merged. Among the many reasons for this were name spellings that differed between carrier listings and postal records, initials and/or first names appearing on one source of information and not on the other, and different addresses or spelling of addresses on the two sets of records. Address discrepancies were particularly problematical since postal records often are not updated when establishments move. The number of possible kinds of minor differences between the two sources of information is enormous, and they all seemed to occur on one set of records or another.

The horrible truth revealed itself: If these records were to be merged with accuracy sufficient for sample selection, they would have to be merged by hand! And approximately one-half million financial records had to be merged into almost 1.6 million carrier listings. For small post offices, the job was not difficult. But for cities like Los Angeles, New York, and Chicago at times it appeared overwhelming. In all, an average of 45 full-time-equivalent employees worked 11 months to complete this project. Quarter-sample PSUs were processed sequentially to permit second-stage selection in time for field operations.

The Second-Stage Sample of Establishments Within Post Offices

The second stage in the development of the sample was the selection of establishments within sample primary units. For establishments with recorded postage expenditure, a sample drawn with probabilities proportional to size (PPS) was thought to provide an advantage with regard to sample precision. The measure of size for each establishment was defined to be its total recorded postage for fiscal year 1977.

A major problem with using this procedure for selecting the sample is that a large number of establishments do not use any services for which post offices keep customer-specific records. Over-the-counter purchases of stamps present the biggest problem. Establishments that use stamps will generally not be credited with a corresponding measure of size in the nonhousehold frame, and data from the frame indicate that approximately 80 to 85 percent of all nonhouseholds rely solely on the use of postage stamps or do no mailing at all. On an individual basis, these establishments are probably not large mailers, but their aggregate impact on the mailstream may be substantial.

Although several approaches could have been used to deal with establishments lacking a postal-expenditure measure of size, the following plan was developed, primarily because of its compatability with a computerized selection algorithm. Establishments with assigned postal-expenditure measures of size were eligible for selection with a probability proportional to their fiscal 1977 recorded postage purchases. This PPS procedure is designed to sample the high-volume users of postal services. Paralleling the PPS selection, but independent from it, was a second procedure aimed at sampling from the entire universe regardless of a priori notions about establishment size. Address locations of all listed establishments were sampled with equal probability. Assuming the theoretically complete coverage of the universe by the sample design, the second procedure provides each nonhousehold establishment location in the coterminous United States a known, non-zero probability of selection. In reality, this assertion must be tempered by the likelihood that the list of nonhousehold addresses has some degree of undercoverage.

Under the PPS procedure, the listed establishment is the sample element even if it has moved from the originally listed address. (This procedure was modified somewhat in the field. Only $20,000-and-over establishments were followed within their postal area, and only $2 million-and-over establishments followed outside of the areas served by the post office in which they were listed.) In contrast, under the second procedure the establishment occupying the sampled address location on the Monday of the assigned data collection week is designated as the respondent unit. Sampling establishments by their location at a randomly assigned point in time increases sample coverage of newly formed establishments and provides a means for coping with movement within the nonhousehold universe. Related to this, locations listed as "vacant" or "under construction" are eligible for selection. Establishments occupying sampled units of this type on or before the Monday of the assigned data collection week are designated as respondents. New construction begun since the listing was performed (winter and spring 1978) is not covered in the frame.

The Postal Service requested special consideration for 12 groups of establishments. The sample size necessary to meet analysis specifications required different sampling rates for each of the 12 groups. Two sampling rates were calculated for each group, one for the PPS procedure and another for the location-selection procedure. A computerized program for systematic selection of establishments at the group-specific sampling rates was run. Input listings from the nonhousehold frame were read directly from magnetic tapes, and selected listings were written to an on-line system file. A second program prepared the selected listings for the field operation by assigning a sequence number, post office code, selection procedure code, random data-collection week, and random validation day(s) to each sample listing. From this prepared sample file, labels for cover sheets and sample address summaries for interviewers were prepared. Subsequently a series of control files was established and summary programs written to monitor the status of each sample listing in the field.

Assignment of Establishments to Weeks

The random assignment of establishments to weeks of the data-collection year results in each week having a legitimate probability sample of establishments reflecting the industrial types to be studied, geographic regions, and size of PSUs. Each week approximately 100 establishments are asked to provide detailed data on their outgoing mail for a one-week period. No establishment is asked to participate more than once in a quarter. (The sample was pulled with replacement for each quarter separately. Consequently some mailers, usually large ones, are asked to provide data for one week in two or more quarters. Procedures were greatly modified for "repeat selections" to minimize the burden of their providing data more than once.) With the data in hand, national estimates of mail flow can be made for annual or shorter periods, and seasonal variations can be observed.

Some Refinements in Sample Design

Federal Government Establishments

The sample design described in the preceding paragraphs contains two weaknesses of a statistical nature for which special remedial action was taken. Under the PPS selection procedure, federal government establishments would not be represented in proportion to their actual use of postal services since in most instances they hold penalty mail privileges. All attempts by SRC to obtain a comprehensive list of federal units with their associated postal expenditure in dollar equivalents were unsuccessful. Record-keeping practices for penalty mail lack detail and uniformity across government units. Current regulations require only that an annual report on usage be submitted to the Postal Service, and this on an agency rather than an establishment basis.

The measure-of-size underrepresentation of federal government establishments results in their having small probabilities of selection, which in turn translate into higher weights for data gathered from them. The application of large weights to potentially large establishments' data produces an increase in the overall variance of sample estimates. A decision was made to reduce this effect by supplementing the sample. But the sample was supplemented in the Washington, D.C., area only for two reasons. First, constructing lists from which to draw supplemental samples is extremely time-consuming. It was thought necessary to do so for Washington, D.C., where the problem of measure-of-size underrepresentation is most pronounced, but not for other areas where there is a considerably lower concentration of federal offices. Second, it was thought that there was likely to be a relatively high degree of undercoverage of federal establishments in the Washington, D.C., nonhousehold list because carriers there normally deliver mail not to individual federal establishments but rather to specified drop points.

A number of sources were used to construct the Washington, D.C., supplementary frame, but none is totally inclusive. As a result the frame is likely to have some degree of noncoverage. Listings in the supplemental frame are organized into two strata, one consisting of major departments, offices, agencies, and commissions, and the other of all federal establishments. The lack of knowledge concerning listed units' mail volume and characteristics discouraged the use of a more complex set of stratification guidelines. A total of 20 federal units in Washington, D.C., were selected into the supplemental sample, 12 from the first stratum and 8 from the second.

Large Mailers Outside of Sample Post Offices

Most large post offices in the United States were included with certainty or selected with high probability in the first stage of the sample. Large users of postal services in these post offices are subsequently selected with high probability in the second stage of selection. Under sampling theory, large mailers outside of sample post offices are represented by similar establishments within sample post offices. It is known, however, that the distribution of postal expenditure across establishments is highly skewed and the largest mail users are not necessarily found in the largest primary areas. Many of the highest volume users of the USPS are located in small- and medium-sized post offices. In these post offices, a single large mailer may account for as much as 95 percent of gross postal revenue. The uniqueness of many of these isolated large users raises questions as to whether they can be represented adequately by other establishments.

If two post offices serve areas that are basically the same except that one includes a large mailer and the other does not, the post office serving the large mailer will have greater revenue than the other post office, and its selection probability will be correspondingly greater. The implication of this for overall sample design is loss of "sample efficiency" relative to a hypothetical design in which such "outliers" do not exist. This loss of efficiency takes the form of increased variances in estimates from the sample data. Sample variances both within primary selection units and between primary selection units in the same stratum are increased by the presence of the large mailers in small- and medium-sized post offices.

Ideally, all large mailers should have been included in the sample with certainty and removed from the universe of establishments prior to the primary-stage selection of post offices. Including large, unique mailers in the sample with certainty eliminates any contribution they would otherwise make to overall sampling variation. Their data simply become a constant in developing sample estimates, although these data may still be subject to nonsampling error or bias.

In planning the sample design, the intention was to follow the above procedure. However, the only lists available from the USPS or other sources were either outdated or limited in scope, and project timing prohibited the development of a new list of large users prior to selection of the primary units. Consequently, primary selection probabilities for post offices reflect the presence of these large users. As expected, several post offices were chosen primarily because of the presence of a single large mailer within their service areas.

A list of big mailers outside the sample PSUs was ultimately created by inserting a notice to postmasters of non-PSU post offices in CAGs A to C in the *Postal Bulletin*, an official publication of the Postal Service. The notice requested a list of the names, addresses, and postage expenditures of all customers that purchased $2 million or more of postage in 1977. A form was provided for this purpose. If postmasters had no such customers, they were simply to check a box on the form indicating this. They were instructed to send the forms to the Survey Research Center, where they were logged in. Post offices that did not comply with the initial request were sent a reminder. When all post offices had returned the forms, the list of big mailers across the United States was compiled. Its degree of coverage should be very high.

The list was organized by industry type and total expenditure. Within each industry-type stratum, the larger mailers were designated to enter the study with certainty. The cutoff level within each stratum was set subjectively after considering the costs and benefits of including units smaller than the cutoff value. The result of this process was the inclusion with certainty of 74 large mailers outside of sample post offices.

DATA COLLECTION: INSTRUMENTATION
AND FIELD PROCEDURES

When the first quarter-sample was drawn and assigned to data collection weeks, it became possible to initiate field operations. Data collection procedures were designed with the understanding that full cooperation of all post offices involved would be forthcoming. This cooperation was assured by having Senior Assistant Postmaster General E. V. Dorsey send a letter to postmasters of the offices selected in the first stage explaining the importance of the study program and their role in it. Throughout the data collection period, the recalcitrance occasionally encountered at the local post office level has been turned around by a telephone call to that office from the technical representative of the Rates and Classification Research Division of the USPS assigned to the study. In fact, local post office problems have been surprisingly few, given the high degree of participation expected of these offices in the study.

Two types of data collection instruments are used for each cooperating establishment: two questionnaires, one addressed to the establishment's executive and one to the "mail handler" or person directly responsible for entering material into the mailstream; and a set of forms designed to facilitate the recording of mail-piece data. In addition, a procedure was set up to verify some of the mail-piece data provided by cooperating establishments.

The Questionnaires

The Executive Interview

Approximately six weeks prior to an establishment's scheduled data collection week, an SRC interviewer initiates the data collection process by identifying the appropriate executive respondent. The interviewer does this by calling the secretary to the president of the establishment (or corresponding appropriate officer) and, through discussion, identifying the person who, first, is involved in and preferably responsible for policy decisions pertaining to the use of mail and alternate delivery services and, second, is in a position to commit the entire establishment to cooperate in mail-piece data collection.

Once this executive is identified, the interviewer sends him or her a letter encouraging participation. The letter attempts to show the executive that his establishment's cooperation will enable the Postal Service to improve services and to structure rates with greater economic rationality. To underscore the importance of the study, the letter is written on the letterhead of the United States Postal Service and is signed by the local postmaster.

After allowing sufficient time for the letter to be delivered, the interviewer calls the establishment and makes an appointment to conduct the executive interview, which requires about one hour. The questionnaire addresses issues such as establishment characteristics (industrial type, size, population served, and so on), attitudes towards and use of the Postal Service and of competing services, and potential demand for new services that the USPS might offer in the future. If the executive is unable to provide factual information requested, an attempt is made to obtain it from others in the establishment.

Upon completion of the executive questionnaire, the interviewer requests permission to interview the "mail handler,"* to have counts of outgoing mail made in the mailroom during a specified week, and to have everyone in the establishment who prepares outgoing mail place codes indicating type of content and type of recipient on the outside of each mail piece they prepare during data collection week. The executive is also requested to send a memo to all employees encouraging participation in content and recipient coding.

The Mail Handler Interview

The interviewer attempts to administer the mail handler questionnaire after the executive interview has been completed. If this is inconvenient, an appointment is arranged. The mail handler questionnaire, considerably shorter than the executive questionnaire, addresses the mail handler's attitudes toward the Postal Service and obtains detailed information not likely to be known by the executive about postal services the establishment uses. Upon completion of the questionnaire, the interviewer sets up an appointment for the week preceding the scheduled data collection week to train the mail handler and others in the mailroom to complete the mail-piece forms.

Mail-Piece Data Collection

Between 10 and 13 items of information are needed about each mail piece sent by an establishment during its data collection week, the exact number depending on the type of mail piece. Examples of required data items include date sent, method of indicia, how it enters the mail stream, size, postage, class, type of contents, and intended recipient. Similar types of information are required of items sent through delivery systems competitive with the Postal Service, such as United Parcel Service.

For an establishment that sends only a few mail pieces a day, providing

---

*In small establishments, the executive may be the mail handler. In this case, the interviewer addresses relevant portions of the mail handler questionnaire to the executive.

the required data is relatively simple and minimally time-consuming. But some establishments, particularly mailing services, send many thousands of pieces each day. One of the most difficult parts of the study was designing forms that would make the job of data collection feasible, even for very large mailers. Many versions were tried in the field before the current versions were printed.

The single most important factor contributing to the feasibility of mail-piece data collection is the fact that huge mailings by a nonhousehold establishment usually consist of identical mail pieces. Moreover, to take advantage of preferential mailing rates (pre-sort, bulk-rate, and so on) or to mail with a permit imprint rather than stamps or meter strips, mailers must complete a Postal Service form of each mailing. This form identifies the number of pieces being sent, the mail class, and other types of information required for the study. Taking advantage of this, SRC designed forms with the top half identical to the Postal Service forms and the bottom half requesting the remaining dozen or so required pieces of information about the mailing. It had these forms made into sets of four pages with carbon paper inserted between them. The top two pages are the regular postal service forms and the bottom two the SRC forms. Therefore, in filling out the padded forms, the establishment need do little more than it does routinely when preparing a mailing.

Designing forms for mail pieces that are not sent in batches requiring Postal Service forms was more challenging. Ultimately seven forms that worked well were designed for different types of mail pieces (three for envelopes in different size groups, one for postcards, one for packages, one for mail using special services, and one for items sent through mail-competing services). In addition, a separate form was created to capture information about each second-class publication sent by the sample establishment during the previous year.

During each day of the assigned data-collection week, mailroom employees of participating establishments complete the mail-piece forms. Because content and recipient codes are placed on the front of mail pieces, these employees are able to provide all of the required information.

If an establishment is willing to cooperate but finds the job of completing the mail-piece forms overwhelming, two different procedures are being used. For establishments that keep good records, an attempt is made to capture much of the information from these records or to make good estimates based on them. If adequate records are not available, employees of the local post office complete the forms. When this is done, establishments sometimes are able to provide good content/recipient estimates so this information is not lost. Some have even been willing to place content/recipient codes on the mail despite the fact that they have felt unable to do the actual data recording.

Post Office Participation

Once an establishment has agreed to participate, the local post office becomes involved in several ways. First, it delivers all of the required forms and instruction books to the establishment before mailroom training is scheduled to take place. Occasionally it assists SRC interviewers with training when mailroom equipment is complex and unfamiliar to them. It picks up all of the establishment's outgoing mail during the week unless the establishment routinely brings it to the post office. This pick-up serves two purposes: it acts as an incentive to encourage participation; and it enables the post office to do independent mail counts that provide verification of the mail-piece data collected by the establishment. Validation counts are made on one day for all participating establishments and on three days for 20 percent of them. To assure consistency in data reporting, establishments are not told that validation counts are being made.

Data Processing

At the end of data collection week, establishments send their completed mail-piece forms to SRC. When they are received, they are logged in and compared with prior information about the types of forms expected from them. When all of the forms and the interviews have been received for an establishment, the data are entered directly to a disk file. Once a month, data on the disk files are transferred to tape and the usual "data cleaning" process is undertaken. Analysis of the first three months of data will begin shortly.

ESTIMATION TECHNIQUES

Data will be presented to the Postal Service in the form of estimates of summary statistics such as means, percentages, totals, and possibly more complex statistics such as correlation and regression coefficients. Estimates will be made for the entire population as well as for a number of its subclasses.

Many of the statistical requirements of the data were anticipated when the sample design was planned. Since the data will be used in the formation (and defense) of policy pertaining to rates and classifications, the precision of estimates must be presented. The probability sampling design facilitates both the development of the estimates and the calculation of sampling errors—statistics that indicate the quality of these estimates.

In the following section, two methods of calculating population and subclass means and totals from sample data will be presented. It is possible that other estimation techniques for analysis of the Postal Study data will be developed. Beginning with the two forms of estimators presented below, as many alternatives as time and resources permit will be investigated. The decision regarding what forms of the estimators to use will be based on precision, ease of use, and continuity across variable types.

Simple Weighted Estimators

A. *Means*   B. *Totals*

$$\bar{y}_w = \frac{\displaystyle\sum_{a=1}^{A} \sum_{i=1}^{n_a} w_{ai} \cdot y_{ai}}{\displaystyle\sum_{a=1}^{A} \sum_{i=1}^{n_a} w_{ai}}$$

$$\hat{Y}_w = \sum_{a=1}^{A} \sum_{i=1}^{n_a} w_{ai} \cdot y_{ai}$$

Notation

$\bar{y}_w$ = Weighted estimate of the population mean for variable y.

$\hat{Y}_w$ = Weighted estimate of the population total for variable y.

y_{ai} = Value of variable y for establishment i in PSU a.

w_{ai} = Weight value for establishment i in PSU a. Generally, it is the product of the inverse of the probability of selection, F_{ai} , and any supplemental weights such as nonresponse weights.

a = PSU subscript ($a = 1, \ldots , A$).

A = Total number of sample PSUs.

i = Establishment subscript ($i = 1, \ldots , n_a$).

n_a = Total number of sample establishments in PSU a.

The estimators y_w and Y_w are thus weighted means and weighted totals.

Ratio Estimators

More precise estimators of means and of totals can be produced if the population mean of another variable, x, can be obtained without error from an independent source. In addition to data pertaining to the variables that are of direct interest, the value of the auxiliary variable x must be obtained from each sample establishment. Then ratio estimators of the following form can be constructed.

A. *Means*   B. *Totals*

$$\bar{y}_r = \sum_{k=1}^{K} \widetilde{\bar{X}}_k \left\{ \frac{\sum\limits_{a=1}^{A} \sum\limits_{i=1}^{n_{ak}} w_{ai} \cdot y_{kai}}{\sum\limits_{a=1}^{A} \sum\limits_{i=1}^{n_{ak}} w_{ai} \cdot x_{kai}} \right\} \qquad \hat{y}_r = \sum_{k=1}^{K} \widetilde{X}_k \left\{ \frac{\sum\limits_{a=1}^{A} \sum\limits_{i=1}^{n_{ak}} w_{ai} \cdot y_{kai}}{\sum\limits_{a=1}^{A} \sum\limits_{i=1}^{n_{ak}} w_{ai} \cdot x_{kai}} \right\}$$

$$= \sum_{k=1}^{K} \widetilde{\bar{X}}_k \cdot r_k \qquad\qquad\qquad = \sum_{k=1}^{K} \widetilde{X}_k \cdot r_k$$

Notation

$\bar{y}_r$ = Ratio estimate of the population mean for variable *y*.

$\widetilde{\bar{X}}_k$ = Independent estimate of the population mean of the auxilliary variable *x* for establishments in stratum *k*.

$\hat{Y}_r$ = Ratio estimate of the population total for variable *y*.

$\widetilde{X}_k$ = Independent estimate of the population total of the auxilliary variable *x* for establishments in stratum *k*.

y_{kai} = Value of variable *y* for establishment *i* in PSU *a*. Establishment is a member of stratum *k*.

x_{kai} = Value of the auxiliary variable *x* for establishment *i* in PSU *a*. Establishment is a member of stratum *k*.

r_k = Ratio of weighted sample totals for variables *x* and *y* from sample establishments in stratum *k*.

w_{ai} = Weight value for establishment *i* in PSU *a*. Generally, it is the product of the inverse of the probability of selection, F_{ai}, and any supplemental weights such as nonresponse weights.

a = PSU subscript (a = 1, . . . , A).

A   = Total number of sample PSUs.

i   = Establishment subscript (i = 1, . . . , n_a).

n_a = Total number of establishments in PSU *a*.

n_{ak} = Total number of establishments in PSU *a* belonging to stratum *k*.

k   = Stratum subscript (k = 1, . . . , K). For most analyses, these strata will be the 12 organizational-type groups used as the strata for selecting the sample. However, certain analyses may benefit from poststratification on other variables such as region and expenditure.

K   = Total number of strata.

In this study, the most promising auxiliary variable is postage purchased by establishments in 1977, the same data that were used to calculate probabilities for PPS selection. Unfortunately, the data in the frame are not perfectly accurate or complete so that $\overset{\approx}{X}_k$ and $\widetilde{X}_k$ will be subject to variation. Since this variation will enter ratio estimation of both the mean and the total, the relative precision of the estimators $\overline{y}_w$ and $\overline{y}_r$, and of $\hat{Y}_w$ and $\hat{Y}_r$, will have to be compared empirically. It is possible that the relative precision of y and y , and of Y and Y , will depend on the type of variable for which estimates are being made.

Error and Bias Analyses

All sample data are subject to a number of sources of error and bias. Proper data analysis requires assessment of the impact that these errors and biases may have on estimates produced from the data.

Sources of Error

A distinction is usually made between sampling error and nonsampling error. Sampling error arises because the value of any characteristic to be estimated varies among the elements that comprise the population. Statistical estimates derived from data provided by one sample of population elements are likely, therefore, to differ from statistical estimates derived from a different sample of the same size. This variation, or "sampling error," is always present in sample estimates of population values, and surveys must be designed to cope with it.

This Postal Study sample was designed to control sampling error by using techniques such as stratification and controlled selection. Sampling error estimates for the first calendar quarter will be calculated as soon as the availability of data permits. When data for the full year are available, sampling error estimates will be calculated for the complete spectrum of variable types and population subclasses. But cost and time considerations prohibit calculating sampling errors for every conceivable estimate that might be of interest. Therefore, a series of general-usage sampling error tables will be developed using average variance characteristics of a representative cross-section of variable types and subclasses of the population. Under the theory of large-scale normal distribution approximation, sampling error entries in the tables can be translated into confidence intervals which, in turn, can be used to evaluate the approximate precision of estimates produced from the data.

Investigation of sampling errors will be extensive in this study due to the unique character of the sample design and the intended use of the data for policy formation. Calculation of sampling error estimates will be performed using software available on The University of Michigan's computing system.

Nonsampling errors may also enter the data and thereby affect the resulting estimates. To control nonsampling error (which has the potential for causing serious problems in any study), the Institute for Social Research maintains professional interviewing and coding staffs and follows verification and consistency-testing procedures at all levels of data handling.

Sources of Bias

Bias can also become embedded in sample data and estimates. Bias can occur in this study for a number of reasons. First, the nonhousehold frame contains duplicate listings because of imperfect merging of postage records and carrier listings. Unless discovered, the weights associated with duplicate-listed sample establishments will be too large. A serious effort is being made to identify duplicate listings and adjust selection probabilities accordingly. The frame also is bound to have some degree of noncoverage because carriers may have forgotten to list some nonhousehold establishments and may have been unaware of the existence of others. Unless there are postage records for the unlisted establishments, they will not appear in the frame. Undercoverage will be investigated through a small coverage check in the field. Also, where possible, comparisons will be made between nonhousehold attributes estimated from the sample frame and the same attributes obtained from independent sources.

Bias can also be introduced through the presence of nonresponse. How bias is introduced depends, in part, on the estimation procedures used. If expansion estimators are used to estimate population totals and some establishments have refused to provide data, the estimates will have a downward bias unless adjustment is made for nonresponse. This adjustment involves increasing the weights attached to data collected from some cooperating establishments. The tricky thing here is to decide which weights to adjust since little is usually known about nonrespondents. Adjustment will probably be less problematical in the postal study than might be the case because the sample frame contains a considerable amount of information about all establishments and thus provides some basis for making nonresponse adjustments.

Ratio estimators can introduce two different sources of bias. First, ratio estimators are, by nature, biased estimators (irrespective of the quality of sample data), although for large samples the degree of bias they introduce is small compared with sampling variance. Second, unless explicit adjustments are made, ratio estimates of population values are calculated on the implicit assumption that respondents are representative of the population. If, in fact, respondents do differ in significant ways from nonrespondents, ratio estimators introduce bias into sample estimates unless appropriate weight adjustments for nonresponse are made.

"Delayed response" also has the potential for introducing bias. It should be recalled that one aspect of the sample design is the assignment of establishments to specific weeks for mail-piece data collection. An establishment may agree to provide data but not for the assigned week. When this happens, a decision must be made: should the establishment be treated as a nonrespondent (with its concomitant potential sources of bias), or should it be allowed to provide data for an alternative week? The primary factor influencing the choice is whether or not a different week can be found that is similar to the week originally assigned in terms of mail composition and volume. If no similar week exists, the establishment must be taken as a nonrespondent. If a similar week can be found, then mail-piece data are collected during this week but are analyzed *as if* they were collected during the week originally assigned. If they were not analyzed this way, estimates of population totals for combinations of data collection weeks might have either upward or downward biases.

In summary, many steps have been taken to reduce error and bias, but they can never be eliminated completely in complex studies. Although sampling errors are estimable, in general most nonsampling errors and biases are not because quantification procedures are not currently feasible. Persons analyzing the data from this survey will need to draw on experience with survey data and knowledge of the subject to assess the degree of any nonsampling errors and biases that may be embodied in the data and the implications they may have.

PROBABILITY SAMPLING, MARKET RESEARCH, AND GOVERNMENT

The advantages of probability sampling for market research for the government sector are exactly the same as its advantages for research for any other sector. Primary among them is that the precision of estimates made from probability samples can be estimated and, through adjustment of sample size, prespecified levels of precision may be built into the survey design. Alternatively, it is possible to design relatively efficient samples for a given level of cost.

In a parallel fashion, the disadvantages of probability sampling are the same for all types of research for which it might be used. Primary among them is cost. In order to draw a probability sample, a reasonably complete, up-to-date frame must be available. But the cost of developing and maintaining probability sample frames can be very great, depending on the nature of the universe to be studied. Also, the cost of adhering to strict field procedures, for example, not permitting interviewers to substitute one respondent for another if the selected respondent is unavailable, may be relatively large.

Needless to say, it is the researcher who must decide, on the basis of his or her knowledge of the problems under study and the intended uses of data collected, whether measuring the precision of estimates permitted by probability sampling is worth the cost. We who are working on the Postal Study are obviously committed to probability sampling and are very excited about the potential uses this new sampling frame may have for all kinds of future research—for the government or others—in which intended respondents are nonhouseholds. We are now beginning to consider alternative procedures for making the nonhousehold frame more manageable and methods we might use for updating it. We are, we believe, at the start of a very exciting venture.

REFERENCES

Kallick, M. et al. (1977), *Household Mailstream Study: Final Report*. Ann Arbor: Institute for Social Research.

SRC Sampling Section jointly with the Postal Study Research Staff (1977), *A Quantitative Description of the Current Nonhousehold Mailstream: Task 2 Report*. Ann Arbor: Institute for Social Research.

16

CONSUMER RESEARCH IN THE FEDERAL GOVERNMENT

Kenneth L. Bernhardt

A review of the consumer research literature over the past few years indicates the greatly expanded interest in applying consumer behavior research techniques to public policy problems. As has been pointed out in many articles and speeches by government officials, this body of research has not always been utilized by government agencies in their decision-making processes, even though the potential for consumer research contributions has been demonstrated (Dyer and Shimp 1977; Mazis and McNeill 1978; Rosch 1975; Wilkie and Gardner 1974). The purpose of this chapter is to demonstrate that a substantial amount of consumer research is being undertaken by government agencies and to provide examples of the types of projects involved. A second objective is to analyze how consumer research conducted for government differs from that conducted for the private sector. While many of the examples of current research described are being conducted for the Federal Trade Commission (FTC), an attempt has been made to identify and describe a variety of studies being conducted for other government agencies as well.

There are a number of indications that consumer research in government has been increasing. An informal group of government consumer researchers formed the Consumer Research Interagency Group (CRIG) several years ago. There are now over 50 people on the CRIG mailing list,

The author expresses thanks to Michael B. Mazis, Federal Trade Commission, and Richard B. Ross, Market Facts–Washington, for their assistance in the preparation of this presentation. The views expressed are the author's and do not represent the views of the FTC or any FTC official.

and the number of individuals attending the monthly meetings during 1978–79 was substantially higher than in previous years. Four large national consumer research firms, Chilton, Market Facts, Opinion Research Corporation, and Westat, have Washington offices, most of which have been expanding recently. The author is aware of several other large national consumer research organizations that have recently been investigating the possibility of opening Washington offices to handle their increasing government business. Richard B. Ross, vice president in charge of the Washington office for Market Facts, estimates that the total market for consumer research among federal government agencies is between $30 and $60 million, depending upon how consumer research is defined.

CONSUMER RESEARCH AT THE FEDERAL TRADE COMMISSION

Several authors have criticized the FTC for not conducting more consumer research (Engel, Blackwell and Kollat 1978; Aaker and Myers 1975). Aaker and Myers provide a list of reasons why the FTC has not employed consumer surveys in deceptive advertising cases, including the argument that survey research is somewhat inconsistent with the adversary system. They state, "To an attorney, agreeing to a carefully conceived and conducted survey might be too much like calling a prestigious witness without knowing which side his testimony will support" (pp. 580–81). This author submits that this viewpoint is no longer prevalent among FTC attorneys and that today many cases and rule-making proceedings are being developed with the use of consumer research.

Wilkie and Gardner (1974) outlined a number of areas of FTC decisions that might benefit from consumer research. A recent article by Mazis and McNeill (1978) demonstrates that much of the potential for increased consumer research input at the FTC has been attained. Eighteen studies are outlined, including descriptions of the studies' research objectives and policy goals. The following section of this chapter will serve to update that report, describing several detailed examples of how consumer research is currently being used at the FTC.

Most of the consumer research now being conducted at the FTC is a part of the newly created Impact Evaluation Program. Three full-time professionals were assigned to this program when the impact evaluation group was created during the summer of 1978. The fiscal year 1979 budget contains over $700,000 for contract research, almost all of which is consumer research. The purpose of this program is to assess the impact of FTC actions on consumers and industry. An impact evaluation can be a prospective study to predict the impact of proposed regulations or a retrospective study to measure the impact after a rule has been promulgated. Examples of each type will be presented.

Contact Lens Study

The FTC is currently considering the possibility of a trade regulation rule allowing opticians thoroughout the United States to fit contact lenses. At the moment there are a number of state laws prohibiting opticians from prescribing and fitting contact lenses. It is believed by the program staff that the strict standards in these restricted states result in unnecessarily high costs of this product to consumers. A major concern expressed by some members of the industry is whether the quality of the fitting of contact lenses would be decreased as a result of FTC regulations removing these restrictions. The purpose of the consumer research study is to investigate the impact of the regulations by comparing the quality and cost of the fit of contact lenses purchased in restrictive (opticians not allowed to fit contact lenses) and nonrestrictive states.

A consumer mail panel is being used to identify people who have recently purchased contact lenses. The total sample will consist of approximately 22,000 households in 12 Standard Metropolitan statistical areas. It is anticipated that the screening questionnaire will identify approximately 700 recent contact lens buyers who will then be brought to a central location to have their lenses examined by a panel of experts who will not be told where the consumer purchased the lenses. If the results show no quality differences in the lenses fitted by opticians, optometrists, and ophthalmologists, the rule-making process will proceed. If the quality of fit by the opticians is lower than that of the other groups, the program will be dropped.

Antacid Rule-making Proceedings

Two consumer research studies were conducted as part of the antacid rule-making proceedings. The proposed Trade Regulation Rule (TRR) would require antacid marketers to include in their television advertising a warning to reduce the amount of contraindicated drug use (for example, use of an antacid containing sodium by people on sodium-restricted diets).

The study utilized an experimental design with subjects assigned to either a control group or a group to be exposed to one of four alternative warnings. Specific impacts measured included: the degree of awareness of the commercial message and the warning message; knowledge of the content of the commercial and warning message; behavior related to label reading and product purchase by "at-risk" and "not-at-risk" consumers; and the generalization of warning information to not-at-risk consumers and to other products. The results of the study showed that the warning messages could be effectively communicated to the at-risk target audience without affecting sales to the not-at-risk group. This evidence was used to demonstrate that the TRR could be effective and should be promulgated.

A second study measured the incidence of contraindicated drug use using a consumer mail panel. The first wave identified a large number of at-risk consumers; a second wave measured the usage of contraindicated products by the at-risk group, documenting a high level of contraindicated usage. This study was used to show the need for regulation. This study can be replicated after whatever FTC action is taken to determine retrospectively the effect of the FTC regulations.

Corrective Advertising

The FTC is using consumer research increasingly to determine whether or not corrective advertising is needed as a remedy and to evaluate the effectiveness of corrective advertising remedies (Cohen 1978). The FTC has conducted a number of consumer attitude surveys to measure perceptions of advertising messages where deception is suspected. Consumer surveys have, for example, been important in the recent Anacin hearings, which resulted in a recommendation by the administrative law judge that American Home Products be required to spend $24 million in corrective advertising.

Studies of the effectiveness of the STP public notice ad and the Listerine corrective advertising campaign are currently being conducted. The STP research design utilizes pre-ad and post-ad telephone interviews; the Listerine design utilizes a longitudinal mail questionnaire methodology in addition to day-after recall measures by telephone.

Appliance Energy Labeling

Several consumer research studies have been conducted as part of this rule-making proceeding. First, focus groups were conducted with consumers to determine the information and format that should be used for the provision of energy consumption information to consumers evaluating alternative appliances. The second phase involved an experiment to test various label formats on perception and comprehension of the labels.

The final phase consists of assessing the impact of the energy labels on consumer purchasing patterns for appliances, shifting purchases to products that use less energy, and promotional practices of appliance marketers. The data will be used in conjunction with a later study to provide pre-to-post analysis of the effects of the labeling program.

Housing Defects Study

This study, jointly sponsored with the Department of Housing and Urban Development, will ascertain the nature, severity, and extent of defects occurring in new housing. Telephone interviews will be conducted with consumers who have owned their home for one or two years. Actual home inspections will be conducted for a subsample of the homes to determine the validity of the consumer responses. This study will serve to determine the need for federal government action in the housing market, provide direction to any programs that are needed, and provide a baseline measure for evaluating the effectiveness of any action taken.

Other FTC Consumer Research Studies

A large number of other FTC-sponsored consumer research studies are being conducted. For example, consumer research studies are being conducted as part of the proposed Funeral Homes Rule, Vocational Schools Rule, and Used Car Rule. Several studies are being conducted of the effectiveness of alternative life insurance cost disclosure provisions.

As the reader can readily see, consumer research has been incorporated into a number of FTC investigations. The new management of the agency is highly supportive of consumer research and has begun to expect its attorneys to include consumer research in the process of determining alternative remedies. Resources are also being provided to the attorneys to enable them to fulfill these expectations. The demands by Congress and the U.S. public for greater efficiency in government, less unnecessary regulation, and increased evaluation of current and proposed regulations should all contribute to a continued increase in the amount of consumer research conducted by the FTC.

CONSUMER RESEARCH IN OTHER GOVERNMENT AGENCIES

The author has made a modest attempt to identify examples of consumer research studies that have been or are being conducted by other federal agencies. The examples below are by no means comprehensive but should be considered as examples of the types of consumer research studies conducted by these agencies.

Consumer Product Safety Commission

The CPSC has recently conducted a number of consumer research studies. One project consisted of four-hour personal interviews on the use of child-resistant containers. The study sought to determine what happens after these containers are brought into the house. Do consumers remove the hard-to-open lids, or do they leave them on? The study used an experimental design to examine behavior with respect to all different types of closures and included the use of interviewer-administered photographs and torque measurements of the lids on bottles in the household.

An example of a consumer survey conducted to determine the potential need for regulation concerned the CPSC's investigation of thermal underwear. Apparently thermal underwear is sometimes used as sleepwear for children. The product is not required to be flame-retardant and therefore might present a danger to those children sleeping in it. The research will be used to determine the necessity for extending flame-retardant requirements to this product.

Another project utilizes an experimental design to determine the effect of information and education on children's use of school playground equipment. The study uses human factors research methodology to determine how children's behavior can be modified to increase their safety on the playground.

A study has been conducted to determine consumer response to public service announcement advertising of a home safety checklist program. The research determined the reach of the program and whether or not consumers provided with the checklist implemented any of the suggested actions.

Department of Energy

For a number of years the DOE has tracked consumer attitudes and behavior with respect to the perceptions of an energy crisis. They also have conducted consumer research on their life-cycle costing program, which has been test-marketed in Denver. This program would encourage consumers to incorporate operating costs into their evaluative criteria in purchasing appliances.

Another DOE study is tracking consumer ownership, usage, and preference for energy-saving and energy-using features on eight major appliances. The study will utilize conjoint analysis to determine the importance of such factors as frost-free mechanisms.

Food and Drug Administration

The Bureau of Drugs has done a number of studies concerning doctors as consumers of drugs and the effectiveness of alternative ways of providing warning information to doctors. These studies have utilized an experimental design and a variety of warning formats. Other studies have been conducted on consumer information processing on patient package inserts for prescription drug products.

The Bureau of Foods has conducted a number of studies of consumers' perceptions and use of information on food labels. These studies have tracked consumer information processing of ingredient labeling.

Department of Agriculture

This agency conducts a number of consumer research studies concerned with measuring the food consumption habits of the U.S. public. These studies measure the diet consumed by households, the menus used, and the amount of food actually consumed. The agency has hired national analysts at a cost of approximately $7 million to conduct a massive study of food habits.

Department of Defense

Twice each year DOD conducts telephone interviews to track attitudes toward joining the military. The studies measure awareness and recognition of the military advertising and measure the effectiveness of different packages of attributes to improve the attractiveness of joining the military. In addition, a number of copy tests are conducted by the ad agencies used by DOD, one of the countries biggest advertisers with a budget in excess of $100 million.

U.S. Postal Service

This agency has conducted a number of product research studies to determine the type and mix of services to market to their consumers. Also, a number of copy tests have been conducted through their advertising agency to increase the effectiveness of their paid advertising campaigns.

Department of Transportation National Highway Traffic Safety Administration

If one is willing to include human factors research in a definition of consumer research, then NHTSA is one of the government's largest buyers of consumer research. In addition, they have conducted several studies utilizing focus group interviews to determine consumer acceptance of fuel economy standards and the tradeoffs necessary to achieve these standards.

Department of Commerce

The Department of Commerce apparently conducts a number of consumer research studies overseas but does not do much consumer research in the United States. Some of their research is designed to help encourage exports of U.S. products, and much of the remainder is used to measure consumer attitudes and behavior of foreign tourists to help the U.S. Travel Service increase the number of tourists visiting the United States.

Department of Housing and Urban Development

HUD has conducted a number of studies of buyers of new and used houses and mobile homes. They are currently conducting a major consumer study to evaluate the effectiveness of the Real Estate Settlement Practices Act. The purposes of this study are to determine whether consumers received the required disclosure forms before closing on the houses they purchased, what they were told during the closing, and how they were able to process the information presented to them.

Library of Congress

The Library of Congress conducts a periodic survey of those who request materials for blind or handicapped persons to determine such things as preference for types of materials, frequency of use, and satisfaction with the services provided. The Library of Congress has also conducted consumer research to evaluate the effectiveness of their public service announcements in promoting the availability of materials for blind or handicapped individuals.

National Bureau of Standards

NBS has established its own testing laboratory for measuring consumer usage patterns for appliances. This information is used to develop testing procedures for evaluating such things as energy usage of different major appliances. In addition, NBS conducts a number of human factors research studies and consumer motivation studies associated with the Energy Technology Incentives Program.

National Institute for Alcoholism and Alcohol Abuse, National Institute for Drug Abuse, and Department of Treasury

The NIAAA and NIDA, two agencies in the Department of Health, Education and Welfare, have developed research programs to understand the motivation of consumers in their use of drugs and alcohol. They have also developed consumer research to evaluate the effectiveness of their programs. The Bureau of Alcohol, Tobacco, and Firearms in the Department of Treasury has conducted research to determine the impact of advertising on consumer perceptions and use of alcohol.

Social Security Administration

The Social Security Administration has conducted a study of consumer preference for direct deposit of Social Security checks. The study measured consumer likes and dislikes of direct deposit and determined the reasons why consumers would not use such a plan.

National Science Foundation

In the past few years the NSF has sponsored a number of consumer research studies in the area of consumer information processing as part of the RANN Program. Unfortunately, this program of pathbreaking research has been discontinued.

Differences Between Public and Private Sector Consumer Research

There are a great many differences in consumer research conducted for the public sector as compared to consumer research conducted in the private sector. Some would say that it differs in every way except for the fact that both involve obtaining information from consumers. These differences will be examined using the stages of a typical research project: (1) problem definition; (2) development of research design and data collection method; (3) sampling plan and data collection; and (4) analysis, interpretation, and final report.

Problem Definition

Problems that consumer research addresses in government are often more complex than the typical industry consumer research study. Often a problem must be defined without prior experience, as opposed to a situation in industry where a problem may have been dealt with previously. The amount of information available to aid the government decision maker is small compared to the information available from past studies for the industry decision maker. Much of the consumer research done in government is on a one-shot basis, compared to industry where often periodic studies are conducted and replicated.

There are a number of constraints inhibiting the amount of consumer research done by government. One example would be the substantial barrier caused by the need to obtain approval from the Office of Management and

Budget (OMB) for all executive branch consumer research studies and Government Accounting Office (GAO) approval for certain independent regulatory agency studies. As a result, a government study will often be conceived as one very comprehensive project whereas an industry counterpart might be broken into a series of much smaller projects. The massive study is thus much more difficult to define and formulate.

The decision-making process in government is often much more complex than the industry process. To the extent that the research must be defined and formulated to fit into this process, the complexity of government studies increases substantially over typical industry studies. In addition to the problem complexity issue, companies usually have marketing research directors and other personnel who are competent in designing research, while government is often deficient in these types of individuals.

Research Design and Data Collection Plan

Government consumer research studies are much less likely to utilize an experimental design. This is largely a function of lack of control over many of the important variables. For example, a company can decide to test market a new product in several markets, but it is impossible for a regulatory agency to test market a new regulation in a limited number of localities.

Government studies are much less likely to utilize consumer mail panels and other mail survey formats, principally because it is virtually impossible to receive OMB approval for these types of studies. Although government consumer research traditionally has not made much use of focus groups compared to industry's use of this technique, this situation is apparently changing.

The OMB requirement for a response rate greater than 70 percent results in a number of often cumbersome procedures in government consumer research designed to increase the response rate.

Unlike industry studies, most government research projects are available to the public and often subject to very close scrutiny. For example, research that is designed to be utilized in regulatory rule-making proceedings will have to be defended in cross-examination by opponents. Thus great care must be exercised to ensure that research has been properly designed. Often expert consultants will be hired in government studies to serve this oversight function during the course of the project. The result, in addition to a better designed study, often is a more costly product that has taken much more time then originally planned.

Sampling Plan and Data Collection

Government consumer research studies are more likely to utilize national samples in comparison with industry studies where, because of cost considerations, a study often is done in just a few markets. Also, government studies are more likely to utilize probability sampling plans than do industry studies. This is probably a function of the larger budgets of government studies and the need many agencies have for obtaining OMB approval. Finally, the sample sizes used in government studies are typically much larger than those used in industry surveys. Once again, this is often a function of utilizing one government survey to serve a number of purposes where industry studies might be more narrowly defined.

Analysis, Interpretation, and Report

The analysis included in government final reports is typically more comprehensive and sophisticated than the analysis in industry studies. In the words of one person the author interviewed in preparing this chapter, "Industry wants to obtain data which they can analyze, but government wants an answer to their questions, not data that they would not know how to analyze."

Typical government sponsored consumer research studies are disseminated to a much wider audience than normally is sent in an industry consumer research study. There is more emphasis on the report itself for government consumer research, with the report often being the only information available for a number of years. Industry, more typically, would view the average research study as only one piece in a stream of studies.

Finally, the much larger data sets usually used in government studies allow more sophisticated analysis of the data. For example, many multivariate techniques require sample sizes of 500 to 1,000 or more, and most industry studies would not meet this requirement.

CONCLUSIONS

Consumer research is alive and well in Washington. The amount of consumer research conducted by government is likely to continue growing as government's information needs about consumer behavior continue to grow. The proposed Regulatory Reform Bill of 1979 and other trends in the environment demand greater accountability by government. These will accelerate the need for government decision makers to obtain information through consumer research.

Consumer research at the FTC was close to nonexistent just four years ago. Since then there has been a dramatic increase in the amount of consumer research, to the point where few major decisions are made without the aid of some consumer research. This chapter has demonstrated that consumer research is also sponsored by a large number of other federal agencies. The next few years should see dramatic increases in both the reach and frequency of consumer research in these other agencies.

REFERENCES

Aaker, David A. and John G. Myers (1975), *Advertising Management*, Englewood Cliffs, N.J.: Prentice-Hall.

Bernhardt, Kenneth L. and Michael B. Mazis (1979), "Evaluating Consumer Protection Programs," in *Public Policy Issues in Marketing*, eds. Thomas C. Kinnear, Bonnie B. Reece and Cynthia F. Rice, Ann Arbor, Michigan: Division of Research, Graduate School of Business, University of Michigan.

Cohen, Dorothy (1978), "Anacin Ruling Indicates Research Role at FTC," *Marketing News*, (December 15): 3.

Dyer, Robert F. and Terence A. Shimp (1977), "Enhancing the Role of Marketing Research in Public Policy Decision Making," *Journal of Marketing* 41 (January): 63–67.

Engel, James F., Rodger E. Blackwell and David T. Kollat (1978), *Consumer Behavior*, 3rd ed., Hinsdale, Ill.: Dryden Press.

Mazis, Michael and Dennis McNeill (1978), "The Use of Marketing Research in FTC Decision Making," in *Research Frontiers in Marketing: Dialogues and Directions*, ed. Subhash Jain, pp. 308–11, Chicago: American Marketing Association.

Rosch, J. Thomas (1975), "Marketing Research and the Legal Requirements of Advertising," *Journal of Marketing* 39 (July): 69–79.

Wilkie, William L. and David M. Gardner (1974), "The Role of Marketing Research in Public Policy Decision Making," *Journal of Marketing* 38 (January): 38–47.

17

IMPLICATIONS OF INCREASED GOVERNMENT REGULATIONS FOR THE QUALITY AND RELEVANCE OF MARKETING RESEARCH

Yoram Wind

Increased government involvement in all aspects of marketing and management is a fact that is unlikely to change in the near future. The pros and cons of this involvement are often colored by the philosophical orientation of the involved parties. Yet, without taking sides on whether one should minimize or maximize government involvement, the question of the implications of the current regulatory involvement should be examined. The objective of this chapter is to discuss briefly the marketing research implications of this involvement. Specifically, the paper focuses on three issues:

Has the increased use of marketing research in government cases improved the quality of research in terms of better research designs, data collection procedures, sampling, and data analysis?

Has the increased likelihood of subpoenaing research affected the topics addressed by research, the nature of the research designs employed, and the relevance of the research findings to management decision making?

What are the implications of the impact of government involvement on the quality, relevance, and cost of research, and what are some of the needed developments to increase the quality and relevance of marketing research?

GOVERNMENT IMPACT ON QUALITY OF MARKETING RESEARCH

Increased government regulation has led to a major increase in the use of marketing research by both government agencies and affected firms.

Regulation has had a considerable impact on the quality of marketing research, including a number of positive results.

First, greater attention has been paid to probability sampling. Traditionally most marketing research projects have not relied on probability sampling due to the cost involved. The use of marketing research in regulatory procedures has led in many cases to the need to project the results nationally; hence much greater attention has been given to the question of sample representativeness.

Linked to the question of sample representativeness is greater attention to the nonresponse bias of most surveys. The representativeness of a survey depends to a large extent on the assumption that nonrespondents have similar response profiles to the respondents. Typical marketing research studies have seldom tested or challenged this assumption. In the regulatory environment, however, the similarity and differences between respondents and nonrespondents are often examined explicitly.

Another positive consequence is that greater attention has been focused on the various sources of survey errors. The Bureau of the Census published standards for reporting the limitations of all estimates, due both to sampling and to response and other nonsampling errors. These standards were also published by the *Journal of the American Statistical Association* (Gonzalez et al. 1975) and have been applied to a number of marketing research studies.

Also, questionnaire wording, order bias, and the reliability of the data has been receiving considerably more attention in studies likely to be used in legal cases, and greater attention has been given to the quality of data collection procedures and lack of bias due to the interviewers and other field procedures.

Most typical market research studies have relied on cross-tabulation, with little or no attention to measures of statistical significance and with very limited use of appropriate multivariate procedures. Survey research data used in regulatory procedures have to be properly analyzed. This additional focus on analysis ranges from the regular use of statistical significance tests to the use of appropriate multivariate statistical analysis. Finally, related to the improved analytical methods is an increased use of cross-validation procedures. Although cross-validation has been a customary component of most academic research, it has often been ignored in commercial research.

Overall, increased government regulation and use of marketing research in regulatory and court procedures have resulted and will most likely continue to result in improved technical quality of marketing research. This projected trend is consistent with the observation of other sources that have evaluated the current use of marketing research as legal evidence (see Morgan 1979).

IMPACT ON RELEVANCE OF MARKETING RESEARCH

Whereas increased government regulation resulted in an improvement in the technical quality of research, it has also generated considerable negative impact on the relevance of research. In particular, the impact of government access to and reliance on research has led to avoidance of risky questions, which might be misinterpreted or used against a firm in the legislative process. Specifically, there is a high likelihood that management would avoid approval of research projects that include questions focusing on: (1) problems consumers face in the use of the specific product, especially given the risks of product liability suits; (2) information on competitive position and in particular market share information for firms that dominate a specific market, as a precaution against both antitrust and civil suits by competitors claiming monopolistic powers and practices; (3) information on consumers' perceptions of product claims, which can be used as evidence against the company in deceptive advertising cases; and (4) sensitive competitive information, which is also subject to considerable scrutiny by management and legal departments, given the possibility that if subpoenaed it could subsequently be given to competitors who enforce the Freedom of Information act.

These and similar considerations have led and are likely to encourage further management censorship of information sought by research. The perceived risk of collecting quantitative information that can be used against a firm either by the government or competitors has started leading to an increased use of focused group interview and other qualitative research procedures that avoid hard data. This trend is dangerous since it could reduce the relevance of research for more critical marketing management decisions. Such a trend, if continued, could lead to an increased use of "seat of the pants" judgment rather than reliance on rigorous information required as an input into management decisions.

IMPLICATIONS AND NEEDED DEVELOPMENTS

Given the increased use of marketing research in the regulatory process and litigation, improved technical quality of research and its associated reduced relevance and increased cost is likely to continue. The desired position, of course, is improved technical quality while preventing the loss of relevance and maintaining a balance between the cost and value of the research.

Government must become aware of the probable negative impact of its activities and policies on the reduced relevance and increased cost of research. Creative solutions should be generated and evaluated including a reexamination of the Freedom of Information act, the government power to subpoena information, and the basic premises of the use of research in government and interfirm litigation cases. Continuation of the current situation is likely to reduce the role and importance of marketing research as input to major corporate decisions. This might in turn be associated with an increased use of research cosponsored by the firm and government agencies. Yet, legal-oriented research rarely compensates for the reduced relevance of research as an input into key strategic management decision.

This dilemma—the impact of increased government involvement on the relevance of research and its value from a user point of view, and on the desired direction of developing increased quality while not affecting relevance negatively—is summarized in Figure 17.1. The major challenge is to find ways of assuring the increased relevance of research; however this is becoming more difficult due to the pressure toward using external marketing research firms (instead of internal marketing research operations), which are often viewed as more objective if research is brought to court or to a government hearing.

The increased use of marketing research in legislative issues has another important implication for the legislative process itself. There seems to be a basic conflict on the nature of evidence as seen from the research and legal points of view. Consider, for example, use of affidavits or definition of

FIGURE 17.1

The Quality-Relevance Matrix

		Quality	
		Low	High
Relevance	Low		Likely outcome as government involvement increases.
	High	Likely outcome if there is no external incentive for improved quality.	Target Position!

a relevant competitive market boundary. Affidavits from affected consumers are used commonly in the legal process. Yet, when viewed from a research point of view, consumer affidavits should not be used as evidence since, first of all, there is rarely any information on the sample representatives and the way in which it was drawn; hence affidavits are rarely representative. Also, affidavits are usually produced in response to a sequence of questions and guidelines offered by an interested lawyer. The questions (exact wording, order, questioning, setting, and so forth) are not specified. Hence, given that there is considerable amount of behavioral science evidence on the possible bias of different lines of questioning, the majority of affidavits are most likely biased. They do not present unbiased positions and so should not be treated as "objective" research evidence.

Definition of the boundaries of a relevant competitive market is a critical issue in many legal cases involving antitrust and merger. The traditional production-oriented definition (for example, SIC class) is inappropriate. Greater use should be made of consumers' *perceptions*, preferences, and actual usage and purchase behavior. Accepting this concept could markedly increase the use of marketing research in legal cases and would require a change in the evidence in antitrust cases. Such developments would also have major implications for marketing research and, in particular, a tendency toward standardization of concepts and procedures for the determination of market boundaries.

CONCLUSIONS

Marketing research has been occupying an increasing role in the legislative process and in the continuing dialogue and negotiation process between industry and government and among firms. Governmental involvement appears to impose serious constraints on management's attitude toward and use of research. These constraints can reduce the relevance of research for marketing management decisions. It is important that this situation be critically evaluated. The primary purpose of marketing research is to serve as an "objective" input to management decision making.

REFERENCES

Day, George S., Allan D. Shocker and Rajendra K. Srivastava (1979), "Customer-Oriented Approaches to Identifying Product-Markets," *Journal of Marketing* (Fall): 8–19.

Gonzalez, Maria E. et al. (1975), "Standards for Discussion and Presentation of Errors in Survey and Census Data," *Journal of the American Statistical Association* 70 (September): 5–23.

Hughes, G. David and Cameron E. Williams (1979), *The Dialogue That Happened*, Cambridge, Mass.: Marketing Science Institute, April.

Montgomery, David B., Anne H. Peters and Charles B. Weinberg (1978), "The Freedom of Information Act: Strategic Opportunities and Threats," *Sloan Management Review* (Winter): 1–13.

Morgan, Fred W. (1979), "The Admissibility of Consumer Surveys as Legal Evidence in Courts," *Journal of Marketing* 43 (October), pp. 33–40.

Wind, Y. (1977), "The Perception of the Firm's Competitive Position," in *Behavioral Models of Market Analysis: Foundations for Marketing Action*, eds., Francesco Nicosia and Yoram Wind, pp. 163–81, Hinsdale, Il.: Dryden Press.

18

THE CHARACTERISTICS OF KNOWLEDGE: CORPORATE AND PUBLIC POLICY INSIGHTS

Rohit Deshpande
and
Gerald Zaltman

One of the most pressing problems of this decade is how best to use the decision-making concepts, theories, and data being developed in various fields. This problem is compounded as the amount of knowledge that is being produced grows exponentially (Bell 1976). Policy makers in both the public and private sectors have referred to their attempts to cope with the knowledge explosion as one of the most difficult tasks they face. Yet social scientists working in the area of knowledge use have recently made some breakthroughs in isolating the major factors affecting the use, nonuse, or misuse of social science information. This chapter describes some of these findings and indicates what directions this research is taking. The findings have great relevance for the use of marketing concepts and tools in the government area. Without an understanding of how knowledge can be transferred from one domain of practice to another, policy makers run the risk of preemptively labeling concepts and techniques irrelevant. The issues in this chapter are presented in the perspective of corporate and public policy patterns of information use. Similarities and differences in these utilization systems are described along with guidelines for decision makers in both sectors.

THE KNOWLEDGE USE PROCESS

Knowledge use is defined as the process whereby users' needs are determined and communicated to producers, producers design knowledge to meet these needs, and eventually new knowledge is developed based on the application of information by users to satisfy their needs. The "knowledge" we discuss in this chapter refers to concepts such as benefit segmentation, test marketing, the buying center, product life-cycle mapping and other tools and techniques of analysis that have been used successfully in marketing.

The knowledge use process is shown schematically in Figure 18.1. Each element in the process describes an activity that has its own set of problems and opportunities. The process is presented in a circular fashion to indicate the nonprecedence of any one particular activity. Knowledge use when carried out effectively is a continuous set of feedback loops. For example, information collected a year ago on issues of energy conservation may be considered relevant by public policy makers faced with the decision of allocating funds between natural gas and coal-producing industries. The information is retrieved from storage and translated into policy, which is then implemented and later evaluated. The evaluation may indicate the need for further research information. And so the process continues. The spokes of the wheel in Figure 18.1 refer to the short-circuiting that may occur when certain stages are skipped (or backtracked upon) in order to complete the knowledge use process.

Social scientists investigating the knowledge use process have focused on various elements enhancing or hindering the effective use of information. Most of this work has been done in the policy sciences area, although more recent work examines marketing research as a subset of social science information (Caplan, Morrison and Stanbaugh 1975; Weiss 1977; Deshpande 1979a). Although the knowledge use literature has been largely conceptual in orientation, several empirical studies have been reported recently (Patton et al. 1977; Rich 1979; Mayntz 1977; Weiss and Bucuvalas 1978). Unfortunately, most empirical and conceptual work has examined only a few elements of the knowledge use process; however, there have been a few more integrative exceptions (Zaltman and Deshpande 1979; Cherns 1979; Lynn 1978; Weiss 1977; Havelock 1975). Narrowing the scope of variables to be studied as having an impacting upon the use of social science information has been lamented, and future work is likely to take a more holistic approach (Lindblom and Cohen 1979; Deshpande 1979b).

This chapter does not attempt to describe in great detail the knowledge use studies that have been reported; rather the major issues that have been studied and basic findings are explored. We present theoretical and empirical perspectives in both public policy and the private sector and then indicate the commonalities between them.

KNOWLEDGE UTILIZATION IN THE PUBLIC SECTOR

Knowledge use researchers in the public policy area have dealt with the barriers to and facilitators of the effective use of social science concepts and data (Lindblom and Cohen 1979). A major distinction is made between

FIGURE 18.1

The Main Elements of the Knowledge Use Process

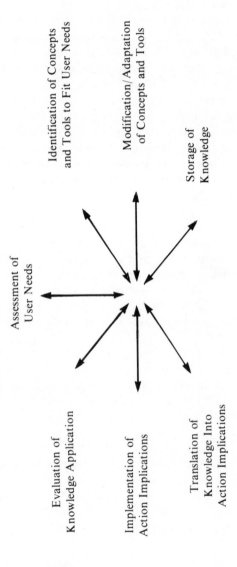

Identification of Concepts
and Tools to Fit User Needs

Modification/Adaptation
of Concepts and Tools

Storage of
Knowledge

Assessment of
User Needs

Evaluation of
Knowledge Application

Implementation of
Action Implications

Translation of
Knowledge Into
Action Implications

"instrumental" and "conceptual" information in order to answer the question, information for what purpose? *Instrumental use* of information occurs when the use of knowledge might be documentable and contributes to a policy decision in the short term. *Conceptual use* is the use of knowledge for general enlightenment rather than specific action. These two types of knowledge have been labeled "knowledge for action" and "knowledge for understanding," respectively (Rich 1977). Most researchers in the knowledge use area have concluded that social science information is predominantly used by public policy makers to enlighten rather than help solve an immediate problem (Weiss 1977). Further work has studied the ways in which knowledge gets used. This work indicates that a problem that was initially conceptualized as one of nonuse of information is actually one that we might call underuse. This distinction is important because it implies that policy makers seldom reject social science studies in their entirety but rather use the available information selectively.

Thus the question arises of what variables affect the selective use of knowledge. Much empirical work is available in this area, and the results point to three chief determinants of knowledge use. The "two-communities" theory of Caplan, Morrison and Stambaugh (1975, 1979) deals with differences in experience and perspective between policy makers and researchers. Public policy makers live in a world of pluralistic demands for equal attention. They must make compromises that lead to the use of particular concepts and research findings on political rather than "scientific" considerations. Researchers, on the other hand, are committed to doing (what they see as) high-quality research and hence are more concerned with the issues of freedom from bias, technical sophistication, and explicitness inherent in research. Timeliness of research information for decisions that need to be made and conformity of the findings to the expectations of users have less importance to them than to policy makers. This can and frequently does lead to conflict between the two "communities" which results in the underutilization of the research information.

A slightly different perspective is taken by knowledge use theoreticians who study the divergence in values between the parties involved in the production and use of social science information (Mayntz 1977; Rein and Schon 1977; Rein 1976). This perspective explores the basic assumptions that researchers and users have prior to the conduct of any research. Rather than proceeding on the basis that there are accepted goals of social policy, this work indicates that the moral and ideological objectives of social policy are open to multiple interpretations, and thus ambiguity is essential for agreement. The approach used by these theoreticians has been referred to in sociology as latent functional analysis. It indicates that all intervention programs of social change have hidden costs and any analysis must use a systemic rather than atomistic approach. Researchers must know what the unintended consequences of social change programs might be and build into their recommendations a flexible mechanism for handling such consequences (Rich and Zaltman 1978; Zaltman 1979). Rather than providing one definitive direction, research information should suggest several alternative courses of action that policy makers can use depending on their own value commitments.

The third perspective investigates the unstable and ambiguous nature of social research knowledge and draws the conclusion that information is underused because it is static and time-bound in a dynamic society (Rich 1979; Weiss 1979). Because the variables that affect social problems are in a constant state of flux, any particular study rapidly becomes obsolescent in its relevance, and policy makers can only use a small proportion of a study for any one decision. The three perspectives described are presented in Figure 18.2.

We turn now to a discussion of knowledge use insights from literature in the private sector.

KNOWLEDGE UTILIZATION IN THE PRIVATE SECTOR

Most of the work described here was developed in a marketing context, a context with which the authors are familiar. Moreover, marketing has strong information-production requirements. Since marketing activities are concerned with the distribution of products and services to consumers, marketing managers need to be constantly aware of the needs of the marketplace. The market research department or division is therefore charged with the task of investigating what consumers wish to buy, in what form they wish to buy it, and how much they are willing to pay. Once this has been determined, the product or service is designed, and research is once again required to ascertain how best to promote and advertise the availability of the product or service. Finally, tracking of the sales of the product is needed to indicate the best time to modify the product or delete it entirely from the line of the company's offerings. Clearly research information is the lifeblood of marketing firms. Equally clearly, research usability should be an extremely important concern in decision makers' minds.

Surprisingly, very little empirical work has explored what factors influence market research usability. Most of this work is of recent origin or in progress. However, sufficient information exists to suggest ways of enhancing the usability of research information.

A pilot study recently completed for the Marketing Science Institute (Luck and Krum 1978) has documented several factors relating to the organizational setting in which the research is performed and to which it is supplied. We can refer to this as the organizational perspective of knowledge use, as presented in Figure 18.3. The findings from this pilot study indicate that those marketing firms identified as better users of knowledge tend to spend more money on specially commissioned research projects to service particular decision-making requirements. Additionally, in-firm staff specialists were enjoined with the specific task of procuring research and seeing that it was correctly implemented, and open communication between researchers and users at all phases of the research process was seen as facilitating the use of the research information produced. Furthermore, there also existed a friendly, favorable climate for research where there was little distrust and a high morale among producers and users.

The chief problems seen by decision-making managers were the limited extent to which research came up with creative or innovative courses of action, inadequate staffing to meet the growing demands for research, and unsystematic research planning. Research producers pointed to problems in tight budget allocations for larger research projects and the limited involvement permitted researchers in senior-level strategy formulation. Also, a lack of feedback from users concerning how research information would be (and was) used led to a lowered relevance of the research for decision-making requirements and consequently a reduced usability of marketing research.

More recently, work in knowledge use marketing has been looking at the research itself as the unit of analysis (Mitroff and Zaltman 1979). This knowledge purpose perspective, presented in Figure 18.4, investigates the research produced by externally contracted suppliers (that is, suppliers in agencies independent of the user firm). An interesting difference has been found in the types of research contracted. A large proportion of the research (over 70 percent) appears to be of a "confirmatory" nature, where the manager already feels he or she knows what decision to make and how to make it. Research is needed to substantiate the decision. This "prior" decision making is generally carried out on the basis of intuition.

The other type of research is "exploratory." Here the manager genuinely does not know what course of action to follow or sometimes even what the alternative courses of action are. In this case, research is contracted for to provide guidance in the decision to be made.

The findings from this knowledge purpose perspective seem to indicate that, for some managers, research is used to reduce the uncertainty in translating experientially based opinions into implementable action. Thus for these managers research has largely a risk-reduction function. If the research findings support what a key decision maker intuits, it will be used; otherwise it will be rejected. Part of the explanation for this finding lies in the variable of "surprise in the research results." Managers tend to be leary of research information that indicates a direction that runs counter to the present practice (if this was not part of the original research design). As a consequence, researchers seem to be encouraged to do "risk-free," confirmatory research. This tendency correlates well with the organizational perspective finding that managers do not find researchers innovative and creative. In a sense, managers create the climate of openness to surprise in research.

FIGURE 18.2

A. Two-Communities Theory of Knowledge Use

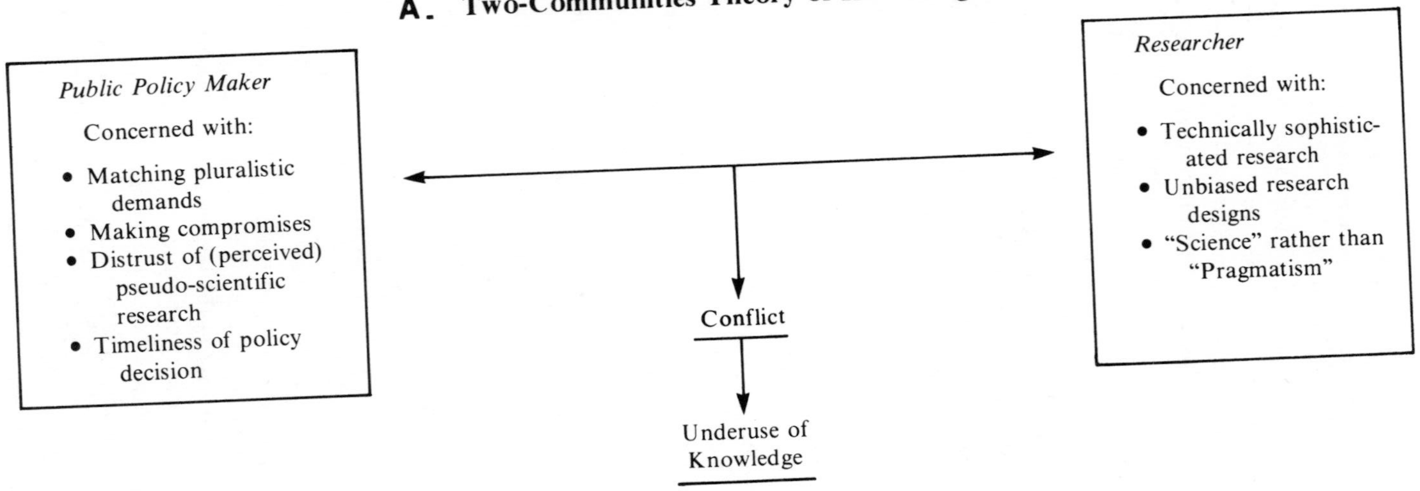

Researcher

Concerned with:

- Technically sophistic-
  ated research
- Unbiased research
  designs
- "Science" rather than
  "Pragmatism"

Public Policy Maker

Concerned with:

- Matching pluralistic
  demands
- Making compromises
- Distrust of (perceived)
  pseudo-scientific
  research
- Timeliness of policy
  decision

Conflict

Underuse of
Knowledge

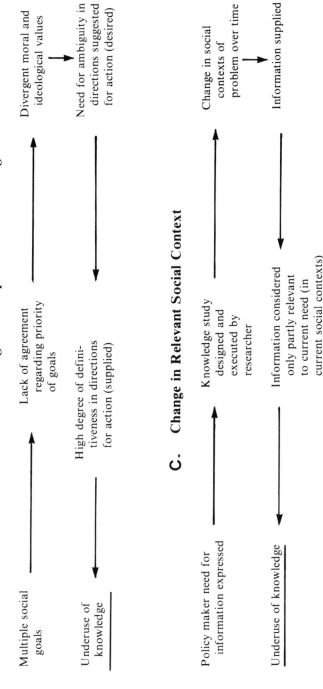

B. **Value Divergence Perspective of Knowledge Use**

Multiple social goals →

Lack of agreement regarding priority of goals →

Divergent moral and ideological values →

Need for ambiguity in directions suggested for action (desired)

High degree of defini- tiveness in directions for action (supplied) →

Underuse of knowledge

C. **Change in Relevant Social Context**

Policy maker need for information expressed →

Knowledge study designed and executed by researcher →

Change in social contexts of problem over time →

Information supplied

Information considered only partly relevant to current need (in current social contexts) →

Underuse of knowledge

FIGURE 18.3

Selected Organizational Factors Relevant to Knowledge Use

Resource Factors

- Manpower specialized in utilization
- Funds allocated for research (given high priority)

Interaction Factors

- Open channels of communication between researchers and users
- High researcher morale

Researchers working in an overly confined and structured environment will produce "expected" rather than innovative knowledge.

These comments bring us to a synthesis of the contributions from the perspectives of knowledge use in both public policy and marketing. We see similarities in the findings of the various studies and also some direction for the future. We comment on these directions by pointing to other bodies of literature that are highly relevant to the diffusion of marketing concepts in government organizations.

CONCLUSIONS

High morale among knowledge producers contributes to better and "more relevant" knowledge. High morale is a consequence of two major factors. First, frequent interaction between producers and users on issues regarding problem definition, conduct of research, types of findings expected, and the quality of recommendations leads to better designed and conducted research projects. Additionally, the involvement of knowledge producers in the utilization process also contributes to a feeling of researcher commitment. These conclusions from an organizational perspective also hold in the case of the two-communities theory model in public policy research. Interaction between producers and users of research can be seen to bridge the gap between the two communities.

Beyond simply increasing the quantity of interaction, improving the quality of each interaction is important because it enables researchers and users to understand each other's values and assumptions. This understanding implies a comprehension of the extent of surprise in research results that particular decision makers will tolerate. It also indicates to researchers the desired degree of confirmatory or exploratory research. The extent of value divergence can be reduced, concomitantly, and the resulting research thus can be made more usable.

Obviously issues of interaction between researchers and users go hand-in-hand with manpower and monetary sufficiency. A short-staffed research

FIGURE 18.4

Impact of Purpose on Knowledge Use

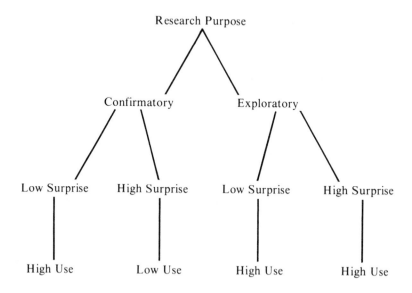

group with limited funds allocated for a project will find it difficult to spend time getting feedback from managers, regardless how important this feedback may be—and it is extremely important. Hence the resource factors of the organizational perspective have parallels with the public policy knowledge use perspectives' conclusions. Our comments indicate there are indeed many commonalities among knowledge use perspectives. For example, Barabba (1978) indicates that, rather than distinguish between knowledge use patterns in the government and private sector, it is more meaningful to distinguish between that in large and small organizations.

The task of introducing a more explicit use of marketing concepts and tools, and perhaps the research resulting from the use of those concepts and tools, poses a problem in planned social change. We assume that an item of knowledge may be perceived as new and thus an innovation. The introduction of knowledge innovations may create social change, and therefore knowledge transfer and implementation may be viewed as a special instance of the field of social change.

In this chapter, our concern has been organizational change in public sector agencies. A large amount of research exists with prescriptive implications for introducing knowledge into public agencies (for example, Beyer and Trice 1978; Bingham 1976; Zaltman, Florio and Sikorski 1977; Schultz and Slevin 1975). A major thrust of this research is that organizational variables may be more important determinants of the acceptance of knowledge than the quality of knowledge or its direct relevance to a problem. These factors are important but become salient only after certain organizational enabling factors have been established. Research concerning the acceptance of new tools and concepts by organizations suggests an important distinction between the adoption of knowledge and its implementation. Organizational factors that may facilitate (hinder) the adoption of a particular marketing concept may also hinder (facilitate) its implementation. Hence, the notions of free space (Holzner and Marx 1979) and switching rules (Zaltman and Duncan 1977) have been developed to correct this, and there are procedures for coping with this knowledge transfer dilemma.

There is also a substantial body of knowledge and practice concerning organizational climate and techniques for making organizations more open to new tools and concepts—such as those discussed in other chapters of this book (for example, see Duncan et al. 1977). Unfortunately, the results of organizational renewal and climate studies have had limited diffusion (Giacquinta 1979). We point to this literature as a source of ideas for the purveyor of knowledge or knowledge advocate.

For the past several years, there has been active exploration of the use of marketing concepts and tools in various public sector settings. Independent of this activity but coterminous with it evaluation research has emerged as a major field of practice and study. The technology exists to evaluate actively efforts to apply marketing concepts and tools in the public sector. This is critical for a number of reasons: marketing may not be as relevant as we think; or it may be far more relevant than anyone believes. In either case, sound formative and summative evaluation research is needed to learn where and how marketing concepts may be used most beneficially. Presently there is a dearth of sound research evaluating the impact of marketing approaches used in public sector agencies. Anecdotal evidence is useful but insufficient. Evaluation research on the use of marketing concepts may be applicable to other concepts in operations research and management science in government.

The major "dependent" variable in the emerging field of knowledge transfer is *use*. Exactly what constitutes use of knowledge and how this use is measured is an important, yet unsolved problem (for example, see Weiss 1977; Rich 1979; Zaltman 1979). There are many types and dimensions of use. For example, Caplan and his colleagues (1975) in a study mentioned earlier, initially found little *instrumental use* of knowledge. This could have suggested negative conclusions. Upon deeper exploration, though, a different type of use, *conceptual use*, emerged. This interpretation provided an accurate and promising picture of the situation. We therefore suggest care when specifying what dimensions or types of use are to be studied. The intense and probing researcher may uncover unexpected types and dimensions of use. Suffice it to say, great care must be exercised when developing and evaluating the use of marketing concepts in public sector agencies.

REFERENCES

Barabba, Vincent P. (1978), "Knowledge Utilization: The Difference Between the Public and the Private Sector," Paper presented at the Conference on Federal Information Sources, Ottawa, December 4–5.

Bell, Daniel (1976), *The Coming of Post-Industrial Society*, New York: Basic Books.

Beyer, Janice M. and Harrison M. Trice (1978), *Implementing Change: Alcoholism Policies in Work Organizations*, New York: Free Press.

Bingham, Richard D. (1976), *The Adoption of Innovation by Local Government* Lexington, Mass.: Lexington Books.

Caplan, Nathan, Andrea Morrison and Russell J. Stambaugh (1975), *The Use of Social Science Knowledge in Policy Decisions at the National Level*, Ann Arbor: University of Michigan Press.

—— (1979), "The Two-Communities Theory and Knowledge Utilization," *American Behavioral Scientist* 22 (January-February): 459–70.

Cherns, Albert (1979), *Using the Social Sciences*, Boston: Routledge and Kegan Paul.

Deshpande, Rohit (1979a), "The Utilization of Marketing Research Information in Consumer Product Strategy Decisions," Ph.D. dissertation, University of Pittsburgh.

—— (1979b), "The Use, Non-Use, and Abuse of Social Science Knowledge: A Review Essay," *Knowledge* 1 (September), pp. 164–176.

Duncan, Robert B. et al. (1977), *An Assessment of a Structural Task Approach to Organizational Development in a School System*, Final Report Grant No. 6-003-0172, Washington, D.C.: National Institute of Education.

Giacquinta, Joseph B. (1979), "The Unwarranted Optimism of Planned Educational Change," *Review of Education*, Vol. 5, no. 2 (spring), pp. 89–95.

Havelock, Ronald A. (1975), *Planning for Innovation*, Ann Arbor: University of Michigan Press.

Heffring, Michael (1979), "Problem Definition and Interaction Factors Influencing Marketing Research Utilization," Ph.D. dissertation, University of Pittsburgh.

Holzner, Burkart and John Marx (1979), *Knowledge Application: The Knowledge System in Society*, Boston: Allyn and Bacon.

Lindblom, Charles E. and David K. Cohen (1979), *Usable Knowledge: Social Science and Social Problem Solving*, New Haven: Yale University Press.

Luck David J. and James R. Krum (1978), "Conditions Conducive to Effective Use of Marketing Research in Corporations," Report of a pilot study for the Marketing Science Institute, University of Delaware.

Lynn, Lawrence E., Jr. (1978), *Knowledge and Policy: The Uncertain Connection*, Washington, D.C.: National Academy of Sciences.

Mayntz, Renate (1977), "Sociology, Value Freedom, and the Problems of Political Counseling," in *Using Social Research in Public Policy Making*, ed. Carol Weiss, Lexington, Mass.: D. C. Heath.

Mitroff, Ian I. and Gerald Zaltman (1979), "Selected Factors Influencing the

Effective Use of Market Research," Unpublished work report, Graduate School of Business, University of Pittsburgh.

Patton, Michael Q. et al. (1977), "In Search of Impact: An Analysis of the Utilization of Federal Health Evaluation Research," in *Using Social Research in Public Policy Making*, ed., Carol Weiss, Lexington, Mass.: D. C. Heath.

Rein, Martin (1976), *Social Science and Public Policy*, New York: Penguin Books.

——— and Donald A. Schon (1977), "Problem Setting in Policy Research," in *Using Social Research in Public Policy Making*, ed. Carol Weiss, Lexington, Mass.: D. C. Heath.

Rich, Robert F. (1977), "Uses of Social Science Information by Federal Bureaucrats: Knowledge for Actions vs. Knowledge for Understanding," in *Using Social Research in Public Policy Making*, ed. Carol Weiss, Lexington, Mass.: D. C. Heath.

——— (1979), *The Power of Social Science Information and Public Policy Making*, San Francisco: Jossey-Bass.

——— and Gerald Zaltman (1978), "Toward a Theory of Planned Social Change: Alternative Perspectives and Ideas," *Evaluation* (special issue): 41–47.

Schultz, Randall L. and Dennis P. Slevin (1975), *Implementing Operations Research Management Science*, New York: American Elsevier.

Weiss, Carol, ed. (1977), *Using Social Research in Public Policy Making*, Lexington, Mass.: D. C. Heath.

——— and M. J. Bucuvalas (1978), "Truth Tests and Utility Tests: Decision-Makers' Frames of Reference for Social Science Research," Working paper, Center for Social Sciences, Columbia University.

Zaltman, Gerald (1979), "Toward a Theory of Planned Social Change: A Theory-in-Use Approach," Paper presented at the second meeting of the Network Consultants on Knowledge Transfer, Carmel, Calif., December 11–13.

Zaltman, Gerald and Rohit Deshpande (1979), "Increasing the Effective Utilization of Scientific and Technical Information: Guidelines for Research Producers and Users," in *The Marketing of Scientific and Technical Information*, eds., William R. King and Gerald Zaltman, Boulder, Colo.: Westview Press.

Zaltman, Gerald and Robert Duncan (1977), *Strategies for Planned Change*, New York: Wiley-Interscience.

Zaltman, Gerald, David Florio and Linda Sikorski (1977), *Dynamic Educational Change*, New York: Free Press.

Zaltman, Gerald and Linda Sikorski (1979), "Unwarranted Pessimism Toward Educational Change: A Reply to 'Unwarranted Optimism of Planned Educational Change,'" *Review of Education*, Vol. 5, no. 2 (spring), pp. 159–163.

IV

EXTENDING MARKETING PRACTICE AND INVESTIGATING THE CONSEQUENCES

INTRODUCTION TO PART IV

Marketing viewed generically as the management of exchange relationships poses significant questions of domain and impact. What public policy
problems are within the parameters of marketing logic? What organizational
decisions are within the scope of marketing strategy? What is the organizational impact of a consciously adopted marketing orientation? How can the
domain of marketing be extended appropriately and the impacts evaluated
accurately? These vital questions have been probed and explored throughout
this volume. The purpose in this final section is to initiate a systematic search
of the broad implications of these challenging questions.

The chapters of this section are often quite provocative. The marketing
of laws as an alternative to coercive enforcement is advocated. The complex
relationships between theory and practice and between implementation and
evaluation are demonstrated in a social program. A state development
program is audited. Public service advertising is reviewed critically. Controversial issues of public management competence, the need for regulation
of government marketing practices, and the ethics of public sector marketing
strategies are all thoughtfully investigated. The firm tone of these chapters
reinforces the basic theme of this volume: conscious and precise marketing
can be an important dimension of government policy formulation, administration, and evaluation; however, identification and comprehension of its
domain and dynamics entails a practical and scholarly struggle.

In Chapter 19, Sandra Huszagh, Frederick Huszagh, and Kevin Buice
prescribe "The Marketing of Laws as an Alternative to Enforcement." The

traditional legal model is based on the presumption of perfect communication. However, ignorance of the law is common; noncompliance is growing. Lack of awareness and uncertainty are significant influences on noncompliance. The authors propose a remedy designing a marketing communications framework for laws. They demonstrate its applicability and prognosticate its impact in the complex field of administrative law. A critical dimension of the proposal is that marketing laws can be cost-effective and preferable to changes (usually additions) in enforcement patterns.

Strategic marketing is an art, albeit one systematically anchored in applied social and policy science principles; textbook approaches to designing and executing marketing programs do not always lead to textbook results. In Chapter 20, Gary Ford and Robert Spekman describe the confounding realities of the social marketplace demonstrated in "Using Marketing Techniques to Increase Immunization Levels: A Field Experiment." The authors formulate a thoughtful marketing strategy based upon social science principles and cautiously design an evaluation field experiment to test the theoretical structure of their strategy and monitor outcomes. However, situational dynamics confounded strategy implementation and contaminated the experiment. The total experience is boldly presented, and its practical lessons are important.

Field experiments require rigid structuring and execution and are "summative" in their evaluative orientation. A marketing audit is a robust and formative evaluation. Although careful design and systematic execution are vital, the marketing audit is a flexible technique highly adaptable to the distinctive characteristics of very different policy contexts and administrative styles. In Chapter 21, Kenneth Roering and Ben Enis use the marketing audit concept to analyze a state government program and to propose future strategic directions for the program. The project focus is "The Marketing Environment Review: Design, Implementation, and Applications for State Development Programming." The authors generate substantive insights into the efforts and effects of state development programs as well as procedural generalizations concerning the nature of market auditing within government.

When naively discussed, marketing is usually equated with advertising. When marketing is naively adopted, advertising is usually the first investment. In the public sector, the investment is typically in "free" public service ads (PSAs). Stephen Weber examines "Government Marketing Through Public Service Advertising" and critically evaluates the myths, powers, and potential of PSAs in Chapter 22. The folklore of public service advertising appears to have produced polar positions—undue optimism or undue pessimism—and has generated the misconception that PSAs are free. In reality, the costs can often outweigh the impact. The author attempts to dispel false hope and naive attitudes by reviewing a set of unpublished evaluative research studies concerning the reach and effectiveness of PSA campaigns. While PSAs frequently reach their audiences, their effects are limited. A marketing strategy based solely on PSAs is seldom sufficient to meet social or public objectives. Contexts and communications objectives for which a PSA approach can be useful are described.

The actual scope of government marketing practices and potential far exceeds the sampling of activities, contexts, and theories presented in this volume. The purpose here has been to stimulate thought and practice by exploring important programs, interesting practices, and novel policy perspectives and frameworks. Advocacy breeds responsibility! The final chapters of this volume search some dimensions of public sector marketing responsibility and provide frameworks for appraising the utility and ethics of government marketing. The necessity of "perspective" called for in the first chapter is exemplified in the concluding presentations.

In Chapter 23, "Governments as Marketers: Issues of Management and Public Policy," Ben Enis critically addresses the propriety of many government programs and practices and the competence of public decision makers to implement conscious marketing practices in the public interest. Explosive issues such as federal abortion payments, state lotteries and liquor stores, and election campaigns are highlighted. In conclusion, the questions are posed, *Who* regulates government marketing? And *how*?

The subject of ethics traditionally has received comparatively little attention in marketing literature, although it has been a vital topic in government. Recently there has been an increased interest in ethical issues within both the marketing and public policy fields. This is a very healthy and challenging development as conscious marketing practices, particularly research activities, are adopted in social and public problem solving. In Chapter 24, Jerry Porrass and Charles Weinberg present "A Framework for Analyzing the Ethics of Marketing Interventions." The framework is a means of anticipating, comprehending, and dealing with the inherent ethical issues of any "planned change" activity. The premise is to identify the actors involved in the change situation and to incorporate their values and views into the policy process. Controversial examples are presented to demonstrate the utility of the framework. The authors neither promise nor promote any simple solutions to the complicated, multifaceted problems of change and ethics. The message is the inevitability of change and the growing responsibilities of policy makers to manage change sensitively, responsively, and effectively—an admonition implicit throughout this volume.

19

THE MARKETING OF LAWS AS AN ALTERNATIVE TO ENFORCEMENT

Sandra M. Huszagh
Frederick W. Huszagh
Kevin B. Buice

Law is a discrete product which government produces to control the behavior of its individual and organizational citizens. Traditionally the public sector has not explicitly "marketed" laws; citizens are presumed to be aware of obligations imposed by legal pronouncements. The maxim that "ignorance of the law is no excuse" has developed from this presumption of perfect communication. Nonetheless, ignorance of the law is common, and noncompliance with mandatory government directives is thus large and growing.

Noncomplying citizens fall for the most part into three categories: (1) citizens aware of a particular law who deliberately do not comply; (2) citizens unaware of a particular law and thus unable to comply; and (3) citizens who do not comply because of uncertainty about a particular law's relevance to their activities. Given an alarming increase in the second and third categories, it is imperative to evaluate whether effective marketing of laws can impose fewer costs upon society.

From an economic perspective, conscious marketing of particular laws and existing enforcement activities are often preferable to additional enforcement for obtaining an acceptable compliance rate. The theoretical constructs discussed herein were developed to facilitate law marketing as a substitute for law enforcement. They are also applicable to efficient marketing of a broad array of public programs (for example, food stamps), public procurement standards (for example, government contracts), and general knowledge (for example, home and farm improvements.)

LAW COMMUNICATION

Research indicates certain law characteristics are major determinants of public assimilation of a law's inherent requirements. These are originating jurisdiction (federal, state, local), message structure (administrative or statutory laws), dominant substantive focus (economic, political, social), and relative stability (old, modified, new) (Huszagh and Huszagh 1978). How these characteristics affect public assimilation is illustrated below in the context of administrative laws that have a multiple message structure (Huszagh and Huszagh 1979). Such "informal law" is the dominant form of public sector law production. For example, in 1963 federal courts handled 7,095 civil trials; federal administrative agencies, after conducting trial-type hearings, handled 81,469 cases (Davis 1972). Today, a single agency—the Social Security Administration—annually disposes of more claims than all civil and criminal cases determined in the federal district courts.

Administrative laws are distributed in full text by official publications ("channels") financed and staffed by the public sector. Unfortunately, such channels as the *Federal Register* seldom communicate laws successfully to intended recipients at the three levels of communication—technical, semantic, and effectiveness—traditionally viewed as basic to full communication. Since compliance correlates directly with communication effectiveness at all three levels, improved compliance necessitates concern about both points of the law communication process where information loss is likely and the remedies for reducing such loss in the context of the current communicative system.

Sources of communications loss and remedies for improved communication are best conceptualized in the simplistic yet descriptive terms of production, distribution, and consumption. Discussion in these contexts, while not reflective of the intricacies of the marketing discipline, can help identify where our productive capacity is encumbered by government action that has little social utility. As public policy makers recognize how such characterizations can improve the utility of their actions, greater details of the marketing discipline can be proffered without danger of being styled irrelevant to the governance process.

Table 19.1 equates basic tenets of the three diverse disciplines of marketing, communications, and law. Production, distribution, and consumption are matched to basic steps in the communication process as well as significant law characteristics that have greatest potential effect on citizen awareness of law content. Subsequent analysis describes these exhibit "symbols," suggests indirectly how attention to them may improve the linkage between government command and citizen response, and identifies sample law areas where a marketing orientation is relevant and can be instructive.

TABLE 19.1

Administrative Law Communication

Stage of Law Communication	Steps in the Communication Process	Factors Contributing to Law Information Loss
Law production	Information source	Multiple sources: legislature, executive, administrative agency, other administrative agencies, courts
		Power to select channels
		Homogeneity and clarity within and among multiple sources
	Message	Multiple messages: original delegation, agency rules, agency decisions, court decisions
		Perishability
		Environmental consistency
		Importance and rationality
Law distribution	Encoder	Capacity to preserve message integrity
	Channel	Accessibility
		Format
		Importance
Law consumption	Decoder: as interpreter of message	Expertise
		Form of message and decoder status
	Destination: corporate citizen	Basic business functions
		Resources
		Allocation of resources

Source: Compiled by the authors.

LAW PRODUCTION

Information Sources

Administrative law is characterized by multiple sources, including legislative or executive delegations of authority to relevant administrative agencies; the agencies themselves, which remain continuous sources of rules, regulations, and quasi-judicial decisions throughout their existence; and judicial review of agency action. The intended recipient of legal information thus must interweave numerous messages produced by diverse sources of law. The problem is particularly acute when more than one federal agency is involved in the regulatory process. The Equal Employment Opportunity Commission's regulatory authority in the area of employment practices, for example, is fragmented among several programs and, too often, confused by programs and regulations resident in some nine other federal agencies. Similarly, the export licensing process involves three major agencies (the Departments of Commerce, State, and Defense), which are joined on occasion by the Departments of Agriculture and Energy.

Citizen surveillance of multiple sources and their continuous output through official channels is difficult by itself. In addition, however, citizens must mesh such information into an intelligible whole. This requires either touching base with each agency source or extracting all relevant messages from the bulky mass of official materials. Quite naturally, the burdens of tracking and integration affect most adversely those small or medium-sized organizations with personnel and resource constraints, for legal decoding skills are of paramount importance. A recent survey of 300 corporations revealed that 16 percent of the top corporate officers surveyed had legal backgrounds; six years ago the same sample resulted in a figure of only 4 percent (*Wall Street Journal* February 6, 1979).

To some extent information overload problems can be reduced if the government sends particular messages over channels selected to match messages with intended recipients. Greater resources at the federal level, compared to state and local jurisdictions, suggest that some agencies have the resources to tailor channels carrying their profuse output to the special needs of organizational and individual subjects. The Internal Revenue Service, for example, is able to supplement its copious issuance of public rulings with private letter rulings, thereby focusing attention upon a single taxpayer's legal problem. Few state agencies, and even fewer municipal ones, can provide such individualized attention.

The communications problem associated with multiple sources, despite the benefits inherent in channel selection power, is compounded by the substantive inconsistencies that flow from each individual source over time; in essence its outputs are not homogeneous or clear. For example, enabling legislation often suffers from a marked lack of clarity, perhaps the result of political gerrymandering behind the scenes when the executive or legislative delegation takes place. Similarly, numerous interest groups often must be appeased in the process of creating a new federal agency, as was the case with the Department of Energy, or in amending the boundaries of an established regulatory framework, such as the export licensing process. Consequently, the administrative agency in question often produces regulations with contradictory and confusing provisions, and the resulting confusion of individual or organizational citizens is anything but conducive to strict compliance with governmental directives. Moreover, the entire economy itself suffers. A recent item in the *Wall Street Journal* (February 28, 1979) noted, "White House economists . . . assert that the costs of complying with complex and often contradictory regulations contribute to inflation."

Additionally, the executive order or enabling legislation setting forth an administrative agency's role as lawmaker may not provide sufficient detail for the agency to determine the boundaries of its own authority. The Department of Energy, for example, has indicated that it may make statistical data supplied by oil companies available to departmental regulators and other federal agencies. Of course, the companies involved naturally have voiced a sharp criticism of the department's proposal; the proposal does appear, however, to present a serious question concerning the department's authority to create new rules governing the acquisition and use of information without specific legislative authority (*Wall Street Journal* February 10, 1978). This absence of detail contributes not only to confusion within the agency itself but also to uncertainty among regulated entities as to whether the agency is acting within the boundaries of its authority. Uncertainty inevitably stimulates at least partial noncompliance and even occasional challenges by those industries most seriously affected. In response to the Department of Energy's proposal discussed above, one oil company spokesman asserted, "If no uses are specified, then companies will be reluctant to supply the information."

Message

As one moves through the communication process from law sources to the messages they produce, several factors critical to information retention emerge. First, it is difficult to gather and interpret multiple messages, as is dramatically illustrated in the interpretation and enforcement of federal equal employment regulations, a task scattered among some 25 separate agencies. Enormous effort is involved in checking with multiple agencies to ascertain precise definitions of violations and to determine what means of enforcement will be applied. Some corporate giants have abandoned these efforts altogether. Sears, Roebuck, & Company recently filed suit against the Equal Employment Opportunity Commission and nine other federal agencies, contending that "conflicting government programs have hurt the company's efforts to avoid discrimination" (*Wall Street Journal* February 5, 1979).

The probability that one or more messages will be lost is necessarily high, given the numerous messages characteristic of administrative law. Their volume, detail, and periodic conflict with one another often preclude meaningful indexing. Without such indexing, message perishability is substantial. Significant redundancy within messages, however, diminishes this risk of loss somewhat. Such redundancy exists because no single message is intended to be free-standing; rather, each message fits contextually within a message series. Redundancy also occurs when citizens are the objects of similar laws at all three jurisdictional levels. Employment discrimination, for example, is dealt with concurrently by the Equal Employment Opportunity Commission, the New York State Commission for Human Rights, the New York State Commission against Discrimination, and the New York City Personnel Department and Civil Service Commission (compare Shapiro 1972). Enlightened and careful drafting can also reduce potential information loss, although the availability of such drafting talent is often limited to official sources at the federal jurisdiction and only the most industrialized states.

Another factor that introduces distortion into the interpretation of all legal information is environmental change. When laws are not updated to fit changing circumstances, considerable confusion and uncertainty in interpretation are likely. With the licensing of new nuclear power plants, for example, the chairman of the Edison Electric Institute recently complained of the government's "changing and conflicting regulatory requirements, actions of intervenors and inherent slowness" in licensing new nuclear plants and called for a change in federal procedures (*Wall Street Journal* February 22, 1979). At the opposite end of the spectrum there are also interpretative problems when laws are frequently amended to reflect a changing environment. Alterations in labor relations illustrate this problem.

A final message characteristic that materially affects citizen cognizance is perceived message importance. Individuals and organizations follow closely those laws having a direct impact on their activities. The primary concern of businesses with certain law subjects and law sources is thus self-evident: unfair trade practices (Federal Trade Commission), unfair labor practices (National Labor Relations Board), taxation (Internal Revenue Service), and regulations directed toward particular industries (for example, Interstate Commerce Commission, railroads; Civil Aeronautics Board, airlines; Federal Communications Commission, communications; Federal Power Commission, utilities; and Securities and Exchange Commission, investment firms). Despite this apparent division of labor, however, numerous federal agencies do become involved in the implementation process when jurisdictional boundaries are not clearly defined. Inconsistent guidelines frequently flow from such jurisdictional overlap, which diminish the citizen's perception of message rationality and spills over even to the credibility of the law producer. Still, laws that are important to individuals or organizations have a lower probability of loss; thus the relevance of a given law to its intended constituency is a critical issue in the marketing of laws.

LAW DISTRIBUTION

While various factors inherent in law production cause considerable law information loss, they are integral to the political process and not easily altered regardless of potential benefits. Existing features of law distribution also cause considerable information loss, but clamor for greater government efficiency could prompt change. Improved encoding of messages for distribution and selective redesign of full text and signalling channels would improve significantly citizen awareness of legal requirements, thereby reducing noncompliance and the need for increased enforcement.

Encoder

Government personnel generally do little to prepare law messages for official channels in terms of interpretative analysis, cross-referencing, and indexing. In essence, they have no incentive to identify and explain interconnections among messages such as overlapping rule-making delegations by Congress to the Justice Department and Securities and Exchange Commission concerning corrupt practices. In contrast, encoders of commercial, annotated services like the Commercial Clearing House (CCH) and Bureau of National Affairs (BNA) fill citizen needs by (1) integrating and analyzing multiple messages; (2) indexing and cross-referencing to place the message in historical context; (3) commenting on side effects that may alter interpretations of the current law; and (4) estimating enforcement probabilities. Federal level encoders and encoders serving sophisticated states bring a rich background to the encoding process, which is analogous to comprehensive product information in marketing terms. This information reduces demands on citizens, particularly when multiple messages contain conflicting information.

Individuals and organizations faced with complex and frequently changing laws and regulations, such as federal taxation or labor relations, invariably rely on annotated channels rather than official channels because their encoding services provide interpretation, cross-referencing, contextual analysis, discussion of enforcement probabilities, detailed indexing, and even clarifying comments on a message's major substantive focus. To appreciate the significance of a new enactment even the most experienced labor lawyer turns to annotated services like the "Current Developments" volume of *Federal Labor Laws* (BNA). Reference to such services may be in addition to regular annotated channels that assemble previous labor law regulations such as the *Employment Practice Guide* (CCH), *Employment Discrimination* (Matthew Bender), *Occupational Safety and Health Reporter* (BNA), *Labor Law Reporter* (BNA), and *Labor Law Reporter* (CCH). The "Current Developments" volume highlights the substantive focuses of multiple messages by its division of regulations, orders, and statements of interpretation into separate sections concerning such distinct subjects as child labor, age discrimination in employment, and public contracts and property management. After setting forth an act, with all relevant amendments thereto, the service provides pertinent provisions of other acts affecting or affected by the principal piece of legislation. Side effects of the act thus are explicitly referenced in the encoding process. The net result is a far more comprehensive treatment of a given field than could possibly be accomplished by official channels and their stringent limitations on encoding.

Clearly the commercial, annotated channels cope far more effectively with information loss than do official channels and associated encoders, which perform a rather narrow and mechanical function. This observation is most true for federal laws that have dedicated commercial services or reporters because of their importance and breadth. Thus by offering production information similar to that of annotated channels, law content can be effectively distributed and promoted through official channels.

Channels

Directivity, accessibility, and perishability are key characteristics of law distribution channels affecting citizen assimilation. Because official channels provide only rudimentary integration of multiple messages and organization of laws by subject, citizen access to legal information is difficult. Legal expertise is essential when an administrative law is complex, lengthy, lacking in detail about interrelationships of messages, and/or susceptible to environmental changes affecting the law's meaning or frequent amendment. When commercial loose-leaf services cover only certain subjects—the situation in most states—or are nonexistent—as in most municipalities—citizens must rely on official channels. For example, on November 9, 1973, the Cost of Living Council announced creation of a Nonunion Construction Advisory Committee within the Office of Wage Stabilization. Without Commerce Clearing House's *Economic Controls* service, access to this release would be difficult, especially for the uninitiated.

Access problems are compounded for businesses requiring a constant update on legal regulations affecting their daily operations in numerous states. The area of labor legislation dramatically illustrates the problem. As early as 1936, John Andrews, an authority in the labor field, stated, "Modern industry . . . has created the need for a quantity, flexibility, and type of labor legislation which legislatures themselves cannot produce." He further noted:

> In recent years the stream of labor regulations has more than doubled in volume through the promulgation by the Department of Labor and of "administrative rules" which have "the force of law." So important have these regulations become in many states that statutory labor laws can no longer be considered complete in themselves. In fact, the legislative acts may be positively misleading to one who fails to find and consider these rules which supplement and modify them. In this country—with the designated authorities of our numerous states acting independently—it is especially important also that administrative regulations be published in accordance with a generally accepted system. Otherwise it becomes increasingly difficult for a business operating in several different states to know how to observe the regulations imposed by the numerous departments of labor or even to discover whether the law exists. To assure the law's distribution, it should be at least as easy to find the law embodied in these regulations as it is to find the statutes in the familiar series law volumes published by the various states. This reasonable minimum condition frequently has not been observed. In every state and the District of Columbia the best remedy is a recognized system for the regular publication of all administrative regulations to enable responsible citizens to know what laws they are expected to obey. (pp. 131–32)

Even the best annotated services, however, may be unable to overcome the barrier to access involved when no single administrative agency serves as the definitive source for regulations and their interpretation. Moreover, when new laws do not fall within the ambit of existing services these laws may go completely unnoticed by annotated channels. The National Environmental Policy Act, for example, required businesses to formulate immediate responses to new and unusual directives with minimal help from annotated services or trade journals serving electric utilities (compare Stewart and Krier 1978, pp. 733–810). Expanded interpretive coverage by official channels would be an effective remedy for information distribution problems, especially when government sources determine that compliance is a necessity. Without the assumption of these functions by official channels, marketing of law information can be entirely co-opted by commercial channels.

Remedies for official channel shortcomings, however, must be congruent with the dynamic nature of administrative lawmaking; the channel should reinforce the message. For example, a physical format like that of loose-leaf annotated services accommodates both the unpredictable sequence and timing of administrative law messages. Channels should be designed to alert businesses regarding specific judicial modifications of agency action, especially since the process represents a general safeguard against administrative excesses affecting business interests (compare Horsky

1952; Gardner 1959). Recently, for example, the Supreme Court agreed to review a lower court's finding that the Occupational Safety and Health Administration had failed to take into proper account cost-benefit factors in setting a standard limiting employee exposure to benzene (*Wall Street Journal* February 22, 1979).

Perceived importance by business citizens of official channels such as the *Federal Register* or *United States Code* greatly affects assimilation of law content of administrative regulations that are either new or lack economic impact. Initial pronouncements of the Environmental Protection Agency, for example, were grossly underestimated in business circles. Such errors could be avoided through use of the administrative agency itself as a public sector channel, enabling direct encoder-decoder contact to clarify message meaning and compliance standards. In describing Washington legal practices, Horsky (1952) states, "More important than the information acquired from [statutes, legislative history, agency personnel background, agency's sense of its mission] is what the lawyer can learn from dealings with the agency and its staff" (p. 117). Personal contact is impossible, however, when citizens are physically distant from the agency channel. Overcoming physical distance requires significant channel "power"—which necessitates a power increase in most state and local jurisdictions. Channel power is the economic and personal resources, promotion capabilities, and any other factors that would enable public sector channels to reach destinations directly. Available channel power can be concentrated on subjects particularly important to business organizations, or commercial, annotated channels can be encouraged to serve nontransient, important subjects presently uncovered.

LAW CONSUMPTION

Decoder

Law information consumers using official channels must first compile and interrelate multiple messages. Consequently, access is generally limited to those with decoding expertise, such as lawyers or paralegals specializing in particular administrative law areas. Even the use of annotated channels requires considerable expertise. Large businesses with adequate resources will turn to these specialists when laws affecting their operation are complex or there is a considerable time lag between the effectiveness dates of such laws and their appearance in annotated channels. Decoder specialists will also be called upon when access to administrative laws at state or local jurisdictions is essential. Thus the potential for information loss is considerable when firms have limited resources to devote to following numerous administrative agencies at one or more jurisdictions. Information loss may also be significant when large companies have not had previous contact with a particular administrative agency.

Despite the availability of expert decoders, the decoder's interpretative skills are useless unless he has an active working relationship with the firm. A strong relationship can determine the firm's responsiveness to complex, new, changing, or inadequately focused laws. Even for large firms such linkages may exist only for important laws at federal or highly industrialized state or municipal jurisdictions.

Receiver

Despite the United States' penchant for terms like *equality* and *melting pot*, differences prevail among individual and corporate citizens' obligations, rights, capacities, and perceptions. For businesses such differences are caused by factors such as size and functions. Each industry has a distinctive task focus. All may engage in selling, financing, distributing, and procuring functions, but their relative concentration on these functions differs. Consequently, personnel and financial resources allocated to each function vary considerably. In turn, these allocations affect the processing of legal information concerning each function. For example, merchandisers are especially concerned with laws pertaining to consumer rights, employer-employee relations, and supplier performance. Manufacturers traditionally emphasize product standard regulations, tax incentives for capital investment, laws relating to conditions of the work place, and various trade regulation laws on the competitive environment. Extractors, as primarily large and capital-intensive enterprises, are most concerned with laws relating to transportation, tax policy regarding capital investment and depleting reserves, work environment safety standards, and various environmental controls.

It can be anticipated that laws dealing with each of these major concerns noted above will be acknowledged and assimilated by the respective company type, despite their generic newness, volume, complexity, and, to some extent, lack of internal consistency. Conversely, simple laws that add to an existing base of widely recognized legal problems for corporate activity will be recognized by most all corporations regardless of relevance to their primary points of focus. Laws that are new, complex, and lengthy, however, have far less probability of assimilation by some company types as opposed to others.

The mismatch between business function and legal focus is further exacerbated by the limited roles most legally trained personnel have in the formulation of company policy. Ideally for the government, new laws, changes in laws, or additions to an existing law base should be anticipated by various business enterprises and, when enacted, incorporated into their long-range planning. This anticipation and integration should facilitate law compliance and minimize subsequent resistance due to extensive financial commitments inconsistent with the law's dictates. For such laws to be assimilated into long-range plans, however, those initially acknowledging and interpreting the laws must have a substantial role in the policy formulation process. Lawyers in many commercial firms have minimal access to broad-range policy in a variety of areas where a substantial volume of informal laws is generated. Admittedly, in many functional areas a general awareness of the legal environment is maintained. The quality of awareness, however, rapidly deteriorates for complicated or lengthy laws or laws representing major departures from existing precedent already incorporated into the routine operating procedures of various functional divisions.

Physical distance between the company and the lawmaking source may also substantially affect law assimilation capacity (Huszagh 1978). Many business enterprises native to geographically remote regions of the country are comparatively ethnocentric and tend to correlate proximity with legal legitimacy in the absence of extensive enforcement. In fact, the homogeneity of business enterprises assumed by lawmakers in Washington does not exist, and the distinctly regional or local outlooks common in such enterprises pose several problems for business consciousness of legal obligations.

SUMMARY

The factors noted above are among the many that affect companies' capacities to acknowledge and respond to diverse laws. With proper incentives, enterprises might overcome these barriers to law assimilation. Unfortunately, the costs to the private sector would exceed government's costs to achieve similar assimilation rates by revising their approaches for preparation and distribution of law information regarding both obligations and enforcement.

Despite the possible cost savings of government action, three major characteristics inherent in law production limit responsiveness to information needs. The first limiting characteristic resides within the law producers—the legislative and administrative agencies. The legislature represents considerable diversity in economic interests, social perspectives, and political theories. The processes of Congress allow law output responsive to daily pressures. Especially when coalition politics prevail, resulting laws are often complex and internally inconsistent. Since most informal law is produced by administrative agencies exercising delegated power, there are several substantial problems. The passage of time may place congressional policies and interests at odds with those of administrative agencies functioning subsequent in time and responding to different pressures both external and internal to the government. The resulting inconsistencies between legislation and agency output cannot be easily eradicated despite the prospects of greater law consumer responsiveness with less enforcement. Furthermore, since most administrative agencies are not judged by the effectiveness of the laws they promulgate, they have minimal incentives to develop new law designs and distribution channels that will be more effective. No doubt, linking agency appropriations to statistical sampling of effectiveness among law consumers could provide incentives not now present.

A second major limitation stems from the fact that many areas of the environment undergoing rapid change, such as technology, defy full synchronization with the legal system. For example, common carrier services, already encrusted with older legal philosophies, have undergone major revision which has surpassed the legal system's capacity to respond. Even if the law sources were able to coordinate their objectives among one another, it is unlikely that they could enact, publicize, and enforce laws with the speed necessary to maintain full compatibility with rapidly shifting environments. In such situations sensitivity to the adage that "less is more" might prove most effective.

Third, apart from the inelasticities of law producers, we presently lack the orientation toward producing law messages that satisfactorily discriminate among diverse consumer needs. In essence, the legal system has not evolved from the Henry Ford era of a single model and color to the endless combinations of models and colors prevalent today. As the physical and social sciences better define the variations among law consumers and computer technology permits analysis of the consequences of according each law consumer different rights and obligations, we should achieve more effective and equitable governance with less cost. Even if we are naturally inclined to move in this direction, the inflationary effects of current governance approaches will surely prompt action.

THOUGHTS FOR REFORM

Government assumptions of compliance, dire threats for detected noncompliance, ignorance of noncompliance, and token enforcement cumulatively do not produce efficient governance but do encourage government complacency with laws that are increasingly complex and mutually inconsistent. Diverse citizen interests also ensure a continuous demand for laws despite the cost implications. Rising resentment of government intervention and linkages between regulation and inflation, however, will stimulate law producers to seek less costly, nontraditional law enforcement modes. Compliance without enforcement will become a primary goal of the federal government. Fortunately, basic marketing principles can assist the government in realizing this goal. They can also enhance the effectiveness of essential laws without resort to excessive threat of saturation enforcement— an approach laden with social, political, and economic costs.

How can these principles be best applied, given the producer constraints and citizen needs noted earlier? The first remedy is to differentiate among citizens in how the law is written and or distributed.

For business citizens, lawmakers must distinguish small from large, simple from complex, new from old, and urban from rural. Laws geared to each can seek uniform consequences through sensitivity to differing relationships between stimulus and response. Innovations in this regard will not be received without resistance by courts or special interest groups, among others, but disregard of the obvious cannot and will not be endured for long.

Our knowledge of corporate structures and their relative impact on knowledge assimilation permits correlations between law structure and probable corporate awareness. Law producers, despite noted limitations, can tailor message form and content to the information assimilation capacities of target citizens. When those governed are diverse in character and geographically dispersed, centrally located law producers such as federal agencies can take a market segmentation approach to message design. Alternatively, regional units of the federal government can be authorized to issue regulations tailored to their areas if consistent with federal objectives. The federal government can also establish policy guidelines and allow state or local units of government to enact detailed messages that implement those guidelines and communicate effectively with the subjects involved. In essence, law producers first need to become conscious of how different citizens perceive various law messages. Then they can fashion messages which, while different, produce relatively uniform perceptions.

Significant progress concerning recognition and assimilation of law can also be achieved through more creative approaches to the distribution elements of law communication. These elements specifically involve selection of encoders and channels. Encoders associated with official channels should seek to understand the diverse needs of consumer constituencies, inform law producers of their needs, and promote distribution systems that bridge the gap between intended messages and perceived messages. Specialized channels should be developed with the power, capacity, and directivity to alert particular citizens, thus avoiding the necessity for saturation enforcement. Such specialized official channels have been developed by the Customs Bureau and the Export Administration Office of the Department of Commerce. As an alternative to additional official channels, existing annotated channels can be franchised to serve official functions and ensure higher levels of reception. This approach has been adopted by many state courts and allows indexing and distribution of cases for timely and extensive use.

Another distribution alternative is for government encoders to develop formal relationships with specialized signaling channels, such as trade association publications. This would establish a direct tie-in to the full text messages carried by official or annotated channels. Currently, most agency public information officers serving as encoders for agencies merely issue press releases. They assume no obligations for distribution beyond making legal information available. This insular view seems to stem from the premise that "ignorance of the law is no excuse." To encourage more responsible action, agency encoders should be subject to periodic performance audits based on surveys of citizen awareness and compliance. In addition, enforcement units should coordinate with such encoders to develop an optimal relationship between information distribution and enforcement. Currently these functions of distribution and enforcement are structurally separate. This separation hinders creative approaches for effective law distribution and inhibits revision of laws based on citizen feedback. Unfortunately, many enforcers favor ambiguity because it allows lawmaking and discretionary enforcement free from the strictures of most due process requirements.

REFERENCES

Andrews, John B. (1936), *Administrative Labor Legislation*, New York: Harper and Brothers.

Davis, Kenneth C. (1972), *Administrative Law Text*, New York: Foundation Press.

Gardner, Warner W. (1959), "The Administrative Process," in *Legal Institutions Today and Tomorrow*, ed., Monrad G. Paulsen, New York: Columbia University Press.

Horsky, Charles A. (1952), *The Washington Lawyer*, Boston: Little, Brown.

Huszagh, Sandra M. (1978), "Reducing Legal Risks to Marketing in Multiple Country Operations," *Columbia Journal of World Business* 13 (Spring): 50–58.

Huszagh, Sandra M. and Fredrick W. Huszagh (1978), "A Model of the Law Communication Process: Formal and Free Law," *Georgia Law Review* 13 (Fall): 193–241.

―――― (1979), "Production and Consumption of Informal Law: A Model for Identifying Information Loss," *Georgia Law Review* 13 (Winter): 515–48.

Shapiro, Martin, "Toward a Theory of Stare Decisis," *Journal of Legal Studies*, Vol. 1, No. 1, January 1972, pp. 125–34.

Stewart, Richard B. and James E. Krier (1978), *Environmental Law and Policy*, Indianapolis, Ind.: Bobbs-Merrill.

U.S. Congress *National Environmental Policy Act*, (1969), 42 U.S.C. §§ 4321–4347.

U.S., Congress, Senate Judiciary Committee (1945), *Report on the Administrative Procedure Act*, 79th Cong., 1st sess., S. Report 752.

"Weary Watchdogs." *Wall Street Journal* CXC, 40 (August 26, 1977), p. 1.

"Senate Conferees Miss Their Deadline on Gas-Price Accord." *Wall Street Journal* CXCI, 41 (February 10, 1978), p. 3.

"What's News—World-Wide." *Wall Street Journal* CXCIII, 25 (February 5, 1979), p. 1.

"Labor LeHer." *Wall Street Journal* CXCIIII, 26 (February 6, 1979), p. 1.

"Green Mountain Power Plans Suit Against GE Over Closing of Unit." *Wall Street Journal* CXCIII, 37 (February 22, 1979), p. 12.

"What's News—World-Wide," *Wall Street Journal* CXCIII, 37 (February 22, 1979), p. 1.

"Carter Pledges Continued Efforts to Cut Cost to Industry of Environmental Rules." *Wall Street Journal* CXCIII, 41 (February 28, 1979), p. 2.

20

USING MARKETING TECHNIQUES TO INCREASE IMMUNIZATION LEVELS: A FIELD EXPERIMENT

Gary T. Ford and Robert E. Spekman

It has been ten years since Kotler and Levy (1969) suggested "broadening the concept of marketing" to include the activities of public and nonprofit organizations. During that time, marketing theory and practice has been applied successfully to a host of social and public problems. In the area of health care alone, marketers have engaged in activities related to breast self-examination, smoking cessation, hypertension, family planning, and other programs intended to bring about socially desirable behavior. It has become apparent that government is turning to marketing increasingly as a promising framework for planning and implementing social change.

Indeed, this chapter is, in part, a result of the Department of Health, Education and Welfare's (DHEW) concern for and response to recent declines in immunization levels among the nation's children. If we define the fundamental task of marketing as managing the level, timing, and character of demand (Kotler 1975), the present state of declining immunization levels necessitates remedial marketing effort aimed at reversing current trends. Viewed as a social marketing problem, programs must be developed that will raise the level of parental awareness regarding the importance of full immunization, gain parental compliance in beginning the vaccination series, and increase the probability that the initial compliant behavior is sustained until the child is immunized fully against all seven childhood diseases.

This chapter describes a field experiment conducted at one of the

This research was funded under DHEW Contract HSA 78-104 (P). The conclusions represent the opinions of the authors only.

Bureau of Community Health Services' (BCHS) funded clinics. It was designed to increase the level of immunization among the clinic's target population. Focusing primarily on methodological issues, our objectives are twofold: to demonstrate to the marketing scholar that there exist challenging, interesting, and relevant research problems in the public sector; and to demonstrate to the public administrator that marketing tools and concepts can be utilized effectively in the development and assessment of social programs. The emphasis on methodology has great value from two perspectives. In the context of the actual study, such a presentation serves to highlight various threats to validity which tended to confound the field experiment. The second perspective encompasses the broader, more long-range impact of a methodological critique of the study. Since the United States has, to a great extent, come to rely on an experimental approach to social reform, information that improves our understanding of the problems associated with social program development in general and field experimentation in particular is, indeed, valuable.

The chapter begins with a description of the problem setting and of the selection of an appropriate marketing strategy. Then we discuss the experimental design and research setting. Finally we outline what transpired once the field work began. Included is a discussion of the various threats to the validity of the study.

THE PROBLEM SETTING

The crippling effect of polio and the potentially severe birth defects resulting from rubella are memories to much of the nation. Many people recall vaguely the cloud of hypervigilence that swept the country during the 1950s and again during the mid-1960s. The fear of these and other childhood diseases (measles, mumps, and DPT) has become a blur thanks to past programs and the efforts of the medical community. The truth is, however, that we have been lulled into a false sense of security. Childhood disease is not a thing of the past! These are some of the sobering facts released by the U.S. Department of Health, Education and Welfare (DHEW) in 1977:

- Of the 52 million children under 15, approximately 20 million have not been immunized adequately against the seven most commonly preventable childhood diseases.
- The rate of immunization for the population at large has been declining steadily, and this drop has been more pronounced among the poor and the disadvantaged.
- The incidence of childhood disease is on the rise; for instance, in 1974 there were 22,000 reported cases of measles. It was estimated that in 1977 this figure would jump to 77,000.

In response to the recent decline in immunization levels, the secretary DHEW initiated a campaign to immunize preschool and school-age children against preventable childhood diseases. Consistent with DHEW objectives, the BCHS of the Health Services Administration (HSA), established a 90 percent immunization rate for its target population as its goal. It is very clear that DHEW is committed to the long-range goal of establishing a permanent mechanism for providing adequate information services to parents of nearly all of the 3 million children born yearly. Moreover, this sense of commitment has filtered down to the various BCHS-funded health delivery programs through either BCHS directives or continued funding stipulations.

As a first step in achieving its immunization objectives, BCHS sought to determine existing levels of immunization among its funded clinics (Medicus 1978). There is no question that an adequate record-keeping system is a necessary component in the BCHS's immunization campaign, but that is clearly not the sole determinant of improving childhood immunization. Once medical records have been audited and updated, the target population identified, and mechanisms enacted for charting accurately a patient's immunization history, there must also be some formal procedure for communicating with the patient so as to ensure that the entire immunization series is completed.

As a component in a much larger and more pervasive health delivery and educational system, each BCHS-funded clinic must attempt to convert part of its federal funds and other resources into programming, campaigns, and so forth, which will result in an increase in the level of immunization among its target population. While a number of states have enacted laws requiring children to demonstrate full immunizations before enrolling in school, these laws are not enforced with equal fervor. It is quite clear that the BCHS-funded clinics cannot resort to force and attempt to coerce the patient to undergo the complete immunization series. The clinics, therefore, must develop marketing strategies to educate—persuade—the patient or, in most cases, the patient's parents to engage in the prescribed preventive immunization behavior.

SELECTION OF AN APPROPRIATE MARKETING STRATEGY

The outcomes of any preventive health care program are effective only to the extent that desirable changes in behavior occur when the information transmitted from the health communicator is translated into practice. Whether we speak of drug abuse (McGuire 1977), dental hygiene or immunization, the payoff of any social marketing program is behavioral change. Marketers have employed essentially two strategies for encouraging behavior modification: persuasion and behavioral influence strategies. Persuasive strategies are based on the assumption that behavior can be modified by influencing its cognitive precursors. There is both an intuitive appeal and theoretical basis for proclaiming attitude change as a precursor to and major determinant of corresponding behavior (Fishbein and Ajzen 1972; McGuire 1969).

An alternative influence strategy entails the direct modification of behavior. While dispositions may be acquired through information provided by others, an equally important mode of information acquisition is one's own experiences. The process by which attitudes are learned through interpretation of one's own behavior is described by attribution theory (for example, Bem 1972). The attribution theory literature has found consistently that people observe their own behavior as cues to their attitudes. This consistent finding has been incorporated into a strategy known as "foot-in-the-door" for modifying the behavior of individuals (for example, Freedman and Fraser 1966).

Persuasive Strategies

Much of the marketing and social psychological literature devoted to the effectiveness of persuasive communication can be traced to research by Hovland and his associates at Yale (Hovland and Weiss 1951; Hovland, Janis and Kelley 1953). Defining communication as the process by which a communicator transmits a message to influence the behavior of other individuals, one basic assumption underlying the Yale research program is that attitude change is dependent on learning the message content and accepting what is learned (Hovland and Weiss 1951). From this research stream it is possible to trace both the development of several more complex models of consumer behavior (for example, Engel, Kollat and Blackwell 1973) and much of recent literature devoted expressly to attitude formation and attitude change (for example, Fishbein and Ajzen 1972).

While the purpose here is not to review the literature devoted to attitude formations and change, suffice it to say that beliefs are viewed as the cognitive building blocks upon which attitudes are formed. Thus any persuasive attempts directed at changing people's health-related attitudes (and, as a result, their behavior) must be focused at one or more of their beliefs regarding the relevant health-related attitudes. Given the repeated findings that attitudes are not highly correlated with behavior and that attitude change does not necessarily cause behavior change, the effectiveness of a persuasive appeal in altering behavior is less than compelling. In fact, McGuire (1977) states that it has proven very difficult to demonstrate any sizable persuasive impact of explicit campaigns designed to change public health practices.

Yet it has not been our intention to set up a "straw man" to be easily refuted by another theoretical scheme. Indeed, there are many scholars who tend to agree with Fishbein and Ajzen (1975) that the poor predictive power of the attitude/behavior paradigm can be traced to methodological rather than conceptual problems. If the objective here is to change behavior, though, we must turn to other paradigms that can serve as a framework for inducing compliant immunization-related behavior.

The Foot-In-The-Door Technique

An alternative to a straight persuasive communication strategy is the foot-in-the-door (FID) technique (Freedman and Fraser 1966; Scott 1977). Whereas the persuasive communication model posits that modifications of the affective or cognitive components of an attitude will cause the individual to modify his subsequent behavior, the FID paradigm involves modifying behavior first. This, in turn, may cause a change in attitude. Operationally FID entails gaining compliance with an initial small request in order to facilitate compliance with subsequent requests (Scott 1977, p. 156). Its use has been illustrated in a number of different settings including requests to support environmental concerns (Miller, Brickman and Bolen 1975), promoting safe driving (Freedman and Fraser 1966), and enrolling in a prepaid health plan (Tybout 1978). These findings suggest that FID is superior to straight persuasion for modifying behavior.

In a now classic study, Freedman and Fraser (1966) found that subjects who had been contacted for an initial small request (to place a small sign supporting safe driving in their window) showed greater intention to comply with a larger subsequent request (to place a large, unattractive sign in their front lawn) than control group subjects contacted only for the larger request. Theoretically, an explanation of the FID technique is offered by attribution theory (Bem 1972): individuals reflect on their compliance with a small request and conclude that they must have a positive attitude toward such behaviors. This inferred attitude increases the probability of compliance with later requests. The crucial element in this explanation is the process of self-attribution. That is, when an individual reflects on his or her own behavior regarding the initial small request in a FID situation, he or she comes to the realization that there was really very little external force for compliance with the request and therefore decides that he or she must have positive feelings and evaluations toward behaviors of that type. Thus, an individual's own explanation for his or her initial behavior will lead him or her to comply with larger subsequent requests.

For illustrative purposes, the FID technique might be applied to the immunization problem in the following way. Since the FID technique appears to be amenable to telephone contact, a parent would be contacted by a BCHS clinic and asked to comply with a small request. This request should be small enough to elicit compliance and, at the same time, large enough to cause self-attribution to occur (Uranowitz 1975). For example, a parent would be asked to provide some information germane to the child's immunization history. Subsequent to the parent's compliance with the small request, the large request would entail scheduling the child to come to the clinic so that either the immunization record could be verified or, if warranted, the necessary vaccination be given. The dependent measures would be the willingness to schedule the child and the actual subsequent behavior of visiting the clinic.

While previous research has demonstrated that the effectiveness of the FID strategy is likely to be influenced by (1) the size of the first request (Cann, Sherman and Elkes 1975), (2) whether the subsequent larger request occurs during the initial or a separate contact (Harris 1972), (3) the other characteristics of the situation (Tybout 1978), and (4) the sense of personal control of the subject (Cialdini and Minels 1977), other literature suggests that other factors may also have an impact on its efficacy. Specifically, it would be interesting to examine whether compliance with the larger, subsequent request is affected by having participants only agree to or agree to and perform the small, initial request and forcing participants to reflect on why they complied with the small, initial request.

Agree vs. Perform

There have been two operationalizations of the "small, initial request" manipulation in the literature. For instance, Cialdini (1975) has relied almost exclusively on gaining only agreement to perform the small request, while others (for example, Tybout 1978) have sought not only to elicit the participants' agreement but to have the participant perform the small request. It is felt that some of the equivocal research findings can be explained by whether the small request was only "agreed to" or was "agreed to *and* performed." Conceptually, it would seem that self-attribution is more likely to be evoked if the participant is asked to agree to and then perform the small request. That is, by actually engaging (agreeing and performing) in the small request, it is believed that the probability of the participant complying with the larger request is greater than if he or she only agreed to the small request but did not perform it. Yet, if self-attribution can be evoked by having the participant merely agree to perform the small request, social marketers (in this case, the BCHS clinics) can reach their target audience in a more cost-efficient manner.

Forced Reflection

Central to the FID hypothesis is that individuals reflect on their compliance with the small request and thus formulate their attitudes. Tesser and his colleagues (1978) have observed the degree of polarization of attitudes to be a direct function of the amount of time intervening between presentation of a stimulus (here, a small request) and the measurement of an attitude. It would be anticipated that forced reflection (asking participants to state why they agreed to perform the small request) would make the small request more salient (Tesser and Cowan 1975). By asking participants to think about and state why they engaged in the small request it is possible to encourage ("force") them to reflect on their behavior, thereby making it more meaningful to them. As a result, the self-attribution process would be facilitated and the effectiveness of FID enhanced.

Summary of Marketing Strategy

For both conceptual and contextual reasons, it appears that the foot-in-the-door technique is a better strategy for gaining compliance to immunization-related behavior. Since it is likely that parents will have favorable (or, at worst, neutral) attitudes toward the concept of immunization, the probability of gaining compliance with a small, initial request is greater. As a variant of the traditional FID paradigm we have sought to examine whether (1) "agreeing to" or "agreeing to and performing" the small, initial request and (2) "forcing" the participant to reflect on his reasons for complying with the small, initial request would facilitate the self-attribution process. Based on the previous discussion, it would be expected that the attribution-related marketing approach, which has the participant "agreeing to and performing" the small request and then reflecting on his or her reasons for doing so, will be most effective in eliciting compliance with the larger, immunization-related request. The actual research design and the operationalization of the dependent and independent valuables are discussed in the following section.

THE RESEARCH SETTING

Up to this point we have purposefully not discussed the influence of situational variables on the selection of a theoretical framework, the research design, and the operationalization of independent or dependent variables. This is not to say that situational variables had a minimal impact on this research; quite the contrary, situational variables exerted a major influence on the design of this study shaping both the broad outlines of the experiment and the specific operationalization of the independent and dependent variables.

On the broadest level, it was clear that BCHS desired a "realistic" field experiment. It must be emphasized that in the present context this had two distinct but related implications. First, *realistic* implied that the experiment be performed as unobtrusively as possible in a natural setting with actual clinic patients as subjects. Second, it was important that the independent variables manipulated in the experiment be selected and operationalized subject to the constraint of a reasonably high expectation that they could be utilized on a continuing basis by BCHS clinics. In addition to reflecting the BCHS concern for a "practical" study, the research design was influenced by interviews with BCHS staff, site visits to clinics, and a literature review. From this background research, several relevant issues came to the fore which served to shape the actual research design. First, some method of interpersonal contact between the clinic and the patient (or more precisely the patient's parent or guardian) is most desirable because of the ability both to persuade and to handle the logistics of appointment scheduling. Second, some variation of a persuasive message coupled with fear appeal overtones is used currently by clinics to encourage immunization. Third, because clinics are short of staff it is imperative that the proposed experimental approach be efficient.

Once these factors were recognized, it became apparent that the experimental manipulations should be carried out by telephone, which is both interpersonal and efficient. Furthermore, rather than attempting simply to vary the wording and emphasis of existing persuasive messages, the use of a different approach appeared desirable. Attribution theory, as operationalized with the foot-in-the-door technique, offered a theoretical framework that was a clear alternative to a straight persuasive communications strategy and could be employed over the telephone. Furthermore experimental results had shown that the FID strategy could be utilized as effectively in one interaction as in two (Harris 1972), thus allowing this technique to meet the efficiency criterion. Finally, attribution theory has been shown to be a useful conceptual approach in other analogous health-related contexts.

In addition to the factors discussed above, it was deemed important to perform the research in a setting that would be as free from the influence of outside factors as possible, have a stable patient population (to increase the probability that patients could be reached by telephone), and have enough unimmunized patients to provide sufficient cell sizes for the experiment. Based on these criteria and the additional one of being somewhat proximate to Washington, D.C. (since the contract could not support large travel costs), a field site in Gary, West Virginia, was selected by BCHS personnel. Gary is located in rural coal-mining country in McDowell County in southwestern West Virginia. The clinic, which is categorized by BCHS as a Rural Health Initiative, provides complete medical and dental care to 700 families in and around Gary.

Although no demographic information was available about the clinic's population, a brief description of the population of McDowell County will help to illustrate better the research setting. According to the U.S. Census (1977), McDowell County had a population of 54,661, 18 percent of whom were black. The 1974 per capita income was $3,071, which at that time was about $600 less than the average per capita income for West Virginia. Moreover, the unemployment rate was 7.4 percent in 1970.

An initial visit was made to the clinic approximately six weeks before conducting the experiment to introduce the researchers, explain the nature of the project, and identify any potential problem areas that could possibly confound the research. At that time, we were assured that the clinic would have complete immunization records on the approximately 200 preschoolers in the patient population, that new telephone lines would be installed to ensure that the experiment could be performed in one week's time, and that two clinic staff members (who spoke with local accents) would be detailed to perform the telephone contacts. Furthermore, we were assured that almost all patients had telephones and that the clinic had records of these telephone numbers. Finally, the clinic director and head nurse were supportive of, if not enthusiastic about, the proposed research. Therefore, we were optimistic about implementing the research design discussed in the next section.

RESEARCH DESIGN

Experimental Design

Since a relatively complete list of preschool-age clinic patients was available before the experiment, children (and their parents) could be assigned randomly to treatment and control groups. In this fashion, a true experimental design could be utilized in a field setting. It was felt that an after-only design with control group would be appropriate. Such a design is suitable here because random assignment eliminates the need to control for a possible testing effect and because it is realistic to expect that the clinic would only contact its patients once. The research design is illustrated in Table 20.1, which indicates that there were five treatment calls and a control group in this experiment.

As can be seen from Table 20.1, the experiment was designed to see which of the four attribution-related strategies would be more effective than straight persuasion in eliciting the desired immunization-related behavior. As stated previously, most of the clinics were utilizing currently a persuasive appeal to schedule immunizations. The control group, of course, received no contact and was intended to allow determination of the effect-history on the experiment. We hypothesized that among the FID manipulations, the "agree and perform/forced reflection" manipulation (Cell 1) would be most effective and that the "agree only/no forced reflection" manipulation (Cell 4) would be least effective. No other hypotheses regarding the two remaining FID cells could be formulated from the literature. Although it could not be hypothesized with a high degree of certainty whether any or all of the FID manipulations would be more effective than straight persuasion, the literature tends to suggest that "agree and perform/forced reflection" (Cell 1)

TABLE 20.1

Research Design for Immunization Experiment

| | Foot-in-the-Door Manipulations | | | |
| | Cue Salience Manipulation | | | |
Small Behavior Manipulation	Forced Reflection	No Forced Reflection	Straight Persuasion	Control Group
Agree and perform	Cell 1	Cell 3	Cell 5	Cell 6
Agree to perform	Cell 2	Cell 4		

Cell 1: Agree and perform small behavior; forced reflection regarding agreement to perform behavior.

Cell 2: Only agree to perform small behavior; forced reflection regarding agreement to perform behavior.

Cell 3: Agree and perform small behavior; no forced (natural) reflection regarding agreement to perform behavior.

Cell 4: Only agree to perform small behavior; no forced (natural) reflection regarding agreement to perform behavior.

Cell 5: Straight (typical) persuasion strategy only.

Cell 6: A control group, not contacted or recruited in any way.

Source: Compiled by the authors.

should be a more effective marketing strategy than straight persuasion (Cell 5) in gaining compliance with the immunization-related behavior.

Operationalization of Independent and Dependent Variables

The operationalization of the independent variables for the FID manipulations was fairly straightforward. In the most complex case, the "agree and perform/forced reflection" cell, the communication proceeded as follows: First, the interviewer gave her name and stated she was calling from the health clinic. Second, the subject was told that the clinic was updating their immunization records on the subject's child. The subjects in this study are the parents of the clinic patients. Thus, the random assignment of a child to a treatment group is equivalent to the random assignment of a parent or guardian to that treatment group. Third, the subject was asked (as the small behavior) if she or he would answer "a few" questions about the child's immunization status. Fourth, the interviewer asked the subject three questions about the child's immunization history (what shots, when given, where given). Thus, by answering the three questions the parent "performed" the small request. Fifth, the interviewer thanked the subject for providing the information. Sixth, the interviewer stated and then asked the subject, "You have been most cooperative. As a parent, why do you think children should be immunized?" (forced reflection).

The above script was modified in the "agree only" manipulation by telling the subject after step three, "Thank you for agreeing to answer our questions. I have a lot of people to call today, so someone else from the clinic will call you in a few days to get the information." If a subject was not in the forced reflection cell, she or he was not asked the last question about why a child should be immunized.

The dependent variable in the experiment was originally operationalized in two ways. First, we intended to ask the subjects to agree to schedule their child for an appointment to get an immunization. The second level was intended to be the numbers of patients scheduled who actually kept their appointments. We use the word *intended* because we were informed two days before the experiment was to begin that the clinic was unable to obtain complete immunization records on their patients. It seemed that the McDowell County Health Clinic, which had the most complete immunization records on children living in the county, decided to release the immunization information only upon the receipt of a written medical release form signed by the child's parent or guardian.

To compensate for this event, the dependent variable was redefined to be a request that the parent bring the child's immunization record to the clinic. The rationale for this redefinition was simply that the clinic's goal was to find a strategy that is effective in causing parents to bring their children to the clinic. The behavior of hand-carrying the record to the clinic (or coming to the clinic to sign a medical record release form if the parent did not have the immunization record) was felt to provide an adequate proxy measure of the effectiveness of the various treatments. As is discussed in the next section, this was only the first of a number of unforeseen events that influenced the experiment.

THE FIELD EXPERIENCE

Two important events occurred while the experiment was being conducted which influenced its implementation. First, the clinic had difficulty with a newly installed phone system during the experiment, with the result that only one outgoing telephone line, instead of the two that had been expected, was available during much of the week. This had two impacts on the experiment: only 50 percent of the interviews that were expected to be completed were actually performed; and, in order to compensate for the loss of the phone line, the clinic director permitted several of the staff members to make calls from their homes. One problem was that the number of subjects in each cell was dramatically reduced. The second problem, however, was potentially far more detrimental. Since a number of calls were made from the interviewers' homes some control over the delivery of the various messages was lost. It is not certain whether potential interviewer bias is a serious problem. However, to the extent that it exists its effects are undetectable.

The second event that might have influenced the results occurred the evening before the last day of the experiment. The evening news broadcast that the FDA had announced the recall of a batch of diphtheria, polio, and tetanus (DPT) vaccine distributed in eastern Tennessee, approximately 200 miles from Gary, West Virginia. The extent to which this influenced the experiment is not known. The interviewers reported that no subject contacted on the last day of the experiment asked them about the recall. However, there may have been a lagged effect, which although not influencing a subject's agreement to bring the child's immunization record, did influence whether the record was actually brought to the clinic.

HIGHLIGHTS OF THE RESULTS AND CONCLUSIONS

It should be apparent that a number of uncontrollable and unforeseen events occurred during the experimental period. When one considers these factors *together* the interpretation of the study result becomes problematic at best and should be viewed with great caution. Simply, the data show the "agree and perform/forced reflection" manipulation (Cell 1) to have the lowest agreement rate. This finding is counter to the hypothesized relationships among the various attribution-related marketing strategies. One can infer, therefore, that conceptual framework employed in the study was faulty or that the experiment was confounded by the occurrence of unforeseen events. There is no way to determine which of the above explanations is correct. However, it is our opinion that difficulties encountered during the experiment did not allow a true test of the foot-in-the-door strategy.

This experience with a social marketing field experiment for the government has left us with mixed reactions. On the positive side, the interest and willingness of BCHS and clinic personnel in the design and completion of a marketing field experiment was extremely gratifying. We found after we were able to overcome the initial pejorative way in which marketing is viewed by nonmarketers that the BCHS staffers were enthusiastic about and could readily see the ways in which marketing techniques could be applied to their organization. This attitude is significant and appears to bode well for the expanded use of marketing by organizations of this type.

We are concerned, however, that the difficulties experienced while conducting this field experiment could have the potential of limiting the use of marketing techniques to increase the reach and impact of social programs. In the present experiment, we are convinced that the theoretical framework provided by the self-attribution/foot-in-the-door literature is sound and appropriate given the objectives of the study. Similarly, the methodology as implemented in the research design and sampling procedures and as operationalized in the independent variables should have worked. The occurrence of uncontrollable and unforeseen events did not permit a true test of the conceptual framework or study methodology. We state emphatically that field research in general, and the utilization of marketing concepts in particular, should continue to be applied to social problems. Field research can provide the most appropriate evaluation of programs and strategies for effecting socially beneficial behavior. Lack of conclusive experimental results should not be used in any way to diminish the encouragement and enactment of field research and marketing studies by public administrators.

REFERENCES

Bem, D. J. (1972), "Self-Perception Theory," in *Advances in Experimental Social Psychology*, ed. L. Berkowitz, New York: Academic Press.

Cann, Arnie, Steven J. Sherman and Roy Elkes (1975), "Effects of Initial Request Size and Timing of a Second Request on Compliance: The Foot in the Door and the Door in the Face," *Journal of Personality and Social Psychology* 32: 774–82.

Cialdini, Robert B. (1975), "A Test of Two Techniques for Inducing Verbal, Behavioral, and Further Compliance with a Request to Give Blood." Faculty working paper, Tempe: Arizona State University.

——— and Herbert L. Minels (1977), "Sense of Personal Control and Attributions about Yielding and Resisting the Persuasion Targets," *Journal of Personality and Social Psychology* 33: 393–402.

Engle, James, David Kollat and Rodger Blackwell (1973), *Consumer Behavior*, 2nd edition. New York: Holt, Rinehart, Winston.

Fishbein, Martin (1967), "Attitude and the Prediction of Behavior," in *Attitude Theory and Measurement*, ed. M. Fishbein, New York: John Wiley, pp. 477–492.

—— and Icek Ajzen (1972), "Attitudes and Opinions," *Annual Review of Psychology* 23: 487–544.

Freedman, J. L. and S. C. Fraser (1966), "Compliance Without Pressure: The Foot-in-the-Door Technique," *Journal of Personality and Social Psychology* 4: 195–202.

Harris, M. B. (1972), "The Effects of Performing One Altruistic Act on the Likelihood of Performing Another," *Journal of Social Psychology* 88: 65–73.

Hovland, Carl and Walter Weiss (1951), "The Influence of Source Credibility on Communication Effectiveness," *Public Opinion Quarterly* 15: 635–50.

Hovland, Carl, Irving Janis and Harold Kelley (1953), *Communication and Persuasion*, New Haven: Yale University Press.

Jones, Edward E. et al. (1971), *Attribution: Perceiving the Causes of Behavior*, Morristown, N.J.: General Learning Press.

Kotler, Philip (1975), *Marketing For Nonprofit Organizations*, Englewood Cliffs, N.J.: Prentice-Hall.

Kotler, Philip and Sidney Levy (1969), "Broadening the Concept of Marketing," *Journal of Marketing* 33: 10–15.

McGuire, William (1969), "The Nature of Attitude Change," in *The Handbook of Social Psychology*, eds. G. Lindzey and E. Aronson, vol. 2, Reading, Mass.: Addison-Wesley.

—— (1977), "Psychological Factors Influencing Consumer Choice," in *Selected Aspects of Consumer Behavior*, ed. R. Ferber, Washington, D.C.: NSF-RANN.

Medicus Systems Corp. (1978), *BCHS 1977 National Baseline Survey of Grantee Immunization Levels*, HSA 240-76-0053, Washington, D.C.: Office of Planning, Evaluation and Legislation.

Miller, Richard L., Philip Brickman and Diana Bolen (1975), "Attribution Versus Persuasion as a Means for Modifying Behavior," *Journal of Personality and Social Psychology* 31: 430–41.

Scott, Carol A. (1977), "Modifying Socially-Conscious Behavior: The Foot-in-the-Door Technique," *Journal of Consumer Research* 4: 156–64.

Tesser, Abraham (1978), "Self-Generated Attitude Change," in *Advances in Experimental Social Psychology*, ed. L. Berkowitz, New York: Academic Press.

—— and C. Cowan (1975), "Some Effects of Thought and Number of Cognitions on Attitude Change," *Social Behavior and Personality* 3: 165–73.

Tybout, Alice M. (1978), "Relative Effectiveness of Three Behavioral Influence Strategies as Supplements to Persuasion in a Marketing Contest," *Journal of Marketing Research* 15: 229–42.

Uranowitz, Seymour W. (1975), "Helping and Self-Attributions: A Field Experiment," *Journal of Personality and Social Psychology* 31: 852–54.

U.S., Bureau of the Census (1977), *County and City Data Book*, Washington, D.C.: Government Printing Office.

21

THE MARKETING ENVIRONMENT REVIEW: DESIGN, IMPLEMENTATION AND APPLICATIONS FOR STATE DEVELOPMENT PROGRAMMING

Kenneth J. Roering and Ben M. Enis

Marketing principles cannot be transferred blindly from the private to the public sector. They can, however, be skillfully adapted to the needs of effective administration in the public sector. The general concept that guided this project is the marketing audit (Shuchman 1959; Kotler 1975; Mokwa 1979).

While the field of marketing is not codified as well as the field of accounting, there are generally accepted principles and procedures by which marketing programs are evaluated. Formally, a comprehensive marketing audit is an examination of an organization's marketing effort covering mission, target markets, strategy formulation, implementation, and control. The purpose of the audit is to assist management in determining what is being done and formulating recommendations as to what should be done in the future.

THE MARKETING AUDIT CONCEPT

In concept, the marketing audit consists of three separate parts (Kotler, Gregor, and Rogers 1977). The first part, the marketing environ-

Support of the Office of Administration, State of Missouri, is gratefully acknowledged. The authors are solely responsible for the contents of this presentation.

ment review, focuses on the organization's markets, competitors, and macroenvironment. The second part, the marketing system review, calls for evaluating the organization's capabilities to exploit opportunities and meet problems noted in the environmental review (organizational structure, resources, management skills, and so on). The third part, the marketing program review, links the desires of customer segments with the organization's marketing program—products, pricing, distribution, personal contact, advertising, publicity, and sales promotion.

The project described here focuses primarily on the first part of the marketing audit—the marketing environment review. The research attempted to establish the status of the main environmental factors—markets, competitors, and macroenvironmental forces—affecting efforts of a state government (Missouri) to attract and retain commercial and industrial development. The potential contribution of the marketing environment review is perhaps best understood by considering the questions the project initially sought to answer regarding the three sets of environmental factors.

Marketers have long recognized the necessity of focusing on a target market. In general, target markets are selected by a combination of searching for individuals with unsatisfied wants and matching those wants with the marketer's products. For the marketing of economic development by states this means identifying businesses that desire to expand or relocate and determining the factors that influence such decisions.

Marketing thinking is based upon the fundamental dictum that customer wants and desires are the starting point for marketing strategy. Once the marketer has determined which customers they want and whether these wants can be satisfied "profitably," then a marketing program to achieve that satisfaction and that profit can be developed.

The activities of competitors constitute a direct constraint upon marketing strategy and therefore are a necessary input to the development of an effective marketing strategy. Fortunately, the study of competitors, who usually are fairly easy to identify, is one of the most efficient means of obtaining background information on markets and on macroenvironmental forces. For this reason, marketing auditors generally focus initial attention in the environmental review upon competitors, in particular, the marketing efforts of competitors, incentives offered by competitors, and the effectiveness of competitive efforts.

The environment in which the marketer functions is dynamic, changing in response to a number of forces. These forces can be categorized as economic (for example, business cycle stage, technological advances, entrepreneurial skill and confidence), sociocultural (people's income and education levels, tastes, opinions, attitudes), political (laws, administrative actions, lobbying, court decisions), and physical (climate, terrain, farmland, rivers, roads, and bridges). The impact of such forces is difficult to measure precisely, but it cannot be ignored.

THE AUDIT PROCEDURE

Implementation of the audit concept requires careful coordination of a number of activities. The procedure for this study was implemented in three stages: (1) systematic review of the situation, (2) collection of primary data, and (3) abstraction and assessment of information from those data.

Stage 1: Situation Review

The implementation of a marketing audit requires a thorough familiarity with the situation. This involved obtaining information from three sources: (1) two cycles of interviews with the professional staff of the unit audited—the Commercial and Industrial Development Division (CID), (2), interviews with experts in the field of state economic development, and (3) examination of pertinent literature. As in any research project, the situation review provided an essential foundation upon which to base primary data collection.

Stage 2: Primary Data Collection

Building upon the foundation developed in Stage 1, a methodology was developed to obtain the necessary primary data. This stage involved respondent identification, questionnaire design, and data collection.

The data collection was as comprehensive as the budget permitted. Numerous factors suggested that competitors would be the most efficient respondent set. Competitors were divided into secondary and primary sets. Competitors in the secondary set, consisting of the 32 National Association of State Development Agencies member states that are not contiguous to Missouri, were asked to provide general information about their marketing activities. Basic questions were asked about mission and objectives, level and targets of marketing effort, marketing strategy formulation, strategy implementation, and efforts to control their efforts. Competitors in the primary set, consisting of the eight states contiguous to Missouri, were studied in greater detail. Questions were structured in terms of the steps in marketing planning: mission statement, target market identification, strategy formulation, strategy operationalization, and evaluation and control (Bowman 1974).

Data were collected in telephone interviews by experienced researchers who were carefully trained and supervised to obtain the maximum amount of data at minimum cost (Black 1970; Ferber 1975). Data were obtained by contacting the principal economic officer in each state and interviewing that individual by telephone. Interviews were conducted during December and

January. Interviews with respondents in the secondary set averaged 15 minutes in length, while the interviews with the economic development directors of the eight contiguous states averaged 30 minutes.

In addition to questions about economic development activities, each industrial development agency was asked to provide the standard package of economic development materials sent to individuals inquiring of the state office, an organization chart, and any other pertinent information. A large volume of material of varied quality was obtained in this manner.

Stage 3: Analysis and Recommendations

The stage of the audit project requiring a large amount of "interpretive skill" is the extraction of meaningful information from the wealth of data obtained and the formulation of action-oriented recommendations based upon this information. The initial steps included compiling and summarizing the data and establishing a file for each participating industrial development agency.

The information contained in each file included the literature provided by each state, the completed questionnaire, and the interviewer's comments. This information was thoroughly scrutinized, summarized, and analyzed to obtain the most meaningful conclusions. This information, together with the literature review and other pertinent insights obtained during the situation review (Stage 1) provided the basis for the auditors' report.

The next section of this chapter presents the audit findings in the categories that typically comprise a marketing plan: mission and objectives, target markets and prospects, strategy formulation, strategy implementation, and evaluation and control.

THE ECONOMIC DEVELOPMENT MISSION

Nearly every director of a state economic development unit mentioned the creation, addition, and upgrading of jobs for the citizens of his state as the fundamental reason for the existence of his unit. Some of the more sophisticated directors elaborated the complement of jobs in terms of improving the tax base and providing incentives for industrial expansion. In short, there was virtually unanimous agreement that the fundamental mission, indeed the basic reason for the existence for the economic development unit, was growth in the number of jobs in the private sector.

It was quite apparent that industrial development units, like many nonprofit organizations, have a difficult time specifying their objectives beyond a pleasant-sounding public relations-type statement. While the directors of industrial development units may understand that specific and understandable objectives are crucial to an organization's long-run success, their actions failed to reflect such an understanding. Moreover, their statements of objectives failed to reflect two key attributes of organizational objectives: first, a hierarchical outline for objectives; and, second, objectives that are measurable.

Short-Term Objectives

The data suggested that few states had done anything that could be described as the formulation of an explicit operational hierarchy of objectives. Most states did have an organizational chart depicting formal lines of authority and responsibility, but few had clearly specified, in operational terms, the objectives to be accomplished at each level of the organization. A few states mentioned efforts to overcome this limitation by various formal planning procedures (for example, Management By Objectives), but results from such methods were quite disappointing. Moreover, respondents indicated a reluctance to commit to specific objectives. One director said, "You know, if we commit to definite goals and achieve them, fine. But if we don't do what we said we'd do, we're in trouble." This view is not unknown in private industry, but it is less pronounced. Such an approach to objective setting is short-sighted, to say the least.

Long-Term Objectives

Very few state economic development units (5 percent) had explicit procedures for planning beyond the next fiscal year. Of course, the political responsive nature of state government, particularly the uncertainties associated with the four-year election cycle, impact heavily upon long-range planning. The point is that long-range marketing planning, which has contributed considerably to the success of private organizations, has been almost completely ignored in the public sector.

The lack of clearly formulated objectives was most noticeable in responses pertaining to determination of the budget for the economic development unit. The responses were quite general; most fell into one of two categories: a percentage increase over last year's budget or an attempt at zero-based budgeting. In most cases there was little, if any, justification for the budget requests. As a result, these units are particularly susceptible to substantial variations in budget appropriations and the ineffective use of resources that inevitably accompanies such variations. That is, the economic development units appear to experience "feast or famine" conditions, which prohibit the systematic development of a marketing strategy so that its programs can have an impact upon economic development.

PROSPECTING AND TARGET MARKET IDENTIFICATION

Marketing begins with the identification of customers. In the private sector, every marketer—from the sales person in the field to the vice president for marketing—is interested in prospective customers: who they are, what they are interested in, how to communicate with them, how valuable they are. Thus, searching or prospecting for customers should be an integral part of any marketing strategy, whether profit-oriented or for a public sector organization.

In general, state economic development units acknowledge this point but apparently do not understand its implications. That companies seeking to relocate and/or expand operations in a state are customers in the traditional marketing sense is recognized but overused; however, meaningful understanding and implementation lags considerably behind concept recognition. The search for customers is generally characterized by ad hoc, "hit-or-miss" procedures. Few states have the type of organized and systematic prospecting efforts that characterize such commercially successful firms as IBM and Procter & Gamble, or even more moderately effective commercial organizations.

The dominant prospecting method is reaction. Most states react fairly efficiently to direct requests for information from prospective customers or referrals by other state officials. In many cases, the standard package of material is voluminous and is produced professionally. Seldom is it tailored to the specific requests of an individual prospect. When the package is tailored, it is usually simply pulled together from standardized materials on a particular industry or area of the state.

The active customer-seeking efforts of industrial development units is frequently limited to advertising, primarily in business and trade publications. Some have a program of managed publicity focused primarily upon activities of the governor and other state officials. About half of the states do some type of "personal selling," that is, state officials venture forth to contact prospective customers. Often these contacts are in response to announcements by companies that they are considering relocation and/or expansion. Some states maintain out-of-state offices (primarily in Washington, D.C., and New York City), and a few maintain offices in other countries (primarily Western Europe).

A few states are using imaginative prospecting techniques. One state contacts suppliers of major firms located in the state and tries to convince the suppliers to relocate to that state. Several host luncheons periodically in major cities for top company officials. Thus "Chicago Day" may draw representatives of Chicago firms considering relocation to a presentation and question-and-answer session. Another state periodically writes to the chief executive officer of each *Fortune 500* company, searching for expansion plans, acquisitions, or relocation decisions.

The emphasis has unequivocally focused upon out-of-state prospects. When asked to allocate total economic development effort between in-state and out-state prospects, most respondents assigned between 60 and 80 percent to out-of-state activities. A few indicated that in-state activities were the responsibility of other agencies.

The research activities conducted by economic development units on behalf of prospective customers is almost exclusively secondary in nature. Research consists primarily of assembling and editing economic data generated by such sources as the U.S. Bureau of the Census, the U.S. Department of Labor Statistics, other units of the state government, and private sources such as trade associations and published economic development studies. Respondents rarely indicated that extra effort would be mounted to do primary research for a particular prospect.

The latter comments warrant elaboration. Obviously, some prospects are better (of greater potential significance, in more of a hurry, able to exert more legislative clout) than others. While this point was acknowledged by most respondents, few had any systematic method of assigning priorities to different prospects or provided better assistance when they recognized intuitively that such action might be appropriate. Most commented that they "tried to serve everyone" or that they "treated everyone fairly." The point is this: the aspect of prospecting that most profit-seeking marketers would recognize as customer qualification was ignored almost totally by state economic development units.

In summary, the dominant mode of prospecting was reaction to requests for information. These requests stemmed primarily from uncoordinated promotional efforts to out-of-state prospects and from word-of-mouth referrals concerning in-state prospects. In marketing terms, industrial development units employ an undifferentiated marketing strategy—which means that they treat the whole market as homogeneous, focusing on what is common rather than what is different or unique. This type of strategy is only appropriate when the needs of all prospects are nearly homogeneous. Obviously, there is considerable room for improvement in the marketing efforts of economic development by states. Simply focusing their efforts to reflect the different needs and different potential level of prospects would increase the efficiency and effectiveness of marketers' efforts appreciably.

STRATEGY FORMULATION

Strategy formulation, the matching of organization capabilities and resources to the demands of individual prospects and market segments, can only be effective if target markets and individual customers are well defined. Unfortunately, the states surveyed evinced relatively little in the way of specifically formulated marketing strategies. The matching of the state's "product" to the needs of particular customers can be categorized in terms of budgetary support by the governor's office and the legislature and a listing of the state's economic strengths.

Resources and Budgets

The survey indicated that in many states the director of the economic development unit reports directly to the governor. The number of staffers in the unit averaged 40 to 50, with some states employing in excess of 100 people. The average budget was approximately $0.5 million annually, although this figure ranged widely. Comparisons of budget figures are suspect because different states include different types of activities within the reported budget figure. For example, various states include manpower training, promotion of tourism, and the encouragement of movie making in their budget. Most of the respondents claimed good to excellent rapport with the governor's office and at least satisfactory legislative support. To guard against receiving "politically correct" responses, interviewers asked strategy formulation questions in several different ways and probed for elaboration and examples. There appears to be evidence that gubernatorial and legislative support is not a reason for the general lack of clearly formulated marketing strategies.

Environmental Strengths and Weaknesses

Most respondents considered marketing strategy to be the enumeration of the economic strengths of the state. In many cases, these strengths involved economic factors such as availability of raw materials, a good transportation network, a skilled labor force, and/or accessibility to major markets. Political factors often cited as strengths included tax incentives or moratoriums on taxes, right-to-work legislation, low or nonexistent corporate and/or personal income taxes, and a general "pro-business" attitude.

Respondents generally were candid about their weaknesses. For example, Iowa's director of the industrial development unit felt their high personal income tax was detrimental to relocation, since executives responsible for making the relocation decision would be directly affected by the tax.

No doubt the legislative and economic strengths of various states are real and should not be discounted. Rather they should become components of a marketing strategy to present such benefits to best advantage, that is, matching the particular benefits to the needs of specific industries or companies. Coordinated, systematic, comprehensive marketing strategies could be developed to exploit strengths and counter weaknesses.

STRATEGY IMPLEMENTATION

Lack of a systematic strategy does not mean that marketing efforts were not performed. Indeed, all states engaged in a great many marketing activities which tended to be concentrated in advertising and publicity, personal contact, and research. Most of the advertising and publicity money was channeled into print media and into the production of elaborate direct-mail packages sent in response to customer inquiries. Many of the states indicated that a professional public relations agency was consulted for specific projects.

Nearly all states had some individuals involved in direct customer contact—personal selling. In almost all cases, these were relatively high-level individuals who were provided considerable resource support, including expense accounts, state automobiles, and in some cases aircraft.

Every state indicated that some research was performed to support personal selling efforts and in response to specific customer queries. Most of this research appeared to involve library research. Since there is wealth of material available from secondary sources, this type of research can be quite beneficial. However, the potential value of primary research appears to have gone virtually unrecognized and certainly underdeveloped.

The lack of overall marketing strategy is clearly emphasized by the possible conflicts among activities. Most of the personal selling efforts and almost all of the tax incentives are focused on out-of-state prospects. Such efforts might well be to the deteriment of in-state firms, who are taxpayers of the state, a point which seldom had been addressed in any systematic way.

EVALUATION AND CONTROL

Some states divided performance into jobs created by expansion of in-state firms and jobs created by immigration from out-of-state firms. Only a few subtract jobs lost from jobs gained. In addition, some states attempted to measure the increased capital investment from economic growth. Apparently, it is common practice for the economic development unit of each state to claim credit for all jobs and capital investment in the state in a given year. Few states made a systematic attempt to determine whether the unit's marketing efforts were influenced in a particular expansion or relocation decision.

In addition to attempts to measure overall mission attainment, some control procedures were instituted with respect to aspects of the marketing program; however, such efforts were relatively primitive. Personal selling effort in many states was documented in a manner analogous to salesperson call reports: when the contact was made, who was contacted, the nature of the location decision, and so forth. Similarly, some states made attempts to follow up with personal contact after individuals or companies had requested information. Almost no attempt was made to assess the effectiveness of advertising beyond the attempt to determine from those inquiring whether advertising prompted the inquiry.

The need for careful follow-up and analysis is acute. Any effort devoted to marketing planning will be wasted unless there is systematic comparison of actual performance with both the unit's mission and customers' expectations. A careful review and appraisal of evaluative findings, such as those summarized above in the preceding audit can provide a foundation for formulating a prognosis of future trends and conditions. This prognosis is a judgmental assessment built on the expertise and general knowledge of the evaluators.

CONCLUSIONS

The preceding discussion suggests the following conclusions:

First, it appears that the marketing activities of any state industrial development unit are not the major determinant in corporate interstate relocation decisions. It is likely that economic and legislative factors are considered more significant. The role of the state industrial development unit is to facilitate considerations and comparisons, placing the state in a favorable light.

Second, there is clearly a need for more systematic and comprehensive identification of target markets by state industrial development units. These units must take the initiative in finding potential customers and relating to them.

Third, strategy development needs to be more systematic and comprehensive. It is essential that state industrial development units formulate a long-range, explicitly stated set of marketing plans to accomplish the objective of facilitating the relocation and/or expansion decisions of clearly identifying target markets.

Fourth, the marketing activities now being performed should be integrated into the comprehensive plan and should be stated such that they can be measured operationally for control purposes.

In summary, the environmental audit provided guidelines for analyzing and developing marketing activities of the CID. An internal audit, in addition to the environmental audit, would provide a sound foundation upon which to build a comprehensive marketing strategy. Sophisticated proactive searches for potential customers would be central to this strategy. This suggests the need for a baseline study of customer behavior plus periodic or continuous updating of relevant information.

Indepth study of customers (and other publics) and formulation of marketing strategy could be formalized into an ongoing program of monitoring and appraisal of state development activities. This would involve establishing intelligence-gathering procedures and operating them on a periodic, if not continuous, basis. If this were done, the state would have a firm foundation upon which to base budget allocations and performance evaluations.

The marketing audit is a powerful concept and should prove particularly valuable in marketing applications to government administration. However, several cautionary notes should be sounded.

First, the procedures necessary to perform a comprehensive audit have not been sufficiently operationalized. A prospective auditor cannot go to the literature and find one neat set of "generally accepted marketing principles" or the proper instruments (questionnaires, outlines, and so forth) or field work steps codified. Consequently each audit must be designed almost "from scratch," particularly for not-for-profit organizations. Considerable research remains to be done in this area. It is hoped that such work will be published and not remain proprietary.

Second, there are behavioral implications to marketing auditing. People in the audited unit feel that they are being judged. Since cooperation with the auditors is essential, it is necessary to establish, if possible, an atmosphere of mutual tolerance, if not trust (Slusher and Roering 1979; Bozeman, Roering and Slusher 1978). The existing auditing literature provides relatively little guidance here.

Third, it is crucial to the success of the project that the auditors have top management support. Auditing takes time and effort—on the part of both auditors and managers in the unit audited. Until a final report is written and presented, there is little to show for the incurred expenditures. Consequently, throughout the project top policy makers—the executive or agency commissioning the audit—must exhibit confidence in the concept, assure administrators that their compliance is expected, and provide sufficient resources so that the project can be accomplished.

REFERENCES

Black, James M. (1970), *How to Get Results from Interviewing*, New York: McGraw-Hill.

Block, Carl E. and Kenneth J. Roering (1979), *Essentials of Consumer Behavior*, 2nd ed., Hinsdale, Ill.: Dryden Press.

Bower, Joseph L. (1977), "Effective Public Management," *Harvard Business Review* 55 (March-April): 131-40.

Bowman, E. H. (1974), "Epistemology, Corporate Strategy, and Academia," *Sloan Management Review* 15 (Winter): 35-50.

Bozeman, Barry, Kenneth J. Roering and E. A. Slusher (1978), "Social Structures and the Flow of Scientific Information in Public Agencies: An Ideal Design," *Research Policy* 384-405.

Enis, Ben M. (1979), *Marketing Principles*, 2nd ed., Santa Monica, Calif.: Goodyear.

—— and Keith K. Cox (1972), *The Marketing Research Process*, Santa Monica, Calif.: Goodyear.

Enis, Ben M. and Richard E. Homans (1973), "A Guide for Appraising Marketing Activities," *Business Horizons* 16 (October), pp. 20–30.

Ferber, Robert, ed. (1975), *The Handbook of Marketing Research*, New York: McGraw-Hill.

Kotler, Philip (1975), *Marketing for Non-Profit Organizations*, Englewood Cliffs, N.J.: Prentice-Hall.

———, W. Gregor and W. Rodgers (1977), "The Market Audit Comes of Age," *Sloan Management Review*. (Winter): pp. 25–43.

Lorange, Peter and Richard F. Vancil (1976), "How to Design a Strategic Planning System," *Harvard Business Review* 54 (September-October): 75–81.

Lovelock, C. H. and C. B. Weinberg (1974), "Contrasting Private and Public Sector Marketing," *1974 Combined Proceedings*, ed. Ronald C. Curhan, pp. 242–247, Chicago: American Marketing Association.

Lynn, L. E., Jr. and J. M. Seidl (1977), "Bottom-Line Management for Public Agencies," *Harvard Business Review* 55 (January-February): 144–53.

Mintzberg, Henry (1973), "Strategy-Making in Three Modes," *California Management Review* 16 (Winter): 44–53.

Mokwa, Michael P. (1979), "Strategic Marketing Evaluation for the Social Action Organization: A Formulative Policy Study," Ph.D. dissertation, University of Houston.

Naylor, Thomas and C. L. Wood (1978), *Practical Marketing Audits*, Englewood Cliffs, N.J.: Prentice-Hall.

Reimnitz, C. A. (1972), "Testing a Planning and Control Model in Nonprofit Organizations," *Academy of Management Journal* 15 (March): 77–87.

Shuchman, A. (1959), "The Marketing Audit: Its Nature, Purposes and Problems," in *Analyzing and Improving Marketing Performance*, Report no. 32, New York: American Management Association.

Slusher, E. A. and Kenneth J. Roering (1978), "Designing a Scientific and Technical Information System: Behavioral Dimensions and Administrative Decisions," *International Journal of Urban Systems* 3, no. 4: 201–10.

Spiegel, A. (1975), "How Outsiders Overhauled a Public Agency," *Harvard Business Review* 53 (January-February): 116–24.

Tirmann, E. A. (1971), "Should Your Marketing Be Audited?" *European Business* 31 (Autumn): 49–56.

22

GOVERNMENT MARKETING THROUGH PUBLIC SERVICE ADVERTISING

Stephen J. Weber

Most federal agencies are prohibited from purchasing time or space for advertising purposes. Public service ads (PSAs), which rely upon donated media, have become a marketing tool which serves many purposes for federal agencies as well as for states and local or national nonprofit organizations. At the federal level PSAs are used for various purposes: to promote health and safety, to inform citizens of their rights or obligations, to substitute for or to supplement regulations. How well PSAs serve these purposes is not known. During the past 18 months the Public Sector Research Group of Market Facts has carried out several studies of federal government public service advertising. While the knowledge we have gained about PSA effectiveness is still elementary, the research has suggested some of the possibilities and limitations of PSAs.

MYTHS ABOUT PUBLIC SERVICE ADVERTISING

Research has been conducted on a rather large number of public service advertising efforts, but most of this research is of indeterminate quality, unpublished, and hard to obtain. Much of what is known about PSA studies seems to be secondhand knowledge: people know something about the operation of PSA campaigns and have heard about studies, but usually they do not have written reports analyzing the program decisions or objectively describing campaign effects. This circumstance can contribute to a considerable body of lore but little systematic knowledge. Some of this lore can be characterized as myths—the myths of naive optimism, of naive pessimism, and of free advertising.

Myth of Naive Optimism

Mythical thinking of this type usually is signalled when certain types of "facts" are cited. For example, it is likely that a case will be made for the awesome might of television advertising when it is noted that more U.S. households have television sets than have indoor plumbing, or that 88 million people watch TV in an average evening, or that the average person watches television more than three hours per day. However, it appears that only a small portion of these mass audiences are likely to be reached through PSAs.

This myth may also appear in the form of "equivalent dollar values" of advertising time that has been donated to a campaign. These dollar values, which can be quite large, are frequently used as an indicator of the cost-effectiveness of mounting a PSA campaign. Often such dollar figures are based upon data presented by the television networks. Networks feed programming and advertising to local stations, but individual stations may override programming and public service advertising with local material. In fact, it appears that local stations typically override network-fed PSAs with paid advertising or local PSAs.

A recent study by Kenneth Rabin (1979) used BAR data to track the play of all network-fed PSAs in 11 media markets during one day in February 1979. (BAR is a commercial service which monitors advertising in major media markets.) By comparing network data on feeds of PSAs to BAR data on what actually aired in local markets, Rabin found that fewer than 15 percent of the network-fed PSAs were actually played by the local stations. While these findings may not generalize throughout the year or across all local markets, it should be clear that dollar equivalencies of network feeds do not represent real dollars at all.

In the case of local PSAs, dollar equivalents are more likely to represent actual airtime and actual audiences. Usually the source of data on play of PSAs in local markets is BAR, although play figures sometimes come from station logs or from estimates by station public service directors. Time given to public service ads by local stations is usually unsold time. For this reason, PSAs often play at odd times, most often during the daytime when audiences are relatively small. Only about 10 percent of PSA plays occur during prime time (Market Facts 1979a; Sherman 1979). Dollar equivalence of time that did not sell is a rather curious concept, because the marketplace largely determines what stations charge for their time. Nonetheless, dollar equivalence of local station airtime provided to PSAs represents, in a loose fashion, the value of this donated advertising.

Myth of Naive Pessimism

Among some observers, public service advertising is felt to be a rather pointless exercise. Few studies have shown that PSA campaigns have been effective in changing behavior. A convincing case can be made that information from other media sources concerning social problems like alcoholism, drug abuse, or smoking usually swamps any effect that PSAs might have on such topics. Infrequent play occurring at undesirable times may suggest that public service advertising is largely a public relations charade on the part of broadcasters or public agencies. Hardly a naive observer, Hanneman (1978) presents a well-argued form of this pessimistic view. He suggests that "purchased media time/space is the only assurance of impact," and he asserts that media campaigns as they are currently realized are a waste of taxpayers' dollars.

A thoroughgoing pessimism about PSA campaigns appears unjustified. PSAs do receive substantial amounts of airtime, some of which is in prime time. PSAs provide an opportunity for a public agency or organization to reach a large audience with its message. People do see and remember PSAs. Smokey the Bear, for example, is a product of public service ads from the Forest Service, and it is doubtful that Ronald McDonald or Tony the Tiger are better known advertising symbols.

Commercial advertising campaigns may provide an unfortunate context for judging public service advertising. Paid advertising enables communicators to reach an audience repeatedly in a short period of time and to select airtime in order to reach specific market segments. Typically, PSA efforts cannot control intensity or target audiences through scheduling. Comparisons with paid campaigns in these respects will almost inevitably be unfavorable. However, some studies suggest that, with modest expectations and with properly selected objectives, PSA campaigns are able to deliver a message to a sizable audience.

Myth of Free Advertising

Public service ads receive free airtime. The lure of free airtime, coupled with the fact that PSAs at worst appear innocuous, may encourage federal agencies or other groups to embark on campaigns without considering the costs involved in undertaking a PSA effort.

In one of the evaluations that Market Facts conducted, an attempt was made to estimate, or at least identify, costs involved in mounting a nationwide, one-year campaign. The campaign included large amounts of printed materials which were developed and distributed to the public. In order to generate grass-roots involvement and to increase play by local media, the campaign was implemented in a highly decentralized fashion through state and local agencies across the country. The evaluation was also conducted on a large scale, employing many test markets and multiple evaluation objectives.

Not surprisingly, all of this was expensive. Adding together the costs for the development and distribution of radio and TV PSAs, the development and printing of several substantial booklets which were distributed in large quantities, the coordination of a campaign across 50 states, and conducting a sizable evaluation, the total out-of-pocket costs to government probably approached $1 million. Even if this figure is 20 to 30 percent in error, the campaign can hardly be thought of as "free." Of this total figure, the development and distribution of the PSAs themselves apparently contributed about 25 percent, or $250,000.

In addition, the real costs of the campaign involved the use of resources that are more difficult to tally, as the following examples indicate.

- The campaign and evaluation involved substantial administrative costs to government for procurement, management, clearances, and so on. Most of such costs were not incremental costs to the government because the personnel were already in place. Nonetheless, three or four person years could easily have been consumed in these activities.
- Because the campaign was implemented through local and state organizations in almost all states, personnel resources were used at these levels also. If the average state allocated 20 person days to the entire effort, probably a low estimate, a total of four person years would have been expended.
- The campaign consumed the airtime on TV and radio stations that is provided for public use. Presumably some other worthy messages may have been displaced by the PSAs.

The PSA campaign that we have been using as an example is probably not typical of the level resources consumed by other campaigns. This campaign was conducted on a large scale and had a very substantial print component. Most campaigns, however, do have similar sources of costs. Attending primarily to donated airtime can foster illusions that PSA campaigns are free.

EFFECTIVENESS OF PUBLIC SERVICE ADVERTISING

Are public service advertising campaigns effective? This question is phrased too simply. Commercial advertising is never universally effective or ineffective. Neither is public service advertising. To address the effectiveness of PSAs requires that at least two types of issues be examined: (1) the conditions under which PSA campaigns may be more likely to be effective, and (2) what is meant by effectiveness.

Conditions That May Affect Effectiveness

Professionals who have worked on PSA campaigns feel that they know some of the factors that can make campaigns more effective. Obtaining airtime seems to be perceived as a primary barrier, and several characteristics of campaigns are felt to promote play: high production values in the spots themselves; localization of the PSAs either through the use of local taglines or sponsorship by local organizations; and personal delivery of spots to television and radio stations rather than mail distribution. Each of these factors is reputed to increase the level of play by local stations, but for the most part they have not been systematically studied.

Other conditions that are generic to effective mass media communications also apply to PSA efforts, for example: the importance of formative research to assess the target audience's baseline knowledge, attitudes, behaviors, and media habits; careful message pre-testing; and persistence in communication efforts, both through repeated distribution of PSAs in a single year's campaign and year-to-year campaigns that repeat or build upon previous themes. These prescriptions have not been the subjects of specific studies but represent current wisdom about methods to improve campaign effectiveness. Staff at the U.S. Department of Transportation (1978) have recently produced a publication designed to assist state and local agencies in preparing public communications programs on the 55-mile-per-hour speed limit. This document, designed for practitioners, reflects much of the current thinking about how to make PSA campaigns more successful.

Carefully planned and well-executed campaigns still may fail, and even PSA efforts that receive considerable airtime may be unsuccessful. One of the most difficult issues that planners of a PSA campaign must face is the selection of the communication objectives. Setting objectives and related expectations about effectiveness may be critical to whether a campaign is ultimately judged effective or ineffective.

Several different classes of campaign objectives can be examined: promoting a direct response; reaching and informing an audience; and producing changes in behavior. The potential of public service advertising for achieving these objectives will be evaluated in light of some of our own research evidence and of the general applicability of using communications for such purposes.

Prompting a Direct Response

Advertising that aims at achieving a direct response from the consumer is a vigorous component of U.S. marketing. Direct response advertising, as the name implies, seeks to induce the consumer to make a direct purchase by mail or telephone. Most of us probably receive direct appeals every day. It may be a direct-mail ad for a professional book that we can obtain at a special prepublication price or a television offer to purchase "20 Golden Hits From the Big Band Era" which is "not available in stores."

Whatever our esthetic opinions about direct response advertising, it can be commercially effective. Furthermore, the outcomes of such direct response efforts are far more measurable than most other forms of advertising. Commercial outcomes appear in the form of purchases and dollars. Accordingly, direct-mail advertisers are continually conducting true experimental tests of their appeals, lists, and pricing strategies. Direct response advertising is open to very hard-headed, quantitative cost-return analysis.

Public service advertising campaigns often have a direct response objective along with their other objectives. A viewer is urged to write to Rockville, Maryland, or Washington, D.C., or Pueblo, Colorado, to obtain brochures containing consumer information, information about one's civil rights, or information about alcoholism. Often the direct response component of the PSA campaign is not carefully evaluated. Most campaigns are multifaceted, and it is difficult to clearly attribute the number of brochures disseminated to a direct response to the PSAs.

Our Public Sector Research Group has conducted three evaluations of PSA campaigns. In each, promoting a direct response was one of the major objectives. The Consumer Product Safety Commission (CPSC) developed a "Home Safe Home" campaign of which a major component was a Home Safety Search Checklist. It was intended that households would obtain this checklist and use it to check areas and items around the house that tend to be causes of accidents. The checklists were distributed in response to queries generated by the PSAs as well as through community outreach activities in several cities, for example, through schools, community organizations, and various public relations activities. Telephone surveys were conducted to evaluate the campaign (Market Facts 1978).

Several thousands of checklists were distributed across six test cities. However, very few of the checklists appear to have been placed by means of a direct response to taglines in the PSAs. The telephone surveys revealed that only 10 percent of those who obtained the checklist did so by writing or by calling a hotline—the techniques recommended in the PSAs. Five times as many respondents reported obtaining the safety checklist through the schools. In one city, the local CPSC staff reported handling about 2,000 requests for checklists, but only two of these requests could be clearly attributed to direct response to the PSAs. Thus direct distribution and community outreach activities appeared to be far more effective in placing the checklists in households than direct response to the PSAs.

This pattern of heavy distribution of printed materials but very light direct response to PSAs is a common one, we suspect. In the 1978 Drug Abuse Prevention Media Campaign, which Market Facts (1979a) evaluated, the findings were similar. Drug abuse prevention agencies in eight cities which served as evaluation sites were queried about their distribution of pamphlets that were part of the campaign. The agency in each city reported distributing at least several hundred pamphlets, primarily through organizations. Four cities were able to provide estimates of the number of requests for pamphlets that were generated by the PSAs themselves during the six-month campaign evaluation. One city reported requests for 21 pamphlets; the other cities each reported that three or four requests had been generated by the PSAs. While determining the stimulus for a pamphlet request may be difficult at times, it seems evident that PSAs, even with local taglines as in this campaign, are not likely to prompt many direct responses in the form of writing for information.

A third study conducted for the National Library Service for the Blind and Physically Disabled, a component of the Library of Congress, presents a slightly different picture (Market Facts 1979b). The goal of the campaign was to inform the public about the recordings and other library services available for blind and physically disabled persons. The campaign was tested in seven cities and states and a tagline presented an 800 number through which further information could be obtained. During the 22 weeks of the campaign evaluation, approximately 1,850 calls were received on the 800 number. While some of these calls may have resulted from local activities such as talk show appearances and posters, the majority were probably stimulated by the PSAs.

Whether 1,850 hotline calls should be labeled success or failure depends upon one's expectations and the campaign's objectives. Relative to the two studies cited previously, this level of direct response seems substantial. The conditions under which PSAs will prompt active information seeking through a mail or telephone hotline request are not yet well specified. Presumably, the available information must be perceived as highly useful to the audience before individuals are likely to take the rather unusual steps of noting the telephone number or address and then making a request. Barring information on an issue of extreme public interest, government marketers probably can find more effective methods of distributing printed information—for example, distribution through schools, use of direct mail, working through community groups—than the use of a PSA to prompt a direct response.

Campaign Reach and Ability to Communicate Information

The great promise of PSAs is their potential for reaching large audiences. Studies conducted by our Public Sector Research Group within the last two years indicate that large numbers of people, in absolute terms, can indeed be reached, even though these large numbers may constitute only a small proportion of a total target audience. Prior to examining the findings from some of our recent research and the generally convergent findings from another research organization, a discussion of the substance and methods of assessing campaign reach is useful.

Many things can affect the reach of a PSA campaign. A campaign that is national in scope will probably reach a larger audience in total but a smaller proportion of a target audience than a local effort, which is able to concentrate its human and financial resources in one or two media markets (see Maccoby and Farquhar 1975). The production values of the ads themselves and the timeliness of the communication issues are additional factors which can affect both how much play a campaign receives and the memorability of individual messages. Because of the varying scope and substance of different campaigns, the reach of campaigns, as operationalized by audience recall, must be generalized very cautiously.

Measurement of message recall in PSA campaigns is often problematic in itself. Twenty-four-hour recall, so common in commercial advertising research, is usually not viable because play of the PSAs is uncontrollable. When the audience is asked to recall a spot which they may have seen days or weeks earlier, their recollections are likely to be blurred, and the stringency of the method of scoring recall can be critical to the estimates of reach that are ultimately used.

Nonetheless, it can be shown that some people do see and remember PSAs. How many? Judging from three large-scale efforts, it appears that the expected reach of a PSA campaign may fall in the range of 5 to 20 percent of the target audience. For example, in the 1978 National Institute on Drug Abuse Campaign, we were able to document that an average of 6.6 percent of the target audience across cities saw or heard and remembered, the campaign in the last month of the evaluation (Market Facts 1979a). The measurement was based upon the requirement that a respondent in a telephone interview report something recognizable about the PSA message. This 6.6 percent estimate was probably conservative for several reasons: the use of stringent coding criteria, the fact that forgetting may have occurred, the tendency of respondents to report other drug abuse messages they had seen, and others. While 6.6 percent may appear small, it represented roughly 330,000 adults in the nine evaluation cities who received and remembered NIDA's message.

In the Library of Congress evaluation, it appeared that approximately 14 percent of adults were reached in the seven test sites (Market Facts 1979b). Once again this estimate of reach was based upon respondents recalling some specific details of the PSAs. Premeasure data were used to correct these postmeasure figures, and consequently the estimates probably are not inflated by guessing.

The objective of the Library of Congress campaign was simply to inform the public about the service for blind and physically disabled readers. Other measures in the telephone survey indicated that this objective was attained with at least some of the target audience. From the pre- to postmeasure, there was a significant increase in the number of persons who reported having heard of a program for persons with reading difficulties, and being familiar with such a program was significantly associated with recall of the PSAs at postmeasure. Furthermore, significantly more persons at postmeasure knew what kind of materials were available and knew that the service was free. From this study, the ability of a PSA campaign to provide information is rather clear. When one's objective is to inform the public about some issue, a PSA campaign can reach and inform a significant, if small, proportion of the target audience.

A third study, conducted by the research department of Compton Advertising, provides some convergent findings about the reach of PSA campaigns (1977, 1978). The study was conducted for the Advertising Council and dealt with a campaign designed to inform the public about the merits of the American Economic System. It appears that measurement of message recall required respondents to play back recognizable elements of the campaign's PSAs, a measurement procedure quite similar to that used in the Market Facts studies. After one year of the campaign, approximately 12 percent of the adult respondents could be designated as aware of the messages; after two years, the reach increased to 20 percent. Both TV and print advertising were used in this campaign.

None of these three studies were small-scale tests of PSA efforts in which the campaign and the evaluation could be highly controlled. In many respects, they probably are typical of well-executed nationwide PSA programs. One paradox of PSA efforts is apparent in these data. If 5 to 20 percent of the audience is a reasonable target for the reach of a national PSA campaign, this represents roughly 10 to 40 million persons. The potential impact of a communication remembered by an audience this large may be socially significant. However, if government or public agencies need to reach a large proportion of the target audience, PSAs may not be an appropriate marketing tool.

Producing Changes in Behavior

The ability of mass media to achieve behavioral change is such a complex matter that a thoughtful treatment of the issues is far beyond the scope of this chapter. PSAs and their potential for behavioral effects represent a subset of the many questions that can be posed about mass media. A few issues concerning PSAs can be treated briefly, however.

A number of studies of PSA campaigns have investigated impact on behaviors such as smoking (O'Keefe 1971) and safety belt usage (Robertson et al. 1974). Typically few behavioral effects have been documented. Certain other studies have shown that PSAs could have small effects on prompting elderly persons to obtain a free medical screening for a disease (Salzar et al. 1977) or even lead to a reduction in the risk factors associated with coronary heart disease (Maccoby and Farquhar 1975). Findings that indicate inconsistent behavioral impacts are quite common across social science research, whether the studies deal with mass media, commercial advertising, educational programs, or other approaches to influencing behavior.

PSAs, by their nature, have some identifiable possibilities and limitations in the arena of promoting behavioral change. A public service ad provides an opportunity for presenting a 30-second or 60-second message. Behaviors that have proven intractable to psychotherapy or other more intensive influence procedures are not likely to be affected by a 30-second message. Moreover, only a small proportion of the target audience will be exposed repeatedly to a PSA. Infrequent exposure to a brief message will seldom motivate people to engage in behavior or change values and will seldom arouse interest in something that they are aware of but not interested in. The best commercial advertising campaign will not induce repeat purchases of a discriminably bad product. PSA campaigns will not sell "bad" products either.

Under the proper circumstances, though, even a 30-second message seen once or twice might prompt behavior. People may seek information after seeing a PSA if they perceive the information to be very useful to them. Some consumer information campaigns may offer such useful material. A PSA may also serve as a cue or reminder. One of the objectives of the National High Blood Pressure Campaign is to remind hypertensive persons to take their medication daily. Similarly, the Postal Service's reminders to mail early at Christmas seem likely to affect behavior.

PSA campaigns can also present information effectively, and, under the proper motivational conditions, new information can lead to behavior change. A 30-second message may contain facts that allow people to make better consumer decisions or encourage them to seek medical care or save energy. The key feature of such information is that it must be highly instrumental for the target audience. If people do not care about a problem or do not feel that it is relevant to them or if the information does not have implications for simple, easy action, behavior change through public service advertising is improbable.

In summary, there appears to be nothing intrinsic to public service advertising that would prevent it from affecting behavior if campaign objectives were carefully chosen. Audience exposure to a message is likely to be low, and repeated exposure lower still. Behavioral objectives that do not require repeated doses of the message should be attainable in a PSA campaign.

Cost Effectiveness of Public Service Advertising

If public service advertising were free, then cost effectiveness would not be a question. Since PSA campaigns are never without cost (even if no costs are incurred in production, there is still cost to broadcasters and to society), cost effectiveness is a legitimate and important question. There has not been enough work on PSA costs and effects to arrive at a sound conclusion, but there is some evidence that PSAs are potentially cost effective.

Earlier, the costs of a large-scale, multifaceted media campaign were described. In conducting the evaluations of the PSA component of this campaign, Market Facts attempted to relate costs to how many members of the target audience were reached by the campaign's message. After making a number of simplifying assumptions, we computed that a meaningfully remembered message was delivered to the target audience at a cost between 2.5 and 10.0 cents per person. The range is wide because it depends upon which costs are allocated to the PSA component of the campaign. Other simpler campaigns are likely to involve lower costs per person reached.

Reaching an audience with a message they remember for a few cents a person suggests that PSAs have considerable promise as a communication channel. Direct mail, for example, would cost several times as much. Whether a given PSA campaign will go beyond awareness and achieve its informational or behavioral objectives depends principally upon the selection of the appropriate objectives and the execution of the message.

SUFFICIENCY OF PUBLIC SERVICE ADVERTISING

The evidence from the few studies discussed here may be persuasive that public service advertising campaigns can be effective in reaching audiences; nonetheless, there still may be circumstances in which PSAs should not be used. One such circumstance is when the communicator's objectives require reaching a large proportion of a target audience. Infrequent plays of PSAs on television and radio can reach large numbers of people due to the mass nature of these media. A small proportion of the national media audience may represent several million people. However, large proportions of a target audience may not be reachable except by repeated campaigning over many years. Smokey the Bear is perhaps the classic example of PSA reach, but this effort has had three decades to achieve virtually 100 percent audience awareness.

In the case of a few government agencies it has been recognized that the reach and frequency of public service advertising are simply insufficient for their marketing objectives. The efforts of the Department of Defense to staff the volunteer military is perhaps the most notable example; the Postal Service and Amtrak also employ paid advertising rather than donated time. From these examples it appears that paid advertising is more acceptable in government when the benefits are more easily monetized in terms of recruits, use of the mails, or ridership. These agencies apparently have made a successful case that paid advertising is required to attain sufficient reach for their marketing objectives.

Another circumstance in which a PSA campaign may be an ineffective marketing tool is when the goal consists of changing certain classes of behaviors. If engaging in a new behavior or discontinuing a current pattern of action provides few payoffs to an individual, then it is not likely that any brief communication will produce the desired changes. Rothschild (1979), in an analysis of the different marketing objectives in the public and private sectors, points out that little latent demand exists for many products marketed by government. While society as a whole, or public officials, may want people to adhere to the 55-mile-per-hour speed limit, use safety belts, or stop using illegal drugs, the target audiences for such communications may have little interest in these goals. Before a behavior is targetted for a PSA campaign, an analysis should be made of what factors control it and what potential impact a brief message might have.

What can public service advertising campaigns do well? At the risk of overgeneralizing (certain local efforts or some campaign goals may be exceptions to the case that has been developed), PSAs can be successful if the communication goals are modest and properly selected. The following objectives seem to be achievable:

- A PSA campaign can reach a large number of people, at least in absolute terms. It appears unlikely, however, that a majority of any given target audience will remember having seen a specific PSA message.
- PSAs can provide information.
- PSAs can affect behavior if the reinforcement environment will support the new behavior. For target behaviors of this type, the message in PSAs can serve as a cue or reminder ("mail early" or "douse your campfire"), or the information may be instrumental for achieving desired objectives (how to reduce home energy costs).

Public service advertising often receives criticism because it must rely upon donated airtime and consequently play may be infrequent and poorly scheduled. Some public service ads are also disparaged because of their lack of creativity and low production values. Such realities ought not be ignored. Within these recognized limits, the core decision about whether or not to employ PSAs seems to be the nature of the marketing objectives. If the objectives are compatible with relatively low audience exposure and can be achieved through a brief informational message, then public service advertising can be a useful technique for government marketers.

REFERENCES

Compton Advertising (1977), "Summary of Research: Study on Advertising Awareness and Understanding of the American Economic System," Unpublished report, Compton Advertising, Inc., New York.

Compton Advertising (1978), "Research Highlights: Study on Advertising Awareness and Understanding of the American Economic System," Unpublished report, Compton Advertising, Inc., New York.

Hanneman, Gerhard, J. (1978), "The Media, the Public and Health Information," Testimony prepared for the Select Committee on Narcotics Abuse and Control, United States House of Representatives, Washington, D.C.

Maccoby, Nathan and John W. Farquhar (1975), "Communication for Health: Unselling Heart Disease," *Journal of Communication* 25: 114-226.

Market Facts (1978), "Evaluation of 'The Home Safe Home' Safety Campaign," Technical report prepared for the U.S. Consumer Product Safety Commission, Bethesda, Maryland.

Market Facts (1979a), "Evaluation of the 1978 Drug Abuse Prevention Media Campaign," Technical report prepared for the National Institute on Drug Abuse, Rockville, Maryland.

Market Facts (1979b), "A Two-Phase Survey of the Impact of Radio and Television Public Service Announcements," Technical report prepared for the Library of Congress, National Library Service for the Blind and Physically Handicapped, Washington, D.C.

O'Keefe, M. Timothy (1971), "The Anti-Smoking Commercials: A Study of Television's Impact on Behavior," *Public Opinion Quarterly* 35 (Summer): 242-48.

Rabin, Kenneth H. (1979), "Network Public Service Announcements Feeds: How Many Do Affiliates Really Use," Unpublished paper, American University, Washington, D.C.

Robertson, Leon et al. (1974), "A Controlled Study of the Effect of Television Messages on Safety Belt Use," *American Journal of Public Heath* 64 1071-80.

Rothschild, Michael L. (1979), "Marketing Communications in Non-business Situations or Why It's So Hard To Sell Brotherhood Like Soap," *Journal of Marketing* 43 (Spring): 11-20.

Salzar, J. E. et al. (1977), "The Use of Cable Television as a Tool in Health Education of the Elderly: Screening," *Health Education Monographs* 5: 363-78.

Sherman, Pro (1979), Unpublished paper on public service monitoring, Broadcast Advertisers Reports, Inc., New York.

U.S., Department of Transportation (1978), *55 mph Model Plan for Public Communications*, DOT HS 803534, Washington, D.C.: U.S. Department of Transportation.

23

GOVERNMENTS AS MARKETERS: ISSUES OF MANAGEMENT AND PUBLIC POLICY

Ben M. Enis

There is no question that government agencies are becoming interested in marketing. Considerable documentation is provided in this volume to that effect. Indeed, the interest in activities of government agencies as marketers is sufficient to warrant careful review of those activities.

This chapter attempts such a review along three lines. The first briefly documents the breadth and diversity of marketing activities by government agencies. Second, the three sections that constitute the heart of the chapter provide a rather detailed appraisal of these activities. The final section then explores issues raised by these activities in the context of the interests of the larger society.

GOVERNMENT AGENCIES AS MARKETERS

The chapters in this volume illustrate the use of marketing concepts and techniques by government. There are reports of armed services marketing, social programs marketing, governmental marketing in several international settings, and the marketing of food stamps, immunization levels, consumer products, and even Susan B. Anthony one dollar coins. There are reports on the use of marketing research and planning techniques, sample surveys, the marketing audit concept, public sector advertising, and the marketing of laws. Each chapter is worthy of careful consideration and serious study. Yet they constitute a small sampling of the marketing activities of governmental agencies.

In the broad sense, every activity of government can be conceived as a "product" to be marketed. In essence, a product is any combination of qualities, processes, and capabilities (goods, services, and ideas) that a buyer expects will deliver satisfaction (compare Levitt 1980; Kotler 1980; Enis and Roering 1980). It is not the purpose of this chapter to present a long and detailed list of such products; A few interesting examples will suffice (*Advertising Age* 1978; *Media Decisions* 1976a, 1976b, 1976c; Menzies 1979). Governments market goods such as surplus war material, books and publications, liquor in state-owned stores, groceries and packaged goods in military commissaries, and curios and souvenirs in state parks and museums. The British government markets steel; the Polish government markets golf carts; the U.S. government markets stamps and used office equipment. Governments are involved in the delivery of such services as mail, savings bonds, municipal utilities, and libraries. The U.S. government oversees and operates Amtrak, the French government manages Air France, and the Soviet Union operates a large fleet of cargo ships. The National Aeronautics and Space Administration markets technical assistance, and the Central Intelligence Agency at one time operated an airfreight line. Governments also market ideas: employment in the armed services, state and municipal colleges, childhood immunization, use of zip codes, completion of the 1980 Census questionnaire, visits to Jamaica, investment in Northern Ireland, and on and on.

The bottom line is that every organization performs marketing activities. For governmental agencies, as for other marketers, the question is not whether or not to practice marketing but how effectively and efficiently to go about doing so (Kotler and Levy 1969). It is appropriate, therefore, to appraise government marketing activities.

APPRAISING GOVERNMENT MARKETING ACTIVITIES: A FRAMEWORK

In an earlier article (Enis and Homans 1973), the author suggested that the satisfaction derived from all products offered to a society could be appraised in terms of the nature of the utility contributed. This concept was visualized as a continuum of the utility of products, ranging from good to bad. Figure 23.1 reproduced from that article, illustrates this concept.

At the good end of the scale, product benefits are so positive that public policy decrees that all citizens of a society should receive those benefits. The individual citizen's ability to bear the cost of consuming the product is not considered; resources are transferred to that individual to subsidize consumption if necessary. Many of the products marketed by government agencies fall into this category: police and fire protection, public education, mail delivery, and minimal levels of food, shelter, and health protection.

At the bad end of the scale, society decrees that product costs are so

FIGURE 23.1

The Product Utility Continuum

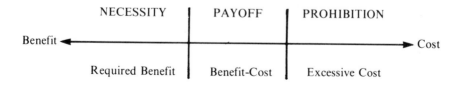

Source: Ben M. Enis and R. E. Homans, "A Guide For Appraising Marketing Activities," *Business Horizons* (October): 27.

high that members of the society cannot be permitted to enjoy those products, no matter how much the individual society member might be willing to pay. Here governmental agencies focus on protecting consumers. The amount and sophistication of marketing applications for this type of product have increased markedly in recent years, for instance, campaigns encouraging people to immunize their children against disease and have their blood pressure checked, "Drive 55 and stay alive," and understand the dangers of drug abuse.

In the middle of the continuum are all products that society neither deems necessary nor prohibits for consumption. This is the marketplace. The individual citizen weighs benefits against costs to determine whether or not to consume such products. Here government marketing efforts exhort consumers to travel Amtrak rather than by private bus or airplane, buy U.S. savings bonds rather than alternative investments, use Express Mail rather than Emery Air Freight, attend a state university rather than a private one.

This framework can be used to appraise the marketing activities of various governmental agencies. Activities in the center of the continuum are examined first, then governmental marketing efforts on the necessary end of the continuum, and finally consumer protection.

GOVERNMENT ACTIVITY IN THE MARKETPLACE

As in the private sector, most governmental marketing is located in the center of the continuum—the marketplace. Here, marketing effort is required to convince buyers that the benefits of a particular product outweigh the costs. This effort must be managed, and it competes with other products.

Management of Governmental Marketing

The management of governmental marketing effort may be one of today's most challenging administrative assignments. Of all organization functions, a good argument can be made that marketing is the most difficult. On the one hand, it shares with production and finance the distinction of being one of the essential line functions of an organization; thus, marketing activities are closely monitored and controlled. Unlike production and finance, on the other hand, marketing is concerned with the attitudes of behavior and people rather than physical quantities or the impersonal orderliness of capital. Moreover, many marketing activities occur outside the organization, spanning boundaries. The management of marketing activities in any organization, therefore, is difficult.

Another point is that it is more difficult to manage in the public sector than the private (Bower 1977). In addition to all of the pressures and complexities of the private sector, the public sector manager faces to a greater extent than his or her private counterpart such problems as conflicting objectives, diffuse authority, political pressures, and frequent top management turnover. The combined effect of these two sets of factors is that the management of marketing efforts by governments becomes an exceedingly difficult task.

Some governmental marketing objectives are similar to those of private industry. For example, U.S. Army recruiters have "sales quotas" to fill, and sales of all products from postage stamps to savings bonds are carefully monitored. However, the cost side of marketing planning is very different. It might be possible to make allocations of costs to marketing activities, for example, variable costs of supplying extra postage stamps for collectors or the fixed costs of renting in a government building. But even if cost allocations are set against revenue projections, the objective of the marketing effort is not unambiguous. It is not to "make a profit"; the governmental unit would pay no income taxes on that profit. The economic surplus from marketing activities should be a secondary objective to some more basic mission—educating the public, helping to provide for retirement, and so on. Few governmental units have specified in operational terms the nature of the basic mission to be accomplished by the marketing effort.

A second managerial point is that government marketing efforts are not coordinated. Different agencies do not seek quantity discounts on goods shipped or warehoused or on media time or space. They do not pool efforts to fund large-scale marketing or technical research efforts or rotate marketing personnel through different assignments. Marketers at a given level—federal, state, or local—do not take advantage of economies of scale.

A third aspect of government marketing management is that marketing activities may actually be "a cover" for some other type of governmental activity. One example is sales of excess products to correct procurement mistakes. Army-Navy surplus stores are one example. Private sector marketers also have sales for this reason, but it is likely that governmental marketers exert less control and coordinate less carefully between procurement and sales of surplus products. A somewhat more disturbing aspect is the use of marketing as a cover for espionage activities. According to a recent *Wall Street Journal* report (Landauer 1979), records on file with the Civil Aeronautics Board show that two cargo airlines owned by the Central Intelligence Agency transported millions of pounds of automotive parts on thousands of flights in the early 1970s. The two carriers handled all kinds of automotive cargo. The Big Three automakers spent more than $100 million a year to ship parts with these two firms. "If you're not doing some kind of legitimate business, you stick out too much, like a sore thumb," says former CIA Director William Colby.

Competition with Private Sector Marketers

In the United States, the Justice Department and the Federal Trade Commission are charged with the responsibility of assuring that competition is "fair." Can competition between public and private marketers be fair? One issue is the treatment of revenues and taxes. Savings bonds and stamps are retailed in government buildings; this is at least a location advantage over marketers of competing products, such as stocks and coins. As noted, it is difficult to match costs against revenues properly. Perhaps taxpayers are subsidizing these governmental marketers to the detriment of their private sector competitors. Private sector competitors pay income taxes and collect sales taxes which raise the final price of products to consumers; public sector marketers do not bear these taxes. On the other hand, it may well be that the management complexities described above place government marketers at a disadvantage relative to their private counterparts. For example, the government agency may have to carry more overhead burden than a private marketer of the same size.

Many of the products that governments market are monopolies: electric power, water, and sewage, postal service, and, in some countries, telephone service. Economists have often warned of the inefficiencies of monopolies, resource waste, weak incentive to innovate, poor customer service. Private firms competing against public monoplies face the problems enumerated above plus the monopoly status of the government marketer. For example, only the U.S. Postal Service is permitted to move first-class mail. Competitors such as United Parcel Service, American Telephone and Telegraph, and Western Union are barred from competing in this part of the business. This point is particularly relevant in these days of rapid technological change, for example, in facsimile document transmission.

The difficulties that private sector marketers face in competing against government marketers are particularly apparent in the international arena.

United States Steel, for example, competes with British Steel, Italy's IRI, and the German government-owned Salzgitter Steel Works. Nor does PanAm stand on equal footing with British Airways and Air France. According to a recent report in *Fortune* magazine (Menzies 1979), state-controlled companies produce 85 percent of the non-Communist world's oil, 40 percent of its copper, and 33 percent of its iron and bauxite. In manufacturing they turn out 54 percent of the steel, 35 percent of polyethylene, and 20 percent of the automobiles. Moreover, Communist state agencies are increasingly active marketers. Soviet shipping, as noted above, carried $2 billion worth of U.S. cargo in 1978, up from $38 million in 1971.

Governmental agencies also compete with private firms for resources. Available time or space in mass media is limited, as is the number of employees and managers with marketing skills. Money invested in U.S. Savings Bonds is not banked or put into the stock market. Government marketing efforts at least increase the cost of such resources to the private sector. Of greater potential significance is the impact upon resource availability if the various governmental marketing agencies began demanding preferential treatment, for example, the quantity discounts dictated by sound management practice.

Finally, there may be to some degree a "halo effect," a predisposition trust, enjoyed by government marketers. To be sure, citizens these days are not enamored of government, but some buyers might tend to trust government marketers somewhat more—or distrust them a bit less—than they do private sector marketers. For example, an undereducated investor might think that United States Savings Bonds would be an outstanding investment. Given current inflation rates, an enlightened investor probably would not agree. Moreover, governmental marketing activities are not confined to the marketplace.

NECESSARY PRODUCTS: DEMAND STIMULATION

At one end of the product utility continuum are products deemed necessary for consumption by all members of society. Resources are transferred among citizens through taxation to facilitate consumption of "public goods and services." Marketing concepts and techniques can play, and indeed are playing, an important role in stimulating demand for such products as immunization against childhood diseases, eligibility for supplementary Social Security assistance, completing the 1980 Census forms, and educational benefits for armed services veterans.

These products are so "good"—so necessary in a social welfare sense—that it appears heartless to question improved marketing of them. One must, however, direct the questions of managerial efficiency and competition with private marketers raised above to these activities. Given that these products are necessary (although it should be noted that even this basic assumption could be questioned), is marketing the most socially useful way to stimulate their consumption?

This question gains salience as the nature of the product for which demand is stimulated changes. For example, in the fall of 1979 the U.S. Postal Service ran a series of advertisements featuring tough he-men who collect stamps as a hobby. Ex-basketball star Willis Reed and movie actor Ernest Borgnine urged consumers to "begin with U.S. commemoratives."

One cannot get too excited about the demand stimulation activities of the Post Office. But consider state-operated lotteries. Gambling is a product—a product which many in our society believe is harmful or sinful. While the debate rages as to whether or not government should prohibit the consumption of such products, some state governments are actually stimulating demand for them (Penn 1974, "Lotteries" 1975). The argument is that people are going to gamble anyway so the state, rather than organized crime, should get the revenue. Perhaps the next step is ads for state-owned liquor stores.

A different type of demand stimulation occurs from the economic byproducts of other types of governmental activities. When noted lawyer Leon Jaworsky agreed to serve as Watergate special prosecutor, he announced that he would accept no salary from his government for such service. What he did not announce was that he would later write a book about his experience. Spurred by public interest in Watergate and Mr. Jaworsky's widely acclaimed handling of the situation, the book became a bestseller. Books by Judge John Sirica and President Nixon himself made fewer profits but illustrate the same principle. Speeches and legal services by elected officials at the state level (the new ethics code at the federal level now severely limits such activities) as well as real estate operations by local government officials clearly present opportunities for using public office to profit from marketing activities.

A final aspect of demand stimulation in the public sector is political activity. Both campaigns for office and lobbying for legislation can be considered aspects of marketing. Some marketing scholars might exclude such activities from the definition of marketing (compare, Carman 1973), but the distinction becomes blurred. President Carter, for example, had his own personal image maker, Gerald Rafshoon. Most candidates for political office avail themselves of the services of advertising agencies, marketing researchers, public relations consultants, and media experts.

Attitudes are measured, positions are test-marketed, advertisements are produced and placed in various media, personal contact skills are honed, and so forth. It is not true, as some critics charge, that politicians are sold like soap. The proper analogy is complex industrial machinery, which must be marketed in different ways to the users on the shop floor, the decision makers on the finance committee, and the purchasing agent who authorizes and oversees the transaction.

The concepts and techniques of marketing are also used in the lobbying aspects of the political process. Simple slogans repeated often, for example, "The right to work is a rip-off" and "Abortion is murder" appear to be as effective as "Put a tiger in your tank" and "Alka Seltzer works fast, fast, fast, fast." Washington, D.C., every foreign capital, every state capital, and many county seats are filled with high-powered, high-paid individuals, many of whom are exgovernmental officials, who attempt to influence legislation through information provision, favor exchanges, and bonhomie. The procedures employed, the techniques followed, and even the words spoken are strongly reminiscent of personal selling efforts.

In brief, governmental agencies do practice marketing, do compete with private marketers, and do stimulate demand for public goods and services. Society must therefore be concerned with whether consumers of these products receive more benefits than the products cost. This is the province of the protection end of the product utility continuum.

PROTECTION: REGULATION OF GOVERNMENT MARKETING

Marketing activities must be regulated by society. Buyers must not be deceived or defrauded, their health must not be endangered, their pocketbooks must not be gouged. Standards of regulation should be no less stringent for public marketers than for private ones. Indeed, one can make an argument for the "Caesar's wife" syndrome: perhaps public sector marketers should be held to higher standards than their private sector counterparts.

Consider fraud and deception. During the 1979 tax season, TV ads by actor Robert Walden and others claimed that citizens should do their own income taxes. "The form is simpler this year," said Walden with a straight face. More serious are the activities of some states that market lotteries. In Illinois in 1976, for example, the state offered a top lottery prize of $1 million. However, the winning number was drawn from all tickets printed, even though some tickets remained unsold, thus reducing the probability of any single ticket holder being the lucky one. Moreover, the holder of the lucky ducat did not receive $1 million cash. Instead, the prize was $50,000 each year for 20 years ("Lotteries" 1975). Given the present value of money, plus contemporary inflation rates, the two sums of money are not equivalent.

Consumers also expect products to perform satisfactorily. The U.S. Postal Service, for example, guarantees "overnight delivery" of its express mail. Consumers who trust this claim and find that their packages have not been delivered overnight can do nothing more than request a refund of the postage paid. No matter how valuable the package, no matter how urgent the delivery date, the consumer has no legal recourse against a government agency (unless the agency agrees to be sued).

The U.S. armed services are spending quite a bit on advertising. They promise "not just a job, but an adventure"; "we build men"; and "feelin' good". Would the Federal Trade Commission allow a private sector marketer to make such claims without significant substantiation? And if, after his or her hitch, the volunteer believes that the product did not live up to its claims, what recourse is available? An army doctor filed suit over this very point but lost. The judge ruled that the army's reneging on its advertised promise to place him in his specialty was "advertising puffery," not a binding contract. Director of the armed services marketing program, A. J. Martin, noted that this case served notice that service marketing efforts should conform if not supersede accepted standards of advertising truthfulness and product performance warranties. He instituted a stringent program of self-regulation.

A final area of regulatory interest in marketing is pricing. One might inquire as to how prices are set for government products. There are regulatory commissions for local utility monopolies, but who prices surplus war materiel? The books published by the Superintendent of Documents? The liquor in state-owned stores? Such questions must be particularly difficult to answer in markets such as surplus military equipment which have no private sector counterparts upon which to base comparisons.

One might also consider the possibility of graft and corruption. The standard answer is that government sales are made on a competitive bid basis. This procedure does indeed combat corruption. But vendors complain about the red tape and delays which increase costs, and many government products are not priced in this way.

The purpose in raising such pointed questions is neither to accuse governmental marketers nor to absolve their private counterparts but rather to demonstrate that, at present, government customers are protected in a less sophisticated fashion than are commercial customers. Indeed, one might argue that governmental marketing activities operate in the sort of laissez-faire environment considered inadequate for the private sector. This concern, indeed the appraisals of governmental marketing activities in all three areas of the product utility continuum, poses significant implications for the public interest.

IMPLICATIONS

The implications of these appraisals are complex and contradictory. By way of summarizing major points made in the chapter and emphasizing its purpose, this final section explores these implications for the management of government marketing and for formulating regulations to incline government marketing toward the public interest (compare Enis 1980).

For Management . . .

There is considerable emphasis today on marketing strategy and planning in the private sector. Scholars and practitioners of public sector marketing should be no less interested. Ideally, one would expect that within any governmental marketing operation attention would be focused upon systematic and comprehensive long-range planning, including articulation of a basic mission and operational specification of the hierarchy of objectives to attain that mission, proactive and creative research to identify customers and market segments, rigorous calculations of the costs and benefits of serving a particular target market, operationalization of the marketing program to exploit that match, careful consummation of transactions required, and comprehensive auditing of marketing activities to attain the objectives specified. This process might be more difficult in public sector marketing, but it will be advocated! This volume attests to that advocacy.

The fact is, however, that governmental agencies are not like private sector corporations (Bower 1977). Governmental objectives extend beyond the rather straightforward hierarchy leading to "maximization of shareholder wealth." In the interest of national defense, the government must mount an intelligence operation. Professional spies maintain that the portion of that intelligence operation which is covert must be concealed by a believable "cover." If that believable cover is in the form of a commercial operation involving marketing activities, how do the various governmental agencies reconcile the competing objectives involved?

The mandate of the Federal Trade Commission is to protect consumers from fraud and deception. Accordingly, the FTC cited the "budget-slashing consumer price survey" advertisements of the Kroger supermarket chain for their lack of methodological rigor (Crock 1979). Federal Trade Commission staffers feared that the poorly conceived and executed surveys would mislead consumers. The Council on Wage and Price Stability, on the other hand, has responsibility for lessening inflation. Its staffers became quite upset at the FTC, claiming that the FTC's charge against Kroger's ads was detrimental to the war on inflation. Further attempts to mitigate inflation involve releasing stockpiles of agricultural products and petroleum reserves. Such activities compete directly with private sector marketing of such products. Who determines when such stockpiles will be drawn upon? What are the criteria guiding such decisions?

Good management practice can also lead to conflicting results. A marketer, for example, might suggest that various governmental agencies combine their efforts in order to obtain quantity discounts. It is likely, for example, that television time for government ads could be purchased at substantially reduced prices. But such concentration of economic clout is feared in the private sector. Indeed, much of antitrust activity on the part of government regulatory bodies is aimed at combating just such concentrations of power. Do citizens and taxpayers want inefficiency and waste, or concentration and clout?

Many advertising agencies have reported that one source of such waste and inefficiency is government buying and selling procedures—red tape, delays, sub rosa deals, and so forth. Attempts to formalize and standardize such procedures on the part of the governmental units involved have provoked a corresponding need for the development of specialization and expertise by advertising agencies and others who buy from or sell to governments. One disturbing result of this trend is that smaller advertising agencies find it increasingly difficult to compete for government contracts. As fewer and larger advertising agencies handle more and more government goods, services, and ideas, there will be increased potential for conflicts of interest between the government accounts and competing private sector accounts.

... and the Public Interest

Inevitably, the public interest enters into managerial questions. As governments become more and more deeply involved in marketing activities, the public implications become more significant and more immediate.

The place to begin is the basic question of role conflict. What are the roles of government, and how can conflicts among them be resolved? For present purposes, the two roles that seem most important are government as arbiter of marketing activities and government as participant in such activities. There are a number of possible examples of conflict here.

Consider first the issue of legalized abortion. The controversy over Medicaid payments for abortions for poor women is essentially a religious question—Does life begin at the moment of conception? The American Civil Liberties Union has taken the position that even discussing this issue is a violation of the constitutional separation of the powers of church and state. But abortions are products in great demand, and that demand will not be lessened by governmental refusal to pay for them.

A similar if seemingly less explosive issue is that of economic development activities by state governments. Almost all states actively engage in marketing their charms to out-of-state corporations. However, the successful "sale" leading to such a relocation has an adverse impact on both competing firms already located in the state and the economy of the state left behind. Even the marketing of such seemingly noncontroversial ideas as "don't be fuelish" might suggest that the government is not interested in the development and marketing of new energy sources and techniques.

It seems clear that the government's role as arbiter of the fairness and equity of marketing activities must take precedence over its role as participant in such activities. All marketing activities—including, or especially, government ones—must be regulated in the public interest. But this begs the question of just what is the public interest. Will the public be better served by policies encouraging the growth of governmental marketing activities or by policies curbing and restraining them? Since poor women will seek abortions whether or not governments fund them, it is surely in the public interest to protect consumers of such products from illegal or incompetent surgeons. At the same time, citizens of the society have the right to worship in the manner of their own choosing. Many choose to believe that such abortion is murder, and therefore should be proscribed by public policy. Where does the public interest lie?

Even after the public interest in such controversial cases is determined through the political process, the classic question remains, Who guards the guardians? That is, who will police government advertising, product claims, and pricing policies? In one case, the Federal Energy Administration proposed commercials that would have shown Arab-like figures negotiating to buy cherished U.S. landmarks to illustrate the need for energy conservation. According to reports, the commercials were in poor taste and were turned down by the Advertising Council. But is it the role of that voluntary, nonprofit, nongovernmental body to police governmental advertising? Is this perhaps the role of the Federal Trade Commission? FTC Chairman Pertschuk recently announced that his agency would in fact "monitor" governmental advertising. But the FTC has no enforcement authority. Or should a new agency be empowered to perform such functions?

This question becomes even more fascinating if one considers political activities to be within its scope. Will political aspirants be held accountable for their campaign promises? And, if so, how will they be called to task? Recall, for example, that President Carter promised during his presidential campaign in 1976 to balance the federal budget by 1980. Knowledgeable observers doubted at the time that it would be possible. But the thrust of regulation of private sector advertising is that it must not mislead even the credulous or the gullible. Were voters mislead in 1976? If so, what types of powers would a regulatory body have to have in order to compel compliance with that claim? Note further that any such compliance might collide with the president's First Amendment rights. Similarly, attempts to restrain Mr. Jaworsky's marketing of his book on the Watergate prosecutions would no doubt be construed as abridging his rights to freedom of speech. And federal actions against misleading state lottery marketing efforts would confront the constitutional doctrine of separation of powers.

This list of implications could be extended. Perhaps the issues discussed are sufficient to demonstrate the magnitude and diversity of questions that could—must—be raised about governmental marketing activities. The amount of such activity is large, and their growth is accelerating. That trend will not abate. Students of marketing should find such questions interesting and challenging. Answers will not be easy to determine, but the search for them should not be neglected.

REFERENCES

Bower, Joseph L. (1977), "Effective Public Management," *Harvard Business Review* (March-April): 131–40.

Carman, James M. (1973), "On the Universality of Marketing," *Journal of Contemporary Business* (Autumn): 1–16.

Crock, Stan (1979), "FTC Told Its Charges Against Kroger's Survey Ads Could Contribute to Inflation," *Wall Street Journal*, March 1, p. 1.

Enis, Ben M. (1980), "Marketing and Public Policy: A Taxonomy," Working paper, University of Missouri-Columbia.

Enis, Ben M. and R. E. Homans (1973), "A Guide for Appraising Marketing Activities," *Business Horizons* (October): 20–30.

Enis, Ben M. and K. J. Roering, (1980), "Product Classification Taxonomies: Synthesis and Consumer Implications," *Proceedings: Second Annual Conference on Marketing Theory*, ed. C. L. Lamb, Chicago: American Marketing Association.

Gordon, Richard L. (1979), "Census Bureau Ponders Ad Drive to Encourage Responses to '80 Count," *Advertising Age*, November 29, p. 56.

Kotler, Philip (1980), *Marketing Management*, 4th ed., pp. 317–54, Englewood Cliffs, N.J.: Prentice-Hall.

——— and Levy, Sidney J. (1969), "Broadening the Concept of Marketing," *Journal of Marketing* (January): 19–33.

Landauer, Jerry (1979), "CIA Has Flown Parts from Auto Makers to Assembly Plants," *Wall Street Journal*, February 16, pp. 1, 13.

Levitt, Theodore (1980), "Marketing Success Through Differentiation of Anything," *Harvard Business Review* (January-February): 83–91.

"Lotteries: States Take the Gamble" *Newsweek*, (1975), December 12, p. 90.

Menzies, Hugh D. (1979), "U.S. Companies in Unequal Combat," *Fortune*, April 9, pp. 102ff.

"The 100 Largest Advertisers" *Advertising Age*, (1978), August 18, pp. 1, 56ff.

Penn, Stanley (1974), "State-Run Lotteries Find Fickle U.S. Public Needs Constant Wooing," *Wall Street Journal*, February 22, pp. 1, 17.

"Uncle Sam, Advertiser—Part 1: $71,000,000 for Volunteers!" (1976a), *Media Decisions* (October): 64ff.

"Uncle Sam, Advertiser—Part 2: The Government Coporations" (1976b), *Media Decisions* (November): 59ff.

"Uncle Sam, Advertiser—Part 3: Where Do All the Dollars Go?" (1976c), *Media Decisions* (December): 72ff.

24

A FRAMEWORK FOR ANALYZING THE ETHICS OF MARKETING INTERVENTIONS

Jerry I. Porras and Charles B. Weinberg

Marketing researchers and managers in both public and private organizations often face situations in which questions of ethics arise. Although marketers have traditionally ignored, or superficially considered, the ethical ramifications of their work, discussions of ethical issues have been appearing increasingly in the literature, for example, Day (1975), and Tybout and Zaltman (1974). The reasons for this increased sensitivity are various. Some researchers are forced to investigate ethical issues because their own institutions and/or federal funding agencies set regulations that compel them to have their projects reviewed for ethical implications. Others may fear colleague reaction to their activities and/or public reaction to their techniques, perhaps in the form of "malpractice" suits or in the more insidious influences of nonresponse or conscious distortion of data by subjects. The utilization of marketing by government agencies and nonprofit organizations can raise the salience of the ethical issues involved in marketing programs (Laczniak, Lusch and Murphy 1979). Finally, some marketing managers, of course, are concerned with the ethics of their activities primarily because of the value system they hold.

Social interventions will always be surrounded by ethical considerations (see Kelman 1965). Public controversies and concerns can arise about the ethics involved in such issues as (1) the use of survey research to select juries favorable to the defense; (2) advertising campaigns that promote the

---

The authors express their appreciation to the many individuals who provided comments on this paper, but especially to George Schement and David Bradford, Edward Deci, Felix Gutierrez, William Ouchi, Michael Ray, and Eugene Webb. The authors, however, retain sole responsibility for its contents.

egg as an economical protein source without mentioning its cholesterol content; (3) the release of a research report on whether former alcoholics can drink again;* (4) a test market (or social experiment) of the negative income tax, of which one apparent consequence is an increase in family dissolution; and (5) deception of subjects of research on family planning. Bok (1978), in her excellent book on ethics entitled *Lying*, provides a dramatic example of how severe ethical dilemmas can be and how profoundly the researcher's and subject's perspective can differ:

> In 1971, for example, a number of Mexican-American women applied to a family-planning clinic for contraceptives. Some of them were given oral contraceptives and others were given placebos, or dummy pills that looked like the real thing. Without fully informed consent, the women were being used in an experiment to explore the side effects of various contraceptive pills. Some of those who were given placebos experienced a predictable side effect—they became pregnant. The investigators neither assumed financial responsibility for the babies nor indicated any concern about having bypassed the "informed consent" that is required in ethical experiments with human beings. One contented himself with the observation that if only the law had permitted it, he could have aborted the pregnant women! (p. 31).

The intent of this paper is not to debate the pros and cons of particular ethical issues or the ethics of specific situations. Nor do we intend to develop a new code or set of guidelines with which to delineate the boundaries of ethical behavior. Instead, our purpose is to present a dynamic framework that can be used to identify and analyze the ethical consequences of marketing activities. This framework is designed to assist the marketer in the development of a systematic approach to dealing with ethical issues. In this sense, the framework should create a process, not a static set of rules, to be used in making judgments about the ethical implications of a set of activities.

This discussion specifically focuses on the use of the proposed framework in a university research setting in which a conflict had arisen over the ethics of a marketing communication research project. However, since we believe that marketing and marketing research are part of a broader set of social interventions focused on creating human change, we describe a general approach which can be used by change-oriented practitioners and researchers to analyze the ethical ramifications of their change activities.†

---

*In the controversy concerning the publication of the RAND report on alcoholism, the focus is not on the study itself but rather on the method of reporting the study's results and how alcoholics will react to mass media coverage (Clark 1976).

†For ease of discussion, the term *social system intervention* will be used to describe both planned social system change efforts and research in individual or social system behavior change. The term *change agent* or *intervener* will be used to mean both practitioners and investigators of behavior change. As stated in the text, marketing fits within a class of social interventions.

APPROACHES TO ETHICS

Ethics in social research are currently regulated by three distinct bodies: professional associations, parent institutions, and governmental funding agencies. The most common method of dealing with ethics in behavior change activities has been through the use of codes to guide intervener behavior. Professional associations, such as the American Marketing Association (AMA) or the American Psychological Association (APA), present representative examples. However, the AMA code is primarily concerned with the client-researcher relationship, not the researcher-subject relationship. Because the AMA code also appears to be less strict than the APA code, we shall examine the APA code for its usefulness to marketers.

The APA code states:

> In planning a study the investigator has the personal responsibility to make a careful evaluation of its ethical acceptability, taking into account these Principles for research with human beings. To the extent that this appraisal, weighing scientific and humane values, suggests a deviation from any Principle, the investigator incurs an increasingly serious obligation to seek ethical advice and to observe more stringent safeguards to protect the rights of the human research participants.
>
> . . . .
>
> The ethical investigator protects participants from physical and mental discomfort, harm and danger. If the risk of such consequences exists, the investigator is required to inform the participant of that fact, secure consent before proceeding, and take all possible measures to minimize distress. A research procedure may not be used if it is likely to cause serious and lasting harm to participants.

Such a code, however, provides little operational guidance. It appears to direct the APA members to be "ethical" but doesn't tell them how to do so or help them directly in being ethical. Further, while the APA code does limit certain practices, it leaves complete control of ethical issues in the hands of the researcher. The difficulty here is that the researcher's prime interest is in carrying out his or her research. As the quotation from Bok illustrates, this focus tends to limit one's perceptions as to what ethical issues should be raised and the appropriate means for dealing with them.

Institutions, such as universities, are a second body which have also sought to guarantee ethical conduct by their members who introduce social intervention. The Human Subjects Committee (HSC) has been the most common mechanism developed by universities. An HSC is typically composed of faculty and other university officers. It is charged with the review of all research projects involving human subjects.

A third body, which attempts to eliminate unethical consequences to human behavior change research, is the governmental or other agency that provides the funding for research projects. For example, all research proposals submitted to the Department of Health, Education and Welfare (HEW) for funding must contain certification from the investigator's institution that the project has been reviewed and purged of any unethical aspects.

In summary, professional organizations appear to have established codes to ensure that their individual members maintain sufficiently high ethical standards in their research activities. Academic institutions, in turn, have established review committees to further police the behavior of the individual researcher. Finally, government funding agencies have begun to require even more rigorous ethical standards in the projects they support.

One explanation for why "higher and higher" levels of organization (individual researcher to professional association to academic institution to government agency) have become concerned with ethical issues is that codes of ethics have been inadequate to control individual research behavior. It is not surprising, then, that recent discussions in the marketing literature have raised issues beyond that of a code of ethics. We now turn to our framework which, we hope, provides a means to anticipate and help resolve ethical dilemmas.

OVERVIEW OF THE FRAMEWORK

A social system intervention can be characterized as a process consisting of a series of actions and events. The intervener can be viewed as a decision maker who must make a choice, or a sequence of choices, among various possible courses of action. The consequences of any course of action depend on an unpredictable event or "state of the world." However, some judgments can be made about the likelihood of occurrence of the uncertain events.

This characterization of the intervention process is based on a decision theory view. We will argue that a useful approach to understanding and dealing with the ethical ramifications of a social system intervention is to cast it in decision theory terms with particular concern for the multiple parties involved in and affected by the intervention. The various parts of the resulting framework can then be used as a basis for the identification and analysis of ethical concerns.

A decision theory analysis of the ethical implications of human behavior change research can be separated into the following five steps:

1. Identification of participants in the change situation.
2. Listing and analysis of the critical actions and events.
3. Assignment of probabilities of occurrence of events.
4. Sequencing of actions and events.
5. Formalization of utility assignments.

These steps comprise a sequential analysis framework for evaluating social interventions. Each of the steps are discussed in detail in the following sections. Application of this framework will de demonstrated in two ways: first, in a conflict setting, and then, more briefly, in a planning setting. The conflict application will be discussed in the context of an actual conflict situation in which one of the authors was a mediator. The conflict occurred during the course of a large-scale communication research study. Although the complete framework was not available during the course of the conflict, the mediators did use some portions of the framework and the concepts underlying the framework. The development of the overall framework was spurred by the need for a systematic way to anticipate and deal with ethical issues such as those which arose in that conflict.

The second application, a planning situation, will be discussed in the context of the current research review processes used by universities to protect the rights of human subjects.

A CONFLICT APPLICATION

The Conflict Situation

In early 1972, the Stanford University Scientific Center on Research (SCOR) began a five-year, multimillion-dollar study designed to investigate a set of medical issues related to heart disease as well as a set of social psychological issues related to the impact of mass communication on behavior change. The specific focus of the project was to use a mass media campaign along with a series of interpersonal communications activities to change those individual habits and behaviors thought to contribute to the likelihood that an individual would contract heart disease.

Three small rural communities near Stanford were selected as sites for the project. In each of the three communities, a random sample of 500 adults were selected. Subjects were given a partial physical examination and interviewed to determine both their media habits and behaviors along four key dimensions: smoking, physical inactivity or lack of exercise, obesity, and diet high in cholesterol, saturated fats, sugar, salt, and alcohol. A composite heart disease risk factor index was constructed for each person based on the results of the physical examination and an analysis of his or her smoking and exercise behavior.

An experimental treatment consisting of a mass media campaign was administered to two of the target communities. The third community received no treatment and served as a control group. The mass media campaign was composed of a series of radio and television spots, weekly articles in the local newspaper, and flyers and brochures mailed to the homes of those in the sample.

In one of the two experimental communities, a subsample consisting of the 100 individuals with the highest probability of developing heart disease was identified and administered an additional, more intensive behavior change treatment. The more intense behavior change treatment, termed the "triggering" mechanism, consisted of a series of small group meetings during which the various desired new behaviors were discussed and reinforced by additional information and experiences. The second experimental community received only the mass media campaign. No additional treatment was to be administered to any of the subjects in this group.

One year after the pretreatment measures, the posttreatment measures were administered. Additional future experimental treatments and activities were based on the findings of the initial research.

During the pretesting of SCOR's instruments, techniques, and approaches, the research team discovered that the target communities contained a large group of Chicanos (about 22 percent), many of whom preferred to use Spanish. In response to this finding, the researchers decided to introduce a Spanish-language component into the research project. This component would consist of Spanish-language questionnaires, interviews, television and radio spots, newspaper articles, brochures, and pamphlets. In some cases the Spanish-language treatment activities were to be specifically created for the Spanish-speaking population; however, the initial plan was primarily to translate into Spanish those media messages already prepared for the English-speaking audience.

The Spanish-language component became an important part of the research. It also became the basis for a complicated crisis situation that developed.

During the early stages of the SCOR project, the researchers approached two Chicano graduate students in the Communications Department and expressed interest in having them join the research team. The students refused, voicing a deep concern over the focus of the research. The following eventually evolved as their major arguments:

1. The Chicano minority, as a suppressed minority, has been heavily manipulated by the majority culture. Developing new techniques of behavior modification derived from experimentation on Chicanos could eventually lead to their usage in additional social control of Chicanos, specifically in various closed institutions. This was perceived as a highly undesireable eventuality.
2. The Chicano community is the most rapidly growing minority group in the country. As such, it presents an attractive target for economic exploitation. The mass media techniques that were to be developed in this project could further that end to the benefit of those outside of the community.
3. The experimental treatment had potential for impact on fundamen-

tal aspects of the culture that exists in the Chicano community—impacts in ways that were not planned by the researchers but because of the nature of the experimental treatment were uncontrollable side effects. For example, a radio spot depicting a family discussing the method of preparation of refried beans delivered *at least* two messages: first, use cooking oil instead of lard because it is lower in cholesterol content, and, second, consider as foolish the 75-year-old grandfather who claims that he has been eating beans fried in lard for over 70 years and has not had a heart attack. The first message was designed and desired by the researchers, the second, a more subtle yet quite powerful message, that is, old people can be quite foolish about modern ideas, therefore don't listen to them, was not intended by the researchers yet had the potential for precipitating attitude change in an area very central to the Chicano culture—the veneration of older people. Other radio spots suggested the substitution of "standard American food" for the traditional Mexican foods.

After some dialogue with the research group in which the two students felt that their complaints had been ignored, they then proceeded to elicit the support of the remaining Chicano students in the Communications Department and began a boycott of the SCOR project. After the larger group of dissenting students had held several additional meetings with the principal investigators to discuss their objections, the students still felt that there were no noticeable changes in the research plan. Student pressure and rhetoric increased against the project. It was not until the student group threatened to go out to the experimental communities and actively campaign against the project that the researchers began to respond seriously to the student complaints.

There thus existed a highly explosive situation in which all the parties believed they were acting in good faith but in which some effects of researcher interventions had strong possible unethical consequences. The SCOR project setting is an example of the potential utility of the framework proposed here. We now turn to an elaboration of this framework.

Application of the Framework

As noted earlier, a decision theory analysis of a situation such as the SCOR project would consist of five steps. Each step will be discussed using the SCOR situation to clarify the application of the framework. It should be noted that the authors' perceptions of the actions and events will be used in the example.

Step 1: Identification of the Actors

In general, human behavior change activities consist of the following components: (1) the *target system*, which contains the subjects of the behavior change activity; (2) the *intervener*, that is, the person or group desiring to institute the behavior change in the subjects; and (3) the *environment*, which includes other social systems of which both the subjects and interveners are members. From these components, three sets of participants or actors in the intervention process may be identified, each set holding a somewhat different view of the process.

The subjects, or targets, of social interventions typically are naive about the ethical ramifications of the change activity. Because they are not normally informed about the intentions of the researcher, the subjects often have limited awareness of the ethical implications of the activity in which they are asked to participate.

The *interveners* should be the most concerned with the ethical implications of their activities. They are the decision makers in the intervention process. It is their responsibility to consider beforehand the ethical implications of their actions and to plan their activities so as to minimize the negative effects of what they do. For example, the APA guidelines state that "the psychologist assumes obligations for the welfare of his research subjects."

The forces acting on the interveners, however, generally result in their having somewhat limited views of the process they create. For example, the researcher often wants to limit the subject's knowledge about the research to minimize data bias and to reduce the percentage of subjects who refuse to participate. The researcher's goals are often more oriented towards the knowledge he or she seeks than the welfare of the subjects.

Concerned others are not always identifiable as a group at the onset of a change intervention as are the subjects and interveners, but they may sometimes emerge during the course of the activities. The concerned others group consists of two categories; those formally responsible and those not formally responsible for reviewing the intervention process.

Formally responsible concerned others are individuals or groups which have been assigned the ethical review task by an institution or by formalization of their own existence. As noted earlier, many universities have created committees to analyze the ethics of any social research undertaken by members of the university community and to determine that the methodologies used are not harmful to the research subjects.* A number of funding agencies also maintain their own ethical review committees.

---

*Stanford, like many other universities, has formed a committee to review all research using human subjects as the source of data. The purpose of this committee is to protect the rights of the subject and to ensure that the subject is not damaged—either physically or

The second category of concerned others, those not formally responsible, is composed of individuals or groups that arise spontaneously to express concern over a specific research project or social intervention. Some examples include members of an intellectual community who band together to express their concern over governmental research being conducted in a disadvantaged community; members of one ethnic group disturbed by attitude change research undertaken with members of their own group; or a group of parents who object to the violence shown on children's television programs.

Using the SCOR project as an example, the three sets of actors were:

1. Subjects—the members of the three target communities.
2. Interveners—the SCOR research team.
3. Concerned others—formally responsible, the University Human Subjects Committee, and not formally responsible, the Chicano graduate students in the Communication Department.

Step 2: Listing Critical Actions and Events

Once the actors in the process have been identified, the second step in the application of this approach is a listing of the critical actions and major events. This step should be carried out in a manner reflecting each actor's perceptions of the process separately.

Ideally, a separate listing of critical actions and major events should be developed by each actor individually. However, in practice this is unwieldly, especially if it is done for each proposed project. As a consequence, in most planning situations the intervener would be the prime specifier of actions and events.

One of the duties of a formally responsible concerned others group could be to decide when to solicit the direct participation of the subjects or the not formally responsible others. Survey research would be helpful in this regard. When direct participation is not possible, either the intervener or the review board can specify actions and events from the viewpoint of the subjects and the not formally responsible others.

In a crisis situation, each actor would be available to generate his or her own list of actions and events. These would naturally be divided into those which have already occurred and those which are anticipated.

In both planning and crisis situations, the listings that are generated by each of the actors can then be compared by those involved in the review process to determine the areas of agreement and disagreement as well as to

---

psychologically—by research carried out by any member of the university community. The committee is divided into two subcommittees. The first subcommittee reviews the medical issues associated with a particular research project. The second reviews the behavior change aspects. A specific research project typically is reviewed by only one of the subcommittees.

identify those actions or events unanticipated by at least one of the parties. Often the subjects or concerned others will perceive critical actions and events very differently and in ways totally unanticipated by the researcher. In this latter case, the intervener can then react by making appropriate changes.

Using the SCOR situation as an example of an ethical crisis in an intervention process, Table 24.1 was developed to demonstrate the initial steps in the application of this framework. It is a representation of the lists of each of the three relevant actors' perceptions. The table is simplified so as to highlight discrepant and unanticipated acts and events.*

A listing such as this, taken from the perspective of each major participant, can be used to identify misperceptions and serve as a basis for their correction. As shown in Table 24.1, some of the SCOR project subjects believed that they would obtain free medical care from Stanford if, during the course of the physical examination, it was discovered that they were ill. Had a chart such as Table 24.1 been prepared by the subjects, this misperception would have been clearly apparent and could have been corrected. Another example of a misperception is that the concerned others (students) were very antagonistic to the development of information describing the media usage patterns of the Chicano community in the target areas. The students believed that this information would be useful to business or other groups wishing to exploit the Chicano community. They further believed that this type of information was difficult and costly to obtain. In reality, organizations desiring the media usage information collected by SCOR researchers could acquire it both easily and comparatively inexpensively. Furthermore, the fact that business had, in fact, not collected such information earlier suggests that they were not at that time overly interested in the Chicano market. The students' perceptions, therefore, were not supported by the reality of the situation.

A listing of acts and events is also useful in identifying areas in which at least one party has no perceptions. The areas of nonperception are often the ones in which the most severe conflicts develop. For example, one of the strongest complaints that the Chicano students had over the SCOR project was that the media campaign was capable of having a negative impact on the culture of the Chicanos in the target communities. A content analysis of the television and radio spots indicated that, in addition to the specific health message, many unintended culturally oriented messages would also be delivered. As part of the conflict resolution, a student-researcher media review committee was formed to evaluate the commercials.

---

*Throughout this discussion, the representations of the opinions of the actors involved are hypothesized by the authors. As mentioned previously, one of the authors was deeply involved as a mediator in the controversy that surrounded the project. Although he is intimately aware of many of the facts concerning the project and the behavior of the various parties, by this very involvement he is also somewhat biased in his perceptions.

TABLE 24.1

Listing of Acts and Events

Interveners (Researchers)		Subjects (Chicano Community Members)		Concerned Others (Chicano students)	
Acts	Events	Acts	Events	Acts	Events
Select communities				Select communities	
	Recognize need to include a Chicano component				Recognize need to include a Chicano component
Enlist community support				Enlist community support	
Media Usage Survey				Media Usage Survey	
Health Data Survey		Health Data Survey		Health Data Survey	
Media campaign	Attitude change	Media campaign	If sick, get Stanford medical care	Media campaign	Subjects expect Stanford medical care if get sick
					Cultural attitude change
					Medical attitude change

Trigger subsample selected Trigger treatment	Behavior change		Trigger subsample selected Trigger treatment	Cultural behavior change Medical behavior change
		Resurvey		
Resurvey Publish results			Resurvey Publish results	Results used for behavior control of Chicanos Media usage survey results used by business to exploit Chicano communities

Note: The dotted line represents the point in time when the table was developed. Those acts and events above the line were perceptions of past acts and events; those below it, expectations of future acts and events.

If a list of acts and events had been prepared beforehand, the differences in perceptions between researchers and students would have been recognized, and the situation might have been resolved without a major confrontation. Improvement in understanding of substantive issues enhances the chance of settlement of the conflict (Walton 1969).

Step 3. Assigning Probabilities

It is often necessary, at least for some events, to estimate the likelihood a particular outcome will occur. For example, if there is only a 1 percent chance that a subject will expect (incorrectly) to get free medical aid, then a review committee would presumably recommend a different course of action than if the chance were 91 percent. Thus, it is often necessary to estimate the probability of outcomes that pose ethical dilemmas.

As in the previous section each actor is expected to develop his or her own view of the situation. In this step, each of the parties first makes its own probability assessments. They then compare their different probability judgments and look for large differences. Through discussion and analysis they then attempt to reduce the differences that they have uncovered.

The degree of precision necessary will depend upon the nature of the particular situation. In some cases it may be sufficient to categorize the probabilities along five levels from very low to very high, while in others numerical values may need to be assigned. A discussion of the probability encoding process may be found in Spetzler and Stael Von Holstein (1975).

If possible, it is preferable to be able to identify and resolve the ethical conflicts that arise by the three steps described above, because the next two steps are more complex and time-consuming.

Step 4: Sequencing Acts and Events

The sequencing process makes it possible for each party to analyze his or her own and others' perception of exactly how the various acts and events would relate to each other over time. By combining the probabilities assigned in the previous step with the expected sequencing, joint probabilities can be calculated and the occurrence of a specific event can be analyzed more realistically.

The importance of recognizing the sequential nature of acts and events can be illustrated in the SCOR project by an examination of the students' concern that the results, when published, would be used by others for behavior control of Chicanos. When considered as a sequential process, it becomes clearer that that action is an immediate consequence not of the research project but rather of a number of other acts and events including (1) a successful outcome of this experiment; (2) replication of this experiment with the same outcome; and (3) people wanting to impose behavioral controls on Chicanos. At a minimum, all of these acts and events must occur before such a consequence is possible.

Analyzing the sequential set of acts and events also raises the question of whether the occurrence of the action being discussed will actually change the likelihood of future events taking place. Using the same example, it is not clear that having a separate Chicano group subject to the triggering mechanism—a controversial issue to the students—changes the likelihood of any actions in the subsequent sequence taking place.

If this step does not lead to a resolution of the ethical issues involved in the situation, the final step, the development of individual utility functions, would be necessary. This last step would be required especially in those situations in which considerable differences in values existed between the parties.

Step 5: Formalizing Utility Assignment

The last step is to assign utilities to the different possible outcomes. This is typically a highly subjective and difficult process to carry out. The problems involved in the development of utilities have been discussed in the literature and are beyond the scope of this paper. However, when decisions are to be reached concerning how social interventions are to proceed and the earlier steps in this framework are not sufficient to result in a mutually agreeable course of action, then the development of utility functions is the next step.

Of course, the different actors in an intervention are likely to have ·different utility functions. However, if the use of the prepared framework has proceeded to the point where utilities need to be constructed, the prior steps should have made all of the actors aware of each others' perceptions and values. Thus, utility functions constructed by any party should be more reflective of the concerns of others than in most situations. Ultimately, a choice may need to be made based on the utility function of one of the actors. Our conjecture is that the utility function of either the interveners or the formally responsible concerned others will prevail but that the utility function of the other actors will influence the final outcome.

The use of decision theory and utility analysis will be illustrated by examining some of the problems arising from the use of radio spots. As discussed earlier, the radio spots generated a series of problems between the students and researchers. The initial decision facing the researchers was whether to include radio spots. When the Spanish-speaking component of the research emerged, the content of the radio spot itself became a decision alternative. There appeared to be four main choices: English language with "Anglo" scenarios; Spanish language with "Anglo" scenarios (direct translation); English language with "Chicano" scenarios; or Spanish language with "Chicano" scenarios. The impact was conditional on other actions, but we will focus on this decision.

The researcher's utility function can be defined in a variety of ways, but for simplicity let it be based on the fraction of the Spanish-speaking segment that changes attitudes on the preventability of heart disease. If the use of the Spanish language has more importance than the scenario but the scenario has some impact, then the alternatives are ranked by the intervenors as follows: $D > B > C > A$. Thus, D is the preferred alternative. However, there is a cost of developing a Chicano scenario, so that alternative B (Spanish language with "Anglo" scenarios) appears to have been the researchers' original choice.

In a single person decision-making situation, the above analysis would be sufficient. However, in the SCOR conflict it became necessary to consider the Chicano students' utilities as well. The students were concerned primarily with the negative impact of each alternative on Chicano cultural values. The students felt that having a Chicano scenario would have minimal or no cultural impact, but an Anglo scenario would have considerable negative impact. This impact would be worse if the Spanish language were used. Thus, the students felt that, in their utility function, alternatives D and C were most highly valued, and both would be preferred to A, which in turn would be preferred to B, that is, $D = C > A > B$.

It now becomes clear that the researchers' and the students' preferences diverge. As a result of a series of interactions, the researchers came to place some value on the students' values. In this particular situation, it appears that the students' negative utility for alternative B was particularly strong. Thus, despite the fact that the cost of going from alternative B to D originally was considered too high relative to the researcher's utility, alternative D was eventually chosen.

Although the utility function was not explicitly determined in this case, the above description very much reflects the process that was actually gone through in the eventual resolution of the conflict. The researchers made an evaluation of the utility of a set of alternatives against their research alternatives. When the mediation of the conflict situation took place, the evaluation then included an assessment of the students' values. The usual outcomes of such adjustments were either that the chosen alternative was modified to meet the student's objections or the no action (no separate Spanish-language component) alternative was chosen. At times the original action was continued as originally planned. The variety of choices made suggests that an evaluation, albeit informal, of costs and utilities did take place.

This section has concurrently developed a framework for analyzing the ethics of social interventions and illustrated its use in a conflict setting. Ideally, of course, the framework should be used in a planning setting to provide ethically sounder social intervention and to reduce the chances of a conflict arising. The next section briefly illustrates how the framework can be incorporated into the planning process.

A PLANNING APPLICATION

Human Subjects Committees (HSC) in universities are charged with the responsibility of reviewing human subject research planned by university members. Figure 24.1, which is based on interviews with the chairman of one university's HSC, illustrates a simplified view of the review process. Two aspects of this review process are worthy of particular note. First, there are several characteristics (presence of deception, use of personality tests, and risk of physical harm) which, if present, serve as warning flags to the reviewers. Three characteristics normally indicate that the research may involve more than minimal risk to the subjects. The review committee must then attempt to ensure that the risks are held to the lowest possible level. It must also determine whether the risks inherent in the research are justified when compared to its potential value. Various heuristics based on past experience are typically used to make these decisions. The second noteworthy aspect of current practice is that the intensity of the review varies on a project-by-project basis.

Taking current practice as a starting point, Figure 24.2 indicates how the proposed framework might be incorporated into an HSC's review process. Since the framework is sequential, the depth of analysis required varies and is determined by the intermediate results of the analysis itself. The more difficult ethical issues will require considerable review, while the easier issues will need only limited analysis.

Another distinguishing feature of the proposed system is the introduction of a screening mechanism to indicate when a sequential analysis should be employed. This mechanism should consist of various screening criteria. For example, two possible criteria are the subject's competence to be informed and give consent and the degree of coercion, or the subject's perceived degree of freedom. A questionnaire study of university faculty would probably be passed very quickly through these two screening criteria while an experimental study of a new drug using prisoners as subjects would need to be analyzed much more deeply. As can be seen from comparing the two flow charts, this approach is primarily a replacement for present procedures as opposed to merely being an additional set of new procedures. This is a distinct advantage.

There are a number of additional operating benefits to be derived from using this approach in a planning process. First, since it is sequential, the effort devoted to reviewing a project for ethical conflicts can be made proportional to the need for review. In other words, many of the gains from using it come about from gathering the necessary information and not from running the full model. Second, this approach provides a structure for analysis. However, unlike some current proposals, it allows review committee judgment to determine the procedures necessary and permits the design of "customized" approaches to unique problems. This is in contrast to pro-

FIGURE 24.1

Research Proposal Review Process

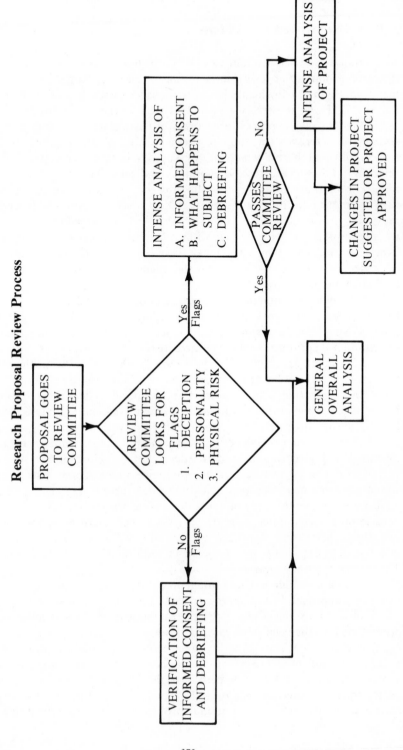

FIGURE 24.2

Modified Research Proposal Review Process

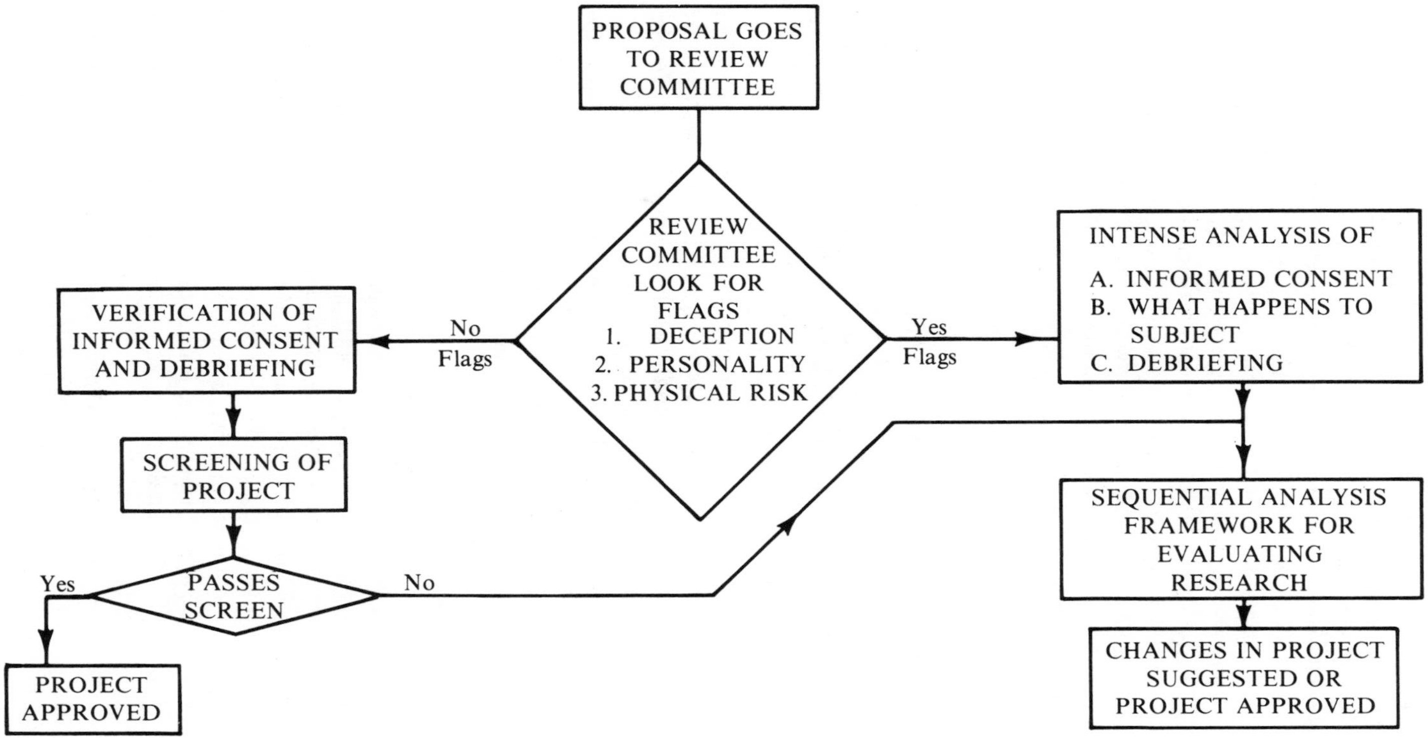

posals that seek to establish standard rules and, in attempting to be all-encompassing, add considerable time and monetary costs to all projects. Research projects that raise no significant ethical issues can quickly move through the review process, while those which are more laden with ethical concerns can be identified and analyzed in more depth. Third, it provides a way of accumulating information systematically so that over time the system can improve in efficiency. Finally, the approach provides a systematic means of integrating the views of different participants, including subjects, into the evaluation of the research. This will allow for political considerations to emerge, including the issue of how the results are to be used. Beyond these operating advantages to HSCs, the use of this approach should lead to ethically sounder research.

CONCLUSIONS

Social interventions will be constantly surrounded by ethical considerations whether or not conflict occurs. Researchers and social interveners need to analyze the ethical impact of their activities prior to engaging in an intervention process involving human subjects. However, researchers in many cases will tend to have limited perspectives on the ethical issues their research raises and the importance of these issues relative to the value of information they seek. In a planning phase, the sequential decision theory approach developed in this chapter can help identify where research projects will be pushing ethical limits. In the implementation phase, the approach can be used if conflict over ethical issues arises.

One of the key aspects of the framework proposed here is that it makes necessary the search for a not formally concerned other group. Techniques of survey research can be used to anticipate the reactions of subjects and not formally concerned others to a project (Wilson and Donnerstein 1976). When conflicts arise, it is often because the perceptions and values of concerned others have not been adequately considered. This seems to have been the case in the SCOR project.

Those who have the task of reviewing the intervener's plans should also find the framework helpful in both planning and conflict situations. If conflict develops, the framework created during the planning process can be updated and used to help deal with the conflict. The perceptions of the parties involved in the conflict can be defined in an organized manner, and, in this way, movement toward solution of disagreements becomes more possible. The application of the framework proceeds in a sequential fashion so that the level of analysis carried out can be adjusted to the needs of the problem being studied.

As the ability to intervene in social systems in deeper and more complex ways increases, marketers and other social interveners are becoming more aware of the need to accept responsibility for the effects of their activities. At a pragmatic level, failure to consider carefully ethical ramifications may lead, over time, to a decrease in society's tolerance for research and social interventions. Methods of guarding against and limiting the negative ethical results that can occur must be developed. An approach such as the one discussed in this chapter assists social interveners in the acceptance of their ethical responsibilities.

REFERENCES

Bok, Sissela (1978) *Lying: Moral Choice in Public and Private Life*, New York: Pantheon Books.

Clark, M. (1976), "Can Alcoholics Drink?," *Newsweek*, June 21, p. 58.

Day, George S. (1975), "The Threats to Marketing Research: More Than a Question of Ethics," *Journal of Marketing Research* (November): 462–67.

Kelman, H. C. (1965), "Manipulation of Human Behavior: An Ethical Dilemma for the Social Scientist," *Journal of Social Issues* 21, no. 2 (April): 31–46.

Laczniak, Gene R., Robert F. Lusch and Patrick E. Murphy (1979), "Social Marketing: Its Ethical Dimensions," *Journal of Marketing* 43 (Spring): 29–36.

Spetzler, C. S. and C. S. Stael Von Holstein (1975), "Probability Encoding in Decision Analysis," *Management Science* 22 (November): 340–58.

Tybout, Alice M. and Gerald Zaltman (1974), "Ethics in Marketing Research: Their Practical Relevance," *Journal of Marketing Research* 11 (November): 357–68.

Walton, R. E. (1969), *Interpersonal Peacemaking: Confrontations and Third-Party Consultation*, Reading, Mass.: Addison-Wesley.

Wilson, D. W. and E. Donnerstein (1976), "Legal and Ethical Aspects of Nonreactive Social Psychological Research: An Excursion into the Public Mind," *American Psychologist* 31 (November): 765–73.

Appendix: EXPLORING AND DEVELOPING GOVERNMENT MARKETING
Yale University, May 2–3, 1979

INVITED PARTICIPANTS

Professor Dale D. Achabal
Graduate School of Business
The Ohio State University

Vincent J. Ahern
Vice President
Studio Center Corporation

Professor Chris T. Allen
Department of Marketing
University of Massachusetts

Ralph I. Allison
General Manager, Marketing
  Services
U.S. Postal Service

Professor Robert W. Backoff
School of Public Administration
The Ohio State University

Blair Barton
Vice President
The Barton-Gillet Company

Dr. Kenneth L. Bernhardt
Consumer Research Advisor
Federal Trade Commission

Professor Paul N. Bloom
College of Business and
  Management
University of Maryland

Elaine Bractic
Chief, Information Projects
National Cancer Institute

Dr. Muriel Converse
Institute for Social Research
University of Michigan

Dr. Rohit Deshpande
Graduate School of Business
University of Pittsburgh

Professor Ben M. Enis
College of Business and Public
  Administration
University of Missouri-Columbia

Paul A. Falcigno
President
Paul A. Falcigno & Assoc., Inc.

Professor William A. Flexner
Center for Health Services Research
University of Minnesota

Professor Gary T. Ford
College of Business and
  Management
University of Maryland

Professor Frederick Huszagh
Dean Rusk Center for International
  Law
University of Georgia

Professor Sandra M. Huszagh
Department of Marketing
University of Georgia

Professor Larry Isaacson
School of Organization and
    Management
Yale University

Professor John R. Kerr
Department of Marketing
Florida State University

Professor Christopher H. Lovelock
Graduate School of Business
Harvard University

John S. Makulowich
Senior Consultant
Booz, Allen and Hamilton

Dr. A. J. Martin
Director, Accession and Retention
    Programs
Office of the Secretary of Defense

Professor Claude R. Martin, Jr.
Graduate School of Business
University of Michigan

Dr. Peter May
Graduate School of Public Policy
University of California-Berkeley

Dr. Jeffrey S. Milstein
Office of Conservation and Sales
    Applications
U.S. Department of Energy

Professor Michael P. Mokwa
Graduate School of Business
University of Wisconsin-Madison

Dr. Richard L. Oliver
Consumer Scientist
Food and Drug Administration

Professor Steven E. Permut
School of Organization and
    Management
Yale University

Dr. J. J. Persensky
Research Psychologist
National Bureau of Standards

Dr. Debra Scammon
Marketing Research Consultant
Federal Trade Commission

Professor Richard Semenik
Department of Marketing
University of Utah

Professor S. Prakash Sethi
School of Management and
    Administration
University of Texas-Dallas

Professor Stanley J. Shapiro
Faulty of Management
McGill University

Dr. Marshall Spatz
School of Organization and
    Management
Yale University

Professor Robert E. Spekman
College of Business and
    Management
University of Maryland

Professor Thaddeus H. Spratlen
Department of Marketing
University of Washington

James M. Stearns
Department of Marketing
Florida State University

Professor Frederick D. Sturdivant
College of Administrative Science
The Ohio State University

Jayne S. Talmage
Director
Media Collaboration, Inc.

Gwene Taylor
Senior Vice President
Management Analysis Center, Inc.

Professor George Tesar
College of Business and Economics
University of Wisconsin-Whitewater

Dr. Stephen J. Weber
Vice President
Market Facts—Washington, D.C.

Professor Charles B. Weinberg
Graduate School of Business
Stanford University

Professor Yoram Wind
The Wharton School
University of Pennsylvania

Professor Gerald Zaltman
Graduate School of Business
University of Pittsburgh

About the Editors and Contributors

MICHAEL P. MOKWA is a member of the marketing faculty of the Arizona State University. Previously, he was on the faculties of the University of Wisconsin-Madison and University of Houston where he received his Ph.D. Professor Mokwa's current teaching and research focuses on strategic policy development and evaluation particularly for non-profit and public organizations. His publications include *Marketing the Arts*, the first text in the Praeger Series in Public and Non-Profit Sector Marketing.

STEVEN E. PERMUT is Associate Professor of Marketing at Yale University's School of Organization and Management. He has served as Chairman of the National Advisory Council, U. S. Consumer Product Safety Commission, and as a consultant to various organizations including the Federal Reserve System, Federal Trade Commission, United Nations, and the Commission of the European Communities. He serves on the National Academy of Sciences Committee on Behavioral and Social Aspects of Energy Consumption, as well as the Editorial Boards of the *Journal of Marketing* and *Journal of Marketing and Public Policy*.

DALE D. ACHABAL is a member of the marketing faculty at the University of Santa Clara where he teaches marketing and retailing management, and marketing in public sector organizations. His primary research interests are in the areas of private and public sector distribution systems. His research has been reported in such journals as *Decision Sciences*, *Geographical Analysis*, and *Social Science and Medicine*.

CHRIS T. ALLEN is Assistant Professor of Marketing at the University of Massachusetts-Amherst. His research interests include evaluation of consumer behavior theories in applied contexts, and examination of the application of marketing methods in public policy areas such as energy.

ROBERT W. BACKOFF is an Associate Professor of Public Administration and Political Science at the Ohio State University. His teaching and research areas include public policy formulation; program analysis, implementation, and evaluation; organization design and innovation; and the comparison of public and private organizations and management. His research has been published in the *Public Administration Review, Administration and Society* and other journals.

J. A. BARNHILL is Associate Professor in the Schools of Commerce and Public Administration at Carleton University in Ottawa, Canada. He has had significant experience consulting with public sector organizations including the Canada Post Office and the Department of Indian and Northern Affairs.

KENNETH L. BERNHARDT is Associate Professor of Marketing at Georgia State University. He served recently as a consumer research advisor for the Bureau of Consumer Protection, Federal Trade Commission.

Professor Bernhardt has published extensively on a wide variety of consumer behavior topics. He received his Ph.D. from the University of Michigan.

DEAN BLOCK is Assistant to the City Manager, the City of Tallahassee, Florida, where he has served since 1975. Previously, he held the position of Director, Office of Management and Budget. He was instrumental in initiating resident opinion surveys in Tallahassee.

PAUL N. BLOOM is Associate Professor of Marketing at the University of Maryland at College Park. He is spending the 1980–81 year as Visiting Research Professor at the Marketing Science Institute in Cambridge, Massachusetts. The author or coauthor of more than thirty articles and papers on marketing, Dr. Bloom received his Ph.D. in marketing from Northwestern University.

KEVIN BUICE received a J.D. from the University of Georgia School of Law and currently is an associate with the law firm of Kilpatrick and Cody in Atlanta.

MURIEL CONVERSE holds a Ph.D. in economics and currently is a Study Director at the Survey Research Center, the University of Michigan. Dr. Converse also teaches economics at the University of Michigan. Her recent publications include articles on inflation, and several research reports for the United States Postal Service.

ROHIT DESHPANDE is Assistant Professor of Marketing at the University of Texas at Austin. He received his Ph.D. from the University of Pittsburgh. His major research interest is in the field of knowledge systems in marketing. Currently, he is studying differential research utilization patterns in the private and public sectors.

BEN M. ENIS holds the Bailey K. Howard World Book Chair in Marketing at the University of Missouri-Columbia. He has written extensively and his books include *Marketing Principles*, *The Marketing Research Process*, and *Marketing Classics*. He serves on the Editorial Review Board of the *Journal of Marketing*, and is coeditor of the *Review of Marketing*.

GARY T. FORD is Associate Professor and Chairman of the Marketing Department at the University of Maryland. His research interests are in the application of marketing techniques in the not-for-profit sector and in the analysis of public policy issues. His research has been published in the *Journal of Consumer Research*, *Journal of Marketing Research*, *Journal of Business* and others.

STEVEN G. HEERINGA is a Senior Research Associate at the Survey Research Center, the University of Michigan. He serves as sampling statistician for SRC research projects; consultant to university, government, and private research groups; and instructor in courses on survey sampling and design.

FREDERICK W. HUSZAGH is Professor of Law and Executive Director of the Dean Rusk Center, University of Georgia. He received both a J.D. and J.S.D. from the University of Chicago. Currently, he serves as staff cochairman of the National Governor's Association Committee on International Trade and Foreign Affairs, and is an advisor to the Governor of Georgia.

SANDRA M. HUSZAGH is an Assistant Professor of Marketing and Coordinator of International Activities, University of Georgia College of Business Administration. Her current research interests include government regulation of export transactions and the role of marketing and distribution in developing nations. She received her Ph.D. from the School of International Service at the American University.

MAUREEN KALLICK is a Program Director at the Survey Research Center of the Institute for Social Research, the University of Michigan. She is a past president of the Division of Consumer Psychology of the American Psychological Association. Dr. Kallick has recently published studies in the areas of pollution control and employment, gambling and public finance, and inflation.

JOHN R. KERR is Professor of Marketing and Director of the Small Business Development Center at Florida State University. He has been actively engaged in government marketing research for the past several years, conducting resident opinion surveys for the City of Tallahassee and for Leon County, Florida. Dr. Kerr has written numerous articles and a textbook, *Marketing: An Environmental Approach.*

CHRISTOPHER H. LOVELOCK is Associate Professor of Business Administration, Harvard University Business School. His present research and consulting focuses on marketing consumer services in the public and private sectors. Before earning his Ph.D. from Stanford University, he worked in both consumer and industrial marketing. His recent publications include *Cases in Public and Nonprofit Marketing* and *Readings in Public and Nonprofit Marketing.*

A. J. MARTIN is Director of Accession Policy in the Office of the Secretary of Defense. His responsibilities involve policy and program analysis for military manpower acquisition including recruiting, advertising and market research. He has taught at the U.S. Naval Postgraduate School, Florida International University, and the University of Delaware. He earned his Ph.D. at the Ohio State University.

CLAUDE R. MARTIN JR. is Professor of Marketing at the Graduate School of Business Administration, University of Michigan. He presently serves as a consultant to the Board of Governors of the Federal Reserve System and was the principal researcher investigating public acceptance of the Susan B. Anthony dollar.

PETER J. MAY is an Assistant Professor of Political Science and Public Affairs at the University of Washington. He received his Ph.D. from University of California-Berkeley. He recently conducted a provocative study of the use of citizen feedback in the public policy process.

ROGER MCGRATH is a doctoral candidate in the Management Department at Florida State University. He has been involved in resident opinion surveys and has 12 years experience in the public sector.

WILLIAM D. NOVELLI began his marketing career in product management at Lever Brothers Company and later served in account management at Wells, Rich, Greene advertising agency and as advertising manager at *ACTION*, the Federal agency for volunteerism. Currently, he is president of Porter, Novelli and Associates, a social marketing firm in Washington, D.C.

JERRY I. PORRAS is Associate Professor of Organization Behavior at the Graduate School of Business, Stanford University. His research interests include the assessment of planned change of organizations and the implications of interventions aimed at changing the behavior of people in organized systems.

KENNETH J. ROERING is a Professor of Business Administration at the University of Missouri–Columbia. His research has been published in leading scholarly and professional journals including the *Journal of Applied Psychology*, *Behavioral Science*, and *Journal of Urban Systems*. He has coauthored a textbook entitled *Essentials of Consumer Behavior*, and is coeditor of the *Review of Marketing*.

S. PRAKASH SETHI is Professor of Business and Social Policy at the University of Texas–Dallas. He is the author of numerous books and articles including *Up Against the Corporate Wall, The Corporate Dilemma: Traditional Values and Contemporary Problems*, and *Advocacy Advertising and Large Corporations: Social Conflict, Big Business Image, The News Media and Public Policy*.

STANLEY J. SHAPIRO is a Professor of Marketing at McGill University and former Dean of the McGill Faculty of Management. His current research and consulting center around the financial dimensions of marketing management, the interface of corporate marketing with the broader social environment, and relevant applications of marketing to government departments and nonprofit institutions. He has published over forty articles and six books.

ROBERT E. SPEKMAN is Assistant Professor of Marketing at the University of Maryland. His areas of research range from organizational buying behavior to managerial issues in social marketing. His articles have appeared in the *Journal of Marketing*, *Academy of Management Journal*, *European Journal of Marketing* and others. He received his Ph.D. from Northwestern University.

THADDEUS H. SPRATLEN is a Professor of Marketing at the University of Washington. His teaching and research interests focus on public and nonprofit marketing, macro-marketing and public policy issues relating to ethnic minorities and the inner-city marketplace. He has written many articles and is currently writing a book on marketing nonprofit professional theater.

JAMES M. STEARNS is Assistant Professor of Marketing at Miami University (Ohio). His research interests relate to government marketing and have focused on the development of a valid measure of citizen satisfaction/ dissatisfaction with public products.

FREDERICK D. STURDIVANT is the M. Riklis Professor of Business and Its Environment in the College of Administrative Science at Ohio State University. His teaching and research interests are in the area of marketing and public policy and the interrelationships between business and its social/political environment. He recently served as the guest editor of a special issue of the *Journal of Marketing Research* which explored social and public policy issues. His publications include *Business and Society* and *Managerial Analysis in Marketing.*

GEORGE TESAR is an Associate Professor of Marketing at the University of Wisconsin–Whitewater. He has a Ph.D. from the University of Wisconsin–Madison and was a Fulbright Lecturer at the Central School of Planning and Statistics in Warsaw, Poland. He specializes in product and service development and serves as a consultant with a number of large corporations and government agencies.

STEPHEN J. WEBER is a Vice President at Market Facts— Washington, D.C., the Public Sector Research Group of Market Facts, Inc. Formerly an Associate Professor of Psychology at the University of New Hampshire, he has conducted planning and evaluation research on a number of topics including public service advertising, consumer behavior concerning energy efficiency, and health behavior. His Ph.D. was earned at Northwestern University.

CHARLES B. WEINBERG is Professor of Marketing and Public Management on the Faculty of Commerce and Business Administration, University of British Columbia. He has previously been on the faculty at Stanford University, London Graduate School of Business, and New York University. His primary research interests are in the areas of marketing for public and nonprofit organizations, and the development and application of management science in marketing. His most recent books are *Cases in Public and Nonprofit Marketing* and *Readings in Public and Nonprofit Marketing.*

YORAM (JERRY) WIND is a Professor of Marketing at the Wharton School, University of Pennsylvania and the current editor of the *Journal of Marketing.* He is an active consultant and the author of several books including *Product Policy, Advertising Measurement and Decision Making, Market Segmentation,* and *Organizational Buying Behavior.* He is a frequent contributor of journals which have included over one-hundred of his articles.

GERALD ZALTMAN is the Albert Wesley Frey Distinguished Professor of Marketing and Co-Director, University Program for the Study of Knowledge Use, University of Pittsburgh. He holds a Ph.D. in sociology from the Johns Hopkins University. His special interests are in the adoption and diffusion of innovations. His current research focuses on the various factors affecting the use, nonuse, and misuse of knowledge. He has published many books and articles including pioneering works such as *Creating Social Change, Innovations and Organizations, and The Handbook for Managing Nonprofit Organizations.*